The Single Parent's Almanac

For Christopher

The Single Parent's Almanac

Real-World Answers to Your Everyday Questions

Linda Foust

PRIMA PUBLISHING

Library of Congress Cataloging-in-Publication Data

Foust, Linda, 1950-
The single parent's almanac : real-world answers to your everyday questions / by Linda Foust.
p. cm.
Includes index.
ISBN 0-7615-0329-3
1. Single parents. 2. Divorced parents. 3. Children of single parents. 4. Parent and child. I. Title.
HQ759.915.F68 1995
306.85'6—dc20 95-31315
CIP

99 00 DD 10 9 8 7 6 5 4 3
Printed in the United States of America

How to Order:
Single copies may be ordered from Prima Publishing, P.O. Box 1260BK, Rocklin, CA 95677; telephone (916) 632-4400. Quantity discounts are also available. On your letterhead, include information concerning the intended use of the books and the number of books you wish to purchase.

Contents

Part 3 Family, Work, and Money

Part 4 Moving On

A Note on Language

I regret the lack of neutral pronouns in English. This book addresses male and female single parents caring for children of either gender. For readability, I generally use male pronouns, but they refer to both genders unless the context indicates otherwise. The alternatives just proved too unwieldy.

Acknowledgments

Though I can't name everyone here, I'm grateful for the faith, support, and encouragement from family and loving friends in both my writing and my life, including those who offered love and assistance after Tony's death.

For the vastly different and equally important ways they helped and guided me in my path, I offer my deepest gratitude to Staci and Randall Hobbet; Tim Bigalke; Wendy Kupsaw and Shelley Rothenberg; René Paufve; Ann Matranga; Bennett and Arlyn Christopherson; Ram Dass; Jannie Dresser; Diane Caliazzo; and Brian Simmons.

A heartfelt thank-you to everyone in my present and former "groups," including the "Resolve group," the Friday morning "moms' group," Mark Greenside's and Marcy Alancraig's writing classes, the "writing group," the "play-reading group;" and my generous neighbors. Special thanks to Beverly Dance, Jean Oakley, and Catherine Haley, the "HR Moms," who provide inspiration, advice, friendship, and practical help.

Thank you to Tina Bennett, Amy Earl, Cruz Fernandez, Rebecca Criss, Carmel Sheerin, and others at Christopher's school, who cared for him so wonderfully while I wrote.

I'm grateful to all the single parents who shared experiences and insights with me. I changed the names of most of the people mentioned in this book, and some are composites of two or more individuals.

Many thanks to Jane Nelsen for permission to summarize her family meeting concepts, Peggy Cabaniss and Ed Hartman, financial advisors, for the record-keeping system, Jim Foust, Jean Oakley, René Paufve, John Peterson, and Catherine Haley for reading portions of the manuscript; and Bananas of Oakland, California, for showing so many the way to enlightened parenting.

My undying thanks to Meg Zweiback, pediatric nurse-practitioner, who set me on the right track at the beginning and continues to guide me along the way.

Any errors in this book are strictly my own.

I am indebted to the Single Parent Support Group supported by the Lafayette-Orinda Presbyterian Church in Lafayette, California. Thank you to every past and present member and to those who make the child care possible, including Crystal, Vimala, and Bobbie, Laura, and Jennifer Frey.

And, finally, my sincerest gratitude and love to support-group leaders Liz Hannigan and Cliff Crain, who teach me so much and give so freely of their time, spirit, and wisdom.

Introduction

Life Preservers for Single Parents

Being a single mother was not a scenario I had ever imagined for myself. Before getting married, I was a student, an attorney, a writer, an artist, a traveler. When I settled down in my mid-thirties, I envisioned an idyllic happily-ever-after with my new husband, Tony, and a child—or perhaps two.

After a few years together, Tony and I had a baby named Christopher. Because of work obligations, Tony felt that he had missed the childhood of his two grown sons from a previous marriage. Now semi-retired, he was determined to give Christopher the benefit of a father's daily nurturing and attention. From the first hour of our child's life, we both fully participated in parenting.

Meanwhile, however, our marriage faltered.

Tony had suffered for years from bipolar ("manic-depressive") disease, and his mood swings worsened. Within a year of Christopher's birth, Tony and I found that we could no longer live together. He established a separate household nearby, and we continued to care for Christopher equally, passing him back and forth according to a complicated schedule. Tony and I reconciled a few times and even bought a new house together, but then our relationship deteriorated further, and we never moved back in together. Despite much couples-counseling, our marriage became unpredictable, rancorous, and impossible to sustain. We talked about making our separation permanent and legal. Finally one Friday afternoon, I told Tony that divorce was the only solution for me. The next morning he killed himself in the house he'd been renting. Christopher was twenty months old.

Overnight I became a single mother, taking on this role in the midst of intense emotional upheaval. Feelings of guilt, fear, abandonment, loss, disappointment, relief, sadness, anger, and inadequacy bombarded me. I felt overwhelmed with emotional and practical issues: family relationships, funeral arrangements, money, Tony's belongings, the new house, taxes. Tony's landlord even threatened to sue on the theory that the suicide had reduced the property value of his rental house by $60,000!

Still, I had to be "Mommy." I consulted a specialist in early childhood development, and I learned that my main job was to convey to Christopher that I was all right and that he would be too. He needed, above all, to feel a sense of security, regardless of what had happened in his young life. I couldn't fall apart for the simple reason that he needed me not to!

What ultimately enabled me to keep functioning those first few months was the love and generosity of other people. I had always found it impossible to ask for help and nearly as difficult to accept it. Now I really had no choice. People brought food, slept on my floor, took turns baby-sitting, helped me organize my new life, comforted me, reassured me, cried with me, made me laugh, shared their perceptions, and listened to me repeatedly describe the shock of Tony's suicide.

After a time, the spontaneous offers of help diminished, and I fended for myself more and more. I began unraveling the complicated emotions of my situation, which was not quite a divorce and not a typical widowhood. I looked forward with dread to navigating potty-training and the "terrible twos" on my own, not to mention sorting out the estate, taking care of my house, selling the new one we'd purchased, and assessing my financial situation. I had thought just being a parent was hard. It was nothing compared to single-parenthood.

I also thought I was unique and alone. I was wrong. A recent Census Bureau study revealed that single parents head one-third of all American families, the majority becoming single parents as the result of divorce or death rather than premarital pregnancy. I began to meet other single parents, both men and women, at a weekly, drop-in support group led by two therapists, Liz Hannigan and Cliff Crain. Both Liz and Cliff were former single parents, and the cost was $3 a week with free baby-sitting. What a deal! What a lifesaver! The group is not a place for tears and sympathy, though there is some of that. Primarily it is a class where single parents learn parenting and survival techniques.

Though two-parent families also contend with many of the same challenges, single-parenting intensifies the difficulties of juggling work, private life, and children. I wrote this book to share some of the "wisdom" I've accumulated from this and other groups, from other single parents, from experts, and from my own experiences. I intend it to be a support group on paper. Read the following "Single Parent's Life Preservers," and then skip around to whatever subject seems pressing. Knowing that harried single moms and dads often can't manage to read more than a few paragraphs at a time, I've kept each topic to the point.

Single parents get bad press. We're blamed for everything from drug addiction to moral decay. We're reputedly lazy, uncaring, ignorant, and self-absorbed, and our kids are T-R-O-U-B-L-E. But the single parents I know don't fit this description, and I could name some married parents who do! Let me be the first to say *I'm proud of being a single parent!* It is the hardest job I've ever had, and the most rewarding. Because of the support and education I've sought out as a single mother, my parenting skills are far better than they otherwise would be. I'm overwhelmed, stressed, afraid, and uncertain, and yet *I'm happy.* I'm happier than I've ever been.

Single parents come in all varieties and they populate every part of the country, every economic class, and every occupation. Most become single parents as the result of divorce, but there are also those who are single parents by choice (or by "accident") from the very beginning and others who end up on their own when a spouse dies. Some, like me, don't quite fit any category.

Your former partner may or may not be in the picture physically, psychologically, or financially. He may be cooperative and caring or vengeful and obstructive, using the kids as pawns. As single parents, we're all different, but we all have much in common: We love our children, we aspire to be good parents, and we need fulfilling lives of our own.

My dictionary defines a "life preserver" as "a buoyant device for saving a person from drowning." That's precisely the purpose of the following Life Preservers. Grasp one when you feel your head slipping beneath the floodwaters of single-parenthood. They will provide you with the general, underlying support for every aspect of single-parenting. Reach for one in a crisis to stay afloat. Rely on them daily for smoother overall sailing.

If I've learned anything from single-parenting, it's that nothing is effective for sure or forever. Parenting requires tuning *out* a certain amount of advice. Some advice is just intrusive, reflecting hidden agendas, and you would be better off simply ignoring it. However, most people who give advice have good intentions, and they want you to benefit from their experience. Their suggestions can get you started, but remember—what works in one family won't necessarily work in another. You really learn best from your own experience.

The tips in this book have been successful for many. Try some and see what works. Adapt them and use them as brainstorming triggers for your specific needs. The suggestions range from the profound (nurture yourself, as "you can't give from an empty cup") to the seemingly trivial (make extra keys) to basic parenting skills, but each is borne of experience and can significantly smooth the way through single life with children.

The Single Parent's Life Preservers

- **Think of Yourself As Your Child's Role Model for a Happy, Effective, Healthy Adult**
- **Make Every Minute You Spend with Your Child a Learning Experience—for Both of You**
- **Get Help—You Can't Do It Alone**
- **Respect Your Child**
- **Set Limits for Your Kids**
- **Communicate with Your Children and Allow Talk about *Anything***
- **Regard Mistakes and Problems As Opportunities for Learning**
- **Don't Blame Everything on Single-Parenting**
- **Consider Your Child's Developmental Stage**
- **Stay Flexible and Creative—Change Is Inevitable**
- **Lower Your Expectations, Forget Perfection, and Set Priorities**
- **Practice, Practice, Practice**
- **Simplify, Simplify, Simplify**

- **Enjoy the Process**
- **Play the Hand You're Dealt—Be Proactive, Not Reactive**
- **Examine Your Anger—It Often Masks Another Emotion**
- **Breathe**
- **Get Organized, but Not Too Organized**
- **Learn and Practice Effective Parenting Skills**
- **Use Humor**
- **Know That You Count**
- **Trust Your Own Instincts**
- **Give Up Guilt**
- **Sharpen the Shears before Trimming the Hedge**
- **Give Yourself Time**
- **Do Your Own Work**
- **Concentrate on What You *Can* Influence**

Think of Yourself As Your Child's Role Model for a Happy, Effective, Healthy Adult

When your kids look at you, they should see the kind of adult you want them to become. Watching you should inspire them to *want* to grow up. Do you *tell* your children how to behave and then *act* another way yourself? Or do you demonstrate daily what it means to be an adult who knows how to have fun? To handle adversity gracefully? To manage stress? To make thoughtful decisions? To set limits? To resolve conflicts? To manage money? To be self-reliant? To respect and care for yourself? To treat other people, especially family members, with love and consideration?

Modeling (demonstrating) desired conduct is the most effective way to influence the behavior of children, and it is worth the effort even if it means changing your own well-ingrained habits. Children learn more from watching you than from all your advising, lecturing, disciplining, and cajoling combined. Even back in the eighteenth century, French essayist Joseph Joubert proclaimed, "Children have more need of models than of critics."

What kids see at home is what they accept as right. If you don't believe that "actions speak louder than words," try an experiment that Cliff demonstrated while leading a single-parents support group meeting: tell someone to touch his ear while you point to your chin.

Despite your verbal instruction, his finger will almost invariably imitate yours and go straight to his chin!

This behavior-modeling principle applies to practically every moment you have with your children. It requires you to be conscious of the message your conduct conveys—even (or perhaps especially) under stress. Use a respectful tone of voice with your child at all times, even when he's driven you to distraction. Otherwise you'll be shocked one day to hear your own ugly intonations coming from his mouth when he's upset!

Practice behaving as you would like your child to behave. It will make *you* a happier, better person, too. Do you fume impatiently in traffic jams and mumble obscenities at rude drivers? If so, you only teach your child to do the same. Instead, show him how to relax and take advantage of the unexpected time together by singing, talking, playing word games, or just enjoying some quiet time. Cursing other cars and pounding the steering wheel have more effect on your blood pressure than on freeway speed anyway.

None of this means you shouldn't get angry, sad, or frustrated, or that you should hide emotions from your children. Indeed, modeling appropriate ways to *express* emotions is one of the most important jobs of parenting.

Make Every Minute You Spend with Your Child a Learning Experience—for Both of You

A parent is an educator. Use every opportunity to teach your child something, and not just with books. Take informal advantage of everyday activities to help him expand his knowledge about the world. Turn errands into educational field trips of a sort. You might just spark an interest in your kid that will affect his entire life. You will accomplish the errands pleasantly and in the usual amount of time, too. My son Christopher, who is now five-years old, absorbs numerous lessons about counting, letters, nutrition, commerce, agriculture, and money from the child's seat of the grocery cart. As your youngster matures, the same daily tasks will offer new and more sophisticated avenues for exploration.

Showing an interest in what your child likes raises his self-esteem several notches. Let your child lead *you* along new paths. Christopher practically emerged from the womb on railroad tracks. He loves trains of any description. By pursuing railway activities together, I learned all about trains and even wrote a magazine article about them. Besides, though you may be too stressed out and exhausted to notice, the world is full of wonder. Seeing it fresh through your child's eyes renews your ability to appreciate it.

Get Help—You Can't Do It Alone

For some reason, this Life Preserver is a hard truth for single parents to accept and implement. Most of us don't know how to ask for help and fear trying. Maybe it's America's independent, individualistic heritage, or perhaps pride gets in the way. Never mind. Learn to ask. Practice asking. Help is a necessity, not a luxury.

Think of the roles you perform each day: valet, appointments secretary, cook, educator, launderer, cleaner, financier, chauffeur, therapist, entertainer, mediator, teacher, consumer, animal trainer, toy-mender, carpenter, plumber, and knee-bandager. And these duties are just some of what you do *at home.* Add commuting and a full-time job, and you really don't have the time or energy to do it all, much less do it well. You will only make yourself and your kids miserable by trying.

> Today only one in four American households is a traditional mom-dad-and-the-kids family.[1]

Get help for jobs you don't know how to do and for those you hate doing. Sometimes just give yourself the gift of a hired housecleaning or a few hours of baby-sitting.

Learn to say yes to offers of help. At the airport recently, Christopher and I saw a woman alone with a toddler and baby, struggling to reassemble diaper bag, stroller, backpack, coats, and luggage after passing through the security check. Thinking of my own travels under similar circumstances, I offered to help. The woman turned me down! I am a not threatening person, especially when accompanied by my little boy. I think she, like many of us, was simply conditioned to just grit her teeth and go it alone. Those offers are all too scarce. Take advantage of them.

One word of caution: Sometimes offers of help, particularly those from family, come with strings attached. This is not to say you shouldn't accept. Just know what you are getting into and evaluate whether the price is too high on an emotional or other level. One single dad moved his girls to an isolated, unfamiliar town in another state in order to live rent-free in a house his parents owned. The use of a car went with the deal, as did financial help and plenty of babysitting by Grandma. Nice package, except that once the dad was settled in, he slowly came to the understanding that his parents expected him to stay indefinitely and care for them when they hit old age. The town held nothing for him, but after a few years of rent-free living, he felt trapped by guilt and perceived obligation. The best course, never easy, is to bring the hidden agendas into the open and discuss the payoffs directly.

So to recap: Get help however you can, on your own terms. Get as much as you can. Buy it, beg it, and trade for it. Be creative. Ask for it on wish lists. Get it from friends, neighbors, acquaintances, and your kids. But get it.

Respect Your Child

Effective parenting ultimately comes down to respect for your kid, a precious human with remarkable machinery inside. Respect his struggles, opinions, emotions, and preferences. Speak to him politely, even when you're upset. Treat his concerns as important instead of dismissing them as being silly. Listen to him attentively. Apologize when you make a mistake. Value his abilities, especially when they differ from yours. Your child will teach you much if you stay receptive. He possesses wisdom you lost along the way.

Respecting your child doesn't mean letting him run the show. Just recognize his value in your interactions. Your respect for him will engender his respect for you.

Set Limits for Your Kids

No child will ever admit it, but limits make him feel safe and secure. That doesn't mean he won't beg and cry and push the boundaries at every opportunity, but still, he will find a certain comfort in a consistent "no." By setting *and enforcing* reasonable rules, you let your kid know that you look out for him and care what happens to him. *Your* being in charge frees *him* to be a child, and your authority relieves him of the anxiety of having to guess where the line of acceptability lies.

Limits make autonomy possible. Setting appropriate boundaries and allowing children to make choices freely within them bolsters both self-esteem and self-reliance. It permits kids to learn from mistakes without suffering major adverse consequences. Your child will also be secretly relieved to have you as a scapegoat. How much easier for him to say that his "stupid mom" won't let him go hang gliding than to admit his fear to peers!

Note, however, that none of this implies that rules should be arbitrary or autocratic. Discuss the limits with your child and explain your reasoning; this will subtly teach him your values and demonstrate responsible decision making.

Think of limits as the wall around a garden in which your child can play safely. The more responsible he becomes, the bigger the garden and the more freedom within it. If he needs a wall to lean on, however, you're always there.

Communicate with Your Children and Allow Talk about *Anything*

"Communicating" is such a clichéd concept that we often don't bother to think about whether we're really doing it. Many of us, however, don't know how to communicate effectively with kids—or with adults for that matter.

You're lucky if your children are young because you can establish openness and good habits from the beginning. I took advantage of Christopher's preverbal years to develop new communication skills, on the assumption, I suppose, that my early mistakes wouldn't harm uncomprehending ears. This may have been overkill, but I needed the practice. As for older kids, expect some resistance at first if you haven't been communicating all along. Seek professional help if necessary to open the channels. Your entire relationship will eventually change for the better.

My consultant on early childhood advised me to tell Christopher about his father Tony's death immediately. Even at twenty months, he needed to know we wouldn't see Daddy again and why. I felt a good deal of reluctance at following this suggestion. How much could a toddler possibly understand anyway? Still, I took the advice and stumbled through the explanation in terms that Christopher was most likely to understand ("Daddy died. His body stopped working. We won't see him again."). I built a foundation of simple truth that wouldn't require contradiction upon later elaboration.

In retrospect, this discussion was as much for me as for my son. I became comfortable talking about Tony's death, and that was the ultimate message for Christopher: It's all right to talk about *anything*, regardless of other people's reactions. Now, I always respond to Christopher's questions, no matter how difficult ("Does Daddy still love us?" "Does he still have a penis when he's dead?" "Why did he die?"). Sometimes his friends ask me about his dad, and I answer forthrightly, which reconfirms that talking really is okay. Christopher is five now, and we'll have many more years of discussing his father. Frankly, I don't know what he absorbs from my explanations, but I've been honest with him, and we've established the freedom to talk.

Regard Mistakes and Problems As Opportunities for Learning

Mistakes represent opportunities for you to learn and to get help from others. They don't mean you're bad or inadequate.

When adversity strikes, ask, "What can I learn from this?" This is a much healthier and more productive response than, "Who's to blame?" or "Why me?"

Ask your kids the same question when they face difficulty or "failure." Actually, there are no failures, just things that didn't work out. Find out why they didn't, and try again. If you hurt someone, apologize, make amends, and move on.

Be gentle with yourself, too. Normal people make mistakes. Everyone does. Recriminations only agitate you. The bottom line is not what happens, but how you deal with it.

Don't Blame Everything on Single-Parenting

Sure, divorce and single-parenting cause problems. But not *all* of them! Raising a child is fraught with difficulties—period. You could have two parents (or the proverbial African village) bringing up your kid, and he'd still fail English. In jumping to the conclusion that Johnny's single-parent home made him set the class wastebasket on fire, you may overlook other, more pertinent factors in his life.

Keep an open mind and communicate with your children. Although divorce definitely affects children negatively, subsequent parental competence controls how they fare in the long run.

Consider Your Child's Developmental Stage

Your kid's developmental stage governs his competence, physical ability, humor, needs, learning, responses, and many other aspects of his life. Consequently, what worked with him at age five won't suffice when he reaches age ten. Sometimes what seems perfectly obvious to you as an adult makes no sense to him as a child of a certain age. And vice versa.

A Georgia metropolitan area of 112,500 people leads the percentage rate for one-parent families. The lowest in the nation, found in Utah, was still 12%. Representative figures are:

Albany, Georgia	37%
New York City, New York	36%
New Orleans, Louisiana	34%
Sacramento, California	28%
Oakland, California	27%
San Francisco, California	24%
San Jose, California	22%
Provo-Orem, Utah	12%[2]

Human development unfolds in a fairly predictable pattern, though at variable individual speeds. A child's behavior reflects the internal issues he confronts and what he's learning to master at certain stages of his life. Toddlers experience separation anxiety, and four-year-olds glory in saying "poop." Teens, on the other hand, struggle with identity and independence (so rebellion and withdrawal from the family are not only normal at this time, but *necessary*).

Realizing that your child's behavior depends on something other than your parenting lets you off the hook a bit and gives you some room to relax. You won't try so hard to alter his actions if "it's just a phase" he'll outgrow naturally as time passes. You won't condemn yourself as a "bad parent" knowing he's *supposed* to act like this now. Just remind yourself, "It's developmental," and don't knock yourself out.

Do use your knowledge about development to arrive at the parenting techniques most likely to work at your child's age. Shape your actions to what you know he needs. For example, whether to spend more time with your child after your divorce, or to leave him alone, may depend a great deal on his developmental stage.

For each stage your child passes through, you also experience simultaneous development. With an infant, you acquire nurturing skills. With toddlers and preschoolers, you learn how to act authoritative. When school-age kids ask hard questions, you decide how honest and forthright to make your responses. With teens, you refine all these skills. You evolve rules at each stage.

Stay Flexible and Creative—Change Is Inevitable

Everything changes—the kids, you, your ex, your situation. If you've found something that works in one phase, great. But stay flexible. Change rules when necessary. Keep yourself in a learning place so you'll recognize a good idea when it comes along. Don't become so invested in one solution that you can't tell when it's time to move on to another.

During Christopher's independent stage, he quickly complied if I threatened to do his job myself. Now, however, when I say, "If you don't pick up your toys, I'll have to do it for you," he says, "Fine." Yelling and nagging don't work, and I don't want that as my style anyway. So I added a new twist: If I pick up the toys, they disappear for a day. *That* is not "fine" with Christopher, and his cooperative attitude returns (at least temporarily).

Use creativity. Try new solutions, even if they seem unusual. Formulate alternatives at family meetings. You can always abandon something that doesn't work.

Often, a transition presents more difficulty than the new situation itself. With everything in flux, try to remember that transitions do eventually lead to the next stage of equilibrium. It's a small comfort, but sometimes it's all you have!

Changes always contain both positive and negative elements. Some long-term good will probably come from unwanted change, and most positive moves also have a downside. Maybe you meet the mate of your dreams, but your kids balk at moving in with "that creep." By all means, take advantage of positive changes, but assume responsibility for handling the negative aspects.

Lower Your Expectations, Forget Perfection, and Set Priorities

Expectations are traps. As Buddha said, "When you cease expecting, you have all things."

Even with help, you can't do everything. Don't expect to. Make a list of how you spend your time. What is really important in your life? Where do your values really lie? Think in terms of what you could give up, at least on a temporary basis. *You can always change again later.*

You *do* have choices. To make yourself aware of them, replace your "shoulds" with "coulds." "I *could* clean the bathroom" creates the possibility of *"could not."* Even if you do end up scrubbing the toilet, you *chose* to. It's a subtle difference, but it's real.

Maybe you spend time cooking because you value good nutrition. Are those hours in the kitchen at the expense of something even more important? It depends entirely on your personal priorities. You could give up home cooking in favor of pizza, cold cereal, TV dinners, and hot dogs. Not an ideal diet, for sure, but probably not fatal! The choice is yours.

Once I tried to set a new routine where Christopher would put on his own clothes for preschool. I really enjoyed that extra morning quiet time, reading the entire newspaper and sipping a second cup of tea, but eventually I began to spend more and more of it nagging Christopher to finish dressing. The more he delayed, the more I steamed. We often stormed off unhappily to preschool at the last minute—with him half-dressed. Finally, I realized that starting the day pleasantly took priority over reading the last section of the newspaper and *expecting* my son to put on his clothes. For now, I settle for one cup of tea and dress Christopher myself, which is fine with him. Soon he'll take over again, and meanwhile, our mornings are peaceful.

Practice, Practice, Practice

Effective parenting—especially single-parenting—requires new skills. Give yourself a break. Just as you don't expect to win the gold medal in figure skating after one lesson, don't expect to qualify for the Parenting Olympics without continual practice. New ways become second nature only after repetition.

At first, you'll make frequent mistakes without realizing you blew it until weeks later. Congratulate yourself! At least you noticed eventually! Apologize and make amends. Keep practicing, and before long you'll see your errors as soon as you commit them. Correct them immediately, even when you have to contradict yourself. If you blurt out, "Can't you ever pick up your dirty clothes?" change it right away to, "Sorry. I mean, I feel frustrated when I find your clothes on the floor because it makes the laundry harder for me to do." With practice, the second statement will flow naturally.

Simplify, Simplify, Simplify

This applies to every aspect of life: your living space, your schedule, your rules. Clear out the clutter in your house. Throw it away, or at least store it out of sight. You'll be amazed at the sense of calm and relief that empty space brings.

Look at how you spend your time. Ask yourself, "What am I doing, why am I doing it, and why am I doing it *now?*" If you can't answer with a good reason, let it go. I spent hours sorting Tony's voluminous slides and photographs. Peering with a magnifying glass at fragments of celluloid became an obsession. I wanted to preserve Tony's history for Christopher, a worthy goal for certain. I stayed up late every night to make time. Finally it hit me. I'd barely made a dent, and none of this would mean anything to Christopher for several years anyway. I shelved the project and had a lot more time for other aspects of my life.

Pare down obligations, too. Learn to say no. The demands of single-parenthood always serve as an acceptable excuse.

Be conscious. If you insist on something merely out of reaction, habit, others' expectations, or blind emulation of your parents, consider it a candidate for the trash heap. For example, do you battle with your child until he eats everything on his plate? Why? Does it really matter? Buy some vitamin pills, give him smaller portions, and throw away the uneaten food without comment. He really won't starve to death, and despite your mother's warnings, the poor children in India won't be affected one way or the other.

Enjoy the Process

You will never be "done," so enjoy the process. Constantly ask, "Is there any way I can enjoy this?" It's *your* responsibility to make your situation pleasant. No one will do it for you. A happy life isn't something you hope for in the future while you suffer in the present. The present is all there is.

> In 1970, single parents headed 13% of American families with kids under 18. By 1980, the figure was 21.5%, and in 1994, it rose to about 30%.[3]

Through a fortunate series of events, the spiritual leader Ram Dass spoke at Tony's memorial. When introduced to me before the service, he said enthusiastically, "Enjoy it!" and, "Ride the roller coaster." As you might imagine, I was quite taken aback. This was not the usual sympathetic murmuring I'd received from others. All I could manage in response at the time was, "No one else told me that!" I soon understood what he meant, though. Don't go numb. Stay conscious. Experience what is happening, good and bad. This is your life; don't miss it.

I've come back to his advice time and again. It allows me to detach, to watch myself acting, to separate from the drama and learn about myself. When I start to get crazy about something, I pull back and say, "Oh, so this is how Linda reacts to this situation. Well, what an experience to have in this life."

The "downs" are as much a part of life as the "ups," and, as on a roller coaster, they may be more intense. Stay on for the ride. Enjoy it.

Play the Hand You're Dealt—Be Proactive, Not Reactive

When you're reactive, you feel stuck. You believe external circumstances control your life, and you blame others for keeping you from what you want. You feel sorry for yourself. At best, you choose among limited choices, often on the basis of emotional reaction. At worst, you wait for something to happen. In reality, when you are reactive, you're choosing to make yourself a victim of other people's needs, desires, and whims.

Be proactive. Accept the reality of your circumstances. Take care of business and accept responsibility for your life. Rather than focusing on the difficulties, become solution-oriented, concentrating on what *you* can accomplish. Reframe problems as challenges, as puzzles to be solved. There is *always* a solution. Look forward, not back. Staying vehemently angry at your ex, for example, only binds you to the past. Remember: Your kids will observe how you manage problem solving. Be a good model for them.

Using positive, proactive language catapults you into action. Say, "I can," "I choose to," "I could," "I don't want to," "I've decided not to," or "I get to." Complaining, bitching, and blowing up are reactions. They are poor *substitutes* for action.

Accepting your current situation doesn't mean liking it, agreeing with it, or staying in it. It means acknowledging that this is where you are and that this is the hand you've been dealt. Once you've done this, you can ask yourself, "Where do I go from here? How can I best play this hand?" Skillful play wins more poker games than good cards do.

My husband, Tony, and I were separated, but not divorced, when he took his life, and so I was left with a mess of practical matters to untangle. In his last manic months, Tony had started business ventures that had to be closed out. In addition, the house he'd initially purchased for himself when we split up had burned in the huge Oakland Fire, and I had to settle the insurance claim. The landlord from whom Tony had rented after the fire insisted on recovering for "suicide damage" to the property value, and I also had to deal with him. In addition, I had to do a complete inventory of Tony's finances, which he'd kept separate from mine, and prepare the estate for probate and taxes. I had to fulfill his commitments for remodeling our newly-purchased house. And despite a depressed real estate market, I had to sell that house immediately, as

I couldn't manage the mortgage payments on my own. I needed to figure out how to live and provide for the future. Tony had no life insurance and left me without sufficient funds to raise and educate Christopher.

All this and parenting too!

Everyone's story differs, but each one is complicated and emotional. There's nothing to do but get moving, minute-by-minute if necessary. If I thought about everything I had to do, paralysis overtook me. Instead, I imposed some temporary order on the boxes piled all over my home office and attacked them one file at a time. I made calls, wrote letters, saw lawyers. It took two years, many tears, and innumerable late nights, and the results weren't perfect, but they were good enough. In retrospect, I scarcely believe what I accomplished, but I feel proud I survived that nightmare. I moved on to another whole set of problems (remember, you're never "done"), but at least I put that first batch behind me.

So get moving! Plans and good intentions call for action. As Horace wrote in his *Odes*, "Seize the day." Or, in Will Rogers' words, "Even if you're on the right track, you'll get run over if you just sit there."

> Nearly 87% of custodial single parents are women.[4]

Examine Your Anger— It Often Masks Another Emotion

When under stress, you may react in anger. Anger serves as protection, shielding you from other emotions that would leave you more vulnerable—emotions like fear, sadness, or pain. Maybe you feel unsafe in revealing those other feelings. Or perhaps you subconsciously believe you're not allowed to have them or that you couldn't survive their intensity. Anger often emerges in a split second and buries them without a trace.

The more vehement your anger in relation to what happened, the more likely another feeling lurks in the background. If your anger strikes a "ten" in response to a wrong of "three," you need to look at what else is going on.

Examining the emotions that underlie your angry outburst will lead to growth and understanding. At one point, I became continually irate at Christopher's crumbs on the floor, even though I knew this was normal and expected. Three-year-olds always drop food. Still, I resented having to clean up the mess that this child blithely created three times a day. I wanted him to be sorry. I wanted him to *care.* One night I broke into tears and finally realized that I really wanted *Tony* to care. Behind the anger was deep sadness and rejection at his abandoning me and Christopher. This resonated with other abandonments I'd experienced in childhood. As I allowed myself to feel the pain, the food on the floor lost its emotional charge. Though I *still* hate cleaning up after every meal, I now do it without drama.

Being able to put the anger on hold long enough to get in touch with other emotions may seem impossible. It requires practice. If you can't observe the old saw about counting to ten, at least take a deep breath. That will create a space between the event and the reaction and perhaps give you a glimpse of another emotion.

Anger is always worth a second look. Maybe your short fuse relates to fatigue or stress. Perhaps you're reexperiencing childhood feelings. You may feel sad or hurt or afraid or powerless. On the other hand, maybe you really and truly are just angry. That happens, too!

Breathe

Yes, meditating forty minutes a day would improve your life. Do I expect any single parent to manage that? No.

You can, however, breathe consciously every so often, which reduces stress and helps you center. It won't cost you a moment of extra time. Hey, you have to breathe anyway! Just do it deeply and consciously.

Take air in through your nostrils and visualize it traveling all the way to the bottom of your lungs, bringing in "good stuff," whatever you need at the moment—courage, self-confidence, serenity, determination. Exhale through your mouth, getting rid of the "bad stuff," tension, judgment, uncertainty, anger. You'll find much more elaborate techniques in books and classes, but this is all you really need. Buy an audio tape if you want a voice to guide you through a longer meditation.

Remembering to breathe is the trick—most people go years without a real breath. Create a system of reminders for yourself. In one company I know, the employees let the phone ring three times while they breathe deeply—practicing "telephone meditation." Try a conscious inhalation at every stop sign. Or every time you get a cup of coffee. Or whenever someone says a certain common word, like "no." (If you have toddlers or teens, you'll get lots of practice with this one.)

Get Organized, but Not Too Organized

Organization makes a real difference in how smoothly your life runs. You find things when you need them, make one trip instead of two, and get where you're supposed to be. But you have to take your personality into account. Your organization method has to be fast and simple, something you will really use. I've seen systems that require goals and sub-goals and steps toward sub-goals and arrows and timetables and checklists. This would either drive me crazy or get me so involved in making things "easy" that I'd never get around to doing anything else. Some people might thrive on such a plan, but ultimately, I'd give it up.

Organizational ability is highly idiosyncratic and sometimes even seems to be genetically determined. Some people's stuff almost finds its own way into neatly labeled files and shelves. Others rely on the shoe-box system. I have a real talent for periodically bringing order out of chaos. Sorting an intolerable mess satisfies some genuine urge in me, but don't ask me to file on a day-to-day basis. Knowing this about myself, I have one basket for papers to-be-filed "someday," one for matters requiring attention "soon," and one for immediate action. I rarely get back to the first basket, but when I do, it's downright enjoyable.

Learn and Practice Effective Parenting Skills

Do you want to parent just as your mother and father did?

Your family may have labored under dysfunctional limitations such as alcoholism or mental illness. Even without clinical dysfunction, advances in child psychology and development mean your parents' methods probably aren't the best. The previous generation's style was often authoritarian, shame-based, controlling, critical, judgmental, blaming, and emotionally uncommunicative. Not something you want to emulate.

Nevertheless, you may not know any other way. How many times have you heard your mother's words coming from your mouth—words you swore you'd never use? Under stress, you regress to parenting in the style you experienced growing up. To change, you must immerse yourself in modern parenting techniques. Just hearing or reading about them isn't enough, though it's a start. Practice until they are as ingrained as the old ways. After all, you had eighteen years of daily exposure to your parents' methods, eighteen years to undo.

Use Humor

Expand the repertoire of your responses. Do something unexpected. Humor is a good place to start, and it doesn't even have to be very good. If you're a natural comedian, great, but sometimes just the surprise value of an unforeseen answer derails a conflict or forestalls a whine. Do something silly. Throw a pillow. Turn a cartwheel. Talk Pig Latin. Drop to the floor and howl like a dog.

Kids learn humor from parents and teachers on one hand, and friends on the other. According to experts, a child's sense of humor goes through a developmental progression. Tune into it and wait for the giggles.

- Very small babies like peekaboo, making faces, and flying games.
- Before age two, toddlers love incongruity and slapstick. To get a laugh, pretend you can't get a hairbrush to work correctly or play a tune on a banana. Wear a shoe as a hat. Fall down.
- Two- and three-year-olds love word-play, purposefully misnaming objects and adding silly rhyming syllables to real words ("table-bable-sable").
- Fours indulge in bathroom humor, though I wouldn't encourage this particular avenue. They also enjoy riddles and word substitutions. Four-year-olds love laughing with others, knowing that another person "gets" the nonsense rhymes or altered song lyrics.
- Slightly older children thrive on rhymes, jokes, and puns that allow them to feel intellectually superior to the listener. Riddles and knock-knocks reverse normal power roles between children and adults. The kid exercises control for a change. He asks the questions and knows the answers, emerging victorious when a grown-

up provides the wrong response. He might even change the answer when you guess correctly. Even if it was moldy back in the dark ages of your youth, laugh at your kid's joke.
- As for teenagers . . . well, who knows?

Laugh with, not at, your child. Kids insult easily. If you really can't keep a straight face when you should, apologize.

Children's humor, like adults,' reflects their concerns and anxieties. Four-year-old bathroom humor is the most obvious example. Bathroom words generate a huge response from adults, which makes the child feel important and part of a group of peers separate from grown-ups.

Making children laugh eases many trouble spots, but also use humor to lighten your own mood. Learn to laugh at yourself and your circumstances. This requires a certain amount of detachment or distance, such as the passage of time. In my support group, Lisa related how she washed her Honda and lavishly praised her preschooler for hosing down the inside of his own kiddy car. Lisa turned her back for a minute to answer the phone and returned to find her little boy expecting more commendation for washing the interior of the *Honda,* too. At the time, Lisa didn't find it amusing to see her car slowly filling with water from a hose through its window, but she laughs about it years later.

> In 1970, single parents headed 10% of Caucasian families, and in 1994, the figure rose to 25%. During that same time, single-parent African-American families went from 36% to 65%. Single parents currently head about one-third of all Latino families.[5]

Similarly, Sharon's son Daniel knew not to play with matches. Four-year-olds make fine distinctions, however, and a barbecue lighter isn't technically a match. He took it inside and set the wallpaper on fire. Sharon can laugh about this disaster—now.

Of course, you can't manufacture distance at will, but you *can* detach psychologically and see the humor in a situation as it happens. This isn't easy, but at least be open to the possibility. One morning, I stared at my mud-caked son delightedly turning the beige house black. Angry at first, I remembered how I'd urged him to paint at preschool. I suddenly saw the Artist at Work, a true master, experimenting with unusual media. Did Picasso start this way? Had I given birth to the next Christo, one who wraps buildings in mud rather than cloth? I took photos, and together we sprayed both him and the house more-or-less clean.

Pull back and reframe stressful situations. The more involved and invested you are, the harder it is to perceive the facts any other way. Play games with yourself to get that psychological distance. You may crack a smile despite yourself or at least keep from boiling over. Superimpose an imaginary animal face on your whining kid, or regard your grouchy boss as a version of Sesame Street's Oscar, who is only happy when he's unhappy. So much of perception is based on how you frame things. I heard about a study in which psychologists asked one group if it was all right to *smoke while praying*. Ninety percent answered no. The researchers asked a second group if it was okay to *pray while smoking*. Ninety percent said yes! Same facts, different framework, different perceptions, different reactions.

Granted, it's hard to be humorous if you're on the verge of tears. Sometimes, though, faking it will help *you* feel better, too. Studies also indicate that laughing affects the immune system positively and reduces stress. Humor has great power to turn a mood around. Writer James Thurber said, "Humor is a serious thing. I like to think of it as one of our greatest and earliest national resources, which must be preserved at all costs."

So, get silly. Hearing a child laugh renews the spirit. And if your teenagers just roll their eyes . . . well, you tried. Enjoy yourself and try something else.

Know That You Count

As a single parent, you focus on your children, as you should. But don't forget you are a living, breathing human being, too, not just a role called Mom or Dad. You count as an individual who deserves respect and courtesy. You have the right to your own opinions. Sometimes you don't have to give an explanation or justification for what you want—your wanting it is reason enough. If you'd rather not listen to blaring heavy metal just now, ask your kid to take it in another room. "Because I say so" can be a perfectly valid answer occasionally.

Trust Your Own Instincts

Get all the advice you want, but make final decisions for yourself. You're the one who has to live with the results. No one knows you or your children better.

Instincts can also open valuable areas of inquiry. Do you have a bad feeling about a teacher? Does your child seem depressed? Is that overnight trip properly chaperoned? Don't ignore those voices at the back of your head. They're on your side. Trust them. Set aside time to sit quietly and listen to your gut. Get information. Then act.

Give Up Guilt

Easier said than done. There's always something to feel guilty about because you will always do too much, too little, or the wrong thing. Lower your expectations. No one is perfect. Forgive yourself. Guilt serves no purpose except to distract you and consume energy better spent elsewhere.

Take comfort in the fact that kids are amazingly resilient. Your mistakes won't "ruin them forever," especially if you apologize, communicate, and learn from your errors.

Parenting by use of "logical consequences" (discussed in Chapter 5) goes a long way toward alleviating guilt. This method focuses on educating your kid rather than punishing him. As he suffers the logical consequences of his behavior, he learns. If he forgets his lunch money, he'll go hungry. You don't have to feel guilty—he absorbs a significant lesson for the long run. How different from tormenting yourself with guilt for the hurtful punishment you inflicted!

Sometimes you can lessen guilt by admitting and acting on something you haven't wanted to acknowledge. For example, all working parents feel guilty for so much time away from home, but knowing the kids enjoy and learn from their caregiver reduces the sting. If your guilt meter consistently hits "high" when you drop them off, however, perhaps you feel unacknowledged dissatisfaction with the child care. Maybe you haven't admitted it because it's so difficult to find other arrangements. You don't have to make any immediate changes, but the question is worth exploring, both by consulting your instincts and getting your kids' input.

Children easily detect guilt and manipulate parents with it. Whatever you do, don't try to assuage it by extravagant gifts or by failing to set limits. You'll only give your kids ammunition and lose their respect.

Depending on the circumstances, your ex-spouse may use guilt to get what he wants or to punish you. Don't, for example, settle for less than you are entitled to in the divorce just because you were the one who "broke up the family." The timing of Tony's suicide—the morning after I insisted on divorce—was certainly calculated in part to punish me with perpetual guilt. I admit to having had guilt feelings, but also to letting them go. What made that possible was knowing, first, that his suicide was the product of a mental illness, and, second, that before his death I did absolutely everything I could have done to help him. At some point, he became responsible for his own actions. The ultimate act was his choice, not mine.

You can't change the past, so work on the present. Relieve yourself of *tomorrow's* guilt by doing your best today.

Sharpen the Shears Before Trimming the Hedge

Besides getting the right tool for a job, you have to keep it in efficient working order. A viny hedge grows along my back garden wall and seems, unlike the flowers, to thrive on neglect. Trimming it had always been Tony's job. At some point after he moved out, I had to cut it back or welcome it as a tenant inside the house. I scrounged in the tools until I found a rusty clipper and set to work. It wasn't the clip-clip-you're-done I'd expected. I spent hours arm wrestling with thick, recalcitrant stems. I knew if I stopped to sharpen the shears the job would end sooner and with more satisfaction. But there was just one problem: I didn't know how to sharpen hedge clippers, so I would have to find out who did, take them in, and wait to get them back—and I was in a hedge-cutting mood *now*. If I stopped, I might never get back to it, I felt. So I continued the hard work hacking and chopping with the dull shears.

Some time later, I did take the clippers to be sharpened. The new edges *sliced* through those vines most efficiently. Of course, I'd already wasted hours doing it the hard way.

Have you ever struggled to finish a letter with a dull pencil, not stopping for the few seconds it would take to put a point on it? Do you clean up the bathroom yourself because getting your child to do it just means trouble? Perhaps you haven't done these, but I'll bet you've done something similar. You know how to make a job easier, but stopping to do it seems too time-consuming or difficult. You're afraid you'll lose your momentum.

I might buy that reasoning, except that writing, cutting, and cleaning occur again and again. Over the long run, you'll save time and energy by stopping to "sharpen the shears." Set your life up in advance to work efficiently and take the load off yourself. Train your children. Learn effective parenting skills. Put an end to whining. Create routines.

Give Yourself Time

However you become a single parent—divorce, death of your spouse, intentional or unintentional pregnancy, or adoption—your life changes drastically. The change can be quite sudden, but adjusting to it takes years. When you first experience the reality of single-parenting, you can't imagine how you will cope, even if you chose and planned for this new life. Exhaustion and stress rule your waking hours. Raw emotions charge everything. Practicalities seem insurmountable. And the kids—how will they fare?

Perhaps you can't believe it now, but *everything will get better.* Take this on trust. "Time heals" is trite but true. Look back and see how much you *have* done already. Give yourself credit. I've repeatedly seen distress turn to acceptance, satisfaction, and even happiness. You will pull yourself up, fall, stand, and take those wobbly first steps. Sooner or later you'll take off running, and—if you do your work—it will be in the right direction.

Do Your Own Work

You can't help kids emotionally if your own unresolved psychological issues keep popping up. They interfere with your ability to assess your child's emotions effectively. You mix up his reactions with yours, and vice versa. When you are unable to detach from your child's behavior, you take everything personally. You might even submerge yourself so deeply in your own problems that you neglect to see your child's. Worse, unhealthy psychology recurs generation after generation—low self-esteem breeds low self-esteem, for example—until someone has the courage to change.

Doing your psychological work takes guts. You give up defenses and take frightening personal risks. Yet the end result is a happier, better-functioning person and parent. Find a therapist or counselor to help, if only to get you started. An outside observer sees so much more than you can alone.

Be patient too. Don't expect overnight changes. Enjoy the process!

By the way, therapy isn't all tears and angst. Sometimes I swear I keep appointments with my therapist because he laughs at my jokes. Of course, he also calls it as he sees it and doesn't let me fool myself. Although my initial crisis ended, I continue to grow in therapy. My therapist is my best and most objective audience—during good times and bad.

Concentrate on What You *Can* Influence

Besides the past, there is much in the present you can't change, at least not right now and not on your own: world hunger, war, urban violence, and pollution, for example. Certainly, these issues deserve your deep concern and devoted activism. But for now don't expend your precious limited time on them, and don't waste your psychic energy obsessing about them.

First figure out life at home, where you do have some degree of control. You can't solve world hunger alone, but you can keep your kids fed. You can't abolish war single-handedly, but you can develop effective methods for resolving family conflict. You can't eliminate urban violence on your own, but you can educate and teach values to your children. You can't cure pollution by yourself, but you can recycle, car pool, and avoid waste.

Think similarly about natural disasters. Especially when you've lived through trauma—like a divorce or death—you anticipate the next "big one" any moment. For a time after Tony's suicide, I obsessed about another death, a fire, or an earthquake. Finally my therapist told me to knock it off. "Do what you can to get ready and then spend your energy where it can do some good." Now I have earthquake kits in the house and car and know how to turn off the gas. I'm as ready as I can be, and I do, in fact, worry much less.

As you become more powerful in your personal and family life, your energy and ability expand for larger issues. The truth is, however, that by teaching your children to be worthy, capable adults, you *are* working on the larger issues.

The following three chapters discuss the first steps for those who become single parents through divorce, death, and choice. Although discussed separately, all have much in common.

ORGANIZATIONS

Full-Time Dads: Networking and support to dads who are the primary caregivers of their kids. Newsletter also (year's subscription is $25; sample issue is $5). POB 577, Cumberland Center, ME 04021.

National Men's Resource Center: National support groups, newsletters, books, general resource for fathers and men. POB 800, San Anselmo, CA 94979.

National Organization of Single Mothers: How-to information for mothers and fathers, referrals to support groups. Publishes *Single Mother* magazine and offers free sample issue. POB 68, Midland, NC 28107-0068; 704-888-5063, 704-888-KIDS (5437).

Single Parent Resource Center: National referrals to local services and support groups, information and material—including a self-help-group development manual. 141 W. 28th St., Ste. 302, New York, NY 10001; 212-947-0221.

BOOKS FOR KIDS

How to Live with a Single Parent, Sara Gilbert (New York: Lothrop, Lee & Shepard, 1982) (ages 9 and older).

Living with a Single Parent, Maxine B. Rosenberg (New York: Bradbury Press, 1992) (ages 8 to 12).

My Kind of Family: A Book for Kids in Single-Parent Homes, Michele Lash, et al. (Burlington,VT: Waterfront Books, 1990). 800-639-6063.

Who's in a Family? Robert Skutch (Berkeley, CA: Tricycle Press, 1995).

Part 1

How You Got Here

Chapter 1

Divorce Recovery

Divorce is an ongoing process, not a finite event that ends when the judge slams down the gavel at your final decree. You have yet to go through grief and emotional recovery. The subsequent adjustment to your new status normally takes at least two years, with the highest stress occurring at the one-year point. The time varies, however. It takes what it takes. Don't ever feel you "should" be at any particular point. And remember your Life Preservers.

The issues you face depend on your kids' ages, where you and your ex-spouse live, whether one of you remarries, the amount of conflict between you, and many other factors. Some questions hit you before or at the time you make the divorce legal. Others—both legal and emotional—appear later.

Legal Matters

To formalize your divorce, you have to enter the legal arena in one way or another. Use the following tips to make the experience as painless as possible.

Hire a Lawyer

Using an attorney makes sense—even in "friendly" divorces—because an attorney will cover bases that might not occur to you. Do your own divorce if you want, but have a legal eye peruse the documents.

Attorneys cost less if you use them wisely. Organize facts and papers yourself rather than paying a lawyer $200 an hour for the privilege. Ask about ways to reduce fees. Volunteer for legwork.

Your lawyer advocates for you one hundred percent where it counts, but don't expect him to snarl and growl at your ex or his hired gun. Divorce attorneys handle hundreds of cases with the same opposing lawyers, judges, mediators, and referral services, so they like to keep interactions friendly and straightforward to maintain their reputations. Besides, cooperation on nonessential points means lower fees for you. Still, if you doubt your lawyer's loyalties, discuss it with him.

If you changed your name when you got married, decide whether to change it back. Usually you don't have to file any legal papers to do this, but check with your attorney. The child's name normally stays the same, but it need not.

Custody, Child Support, and Visitation

Until the early 1900's, children automatically went to the father as his "property." Later judges generally awarded custody to the mother as the "best" parent, with limited visiting rights for Dad. Then research revealed that children do best when *both* parents stay involved. Current trends therefore favor joint custody, both legal and physical.

Joint *legal* custody gives both parents authority to make decisions about the child. Joint *physical* custody officially establishes the kid's time with each parent, usually stated in percentages. The actual possible arrangements vary infinitely, from frequent shuffling back and forth between the parents' homes to school years with mother and summers with father.

Both parents' involvement positively affects a child's transition through divorce. Don't insist that your kid never see your ex. This not only deprives him of half his identity, but it usually backfires anyway. Taking this position could cost you custody *and* your kids' trust.

Courts don't force children to choose between Mom and Dad. The judge considers the kids' desires, but even older children don't have final say. Based on the facts, the court decides what's in their "best interest," which usually means maintaining contact with both parents. State laws vary, and a local attorney will thread you through your particular legal maze.

Whatever your custody situation, try to see its positive aspects. Each one has advantages and disadvantages. If there is no other parent in the picture, for example, you have all the responsibility—emotional, financial, and physical. You suffer for your child, knowing he feels abandoned and unloved by one of his parents. On the other hand, your kid has one stable home, and his friends know where to reach him. You experience all his "firsts," like riding a bike or driving the car. You have no hassle over decisions and no worry about someone else's substance abuse, degree of care, or parenting skills. Your child needn't constantly haul belongings between two houses. No one competes for the title "Better Parent."

Joint custody, when shared by cooperating parents, reduces the stress of single-parenting. Even a hostile spouse gives you time for yourself when he takes the kids. If you're lucky, he cares about your child. He may provide some financial help, too. There is, however, potential for disagreements, trips to court for changes in custody arrangements, competition, and loss of control. No custody situation is "better." You have what you have. See what you can do with it.

Work Out Agreements As Much As Possible, Using Mediation If Necessary

If you and your ex-spouse can't reach agreements on your own, the court will decide for you, perhaps disappointing everyone. Instead of going this route, submit complicated matters like custody to mediation, where trained, neutral mediators help the involved parties to communicate and formulate workable, creative solutions. Mediation is not binding.

Here are other issues to resolve by agreement, if possible:

- Have the divorce settlement provide for future college expenses of even very young children. No law requires payment for college, and a voluntary commitment comes more easily now than in fifteen years. With the obligation in mind, the parent responsible for higher education will be more motivated to save for that goal (see Chapter 15).
- Spell out responsibility for maintaining medical, dental, and life insurance for each adult and child.

Beyond strict legal issues, explore assumptions about logistics and underlying expectations. Iron out differences before they create problems. Tackle questions such as:

- How to handle emergencies.
- Who takes the kid to the doctor.

- Who stays home from work when the child gets sick.
- How to share information.
- How much contact to have with one another.
- Whether siblings will move back and forth separately or together.

Protect Yourself with Formalities

Ask your attorney for exact procedures in your jurisdiction. Make sure to do the following:

- Get your name off joint credit cards by closing accounts. Make your request in writing and obtain *written* confirmation from the bank. If a joint card has an outstanding balance when you divorce, normally one party assumes it and transfers it to a new credit card in his name alone.
- Change pension-plan and life-insurance beneficiaries, in writing.
- Freeze any home-equity line of credit.

Don't Rush into Decisions

> "Consider, Sir, how insignificant this will appear a twelve-month hence."
> SAMUEL JOHNSON

Think through what you really want—what really matters for your new life—and what best serves your kids' interests. Don't relinquish something important just to "get this over with." Likewise, resist the temptation to skewer your ex for the sheer pleasure. Listen to your lawyer's advice. You pay him for his ability to view the facts dispassionately when you can't. Unnecessary, emotion-driven litigation over minor issues only costs you money and serenity, not to mention the fact that it adversely affects your kids.

Beyond the Legal Considerations: Emotional and Physical Aspects of Divorce

Knowing that divorce spawns emotional and physical reactions helps you reduce their negative impact.

Some People Hold a Divorce Ceremony, with or without the Ex-Spouse

If both of you participate, the ritual marks the family's change. You bid the marriage good-bye but recommit to your roles as parents. The children speak if they wish.

Confusion about the Decision to Divorce

As you move through the divorce process, one or both of you may start to question your resolve. Suddenly you think you see why you married him in the first place. He wants to start dating you again. Maybe life wasn't so bad together.

This reaction is normal—ten to twenty percent of divorcing couples do date again. Some even resume sexual relations for old time's sake or to avoid exposure to AIDS.

Be very careful if these feelings emerge. Question their genuineness. Don't act on them. They're probably just a stage of the recovery process.

Recognize Physical Reactions

Divorce (or spousal death) affects you physically. Physiological symptoms signal the degree of trauma you've experienced, even if you've repressed it. They'll fade—and recur from time to time. See a doctor if necessary. Go easy on yourself.

The symptoms include:

- Inability to concentrate; forgetfulness; absentmindedness (during the holidays and about six weeks before each anniversary of Tony's suicide, I start losing my keys—all five sets; I search everywhere in frustration—and two minutes later I find a key ring *right there on the counter where I looked three times*—it makes me crazy until I finally recognize the time of year)
- Insomnia
- Headaches
- Tightness or heaviness in the throat, chest, muscles
- Anxiety, nervousness, panic
- Loss of appetite or overeating; intestinal upsets
- Fatigue
- Self-destructive behaviors such as indulging in alcohol, drugs, promiscuity, food binges, or other compulsions

Recognize Emotional Reactions

You will also feel at least some of these common emotional responses after divorce or the death of a spouse:

- Numbness and denial of feelings; disbelief
- Anger
- Abandonment; sense of betrayal; feelings of being duped and cheated
- Becoming very busy to avoid emotional pain
- Social isolation and withdrawal—or fear of being alone
- Sense of unreality
- Sadness; depression
- Emotional volatility; mood swings
- Responsibility for the divorce; self-blame; self-doubt
- Lowered self-esteem; feeling like a failure
- Guilt; fantasizing "if only" scenarios
- Paralysis and fear
- Lack of energy for social interactions
- Concern that the children will reject you
- Insecurity
- Shame
- Compulsion to call or know about the other, just to maintain some sort of connection; confusion over whether divorce was the right course
- Desire to jump into another relationship immediately to prove yourself worthy
- Mistrust of the other sex
- Hopelessness and depression
- Minimizing the importance of the relationship
- And yes, feelings of liberation and freedom

Breathe and examine your emotions. What *do* you feel? You may first have to excavate your anger to discover other feelings.

Acknowledge Your Anger

Right after the separation, you may go through a month or so of numbness, keeping busy with new arrangements. Then emotions emerge, most often starting with anger.

Anger often underlies even a "friendly" divorce, and most divorces aren't all that friendly. You resent your spouse for not being the person you thought. You seethe that he dumped you for someone else. He opposes you at every turn. He makes unfair offers and unreasonable responses and extorts cooperation by using the children as pawns. You're angry at yourself for sticking around so long or for not admitting your unhappiness sooner. Whatever the precise source and intensity, d-i-v-o-r-c-e almost always spells anger.

You think I'm going to tell you to let go of the anger, right? Well, yes—later—but in the beginning, I suggest that you *indulge it.* As an exercise, set the timer and take ten minutes to feel how enraged you really are. Enumerate your resentments and feel the full impact of your outrage at each one. Yell if you like. Find someone besides your kids with whom you can ventilate. Take a drive on the freeway and scream your lungs out (assuming you can express anger and drive safely at the same time—some people can't!).

Experience and express these feelings now or risk bottling them up into a tidy Molotov cocktail for future explosion—perhaps aimed at your kids. Don't hold back for fear the emotions will overwhelm you or become permanent. They won't. Quite the contrary. Doing this exercise helps release them so they won't burst forth inappropriately later.

Right now everything seems black and white. Your emotional thermostat operates only at "high" and "off." In time, you will experience different states of being about your divorce. You will cycle through the same emotions several times, but you're in a forward spiral, not a backward tailspin. Each cycle teaches you something new. Blaming yourself, your ex, or some third party ultimately does no good. Some day, believe it or not, you will learn from this whole experience.

Grieve the Loss of Your Dreams

When you let go of anger, other painful emotions surface. Being enraged keeps you from having to feel hurt, which is why some people stay angry forever. The pain doesn't disappear, however; it just remains locked inside and intensifies the rage. Every loss you experience brings up previous ones, many of which originated in childhood, and anger escalates to keep them at bay. Getting beneath the anger lets you process and release the stored-up emotions. The only way out is "through" them.

The divorce-recovery process resembles grieving after a death. Indeed, divorce represents the death of a dream you once held dear. Even if you rejoice at your ex-spouse's departure, the end of your marriage signals the death of the hopes with which it started. Nothing will be the same from here on—the living arrangements, the family, the traditions. No matter how bad life was with your ex, divorce represents, in some measure, a loss. You remember sweet times of past years. You hear the echoes of broken promises. The loss is painful.

> Population Council studies found that marriages are dissolving with increasing frequency worldwide. The rate doubled from 1970 to 1990 in many developed countries. In less-developed nations, about 25% of first marriages end by the time the woman reaches her forties.[1]

Remember your Life Preserver: Breathe. Acknowledge the sadness and mourn the loss. Don't deny the pain and "tough it out." Try to "enjoy the process" of grieving and moving on in your life. Experience and ritualize the loss in some way. Use candles, music, flowers, or whatever appeals to you. Cry. Mourning releases you from intense feelings so that every new reminder won't thrust you back into them. Concentrate on what you can influence now. Mourn what you can't change and let the rest go. You are becoming a new person.

In the recovery process, you move through stages of grief, defined somewhat differently by various people: numbness, shock or denial; blame or anger at yourself or the other; depression or hopelessness; awareness of your own psychological issues; acceptance of your pain and losses; integration of new realizations into your life; and moving on. You may be in two or more phases at once and cycle through them all several times in different orders. Some seem endless and others momentary.

Everyone experiences these stages at different rates, but the progression normally lasts at least two years. No quick fixes here. In fact, those who rush into a quick remarriage deny themselves the growth this process provides.

Among the times you may feel the most pain are:

- When you realize that you *will* divorce, often after repeated attempts at counseling or reconciliation.
- When dividing possessions, especially items you purchased together or received as wedding presents.
- When you doubt your previous concept of yourself as a person who can sustain a trusting, deep, lasting relationship.

- When you lose the sense of belonging. You're losing your identity as "wife" or "husband," "couple," and "family."
- When you understand that your ever-after will not be as you assumed.

As you mourn what is gone, take some time to appreciate what you *haven't* lost. Feel thankful for what you have. I'm grateful to Tony for giving me Christopher. Though I'm sorry Tony chose to leave the world, I appreciate that I didn't have to endure a horrific custody battle. Being solely responsible for all decisions about Christopher's life frightens me, but I don't have to fight with anyone about them. It's not appropriate to share these thoughts with Christopher, but I do let him know how happy I am to be his mom. Do the same for your sons and daughters.

Practical Steps

Take proactive steps to help yourself through the recovery process.

Reach Out for Support

Seek out the many resources for those going through divorce—legal, psychological, financial—whatever helps you make the right decisions and survive the trauma. Talking and sharing experiences with others reduces your loneliness and puts your situation in perspective. Look for:

- Divorce recovery workshops offered by churches, counselors, and other organizations
- Peer-organized support groups and networks
- Therapists and counselors
- Friends, divorced or not, to help you through difficult times (Ask for what you need—see Chapter 4.)

Limit Other Alterations in Your Life for Awhile

Change of any kind creates stress, and you don't need any more of that just now. Postpone new commitments when you can. Divorce takes extraordinary time and energy. Conserve yours. Devote attention to yourself and your kids.

Prepare for a Change of Friends

Some people take sides in your divorce. Others just drift one way or the other. Friends developed through your spouse and his job follow him. Some acquaintances stay away out of embarrassment or uncertainty—not wanting to favor one of you, they avoid both. Couples don't call because you no longer fill out the dinner table or make a doubles team at tennis.

Don't assume everyone has abandoned you, however. Be proactive. Make contact with people you consider friends. Stay connected if you still feel kinship. Talk about the divorce's effect on your friendship. Let them know you haven't divorced *them.* If they fail to respond, that's their problem. Find others who will.

Nurture Yourself During the Divorce Process

You need some TLC, even if you're the only one available to administer it. While having "fun" may be asking too much, at least relax. Pamper yourself as you would a beloved friend going through tough times. Most importantly, treat yourself with compassion.

Take care of yourself physically. Refer to Chapter 4, but in the meantime, be sure to:

- Get plenty of rest.
- Eat healthy foods and only as much as you want.
- Exercise to relax.
- Avoid alcohol, which is a depressant and which may interfere with your sleep.
- Give up caffeine if you're anxious or nervous.
- Realize that your reactions are normal. Don't expect too much of yourself.
- Avoid self-criticism.
- Be patient and allow healing to occur at its own pace.

Dealing with Your Ex-Spouse

So you thought you were getting him out of your life? Not so. Because you have children together, you are, in some ways, linked for life. Find ways to make it work.

Separate Your Perceptions of Your Ex As a Mate and As a Parent

You may hate the air your ex breathes, and with good reason. He's mistreated you, cheated on you, and left you with nothing. But consider—just consider—the possibility that he *might* at the same time be a decent dad. One person can be both a rotten partner and a good parent. Could this be true of your former spouse? If so, be grateful that you at least have half of what you wanted from him. Let him be a parent to his kids in his own way, even if he intends his good parenting only as a means of making *you* look *bad.* So what if he *really* bought your girls a puppy because he knew you couldn't afford one? A puppy! How can you compete with that? Don't. Your kids love the dog. Just appreciate that your former spouse did the right thing for the wrong reasons. He's a lousy partner (and a rotten ex-partner) but he might be a good dad.

Avoid Conflict with Your Former Spouse

With luck, both you and your ex have your child's best interests at heart. You communicate and compromise for his sake. Maybe you even still respect each other. Count your blessings.

Even if you hate each other's guts, try to make one all-important agreement: No fighting, no warfare—even when you're "right." *More than any other factor, the degree to which parents avoid conflict determines how well a kid fares after divorce.*

> For the American Automobile Association's (kids) *Flying Alone* pamphlet of practical tips, send a self-addressed, stamped, legal-size envelope to Flying Alone, Mail Stop 800, 1000 AAA Drive, Heathrow, FL 32746-5063.

Whenever a parental dispute arises, place your child's best interest front and center. Otherwise, he will think he caused the conflict and, therefore, there is something wrong with him.

A raging, vindictive ex-spouse makes conflict almost inevitable, as does a neglectful, uncaring one. First, make sure *you* aren't either of those. Then, simply put, do whatever it takes to avoid hostility and fighting. You won't like this because it means losing face, restraining reactions, foregoing commentary, swallowing angry words, and giving up on issues that matter to you. Just remember that your child benefits in a major way.

Your kids may go without coats at your ex's house. They may skip homework, watch too much TV, play Mortal Kombat endlessly, stay out late, eat junk food, dye their hair green, pierce their eyebrows, eat like animals, and swing from the trees over there. Your former spouse may "forget" appointments, miss pickups, bollix up your schedule, and mess with your mind. You can't prevent any of it. Making a fuss just highlights areas for the next attack. You'll run yourself ragged, but you won't change a thing.

Don't imagine that you can have it both ways—battle with your ex and keep it from your kid. Children have radar. You can't fake it. Even if you don't fight in front of your child, he'll know about the conflict. He'll trust and respect you less for trying to fool him.

It's another question, of course, if alcohol, drugs, abuse, neglect, unsafe housing, guns, or other dangers threaten your child when he's in your ex's home or under his care. You must intervene, with outside authorities if necessary.

Two Houses, Two Sets of Rules

You *do* have control at your house, and that's where you counteract other influences. Your rules prevail there, and they can be 180 degrees from what goes on at your ex's. (Your poor teen will have to re-dye his hair once a week! But maybe you'll let that one go. . . .) Kids adjust very well to two sets of rules. When they protest, "Dad lets us do it," they're testing. Take a breath and say, "Maybe so, but I don't. My house, my rules."

Obviously, some issues don't lend themselves to a my-rules-at-my-house approach. If you and your ex can't agree on your kid's school, for example, he can't go to Mom's High one day and Dad's High the next. Don't fight. Show your child how mature adults handle disagreements. Either your divorce settlement made some provision for this, you seek counseling or mediation together, or one of you gives in. If that has to be you . . . okay.

If You Can't Work with Him, Work around Him

Someone once said that if you stumble over furniture in the dark, you don't get mad at the furniture—you turn on the lights and go around it. If your ex-spouse remains as immovable as Aunt Bessie's maple armoire, work around him.

- Keep your expectations realistic. You know this person well and can probably predict his actions. Don't hope for anything more.
- Don't take his problematic behavior personally. Stay detached emotionally. Realize that his actions probably arise from his own feelings of inadequacy and insecurity. Be an anthropologist. Watch his behavior as if trying to document the tribal customs of a long lost, primitive race. Make him a subject of observation, not irritation.
- Avoid critical remarks, even constructive criticism. His insecurities will invariably read your comments as an attack.
- Don't respond in kind to anger or confrontations. Stay calm. Easier said than done? He *wants* you to get angry. So thwart him with serenity.
- If you can't communicate with your ex, stop trying. Find a way to convey information that doesn't trigger argument and insult. Try letters or notes. Communicate solely through your lawyers or therapists or their secretaries if necessary. Try anything but using your kids as messengers.
- If you can't stand to be in the same room, arrange separate parent-teacher conferences. Watch your child's soccer games on opposite sides of the field. Take turns attending functions. Just don't fight.
- Let your ex-spouse have his way sometimes. He may never reciprocate, but perhaps giving him some of what he needs will defuse the underlying insecurities.
- Give it time. If he doesn't repeatedly get a rise from you, he may forget to be obnoxious. Maybe he'll mellow with age.
- If your ex is a rotten parent, accept it. You agonize over your child's pain, but you learned the hard way that reminders, shouting matches, and guilt trips have no effect on your ex. He's going to keep disappointing your kid forever, and that is a fact.

Give Up Your Anger

Blame and anger hook you into the other person, even (especially?) when they have no effect whatsoever on his behavior. Your incessant resentfulness chews *you* up and washes right over him. Some divorced couples fuel conflict for years, staying "half-married," bonded together in mutual hatred and retaliation. Having gone through legal divorce, you must also experience "psychic divorce," the final letting go of intense involvement, both positive *and negative*. You can't move on without doing this.

At some point you will simply get tired of always being riled and you will be ready to move on. You will finally realize that anger is a choice and that you can give it up! You just accept that everything is what it is. Let go of the bait and swim away. Anger may return periodically, but it won't power your life anymore.

Repeat the exercise of listing your resentments, but this time state what makes you angry—and then add, aloud, "and so it is." "She fills the kids' heads with lies about me . . . and so it is." "He buys their love with expensive gifts that I can't afford to match . . . and so it is." Giving up anger takes time. Don't demand perfection of yourself. Just let go as much as you can now.

You have absolutely no control over your ex. Accept that. Give up. Repeat your mantra: ". . . and so it is."

Nobody says you have to *like* anything. Just *accept* it. It is, after all, reality. You cannot remake your ex. If you could, you would have done so before the divorce! An old saying defines *sanity* as giving up the attempt to convince an insane person that he is insane. It simply can't be done—the frames of reference don't even overlap. Divorcing spouses can lapse into a form of "insanity" that rationality can't reach. Stop trying. Deal, instead, with where to go from here.

Your ex-spouse can cause you unlimited pain. He dishes it out and gloats at your misery. He anticipates ruining your life and destroying you emotionally. My reactions to Tony's death have been complex, and sometimes I know he intended to punish and hurt me. This raises my ire until I realize I can foil his intent . . . my best revenge is to be happy!

Helping Children Cope with Divorce

Divorce changes—but doesn't end—family relationships. Unlike their parents, who must *stop* belonging to each other, kids must find a way of belonging to *both* of them—*separately*. As children, they are inexperienced, developmentally incomplete, and powerless to affect the situation. They desperately need your help in coping. They seldom see positive aspects to the change in the family. To them it's just a loss.

A child's ultimate adjustment to divorce depends on gender (boys have more trouble), age and developmental stage, the nature of family life before separation, and the parents' coping skills and relationship after the divorce. The last two—what happens after the family splits up—outweigh the other factors.

Telling Your Child about the Separation and Divorce

Talk to your kid about the divorce, providing special reassurances in areas that intersect his developmental tasks.

> "He that is slow to anger is better than the mighty . . ."
> PROVERBS 16:32

- Tell him sooner rather than later. Don't wait until the morning one of you moves out to inform your child about what's going on. Via the highly sensitive Kid's Radar Warning System, he knows something is up anyway. Being kept in the dark about what will happen only creates high anxiety for your child.
- State the truth clearly and simply. Explain the facts in language he understands. Give general reasons for the split-up, but spare him detailed explanations, especially if they involve adultery. Tell the truth without blaming anyone or suggesting that divorce is shameful. Never use euphemisms that, for instance, suggest that "Mommy is going away for a while."
- Informing all your children at one time, even with large age differences between them, prevents feelings of favoritism or lack of trust. Have individual conversations later. The children will help one another.
- Make it okay to talk about the divorce. Never burden kids with having to keep a "secret" from siblings or friends—an impossibility anyway. Research shows that children of divorce don't get much healing from their friends. Your child may even be reluctant to talk to them about divorce. Nevertheless, give them permission. Forbidding mention of a subject shrouds it in shame.

- Give details about where your child will live and how often he will see each parent. He has a right to know what's in store for his future. If the non-custodial parent intends to move some distance, talk about traveling. Explain any name changes.
- Assure your kid that although his parents don't love one another, they both love him.
- Don't be Santa Claus to make up for the bad news. The only present your child needs at this time is your love, time, and attention.

Children's Emotional Reactions to Divorce

Depending on age, the emotional repercussions for your child may include:

- Feelings of abandonment and withdrawal of love.
- Insecurity and anxiety about what will happen to him. He's always believed that parents love each other forever. If that's not true, then what other erroneous assumptions has he made? Can parents stop loving their kid, for example? Can they "divorce" him?
- Blaming himself for the divorce; thinking he could have done something to prevent it.
- Anger at himself and parents or displaced anger at siblings, teachers, friends; temper tantrums.
- Shame at parental behavior.
- A shaken sense of identity.
- A deep sense of loneliness.
- Blaming one parent or the other for the separation.
- Despair of ever having successful relationships (most often experienced by teens).
- Caretaking of wounded parents.
- Social-emotional regression.
- Dependency.
- Aggression.
- Changes in patterns of eating and elimination.
- Nightmares.
- Physical accidents.
- Misbehavior at school.
- Decline in school performance.
- Extreme "good behavior" to prevent rejection by parents. The stress of sustaining such control can produce anxiety attacks.
- Extreme misbehavior to precipitate the abandonment and get it over with.

- Reunification fantasies. Even a kid who observes that his parents are happier apart often dreams of reuniting the family.

Developmental Stages Affect Children's Reaction to Divorce

The same events have varying impacts on kids who are tackling different developmental tasks. Knowing what struggles your child normally faces at his stage of development helps you assess and address his reactions to divorce.

- An infant works on trust, learning that someone will be there to care for him. He's most sensitive to his primary caregiver's ability to function. As long as that person copes and continues to provide what he needs, an infant generally handles divorce well. Maintain routines and keep him from excessive emotional turmoil.

  If you must suddenly put an infant in day care so you can go back to work, seek continuity. Aim for a place with low turnover, a warm affectionate staff, and a stimulating environment (see Chapter 11 on finding child care).
- Developmentally, a toddler or preschooler struggles with independence and separation. He fears you'll respond to his new assertiveness by abandoning him, and divorce seems to confirm that. Explain what is happening. Most parents underestimate a child's ability to understand, leaving him alone to deal with the confusion and fear. He imagines far worse than the reality. His egocentricity and beginning conscience lead him to believe he caused the separation. Whatever the custody arrangement, explain the parental "disappearances" in terms that have nothing to do with his behavior.

  Be prepared for the same questions over and over. Preschoolers need repeated explanations over time.
- Developmentally, school-age children work on mastery of intellectual, emotional, and physical skills. They solidify sexual identification and undergo socialization. Their normal focus shifts from family to school and peers. They're driven to achieve, and formation of a healthy self-concept depends on opportunities to express that need. Divorce interrupts these processes. Kids of this age feel less responsible for the divorce but more lonely and helpless. Most children with divorcing parents are of school age.
- Around seven or eight, kids understand the concept of the future and "forever." Your child can now understand that the divorce is

permanent. Although he doesn't want to choose sides, he may feel pressured to do so in order to resolve uncomfortable conflicts of loyalty.

A child of this age will be deeply aware of his suffering but won't be able to find relief through reunification fantasies, denial, or activities. Fearing deprivation, he may hoard or have trouble sharing. Some kids are afraid of antagonizing their mother; she might "get rid of them" as she did their father.

- From nine to twelve, children develop empathy and a sense of reality. It's common for them to aim anger at one parent, and they may take care of the other to the point of premature "adulthood." To deal with feelings of powerlessness, they may try to master more and more activities.

> - The U.S. divorce rate is the highest in the world. It has quadrupled since 1960.[2]
> - A divorced parent heads 37% of single-parent families.[3]
> - 40% of American kids do not live with their biological fathers.[4]

- An adolescent's developmental tasks are to separate from you, form his own identity, and adjust to his sexual maturation. His response to divorce includes withdrawal and rebellion, typical teen behavior in any event. He might accelerate into adult behaviors—either becoming super-responsible or experimenting with drugs and sex. Conversely, he may delay separating and become quite dependent. A teen often tests limits. Resolving intolerable ambiguity with black-and-white judgments, he might assign the role of the bad guy to either you or your ex during the divorce. To counteract this, remind him that everyone is complex, both good and bad. Encourage him to spend time with both parents. Avoid exposing him to your anger toward your ex.

  Because your teen struggles with his own sexuality, he normally begins to regard his parents as sexual beings, which threatens and confuses him. After divorce, this conflict grows sharper. He loses a role model for mature heterosexual relationships.

Also, when you begin to date again, you invade his adolescent "territory" with your own concern over *your* appearance, preoccupation with the opposite sex, courting behavior, and so on. You're his "competition," a threat. Therefore, downplay your sexuality (and at least hope your ex will do the same) for a year or so after the divorce.

A teen of divorced parents also often questions his own ability to form lasting relationships. Assure him he isn't doomed to repeat your mistakes; rather, he can learn from them. Divorce isn't hereditary (though, having lived through one, a child might be more willing to consider it a solution to an unhappy marriage).

Finally, let your teen be a teen. Don't ask him to fill in for the missing parent emotionally.

- Only-children seem more vulnerable to negative effects of divorce. Kids with siblings support each other. Sometimes, however, sibs may suffer displaced anger from other kids in the family.

Don't Put the Kids in the Middle

Your child must disengage from the conflict between you and your ex. He can *love* the two of you but he cannot *agree* with both. He shouldn't have to try. Don't ask him to take sides. Involving him in your marital war leads him to expect similar dynamics in his own future family. Using him to work out *your* anger impairs *his* ability to form future, solid adult relationships. To keep your child out of the middle:

- Assure him explicitly and repeatedly that he did nothing to cause the family problems or the separation.
- Don't cast him in the role of messenger or news reporter. Find other ways to communicate with your former spouse. Satisfy your curiosity about his present life directly. Even better, give up caring. Pumping your kid for information leads to distrust and provides a poor role model.
- Don't use your child as a weapon. One man, Paul, has an ex-wife who told their daughter, for example, that the reason he didn't go to her piano recital was that he didn't love her. Paul had wanted to go, but experience had convinced him his ex would make a scene. Fortunately, his daughter questioned him about her

mother's statement, and Paul reassured her of his love. But the little girl suffered nonetheless.

Maintain Discipline

Children need consistency and limits to feel safe. Don't abandon the rules out of guilt, emotion, or hope of winning your kids' favor. Kids learn instantaneously whether you can be manipulated. They'll test you. Be loving but firm.

People used to worry most about the negative effect of the "absent father." No one denies that children fare better when Dad stays in the picture. Except when the absent parent is abusive or seriously disturbed, even minuscule contact benefits the child by reducing fears of abandonment, vulnerability, and dependency on just one parent.

Nonetheless, the more crucial factor is the quality of post-divorce parenting, whether by Mom, Dad, or both. Security, control and limits, parental emotional stability, structure and order, clear boundaries, emotional support, and routine are essential.

Don't Let Your Child Take Care of You

If you don't take care of yourself, your child might bury his own needs and attend to yours. Distraught parents sometimes fail to see a kid's problems or connect them to the family breakup. Your child loves you and needs you to be stable and functioning. His survival literally depends on it. Demonstrate that despite the upset, you remain competent and capable of caring for him and yourself.

Avoid using your child as a confidant, but make clear your willingness to listen to him. Otherwise, he'll get the idea you're too delicate for difficult subjects and will protect you with his silence.

Don't Badmouth Your Ex-Spouse

However much you detest your ex, however despicable his actions and character, refrain from saying so to your child—or within his hearing. Remember, this nasty, vindictive, vile person is the parent of someone you love most in the world. Half your kid's genes come from this rotten, hopeless excuse for a human being. How can your child believe you love *him* if fifty percent of his being consists of so much scum? How can he love himself? He can't.

Besides, he loves your ex. Denigrating your former spouse insults your child's judgment about whom to love.

Look at your motivation for trashing your ex. Aren't you really trying to influence your child's opinion? You want him to love you more than his other parent, to consider you "right"? Forget it. Divorce isn't a competitive sport. Your kid loves you, and his loving your ex doesn't change or diminish that.

Don't just *allow* your child to love his other parent—*support* him in an active, separate, private, loving relationship with that parent. While getting him to blame your ex for all manner of things may satisfy you, it's not in your child's best interest. Keep the boundaries intact between you and him. Allow him the freedom to think what *he* thinks, feel what *he* feels, and love whom *he* loves. Letting him honestly share his affection for his other parent imparts the message that he can be real with you.

If your child shows antagonism to your ex-spouse, don't reinforce it. Instead, help him see that people aren't all good or all bad. Like you, your ex is a complex human being.

Your child may hear horrible, negative things about you from his other parent. Don't get defensive. Just be the good person you are, even if your ex paints you as an ogre. Your kid will make his own judgments. Refrain from debating who's right and who's wrong. Remember, avoiding conflict helps your child.

Reassure Your Child You Will Not Abandon Him

Divorce means you and your spouse no longer love one another. "Love" is suddenly a disposable commodity. If you stop loving your spouse, can you do the same to your child? Do all relationships end in abandonment? Abandonment is, in reality, one of the greatest fears of all children.

Assuage your child's fears of desertion with both words and actions. Tell him often that you love him, that you always will. Explain that you and his other parent loved him together, that you wanted him and were so happy when he arrived. Now you're going to love him separately but just as much.

Always be on time when scheduled to pick your child up, whether from school or your ex's. Small kids, especially, suffer during even short waits, wondering if you've abandoned them. Call if delayed, and urge your former spouse to do the same. Clue him in to the importance of punctual, regular times with your child.

Avoid leaving your kid for any extended period in the early months of your divorce. If you *must* go away, explain why beforehand. You have business, or you have to transport Grandma, or whatever. Emphasize that your child did not cause your absence and you're not leaving forever. When you return, remind him you promised to come back and tell him how much you missed him. Encourage him to talk about the feelings he experienced during your absence, and *listen* to what he says (see Chapter 5).

Don't Raise False Hopes

Some children of divorce never really give up thinking their parents will reunite. Remember Hayley Mills as scheming twins in *The Parent Trap*?

Parent "traps" can be subtle. Both physical accidents and acting out at school may represent an effort, probably unconscious, to bring the family back together. Your kid thinks if his parents love him so much, they'll reunite over his injury or behavioral problems. Perhaps a doctor or teacher will insist they remarry for his benefit!

Grieving requires overcoming denial. Your child must acknowledge reality. Tell him Daddy and Mommy won't live together again. Recognize your kid's feelings without raising his hopes. "I know you feel sad Mom and Dad aren't married anymore."

Don't Take Away Your Kid's Pain

It hurts to see your child in pain, especially if you feel partly responsible for causing it. Don't try to convince him you're all better off now. That may be true, but your kid won't experience it that way, even if pre-divorce life was hell. He doesn't see *any* positive aspects to separation. For him, it's all loss. Everything changes profoundly.

Because it's painful for you to see your child hurt, you may unconsciously try to "fix" his pain, to smooth over his feelings. Don't. Depriving your child of his pain and growth is really an attempt to make *yourself* feel better. Letting him honestly share his feelings, even if you don't share the sentiments, imparts the message that he can be real with you.

If your former spouse disappears or shows up unreliably, help your child come to terms with his other parent's apparent lack of love. Emphasize that the defect lies with the parent, not the child. Explain that your ex may simply be unable to show affection now—or perhaps ever. Don't cover for him or make excuses, and don't berate him. Tell your child the truth: "Some people make promises and don't follow through on them. It's disappointing when that happens." Painful as it may be, your child is better off hearing this and working to accept his parent's faults than constantly losing himself in futile efforts to win love or feeling he is unlovable.

Help Resolve Your Child's Anger

Because anger at a parent frightens a child, he may displace it and instead act out his feelings with friends, siblings, or teachers. Often he'll lash out at the parent with whom he feels safest, trusting that person to "take it" without dishing out severe consequences. Don't be surprised, therefore, if your good parenting only seems to bring strife. It's a sign your kid trusts you. Rather than squabbling over the immediate dispute, address the underlying emotion. Then deal with the superficial issue using your conflict resolution techniques (see Chapter 5).

When your child's anger is direct, detach from it. Don't take it personally. Tell him you encourage discussion but would prefer a calmer one.

Encourage Talk and Expression of Feelings

Emotional problems develop when a kid can't express feelings and communicate with parents about the divorce. He needs a way to tell you even what you don't want to hear—things that will make you sad, angry, or scared. If confiding in you results in hysterics, rages, or punishment, he won't be back for a second helping. Be receptive to hearing anything he says.

Become an archaeologist for your child's feelings. Gently prod him in hopes of bringing them to the surface. "You really seem angry. Do you want to talk about it?" Sometimes he will, and sometimes not. Accept that. Don't pressure him for conversation, but make your availability clear. Say you will listen whenever he's ready. "If you change your mind, let me know." Convey the message, "It's okay, and I still love you."

Every four to six months, inquire into your child's feelings about the divorce. Get a good children's book, such as *Dinosaur's Divorce*, and read it together occasionally. A child reintegrates the divorce experience in different ways as he grows.

Don't Tell Children What They're Feeling

When encouraging children to express feelings, indicate acceptance without implying some particular emotion is "right." Make sure they know they don't have to feel any particular way in order to preserve your love.

Feelings "are," period. They're not right or wrong. Try "I could understand if you felt angry," or "That sort of treatment makes some people sad." If he feels this way, he'll probably admit it, and you can go from there.

Minimize Other Changes

Setting up a separate household creates chaos. Routines for regular meals together, bedtimes, reading, getting to school, and so on, fall by the wayside. Some parents have to learn how to shop, cook, clean, and do laundry on their own. Life tends to be disorganized for at least a year after divorce. Kids who undergo many changes at once—joining a stepfamily, moving, enrolling in a new school, losing old friends, even falling in socio-economic status—take longer to adjust. Some of the reactions you witness in your kids may result not so much from the divorce itself as from the readjustment of daily life. Keep everything as stable as possible and work to reestablish routines.

Deal with Regression by Addressing Underlying Emotions

"Baby" behaviors you never expected to see again may reemerge after divorce, signaling a desire for comfort and reassurance. Address that need rather than the behaviors themselves. Look for the underlying emotions. "Are you feeling scared today?"

Be Aware of Delayed Reactions

Although divorce is probably the most traumatic incident of a kid's early life, some breeze through it with no apparent upset at all—initially. Later, when they're sure *you're* okay, they experience a delayed reaction. Sometimes it surfaces when you break up with a subsequent lover, for example. That separation triggers and intensifies the feelings your child never expressed earlier.

The kids who *never* show upset are the ones to worry about. Often, children of divorce feel they must be perfect, believing this will mend the family. Let your child know emotional reactions are normal and expected.

If any of this seems too frightening or difficult, get help from a therapist or counselor for you or the kids. It needn't necessarily be long-term. Even a session or two with a sympathetic professional about a specific issue can work wonders.

Find a Support or Therapy Group for Children of Divorce

Twice yearly, my single-parent support group offers eight-week groups for the children. Even in this age of fifty-percent divorce rates, many kids believe they are the only ones living with single parents! These therapist-led groups cure them of that notion and offer the opportunity to talk with others in the same situation. This, in itself, aids recovery. The children have a forum for expressing their feelings, exploring new family roles, and validating their perceptions.

The groups teach kids that they *do* have power in relationships and can make choices in how to use it. They can be passive and reactive or responsible and proactive in solving problems. Other members offer suggestions and share similar experiences. Close bonds form among these kids. As they tell their stories, they better understand themselves and their parents.

The approach differs depending on age, but all aim at normalizing the single-parent home. My son joined his first group at age four. The kids sat in a circle and held "Henrietta the Hippo" whenever they wanted to talk. They drew pictures of their families, sang songs, played musical chairs, and ate cookies. Although his dad's suicide makes him a minority within a minority, Christopher has many issues in common with other single-parent kids, especially the need to express feelings and permission to speak about the unspeakable.

If nothing else, Christopher's participation in the groups reassures *me.* In the parent-therapist conference, I learned that he listens to others and matter-of-factly shares that his daddy is dead. I appreciate knowing that he talks freely.

Groups like this sometimes form at schools. Ask guidance counselors about initiating one.

Create a New Sense of Family

Family meetings speed divorce recovery. Use them to form new routines, resolve conflicts, explore feelings, and create a new sense of family. Involve your children in as many decisions as possible about your lives in order to give them some sense of control (see Chapter 5).

Establish New Rituals and Routines

New routines necessarily replace the old. Putting them in place dissipates the feeling of chaos after divorce. Some things that you can do are:

- Ease the kids' transitions between households. Single parents often find their kids unbearable for a day or two after returning from the other parent. This probably results from the transition itself rather than anything your ex did during the visit. Imagine picking up your entire life and moving it from house to house twice a month, every weekend, or even every three days! Whatever the custody arrangement, most kids find having two homes at least somewhat disruptive and unnerving. They need a few hours to settle in after the transition. Think of how you feel when returning from vacations. Shifting back into usual routines comes gradually, and you want to do it your own way. Some people flake out with the TV, while others get busy on the mail or chores.

  Likewise, kids differ in what they need to ease the transition from house to house. Some want to be alone for a while. Others need gregarious welcomes and quick interactions. Ask your child, "What would make the transition back to this house less stressful for you?" He'll appreciate both your asking and your accommodating him.
- You can retain many important routines despite divorce. Carrying on the same way as before brings comfort. Preserve the way you leave home in the mornings, how you say good-bye at school, when you have family meetings, and so on.
- Think ahead about rituals the divorce will change. How will you handle birthdays, for example? Will your child see both you and your ex that day? Or talk by phone? If you have joint custody in the same

geographic area, can you agree on party plans? Can you be together at the party? If not, maybe another year. If one parent attends the party, when will the other celebrate with your child, and how? Can he take the siblings during the party? Communicate all decisions clearly to younger kids, and let the older ones participate in making them.

Don't forget your own new role in all this. I know from experience that giving a party for kids by yourself makes you crazy. You have to supervise as well as run the "show." In the early years, parents always stick around for birthday parties and pitch in. But around age five, they start dropping their kids off and leaving. You could find yourself alone in charge of twenty wild animals and end up pinning the tail on the presents, cutting and serving the piñata, and lighting the tablecloth instead of the candles. Line up assistance ahead of time, even if you have to hire a "mother's helper," and be very specific about what you need. Enlist friends and other parents. Be sure to designate a photographer so you'll end up in some of the pictures!

Alternatively, just "buy" a birthday party from people who produce them for a living. Some facilities, such as science museums, amusement parks, swimming pools, or commercial play areas, supply everything—including the cake, a simple meal, and loot bags. They even preside over an orderly opening of presents and recycle the paper. The kids take advantage of the environs, and you sit back and relax. Remember, you count, too.

See Chapter 13 for a discussion of new holiday rituals.

- When the time comes, decide how you'll handle "Father's Day" or "Mother's Day" and corresponding birthdays. You can help your child pick out and buy a gift or card, or just consider it none of your business. Find out what he prefers. To some degree it will depend on your relationship with your former spouse and his plans for the occasion.

Travel to Visit a Distant Parent

Airlines estimate that hundreds of thousands of children, some as young as five, trek unaccompanied across the country—or the world—each year to visit "other" parents. If your child joins this number, planning ensures success.

- When your child travels alone by public means, inform the carrier. There may be age requirements for flying direct or nonstop. Some airlines now impose a fee of about $30 to supervise unescorted children. Some maintain special kids' rooms for layovers.

- Call ahead a day or two for any special instructions. For air trips, order your child the special meal of his choice. Most airlines feature kids' selections, or he might enjoy the seafood. Let him decide.
- Explain all aspects of the trip ahead of time so he encounters few surprises. Go over details: Will he travel alone? By what means? How long will the trip take? Who will meet him? What should he do if he gets lost? If (let's hope not!) your ex arrives late to pick him up? Explain how and when your child will eat on the trip. Inform him that he may talk with flight attendants, bus drivers, conductors, and the like, even though they are "strangers." He can ask them for help.
- Talk about any changes in your ex's circumstances since the last visit. Put a positive spin on the new developments, regardless of your own feelings: "Daddy has a new baby now named James. Remember the picture he sent you? James is your little brother. You'll have fun playing with him, and I'm sure Daddy will have fun playing with you."
- Tell him you'll miss him. Emphasize that you'll still love him while he's away and will be waiting for his return. Given his personality and age, decide whether frequent communications from you will be helpful or only encourage homesickness. Let him know how and how often you'll communicate with him over the distance—by phone, letter, or e-mail.
- Help him pack, giving him wide leeway to choose what to take. Check for necessities he might overlook. Let him take pictures of you and your life together and, if he's young, any "loveys" or other comfort items to ease the transition. Don't pack anything you (or your child) couldn't bear to lose, however. Pin a list of what he should bring back with him to the lining of his suitcase.
- Provide a carry-on stuffed with books, games, cards, snacks, activities—whatever will keep him busy and comforted. Include some gum for takeoff and landing if he's going by air. He'll need money to pay for an in-flight movie or buy ice cream on a layover.
- If you have more than one child going, give attention and age-appropriate instructions to each. When you send mail, use just one envelope—preventing the U.S. Postal Service from delivering one late or not at all.

- Remind teens to identify themselves to flight attendants if their flights are delayed or diverted. The airline will arrange food and accommodations as necessary.
- Before your child leaves, mail a reassuring, positive letter or card to await his arrival.
- Leave early on the day of departure to allay anxiety and take care of any last-minute problems.
- Pin an information card on your kid's clothing (or inside, if he prefers), stating his and your names, address, destination, name and telephone number of your ex and any other relevant person at the other end. Include any allergies or special health needs on the card. List every emergency phone number you can.
- Ask him to call so you'll know he arrived safely.
- If homesickness strikes and he wants to return to you, don't jump into action, even assuming changes are possible and your ex would let him go. Listen to him and validate his feelings. Get him to talk about his experience so far and find out whether something specific troubles him. Depending on the relationship with your ex, a conversation between you two might prove fruitful. Reassure your child and encourage him to talk with his other parent to make improvements.

  If there really is no possibility of an early return, be honest. Airline reservations may require a certain stay or forbid changes. And then of course, you may have plans yourself (you'd better have something fun planned for yourself!—see Chapter 4).

Preserving Ties with Ex-In-Laws

If your families took hostile sides in the divorce, you may have nothing further to do with your former in-laws. On the other hand, some extended families maintain friendly contact even in the face of discordance between ex-spouses.

Your ex may disappear completely, in which case your child's only chance to connect with his other parent's family depends on you—and their willingness, of course. Play the ex-in-law song by ear. Even if relations prove uncomfortable for you, remember that the other side of the family is half your child's heritage. Besides, those ex-in-laws may turn out to be some of the best financial, emotional, and practical help *you* get in the difficult task of single-parenting.

If ex-in-laws reside at a distance, your child may have little established relationship with them and no means of independently creating one, especially if he's young. Be proactive in making those grandparents part of his life through the mail. Use some of his arts and crafts as gifts. Send a paint-imprint of his hands and feet every year while he's small. Let him call long distance as often as you can afford it. Send pictures frequently. Ask them to write him a story—or let them and your child create a serial story, each adding a chapter and returning it for the other's next installment. Send audio or videotapes. You needn't edit them if you don't have time. Just duplicate and send. If the recipients get bored, they can fast-forward.

As you proceed through the divorce process, stay open to the people who love you and your child, and put your energy into being the best parent you can be. This is surely the quickest way to recovery and the future.

ORGANIZATIONS

Joint Custody Association: 10606 Wilkins Ave., Los Angeles, CA 90024; 310-475-5352.

Mothers Without Custody: Information and support. POB 36, Woodstock, IL 60098 (include a self-addressed stamped envelope and two 1st-class stamps). Crisis Line: 815-455-2955.

BOOKS FOR PARENTS

Mothers without Custody: How Could a Mother Do Such a Thing?, Geoffrey Greif and Mary S. Pabst (New York: Free Press, 1989).

Rituals for Our Times: Celebrating, Healing and Changing Our Lives and Our Relationships, Evan Imber-Black and Janine Roberts (New York: HarperCollins, 1993).

Talking about Divorce and Separation: A Dialogue Between Parent and Child, Earl A. Grollman (Boston: Beacon Press) (grades K–4).

BOOKS FOR KIDS

At Daddy's on Saturdays, Linda Walvoord Girard (Morton Grove, IL: Albert Whitman & Co., 1987) (grades K–3).

Break-Up: Facing Up to Divorce, Gianni Padoan (New York: Child's Play, 1987).

Dinosaur's Divorce: A Guide for Changing Families, Laurene Krasny Brown and Marc Brown (Boston: Little, Brown, 1986) (ages 4 to 10).

The Divorce Workbook: A Guide for Kids and Families, Sally B. Ives, et al. (Burlington, VT: Waterfront Books, 1985) (ages 4 to 12).

Families Are Different, Nina Pellegrini (New York: Holiday House, 1991).

How It Feels When Parents Divorce, Jill Krementz (New York: Knopf, 1984) (ages 12 to 18).

Kids Are Nondivorceable: A Workbook for Divorced Parents and Their Children Age 6–11, Sara Bonkowski (Chicago: ACTA Publications, 1987), 800-397-2282.

Mom and Dad Don't Live Together Any More, Kathy Stinson (Toronto: Annick Press, 1984).

My Mother's House, My Father's House, C. B. Christiansen (New York: Atheneum, 1989) (grades K–3).

Why Are We Getting a Divorce? Peter Mayle (New York: Harmony Books, 1988).

Chapter 2

When Your Spouse Dies

The initial numbness after your spouse dies gets you through the immediate crises—the children, the arrangements, the visitors, the estate. Later, emotions emerge slowly so you can handle them. Honor those feelings. Take time for them. Utilize all available support and let yourself mourn. Read the sections about grieving and emotions in Chapter 1. They all apply to you.

A word about anger: even if you adored your spouse, you'll experience tremendous anger at him for leaving you and the children. This may not seem "appropriate," but it's completely normal, part of the grieving process. Let yourself experience it fully.

Find a grief support group through local mental health agencies or private therapists. I benefited from a group for survivors of suicides.

Don't Make Any Quick Decisions about Your Life

Avoid drastic changes during the first few months on your own. Don't sell your house, for example, or move across the country. With your emotions in turmoil, you're vulnerable to mistakes.

Do immediately make a new will for yourself, execute a new durable power of attorney and living will, and appoint a guardian for your kids (see Chapter 18). Get legal help for the estate and any related legal issues.

Children and Death

When your spouse dies, you must help your children cope with the loss while in the midst of your grief. It isn't an easy job, but the following discussion will help you feel less confused and uncertain.

"Death Education"

If we have sex education, why not "death education"? We're now open about the beginning of life, why not the end? Kids *see* death all the time—the seasons change, a pet dies, a possum lies squashed in the street, a grandparent gives in to old age, TV and movie characters bite the dust in various ways—but kids don't understand what they see. If no one tells them the truth, they come up with their own explanations. Worse, avoiding the subject of death conveys the idea that denial is an acceptable way to deal with it.

Death is like sex—talk about it early, in age-appropriate ways, and it won't loom as an enormous, unapproachable subject when it suddenly becomes relevant. Use reality words, not euphemisms. Don't fear the topic because you don't know the ultimate answers. Who does? If you wait until you do know, you'll be beyond telling anyone! Go with what you believe. Maybe your children have something to teach *you*. At least you can search for wisdom together. Use death to introduce your spiritual beliefs.

Early on, children develop a healthy, natural curiosity about dying. Allow them to pursue it. Comment on death in your everyday environment. Answer questions simply and honestly and only in enough detail to satisfy what your kids want to know. Use terms they understand. Reintroduce the concept from time to time so they can integrate it into new developmental stages.

Because even school-age kids don't necessarily "hold" information about a subject as abstract as death, expect to hear the same questions again and again. Just keep answering them.

Help children view death as natural and inevitable. Those exposed to death through previous calm discussion or prior loss of a pet or distant relative fare better and seem less fearful if a parent dies.

Pay Attention to Your Child's Developmental Stage

From three to five, children don't understand the finality of death. "Mommy died, but she'll be back tomorrow."

From five to nine they form a somewhat clearer picture. They often personify death as some creature who comes and gets people. Could it happen to them? No way. They're so strong and powerful they'll easily escape! Kids of this age have plenty of questions: What happens to the body, how do the worms get inside the casket, why do you get cold when you die?

Finally, around ten, kids understand that they themselves must die.

Recovering from the Death of a Parent

While you and your children grieve simultaneously, you do so differently.

How Children Grieve

A child grieves differently than an adult. He works out his response to loss in play and art. His sadness may appear callously short. Noisy and mischievous one minute, he's disturbed the next, then curious, then sad, then disinterested, then playful.

To adults, the child seems uncaring, but he's really in denial—a defense. The loss would simply be too great to accept yet.

Some adults feel relief at the child's lack of emotion because it lets them off the hook. If the kid doesn't suffer, they don't have to figure out what to do. One girl I know lost her mother at age seven. Withdrawn, guilty, and inexpressive, the child heard people comment that she was "taking it so well," a complete misinterpretation that left her no room to express feelings or ask questions then or later. She had to keep "doing well," though inside she "knew" she had killed her mother—who had died in childbirth—by wishing for a little brother. Children's surface behavior after a death usually masks deep feelings that need the light of day.

As time passes, expect symptoms similar to those after divorce: depression, withdrawal, physical ailments, school troubles, inability to concentrate, emotional outbursts, and the like.

Your child may regress socially or developmentally. He might cling to someone as a "replacement." Some children idealize the deceased parent to block unhappy thoughts and memories or to avoid panicking about the future. Perhaps your kid will identify with the dead parent by taking on his mannerisms, trying to assume his role in the family, or convincing himself he has the physical symptoms that caused the death.

Kids fantasize about reuniting with the dead, creating a real risk of suicide, *even in very young children.* Be on the look-out for signs and take quick action if you see them (see the discussion of suicide in Chapter 17).

Helping Very Small Children Deal with a Parent's Death

My experiences after Tony's suicide illustrate how to help a very young child after parental death. The immediate impact you make may seem minimal, but you build a foundation that will serve your child for the rest of his life.

Leaning over Christopher's crib as he slept that first night, I wondered what, if anything, I should tell him about what happened. I felt he shouldn't view his father's body, but should he attend the memorial service? Should he see my emotions? At twenty months he couldn't possibly understand death. Still, Tony had participated in parenting. Christopher would miss the daddy who had fed him, changed his diapers, and made him laugh. I had to tell him something.

Now five, Christopher is happy and well adjusted. I made the right choices in the crucial first weeks after Tony's death. Most importantly, I sought next-day advice from Meg Zweiback, a pediatric nurse-practitioner who is an expert in early childhood development. I felt the press of so many people, so much to do, so much uncertainty about the future. Professional guidance gave me confidence that I was on the right course with Christopher from the beginning. The first bit of advice, however, was for me: eat, rest, get counseling, and accept love and assistance. To help my son, I had to stay healthy and functional.

I knew Christopher would notice the heightened emotions and activity in the house those first few days. Even without being told, children sense when something momentous occurs. The phone rang continuously. Friends tearfully arrived with food. "Protecting" Christopher by pretending nothing had occurred would have undermined trust in his own perceptions. Therefore, I confirmed what had happened and presented emotional expression as normal and natural:

"Daddy died. That means we won't see him anymore. You may see us cry because we're sad and will miss him." Because young children are especially self-centered and may feel responsible for everything, I emphasized that Christopher was not the cause of Tony's illness or death.

Although Christopher knew Tony was gone, toddlers have no sense of time or loss and think death is temporary. I was tempted to let him think that indefinitely, but he would have come to mistrust me later when he understood the true nature of dying. I used no euphemisms and told Christopher the truth, or a limited version of it that I could build upon afterwards without contradicting earlier statements. Daddy had not "gone to sleep," "passed away," "gone to heaven," or "left for a long visit." I used simple words and concepts to which Christopher could relate: "Dying means Daddy's body stopped working. He can't eat or breathe or walk anymore." Having experienced eating, breathing, and walking for himself, Christopher gained some sense of death in this way.

In the days before Tony's memorial service, I safeguarded Christopher by making our house a private haven. Crowds of unfamiliar faces can overstimulate even the mellowest child, especially if attention focuses on him, as it inevitably will if a parent dies. Out-of-town family and friends found accommodations elsewhere and visited in small groups. I maintained our usual routines as much as possible, keeping to normal mealtimes, playtimes, naps, and bedtimes. Although I postponed further efforts at weaning, I discouraged breast-feeding solely for comfort. Instead, he and I had private "loving time" each day, which benefited me, too.

> "Time passes,
> Time the consoler,
> Time the anodyne."
> WILLIAM THACKERAY
> (1811–1863)

Although I talked with Christopher about people's sadness, I shielded him from intense, raw emotions that would frighten someone his age. He did not attend the memorial service, not only because he wouldn't understand it, but because someone might lose control there. While he saw me cry, I took special care that he not witness me becoming overwrought. Freely releasing my emotions with supportive friends was essential to my own grief process, but I took care not to do so in front of my son. Despite the enormous change in my life, I was still "Mommy" to him. As long as I was firm and capable, he would feel safe and secure. I couldn't fall apart for the simple reason that he needed me not to! I scheduled much child care. Just knowing relief was coming often enabled me to get through until it arrived.

In the weeks after the service, I couldn't bear thinking about my son's future questions: *Why don't I have a daddy? If he loved me, why did he die? Did you make him kill himself?* My first instinct was to spare Christopher (and myself) the pain of our situation. Parenting, however, involves helping a child experience and label his emotions while avoiding the message that he "should" feel any certain way. Instead, I told Christopher how *I* felt. "It makes me sad that Daddy died," but not, "You're sad, too."

In fact, I didn't know whether he *was* sad, as none of my talks with him had produced much visible reaction. Once he asserted, "No!" and another time he stated calmly, "Daddy be here." Instead of trying to guess what, if any, underlying emotion these statements represented, I just reflected back his comments so he would know I heard him: "You're thinking about Daddy." I introduced emotions in a more general way, simply and in age-appropriate terms: sad, glad, mad. I made up stories and explained that some are sad, some happy, and some both. This planted the seed that feelings can be complicated and that complex feelings are okay.

Though practically any response to discussions of Daddy's death would have been "normal," after a few weeks I began to worry that Christopher's continuing lack of reaction signaled unhealthy, unexpressed pain. At Meg's suggestion, I used the third person to approach the topic in a more distant, safer way. "A boy may wonder why Daddy doesn't live with him now." Although this still produced little verbal response, Christopher listened intently. Perhaps his silence represented a postponement of defiance or clinginess until he sensed I had recovered enough to "take it." Indeed, he completely bypassed the "terrible twos" but went through an obstinate period after age three, when I had regained my equilibrium.

My next concern was whether and how to tell new acquaintances about our circumstances. When the time came for preschool, for example, both teachers and playmates would surely ask about his father. Children pick on those who are "different." Adults, uncomfortable at the mention of death, don't know what to say, so they mutter awkwardly or avoid talking at all. Suicide is traditionally even more taboo, and forbidden topics generate shame. I wanted

Christopher to become comfortable speaking about what happened without feeling there was something wrong with him or our family. One important function of my very early talks with him had been to accustom *me* to discussing Tony and his death freely so I could provide a good role model.

Granting Christopher permission to talk didn't mean discussing the death often, at length, or in every circumstance. Rather, it involved letting him know I would listen whenever he was ready to talk. It also meant teaching him that others' discomfort shouldn't silence him. Their awkwardness was their problem, not his.

I continued to raise the subject occasionally in a matter-of-fact way. Household pictures of Tony at Christopher's eye-level and a small photo album still serve as silent "triggers" for permissible conversation. (I won't show videotapes of Tony until Christopher is at least six—as young children may mistake television for real life.) At the memorial service, I had provided paper and pen and appealed to Tony's family, childhood playmates, college classmates, and friends to write letters to Christopher about his dad: anecdotes, things they would miss, reasons they loved him. Some of these letters won't be appropriate to share for many years, but others quickly highlighted aspects of Tony for discussion.

As more time passed, I grappled with my own complicated emotions in response to Tony's suicide. Anger and resentment loomed large, especially on trying days as a single mother. Often, I wanted to let Christopher know in no uncertain terms that his father had let us down in the most selfish way possible.

I resisted that temptation, however. Despite Tony's mental illness, he had tried to be a caring parent. Christopher's self-esteem will depend in part on feeling he was fathered by a loving, admirable man. Because he will have very few, if any, recollections of Tony in the flesh, I am his main repository of "daddy memories," and I want them to be positive ones. I tell Christopher the truth but limit it to what will help him feel worthy, loved, and connected: "Daddy and I really wanted to be parents together." I relate concrete details of experiences with Tony rather than making broad statements that I can't in good conscience defend—statements such as, "Daddy was always wonderful." By saying, "Daddy used to carry you in his backpack all the time," Christopher gets the message that Tony loved and cared for him. At least until he is much older, my difficult times with his father are matters for my private therapy.

Another psychological issue for me was separation. After Tony's death, my emotional connection to Christopher intensified, and I feared losing him. My instincts urged me to keep him in sight at all times, to protect him from every remotely conceivable danger. Meg reminded me, however, that becoming overly protective or making our relationship too exclusive would be unhealthy. I had to set boundaries and maintain our individual identities (see Chapter 5). I searched out ways for Christopher to distance himself from me (and me from him!). We each created special, private space in the house. We talked about our different food preferences and clothing sizes. My going out with friends at night forced him to go to sleep without me. Those evenings also reminded me that I am an adult with needs and interests other than parenting.

Though he is thriving now, Christopher's future will inevitably involve challenging emotional periods. My explanations when he was twenty-months old set the stage for answering further questions by simply adding detail to the foundation of truth and openness: "Some people die from accidents, some from sickness." Later, "Sometimes the body gets sick, and sometimes the feelings and thoughts do." Bit by bit through the years, I will arrive at an explanation of the difficult subjects of manic-depression and suicide. I will help Christopher know his father and, perhaps eventually, understand his final act.

In summary, when a small child's parent dies:

- Promptly consult an early childhood specialist for individualized guidance
- Avoid crowds and overstimulation
- Tell the truth in simple terms
  - –Avoid euphemisms
  - –Use the third person to make the topic feel safer
  - –Emphasize that the child is not to blame
- Describe and express normal emotions
  - –Shield the child from intense, raw emotions, especially of the surviving parent
  - –Don't take him to the funeral or memorial service
  - –Don't tell him what he feels or should feel
- Maintain routines and assure him the surviving parent is okay
- Make it okay to talk about the death and the deceased parent
- Create "memories" for the child
- Maintain boundaries between him and you

Helping Older Children Deal with the Death of a Parent

The guidelines just outlined apply to older children as well, but those kids also need more. Because they're verbal, you can communicate with them effectively. Give them love, support for their grief, and reassurance about the future. Because you're in emotional upheaval yourself, you doubt you're up to the challenge. Helping your child actually gets you through, however. You feel better knowing you're being a good parent in spite of it all.

Read the sections in Chapter 1 about aiding a child's grief and recovery. In addition, for an older child:

- Decide together whether he should go to the funeral or memorial service. Attending enables him to experience the reality of death and ritualize his sense of loss with others. It keeps him from getting stuck in denial.

  If he does attend, prepare him in detail for what will happen. Include him in any gathering after the service, whether joyful with memories or sad with grief. Afford him the choice of opting out of any part that makes him uncomfortable, such as viewing an open casket, attending a burial, or scattering ashes. Accept and value his choices. Never shame or guilt-trip him into participating by insisting he "prove" his love. Provide lots of understanding and comfort.

  If he doesn't attend the service, devise a private ritual with him for another time. Plant flowers or burn a candle, whatever you come up with together. (When Christopher's favorite cat died last summer, we planted a purple flower to match the heart she wore on her collar—and watered it from her cat dish!)
- Be honest without explaining more than the child asks. If he wants to know what happens to the body, for example, you could tell him it "goes back to the earth." When he wants more, explain that burial aids this process by placing the body underground; cremation uses heat to give the body back to the earth a little faster. Again, tailor your explanations to his age.
- Recognize that the fear of abandonment inherent in the situation of a parent's death raises your child's sense of fragility and helplessness. He fears you will die and leave him, too. Tell him most people die only when they're very old and you will be around for a long, long time. And so will he. If your spouse died in an accident, emphasize that you're very careful to prevent mishaps and if they do

occur, they usually aren't fatal. Inform him that you are well prepared for accidents and emergencies (and then make sure you are).

- Be aware of the guilt and responsibility your child feels despite his lack of actual connection to the death. To fill in gaps of understanding, kids often rely on magical thinking about how they "caused" the parent to die. Even if your child doesn't voice these thoughts, reassure him repeatedly that he was in no way responsible for his parent's death.
- Don't deny or deprive a child of his pain, either for your sake or his. Freedom to talk is the key to his recovery. Encourage him to identify and express his feelings, but don't pressure him.
- While letting your child know you're still capable and in control, allow him to see your grief and tears.
- Talk about specific memories of the dead parent: "Tell me about that time you and Mom went camping at Mt. Shasta."
- Limit additional changes in your child's life.
- Expect delayed reactions. A later loss, even an insignificant one, may trigger another round of grief. If this happens, talk about it. Explain that this loss reminds him of others. Never minimize a pet's demise, especially with a child who previously lost a parent—the pet represents a serious loss to him. Just as you wouldn't talk about replacing the dead Mommy, don't suggest getting another pet right away to "take his mind off the death." It will only leave his grieving process unfinished.

Death from Illness

My spouse's death came suddenly and unexpectedly, as do murders and fatal accidents on the highway or work site. Other deaths arrive with more warning. Terminal illness can end rapidly or inch through painful months or even years. While long illness allows time for preparation, planning, and saying good-bye, the anticipation of life's end is difficult and painful.

- When a child witnesses a death by illness, he often fears that any sickness is fatal. Then when you complain of a headache or he gets the flu, his anxiety level shoots off the scale. He expects imminent death. Without raising false hopes about your spouse, tell your child that only very serious illness makes anyone die. Remind him of times people—including him—have been sick and recovered.

- Allow your child continual contact with his dying parent. If possible, that parent should talk about death and reassure your child of his love.
- Offer opportunities for your kid to care for his ailing parent. He can read to him, massage him, feed him—whatever seems appropriate. Letting him help alleviates fears or fantasies about his parent's pain and suffering.

No death is "easy," but a parent's death can devastate a child. As the surviving parent, you can significantly help your children to understand and grieve the end of life.

Then you have to start learning how to be a single parent.

ORGANIZATIONS

The Widowed Persons Service of the American Association of Retired Persons (AARP) has information on local support groups for widowed parents. 601 E St., N.W., Washington, D.C. 20049; 202-434-2260.

BOOKS FOR KIDS

A Taste of Blackberries, Doris B. Smith (New York: HarperCollins Children's, 1988) (death of best friend) (Grades 3–6).

About Dying: An Open Family Book for Parent and Child, Sara B. Stein (New York: Walker & Co., 1974) (explains the life cycle) (grades 1 and up).

Books and Films on Death and Dying for Children and Adolescents: An Annotated Bibliography (1985); First Supplement (1988), (Good Grief Program, Judge Baker Children's Center, 295 Longwood Ave., Boston, MA 02115) (excellent overall resource) (distributed by New Dimensions Media: Eugene, Oregon, 503-484-7125).

Charlotte's Web, E. B. White (New York: HarperCollins Children's, 1952) (grades 2–6).

Everett Anderson's Goodbye, Lucille Clifton, et al. (New York: Holt, 1983) (fiction in rhyme about boy coming to terms with father's death) (preschool–grade 2).

About Death, Joy Berry (Danbury, CT: Children's Press, 1990) (straightforward explanations).

How It Feels When a Parent Dies, Jill Krementz (New York: Knopf, 1988) (ages 12 to 18).

I Had a Friend Named Peter: Talking to Children about the Death of a Friend, Janice Cohn (New York: Morrow Jr., 1987) (excellent introductory parents' guide) (preschool–grade 2).

Lifetimes: The Beautiful Way to Explain Death to Children, Bryan Mellonie, et al. (New York: Bantam, 1983) (life as the time between beginning and end).

Saying Goodbye to Daddy, Judith Vigna (Morton Grove, IL: Albert Whitman & Co., 1991) (fiction about father's death in car accident).

Straight Talk about Death for Teenagers: How to Cope with Losing Someone You Love, Earl A. Grollman (Boston: Beacon 1993).

Talking about Death: A Dialogue Between Parent and Child, Earl Grollman (Boston: Beacon, 1991) (simple language with good parents' guide).

Timothy Duck: The Story of the Death of a Friend, Lynn B. Blackburn (Omaha, NE: Centering Corp., 1989) (illness) (grades 1–6).

When My Dad Died and When My Mommy Died, Janice Hammond (Flint, MI: Cranbrook Publishing, 1981) (simple drawings and text) (ages 3 to 12).

When I Die, Will I Get Better? Joeri & Piet Breebaart (New York: P. Bedrick Books, 1993) (rabbit grieves death of younger brother) (grades K–4).

Where's Jess? Ray Goldstein, et al. (Omaha, NE: Centering Corp., 1982) (a good "first book" on death; death of brother).

Why Did Grandma Die? Trudy Madler (Austin, TX: Raintree Steck-Vaughn Co., 1993) (grades K–6).

Chapter 3

Single Parents by Choice

Single-parenthood can arrive "by choice" in various ways. You may have heard the biological clock ticking and adopted a child, "arranged" a pregnancy, used a sperm bank, or a surrogate. Perhaps you found yourself accidentally pregnant by a man you barely knew or wouldn't permanently invite into your life. Maybe he abandoned you on learning of the pregnancy. Most, but not all, single parents by choice are female.

As a single parent by choice, you (and others with full-time custody) can be grateful not to have disputes with another parent. Not going through divorce, you don't have to deal with adversarial attorneys. You *know* you're on your own from the beginning and can contemplate what that means before it hits you full in the face. Your relationship with your child becomes very close.

On the other hand, you may have little emotional support and even less relief. You're "on" twenty-four hours a day, every day. That closeness may make it exceptionally hard to separate and detach when it would be best to do so.

Dealing with Disapproval

Although the stigma of out-of-wedlock birth has declined tremendously, expect at least a few whispers of "tut-tut" or "I-told-you-so" when you feel overwhelmed or needy. It can even be worse. Jennifer, a woman I know, lived near her brother's family before deciding to become a mother. She enjoyed close relationships with her nieces and nephews and expected to share her joy in parenting with them. But when she became intentionally pregnant, her sister-in-law barred her from the house completely and refused to see her new daughter Chloë or give any gifts. Jennifer's brother, caught between his wife and his sister, chose the wife, and his family disappeared from Jennifer's life.

Grieve the loss involved in such a situation. Then let it go. Ignore the people who don't support you and be with those who do.

Allow Yourself Negative Emotions

Although you love your kid, sometimes you absolutely hate being a parent, especially a single parent. Whatever made you voluntarily take on such an impossible role, made even harder by society's indifference? Don't bash yourself for breaking down in tears wondering why the hell you got into this mess. The fact that you put yourself in this situation doesn't mean you have to enjoy every minute of it. Your choice to have a child on your own didn't deprive you of the normal feelings of all parents.

You may be a single parent by choice, but in reality the "choice" probably wasn't your first one. You made the best decision for yourself under the circumstances, but you didn't choose those circumstances. Your desire for a child outran your biological capability before you met a mate. Your birth control failed. Your lover left you pregnant and alone. While you chose to become a parent, you made your choice within a context. Jennifer emphasized that giving up on the idea of marriage and a "regular" family requires a grieving process. Read the sections in Chapter 1 about grief, anger, and other emotions. They apply to you as well.

Despite anger and grief, you, like Jennifer, will probably never regret your decision. As she said, "I can't imagine wishing I'd made the choice *not* to have Chloë."

Prepare Early

Whatever the precise circumstances, a single parent by choice has one advantage—the ability to put a support system in place *before* the child arrives. You may even enlist support for *making* the choice.

- About one-third of U.S. births are now to unwed mothers.
- From 1980 to 1992, the birth rate among all unmarried women rose 54%.
- In 1973, 50% of unwed births were to teenagers. By 1980, this figure dropped to 41%, and then to 30% in 1992, as more and more older women become single mothers.
- Women over twenty, not teens, are now the largest group of unwed mothers.
- White women are the fastest-growing group of unwed mothers. From 1980 to 1992, the birth rate among unwed, white women rose 94%. Among black women it rose just 7%.
- American women of various ethnic backgrounds have the following rates of unwed births:

Chinese	6%
Japanese	10%
Filipina	17%
Caucasian	18.5%
Mexican	36%
Hawaiians	46%
Puerto Rican	57%
African-American	68%[1]

- Unwed motherhood is increasingly common everywhere. It amounts to one-third of all births in Northern Europe.[2]

Organizations offer classes and workshops for evaluating the alternatives. You will benefit from talking with people in different stages of the process.

Here are some suggestions:

- Set up a support network. You're as scared and uncertain as you are happy and proud. Ask for commitments from friends and relatives, both short- and long-term. Be very specific about what you need, from guardianship to grocery shopping. One prospective single mom held a How-Can-You-Help picnic at which she asked for support when the baby arrived. Some people followed through without asking, and others needed prodding.

  Find people who will commit to spending time and developing their own relationships with your kid. Provide him a "family" of stable people who will be around for a long time.

Do you have trouble asking? Perhaps formulating a more "official" commitment will make it easier to remind people of their promises. Instead of cute little rompers, request "chore chits" at your baby shower. People sign up for so many hours of errand-running, cooking, or baby-sitting. When you call, just say you'd like to spend that chit now.

Don't use these up all at once. From sheer novelty, you'll get lots of volunteer help right after you come home with your baby. Save the chits for later when you think you might go crazy if you don't get a break!

Try alternatives, and if they don't work, do something else. After adopting an infant, Carly took a leave of absence from work and moved in with friends living in a neighboring city. While this had sounded ideal at first, Carly found herself lonely at "home" with the baby all day while her friends worked. While sympathetic, they didn't have time or energy for child care, nighttime feeding, or extended emotional support. Carly felt obligated to keep their house cleaner than she kept her own. Isolated from other friends, she soon moved back to her house and immediately felt more relaxed.

- Hire help. Consider a *doula,* a trained and certified professional who helps before, during, and after birth. *Doula* is a Greek term meaning "to mother the mother," and if you're on your own, you can use some of that! *Doulas* take on all sorts of tasks, from housekeeping to cooking to caring for older kids. Quite simply, they give the new mom a rest. Baby nurses provide a similar break, although they focus on baby care and do no housework. For the least expensive alternative, hire a local teenager as a "mother's helper."
- Resolve legal issues ahead of time:
  –How the birth certificate will read
  –The child's last name
  –Relinquishment of paternal rights or child support (if relevant)
  –A will
  –Appointment of a legal guardian (see Chapter 18)
- Look into child care well before you need to go back to work (see Chapter 11)

Do all of the above—and then expect everything to go wrong. As Jennifer said, "You can prepare and prepare, but you'll never know what will happen." Her employer laid her off when she was five months pregnant!

Explaining Your Single-Parenthood to Your Child

Having an infant gives you time to consider what to tell him about his origins. His first couple of years will give *you* a chance to practice and become comfortable discussing the subject. You may want to seek professional advice for your particular situation.

- Most modern adoption experts advise beginning to explain the process to a child very early. Introduced matter-of-factly at a young age, adoption becomes just one more fact about the child, such as brown eyes and red hair.
- If the other parent abandoned you, tell the truth. Keep it simple while your child is young and build on this foundation. Be honest and positive.

  If the father was a lout, find something good to say anyway. "He decided he wasn't able to help us be a family." "We loved each other before you were born, but he didn't know how to be in a family." If you really can't say something positive, give your child concrete details: "He could fix any car." Or "He made great spaghetti."

  Take special care not to project your feelings for the absent father onto your child. He may look just like his biological dad, but he is himself. Find a place to work through your own abandonment, disappointment, and anger. Therapy is a good place to start.
- If the other parent has never been in the picture, your child will ultimately want to know why. If *you* never really knew your child's father, don't fake it: "We didn't know each other well, and we didn't plan to have a baby, but I'm very glad I have you." The object is to let your child feel all right about his life, and yours. He won't feel okay about yours unless you do.

  My friend, Silvia, explained to her son, Scott, that she and his father became angry at each other before he was born, so she and Scott probably wouldn't see him. She phrased it as mutual dislike so Scott wouldn't blame her for driving Dad away. This also clearly put it out of her power simply to change her attitude and bring Daddy back.
- Several years ago Samantha used a sperm bank after unsuccessfully trying to get pregnant "by appointment" with a man friend. For now, she tells her young daughter Rhonda (and everyone else) that she "doesn't have a father." When Rhonda understands biology, Samantha will have to decide when and how to answer her questions

and explain her origins. Because there really is no alternative, she'll rely on the truth. If the sperm donor agreed, Rhonda can learn his identity at age eighteen and, perhaps, meet him.

- Whatever your "story," encourage your child to share his feelings about it.
- Be prepared for fantasies about the "missing" parent to surface at some point. This is normal.

However we arrive at single-parenthood, our first, tentative steps involve dealing with emotions—ours and our children's. From there we move into more practical aspects of living alone with our kids.

ORGANIZATIONS

Adoptive Families of America, Inc.: Free information regarding single-parent adoptive families. 333 Highway 100 North, Minneapolis, MN 55422.

Committee for Single Adoptive Parents: Resource list and support information. Publishes newsletter ($18 for 4 issues) and the *Handbook for Single Adoptive Parents*, $15. POB 15084, Chevy Chase, MD 20825; 202-966-6367.

Single Mothers by Choice: Local support groups, some open to single fathers. Membership and newsletter, $45; newsletter only, $20. Call or write for local group contacts. POB 1642, Gracie Square Station, New York, NY 10028; 212-988-0993.

Single Parents Adopting Children Everywhere (SPACE): Support and information; hosts National Conference on Single Parent Adoption each fall. 6 Sunshine Ave., Natick, MA 01760; 508-655-5426.

Single Parents with Adopted Kids (SWAK). 4108 Washington Rd. #101, Kenosha, WI 53144; 414-654-0629.

BOOKS FOR PARENTS

Having Your Baby by Donor Insemination: A Complete Resource Guide, Elizabeth Noble (Boston: Houghton Mifflin, 1988).

Single Mothers by Choice: A Guidebook for Single Women Who Are Considering or Have Chosen, Jane Mattes (New York: Times Books, 1994). Comprehensive how-to book.

Single Mothers by Choice: A Growing Trend in Family Life, N. Miller (New York: Plenum, 1992).

BOOKS FOR KIDS

Do I Have a Daddy? Jeanne Warren Lindsay (Buena Park, CA: Morning Glory Press, 1991).

Part 2

Single-Parenting Issues and Skills

Chapter 4

Nurture the Family's Most Important Asset—You

Car maintenance always took a back seat to my obligations as a student and neophyte lawyer. I managed to keep some gas in the tank, but tune-ups and fluid checks were erratic at best. Why waste valuable time on maintenance when the ol' wheels zoomed along just fine? Those little dashboard lights would warn me of anything amiss. And so they did—on a deserted, country road miles from the nearest mechanic. Still, the buggy kept running, and I figured I could probably coax it to the next town. I putt-putted into a gas station with virtually no oil in the engine and a "cracked head"—a term that also applied to me when I heard what fixing it would cost in time, hassle, and dollars. A short date with a dipstick every few weeks would have spared both the car and me a painful experience. To all appearances, my trusty auto rendered loyal service while I ignored its requirements, but regular maintenance would have ensured true mechanical health and longevity.

As the mighty engine now driving your family's life, you, too, need regular care. You burn a lot of "oil" providing for your child materially, psychologically, emotionally, academically, and socially. Whatever your child's age, you sometimes feel like a slave to the needs of a demanding tyrant. You hope to meet every requirement, from dealing with tantrums to constant chauffeuring. You do without sleep, healthful food, and fun. It may happen next month or next year, but without nurturing, you will burn out, and you will be of no use to anyone. As a single parent, you can't afford to let that happen.

Why Giving to Yourself Is So Difficult

You have no problem nurturing your children. What stops you from doing the same for yourself? Some reasons probably stem from childhood. Maybe your parents, like mine, counseled you not to be "selfish," to look after everyone else first. Mothers of the previous generation often modeled caretaking behavior, becoming martyrs to the family's needs. Most of us had no strong role models for self-nurturance (self-indulgence, perhaps, but that's not the same). Some parents engendered low self-esteem in their children by implying or even saying they deserved little, and this belief carried over to adulthood.

Most people who have been divorced for a while regret that they waited so long to start taking care of themselves.

> "Know Thyself."
> INSCRIBED ON THE TEMPLE AT DELPHI, ACCORDING TO THE GREEK PHILOSOPHER, PLATO (427–347 BC)

I know, I know—you don't have time. With so much to do, "unnecessaries" don't even make a single parent's list. Maybe you "have to" do all you do—but you also "have to" take care of yourself. If you broke a leg, would you go to the doctor? If your house burned down, would you find new housing? You *make* time for crises and important obligations—you just haven't put nurturing yourself in those categories. It is. You count. This is one area of life you *can* influence. Your responsibility to the family includes loving care of its most important asset—you.

Give Your Child the Gift of a Happy, Functioning Parent

Being happy and functional yourself represents the greatest gift you can give a child. Abandon any guilt feelings about sometimes putting yourself first. *Taking care of yourself is taking care of your kids.* Relieving stress, staying healthy, and achieving contentment make you a better parent: You stay detached during conflicts, don't take out frustrations on your children, and become emotionally available. You can even kick up your heels and have some fun together.

If you must, *trick* yourself into nurturing the family's prime asset—whenever you do something nice for yourself, think of it as a present to your child! You simply must have a night out dancing or a game of tennis "for the kid"! Taking care of yourself *is* taking care of him.

Nurturing Yourself Models Healthy Adult Behavior

Do you want your children to grow up frenetic and frazzled? Do you want them always to delay or negate pleasure and put someone else's needs above their own? Of course not. But if that's how you go through life, you're teaching them to do the same.

- Demonstrate that happy adults and good parents give to themselves. Let him see you enjoying your own activities. If someone should ask him what his parent is really like, he should know more than the fact that you work, cook, clean, and take him swimming. You also make pottery, run races, meditate, strum the guitar, play league softball, read mysteries, and go away for a weekend by yourself once a year. You laugh at yourself sometimes. You get goofy instead of preparing the income tax return. When your kid sees you like this, he views you as a more complex, complete person. He'll create himself in that mold.
- Ask for what you need. Getting your needs met not only makes you a better parent—and person—but it teaches your kid to say directly what he wants instead of waiting for a mind reader to come along (see Chapter 9).
- See friends. Your kid needs to experience his parent being real with other people. Model for him how to get along with peers. Let him see his parent admit and resolve problems with the help of others. Show him how adults enjoy their lives so he'll want to grow up to be one!

Find Out Who You Are Now

When you divorce or survive a death, you don't suddenly revert to the single person who existed before marriage. However long your relationship, it changed you. Having children also altered your perspective. You're older, too. Becoming a single parent leaves you with the uneasy sense that you don't know who you are anymore. You get a moment's respite from work and the kids, and you stand in the middle of the room, lost, wondering what you'd like to do. Then the obligations resume, and the question remains unanswered.

To nurture yourself, first find out who you are *now*. Ask, "What am I besides a 'single parent'?" Initially, other facets remain hidden. Don't worry, they do exist. Employee, that's an obvious one. Then . . . well, maybe artist. And . . . basketball player. Maybe . . . crossword-puzzle solver. This process requires time. Allow yourself to take it.

Second, admit and accept your present limitations. No matter how smart, efficient, and organized you are, at some point the tasks outpace your ability to do them. Accept this. Consider your limitations as part of a developmental stage rather than as permanent disabilities. Becoming a single parent unfolds through many phases. Where you are now is simply one of them. Tell yourself, "I can't cook dinner every night anymore," and don't wear yourself out trying. Later, if you want, you can resume more of what you used to do. But for now, give yourself a break.

Third, gradually try out activities and experiences to learn what you enjoy. Think of this as a lifetime discovery adventure. Go back to hobbies you abandoned. Dig out the oil paints or golf clubs. Sign up for an introductory class in something new. Accept an invitation. Who knows, maybe rock climbing expresses the real you!

Make Time for Self-Nurturing

You can spend years thinking you don't have time to care for yourself. Or you can become proactive and *make* the time.

You Have Choices

Making time for yourself requires a big step—realizing you have a *choice* about how to spend your day. You really aren't just a victim of circumstances. One of the exercises that therapists Liz Hannigan and Cliff Crain presented at the single-parents support group will prove it:

- Divide a sheet of paper into three columns called "nurturing activities," "nurturing places," and "nurturing people."

In the "nurturing activities" column, list what you enjoy doing. Include small pleasures such as reading the paper or sitting with a cup of tea after dinner. "Nurturing places" can be spectacular and far away, but don't forget the tiny, close ones—the little creek that runs through your neighborhood, the hillside of wildflowers, the shade of that elm in the park. "Nurturing people" leave you feeling refreshed and hopeful. They make you laugh and let you cry. They share themselves and ask you questions. They let you disagree without becoming defensive.

> "He has spent his life best who has enjoyed it most."
> SAMUEL BUTLER (1835–1902)

In contrast, non-nurturing people suck you dry with complaints and judgments. They focus on themselves and relate everything you say to their own experiences. You find non-nurturing people among your friends for various reasons. Perhaps they once came through for you, or maybe you've just known them forever. Some are relatives. Whatever the explanation, you've maintained contact despite feeling drained after every encounter. *They* probably initiate all your get-togethers. They're not nurturing you—they're *taking* life blood. You don't have to break off the relationships, but recognize them for what they are, and don't list these people as "nurturers."

- Review the past few months. How often have you done any of those nurturing activities, visited those nurturing places, spent time with those nurturing people? Probably not very often. Save this list.
- Now make a "to-do" list for tomorrow. When you finish, go back and realistically estimate the time required to complete each task. Most people grossly underestimate by a half to two-thirds, but let's use your low numbers anyway. Adding up all the time, you'll probably find you've still planned twice as much as anyone could do in a day.
- For each entry on your to-do list, ask, "What is the worst that would happen if I didn't do this tomorrow?" If the consequences fall somewhere around "catastrophic" or "end-of-the-world," star the item. We're not talking bad hair days here—or impatient looks from the boss. "Catastrophic" means black mark on the credit record, eviction, illness, safety hazards (including low batteries in smoke detectors), being fired, and so on.

Okay, you have permission to do the starred items tomorrow.

- Next, select something from your "nurturing" lists and add it to the to-do list. Activity, place, or person. Star it. You can (must) do that tomorrow, too.
- Number the unstarred "noncatastrophic" items on your list in order of priority. Do what you can of these tomorrow. The rest you will do, but not necessarily tomorrow. Keep track of them.

If you like, organize a simple list system like this daily. Some people love lists and break tasks down into mini-steps to extend the pleasure of crossing them off as "done." Some save the marked-up lists as reminders of all they accomplished already. A mental list will do, as long as it includes nurturing yourself.

Remember: Retrain your mind to regard caring for yourself as an "end-of-the-world," every day item, *by definition.* It *never* takes second place to anything except another "catastrophic" task—and that should happen rarely.

Take the Long-Term View

The preceding list-making exercise expands your vision to the long term. You can't accomplish everything in a day, but you'll get it done over a week, or a month, or six months, or a year. Give yourself credit for that, rather than berating yourself for being slow or unproductive.

> "There are two things to aim at in life: First, to get what you want; and, after that, to enjoy it. Only the wisest of mankind achieve the second."
>
> LOGAN PEARSALL SMITH (1865–1946)

Give Up Some "Have-to's"

You just admitted that you *could* live with the consequences of postponing some "have-to-do's." You can't get the rug vacuumed before your friend visits? It won't affect your friendship, even if he notices. Not enough time to bake that chicken tonight? Take the kids to the burrito place. Or warm up that pasta again. If the chicken spoils, you're out $5.98, and next time you'll do better. Not a life crisis.

Simplify your requirements and set priorities. When you get frenzied, take a few moments to remember what's most important in your life. Then ask yourself, "Does what I'm doing now contribute to that?" If not, why are you doing it? What are you so busy going after? How do you want people to remember you—as the person with the cleanest bathroom corners in town?

My housekeeping standards sank ever lower after I became a single mom. I really *like* a clean, orderly house. At first I tried to keep up. Then I *gave* up. No, we don't toss our banana peels on the floor, but the idea of a pristine household evaporated long ago. Occasionally, I hire help. Mostly I do what I can, taking care of what bothers me most. I make the choice to spend my limited time in other ways. So far, at least, the house hasn't spontaneously combusted.

Learn to Say No

As you made your lists, you no doubt included some items to do for others, including your kids. On top of those known needs, people come at you all day with requests. You somehow manage to squeeze them in, further limiting your available time. Imagine how much you could accomplish elsewhere just by saying no to requests you can't easily fulfill.

- "No" is a complete answer. You don't have to give excuses or explain or justify. Just say, "No, I'm sorry, but I won't be able to do that." Say it with a smile or a look of regret. Be polite but firm. You can say no to friends, relatives, children, your ex, volunteer organizations, schools, neighbors who drop by, acquaintances, telephone callers, your employer (see Chapter 11)—anyone.
- Again, consider, "What is the worst that could happen if I say no?" Will you lose a friend? Doubtful, but someone who objects to your caring for yourself isn't a friend anyway. Will you drop in popularity? Probably not. You may hear complaints, but most people respect someone who looks out for himself.
- People often ask favors without really expecting results. Naturally, they'll take what they can get, but if that's nothing, they'll shrug and move on. They may ask *you* more often than others because you so frequently say yes! Replace that sign on your forehead reading "Use Me" with one that says "Don't Ask."

Set Realistic Long-Term Goals for Yourself

Say you want to move or change jobs. Or maybe you've always meant to take up ceramics. Breaking a long-term goal into intermediate steps allows you to succeed many times on the way to achieving what you want for yourself. Choose a realistic time to begin and take the first step. Stay flexible and redefine the steps and ultimate goal as you work toward it. Maybe you can do more, or maybe you've set yourself up to accomplish too much. If you give up, make sure you do so by choice and not from frustration. Probably you should just change your timing or the details of your plan.

Nurture Your Body

Take care of your body for the short term *and* for the long term. You need energy and stamina for current obligations, and you don't want to burden your children later with an aging parent suffering from preventable health problems. Besides, nurturing your body feels good—if not right at the moment, then later!

You already know what to do: Exercise aerobically. Achieve your ideal weight. Eat a low-fat, high-fiber diet. Reduce stress. Stop smoking. Avoid recreational drugs. Pay attention to medical conditions. Get adequate sleep. For detailed instructions on any of these, visit Weight Watchers, your local bookstore, or any supermarket checkout stand.

Here are some other ways to take care of your physical being:

- Drive carefully. Stop jumping those lights, and don't race through yellows. Slow down. Those couple of minutes you shave off your arrival time add up to very little in real life. Drive defensively—injuries hurt just as much when the other guy's at fault—and drive courteously. You'll arrive safely and in a better mood.
- Don't drink and drive.
- Get a flu shot in the fall. Clinics, hospitals, and even supermarkets offer them to anyone at little or no cost. While not foolproof, they diminish or eliminate a nasty bout of illness. With kids, you're likely to catch every virus in circulation.
- If you're a woman, do monthly breast exams and annual pap smears.
- Check out those chest pains or that high blood pressure. Get your cholesterol level checked. If you suspect any medical condition, see a doctor sooner rather than later and take care of it. Remember, if something happens to you, your dreaded ex takes the kids full-time.
- Consider all alternatives for exercise. At lunch, early morning, late evening. A machine at home, a club near work. Pushing a stroller up the hill. Pumping iron in the basement. Running with your kid. There is a way. Find it.

Can't get yourself out the door? Get a partner. Exchange gym bags after every workout so you both feel obligated to show up every time.
- Take a nap when you're tired. Forget guilt. You don't have to "do" anything to nurture yourself.
- Reduce your stress—this helps both you and the kids. Stress management comes in many forms. Find one you like: biofeedback, meditation, five-minute naps, massages, hot water. Many community services offer stress reduction classes. Exercise helps, too.

  Know that the more you view life as within your control, the less stress you feel. "Choosing" rather than "having" to do something gives you a fresh outlook and renews your commitment.
- Take safety precautions in whatever you do, whether at home or away, working or having fun. Wear goggles or life jackets, sturdy shoes or a reflective vest—whatever it takes to add that measure of safety. Accidents can happen anywhere, especially when you're tired.

Nurture Your Mind

Single parents' brains turn to mush without time to read, reflect, or exchange ideas with others. Don't let your mental capacity atrophy with disuse. Here are just a few possibilities:

- Read, even just a few pages before bed.
- Set your VCR to tape a favorite TV show every week, then watch at your leisure. Fast-forward through the commercials to save time and avoid insult to your cerebral cortex.
- Subscribe to a local theater season. With the tickets in hand and already paid for, you'll be more likely to get out and go. I buy two subscriptions and take a different friend each time. We often share dinner and talk about the play on the way home.
- Start a book group or a play-reading group. I belong to both. The first ensures I'll read at least one book a month, which we discuss over a pot-luck dinner. The play-reading group requires no

> "While you are upon earth, enjoy the good things that are here."
>
> JOHN SELDEN, ENGLISH LEGAL HISTORIAN (1584–1654)

preparation at all. After a pot-luck meal (obviously, a popular way to get people together in my part of the world), we each take a role in the chosen play and read it cold. The accents and interpretations vary in quality but not in enthusiasm. At the end, dessert spurs us to spirited discussion of the play.

- Take a class in a subject that interests you.
- Visit museums and take docent tours.
- Attend a concert or opera.
- Delve more deeply into a subject your child studies at school. Use excursions with your kid as learning experiences for yourself. As Christopher watches the fish in the aquarium, I read the educational commentary outside the tank.
- Subscribe to a magazine in an area of interest (but only if you're sure you will read it; otherwise it's just clutter).
- Perhaps most importantly, if you get halfway into something and find you don't enjoy it, stop! Put down that boring book. Walk out of the concert. Cancel the subscription. Leave the tour.

Nurture Your Emotional Life

Single parents spend their "free" time taking care of the kids or racing around on errands. Neither affords much emotional support. Parenting alone, you need far more than average emotional nurturing, and you get far less. Make up that deficit.

- Establish "listening sessions" with someone. Either in person or over the phone, take five- or ten-minute turns letting the other talk without interruption. Just listen. Don't offer advice or bring up your own similar experiences. It's hard. Practice. (See Chapter 5.) Truly being heard heals profoundly.
- After you've been angry, sit for a while and see if you can identify any other emotions that anger might mask.
- Vent difficult feelings with a trusted adult (never with your child).
- Ask your best friend to tell you why she loves you.
- Take a cue from your kids. If they tell you not to sweat the small stuff, consider the possibility you were doing just that.
- Rent a sad movie and let yourself cry. Acknowledge any sadness the crying releases and sit with it.

- Rent a funny movie and laugh until you cry.
- Turn on some music and dance by yourself for twenty minutes.
- Browse in a book store. This might nurture your mind, too, but it always brightens my spirits.
- Don't even hope for perfection in anything. Whatever you can do is good enough, at least for now.
- Attend a personal growth seminar.
- Write a letter outlining what you love about yourself.
- Treat yourself to a massage, new hair cut, or pedicure.
- Learn to identify, experience, and express your feelings appropriately through therapy or a self-help book.
- After work, greet your kids and then take some time alone to shift gears and let go of the day before you start the nightly routine. Stay in your room or go outside. Take a shower or stretch into a yoga posture. Listen to music. Dance. Breathe.
- Find a support group. There's one for almost every person, malady, and situation these days. At the right time in your life, groups offer solace, information, and friendship.
- List your fears. "Running out of money," for example. After each entry, write "What I'm *Really* Afraid Of." You might find some surprises. For example, besides the obvious, fear of running out of money could signify you've failed to meet your parents' expectations for success.
- Realize that stressing out about things ahead of time doesn't prevent them from happening. Likewise, you may drive yourself crazy anticipating a disaster that never materializes. Stay in the present. Breathing helps.
- Create designated "Worry Times." Rather than letting vague anxiety gnaw at you all day, pick a time and *really* worry about whatever is on your mind. Chew it over, let it tie you in knots. Then stop worrying until the next Worry Time. As anxieties raise their annoying little heads during the day, tell them, "Quiet! I'll deal with you at Worry Time and not before." Then think of something else. Constant worrying saps your energy and obfuscates solutions. I

> "Resolve to be thyself; and know that he Who finds himself, loses his misery!"
>
> MATTHEW ARNOLD (1822–1888)

often choose the morning shower as Worry Time so I can imagine my problems whirling down the drain.

- Ensure some time alone. Give yourself a "Time Out." You don't have to *do* anything. Just recharge your batteries. If you're out of juice, everything will be hard, no matter how well your kid behaves.

  Starting to resent your kids is a sure sign that you need some alone-time. By the way, you're not the only parent to feel this way about your children sometimes. Ask anyone!
- Take some time for yourself out of the hours allotted to your kids. Don't worry, it's really okay. Christopher talked incessantly for a few months. He jabbered every minute I spent with him, and he expected responses. I tried so hard to pay attention, but minutiae about his railroad cars held only so much interest. I found myself drifting off, sneaking glances at the newspaper, and even wearing a Walkman with music playing in one ear. Then, of course, I felt guilty. Liz and Cliff let me off the hook by suggesting that I set the timer once a day for ten or twenty minutes and listen to Christopher fully and attentively until it rings. When the bell rings, I tell him to talk to his favorite animal or toy: "You have so much to say, Christopher, tell some of it to your engine."

  This piece of advice saved my sanity. I explained to my son that I needed some quiet time. By phrasing it as my need, I avoided implying he'd done anything wrong.
- Inform your kids of your needs. Back to this one again, but it bears repeating. No one expects a four-year-old to know Mom needs some quiet time. Even older kids seem blissfully oblivious to a parent's needs. You have to tell them.

  When you anticipate a situation in which you need something in particular, arrange that you'll get it. On Mother's Day, for example, gently channel your child's sweet desire to honor you into an activity that won't leave you crying or screaming. The gift has to be something *you* want, too. Talk and plan ahead. Breakfast in bed doesn't have to be a surprise, especially if it means a second one in the kitchen later. Teach your child *how* to cook your breakfast in the way least likely to wreak havoc. Let him know how you like your coffee. Show him the toaster setting you like. Eliminate the risk that you'll be stuck with a mess to mop up. Sure, the thought counts, but the *fore*thought keeps you sane.

- Surround yourself with positive influences—books, people, movies. Read uplifting books, perhaps biographies of your heroes. Spend time making your home a pleasant retreat. Buy cut flowers once a week. Give up the TV news for a while, maybe forever. You don't need negative images. Stay away from people who drain you. Find supportive, truthful friends. Build loving relationships with other adults.

Nurture Your Spirit

When the notion of spiritual growth arose in my single-parent support group, one newcomer asked Cliff shrilly, "What does that have to do with single-parenting?" Newly separated, highly emotional, and entangled in custody battles and property division, she saw no relevance whatsoever to spiritual life. Group veterans, with their daily lives more in order, however, quietly accepted the idea that feeding the spirit is part of effective single-parenting.

While some find solace in their religious communities, spiritual nurturance involves neither religion *per se*—nor interactions with other people. Rather, it represents a means of achieving serenity, getting in tune with your own inner rhythms and connecting with whatever metaphor draws you to those goals.

- Once your immediate life crises abate, consider what nourishes your soul. You needn't join a church or find a guru. Some pray, others meditate. Some people have a God, some a god, and some a goddess. Others visualize oneness with the universe. Some delve into their inner being, while others find the deity in nature. Breathing deeply and purposefully every time you come to a stop sign may be enough.
- Nurturing your spiritual life requires time alone to experience the "inner you" without external demands. Build alone-time into your daily routine. Do something to boost yourself to another plane. Start small and expand later if you like. Set the timer for just two minutes and watch a candle burn. Say a prayer as you climb into bed. Inhale the morning air when you rise. I step outside onto the deck off my bathroom every day for a minute or two. Admiring my pitiful garden, I take in the crisp air and imagine the sun (or the fog) energizing me for the day.

- Stop for ten minutes in the middle of anything. Sit or lie comfortably, or even stand. Stretch a little. Relax, breathe, and be perfectly still for ten minutes. Then resume your day.
- Take an entire weekend or longer period alone once or twice a year, just to be quiet and look at your life without interruption. Various retreat centers provide simple accommodations where you have no obligation to talk to anyone, and the prices are shockingly low (see book list at end of chapter).
- Incorporate unstructured time into your schedule. Write it on your calendar and consider it an unbreakable date. Use the time not to *think* or *do,* but just to *be.* Watch the grass grow or follow the clouds.
- Display a favorite picture of yourself. Each morning, ask that person what he needs today. Honor him, nurture his fragile spirit.
- You function better on every level when you resonate with your own inner rhythms. When out of sync with your inner being, you make mistakes and experience frustration. Whenever that happens, give yourself a break. Don't forge ahead, but take some time to become centered again. In the long run, you'll finish more quickly. If doing your taxes makes you crazy and frustrated, for example, *stop.* Do something else until you've regained serenity.
- Practice kindness—to yourself. Although clichéd, the "inner child" remains a powerful metaphor. No matter how harsh your self-judgments, you can relate lovingly to the image of yourself as a child. "Reparent" that youngster as you parent your children. Extend sympathy, praise, understanding, and forgiveness.

> "Who in the world am I? Ah, that's the great puzzle!"
> LEWIS CARROLL (1832–1898)

Have Fun

Is having fun sinful and selfish in the face of all those unfinished commitments, obligations, and problems? If that's the way you feel, then remember that having fun *is* an obligation. You help your kids by having fun, both with and without them.

Choose a special activity from your "nurturing" list or come up with a new, wild idea. Anticipating fun lifts your spirits during difficult times. Plan ahead, whether it's a vision of a full-blown vacation or a night out. Give yourself something to look forward to.

Have Fun with the Kids

Though it's a responsible, momentous job, raising children doesn't have to feel serious and controlled. The character of an experience depends completely on your attitude—which you can change. Refuse to buy into the usual button-pushing interactions. Laugh at yourself, gently tease your kid. The more fun you have parenting, the easier it is. Enjoy it. Your kid's childhood won't last forever. What a tragedy to miss it and look back with regret.

- Aim for full involvement with the kids when you're together and full freedom when you're apart. Whether they go to your ex-spouse or just to school or camp, times without them replenish your ability to attend them fully when you reunite.

  When we had unlimited hours together, Christopher sometimes overwhelmed me with requests to play train, incessant talk about magic, and sheer preschooler exuberance and crankiness. At those times I really just wanted to get away from him, but I didn't think I *should* feel that way. So I listened to him with one ear and read the paper or cleaned the house. Present physically, I was really neither *away* from him nor *with* him, leaving us both unsatisfied. Like one of those parents at the weekend tot-lots reading the Wall Street Journal and sipping lattes while the kids languished unattended on the playground equipment, I wasn't using our time well. Now we're together less, but I'm fully engaged when we are, making us both happier.
- Remember the Life Preserver: Get organized, but not too organized. Planning enhances outings by, for example, saving you a trip to the planetarium on its closed day. Don't tie yourself into a rigid schedule, however. Be flexible and open to changes of mood, weather, and enthusiasm. Plan unstructured days sometimes and decide on the spur of the moment whether and where you will go. Maybe you'll all just stay home and read.

  Simplify your planning, too. I skim newsletters and newspapers with my calendar in hand. When an event catches my eye, I write it on the appropriate calendar date—sometimes months in advance—with its time and phone number. This gets the paper off my desk and into the recycle bin. Penciling in the events commits me to nothing, but it results in a handy reference for all potential activities on a given day. I don't have to remember anything. As a free day nears, I survey the possibilities and, with Christopher, choose among them. One weekend, for example, we had the choice of participating in a Rubber Duck Derby, a clay class, a potato harvest, an Alice in Wonderland tea, a campfire, or a bug show.

I also taped descriptions of permanent local attractions in a three-ring binder as a ready reference for hours and costs. Using the Sunday newspaper listings, this took about five minutes. I never have to shuffle papers and make calls when we decide to visit one of these places.

Too many possibilities sometimes tempt us to overdo, however. I learned the hard way that more than one activity per day tires and overstimulates us. We both need do-nothing time at home. After an outing, we're usually content to settle in alone for a while. Always remember that doing nothing is a valid choice.

For older kids, use family meetings to chart activities (see Chapter 5). List places you would like to visit in the next month or even the next year. Include both free activities and ones that cost money. Select one each week, and decide whether to invite friends along.

- Laugh.
- Play cards and board games.
- Include the children at some adult social events. This allows them to observe you functioning and having fun in the society of your peers. Naturally, you won't bring the kids to a formal adult event, but let them attend potluck dinners or picnics, for example. My book and play-reading groups meet at my house so I don't have to hire a sitter, and sometimes another child attends. The kids join us for dinner and then play together while we talk. A preteen who once attended the play reading migrated back and forth between the emoting adults and the train project in Christopher's room.
- Get together with your kids and others to watch a video. Rev up the popcorn popper.
- Learn together. "Learning is fun," remember? Take hikes or classes with your kids. Visit special exhibits. Formerly phobic about insects, I grew to admire them at the local botanical garden's "Bug

Days." Christopher's interest in slugs and snails led to a class at the science museum. Coaxing snails across high wires and rigging them to pull heavy loads qualifies as "fun" in our book. I never would have done these activities on my own.

- Make everyday activities into fun learning. Ask questions at places you visit. Explain what you see. Look up unanswered questions when you return home. Life is mysterious to younger kids, and even older ones love hearing how things work. See Chapter 12 for other examples.
- Schedule alone-time with each kid, even just five minutes at bedtime. Keep it inviolate. Inject some lightness into the encounter to end the day.
- As often as you can, which may be only once a year, take each child alone with you on a special fun "date." Make it a tradition, something you both anticipate eagerly.
- Share a sport. Learn a new one together or let your child teach you his skateboard techniques. Have a family softball game. Jog together.

Have Fun with Other Adults

Exclude the kids and enjoy some adult fun. Children benefit both from seeing you in a social context and from perceiving you as an independent being with friends and interests of your own.

> "All work and no play makes Jack a dull boy."
> JAMES HOWELL (1594–1666)

- If you can't yet face the opposite sex, go out with friends to whatever sounds like "fun" to you. Dinner, movies, sports, walks. (When you are ready to date, see Chapter 17.)
- Stay involved with childless friends. You expect them to be part of life with you and your child, but you should also spend time with them alone. Schedule some fun activities and talk about anything but kids and divorce.
- Share a baby-sitter and have a night on the town with another single parent.
- Try a singles' club activity. Keep your intentions platonic if you wish, but attending a concert or a horseback ride with a group of other adults might be just what you need.
- Keep up with married friends. Couples Tony brought into our social circle became history rather quickly, but I maintain good

friendships with a number of others. In fact, my relationships with the male members of those duos deepened. As a threesome, we interact as a unit now because we can't dissolve into male and female conversation groups, as often happens with two couples together.

- If you feel close with only one member of a couple, see that person separately. Redefine the relationship and have some fun together.
- Leave the kids behind and take a weekend trip with friends. Go gambling or attend a music festival. Visit a resort. Go fishing. Check out the drag races.

Have Fun Alone

I touched on time alone earlier. I repeat it with an emphasis on having *fun* alone. Maybe nothing sounds more fun than relaxing and recharging. Fine. Also consider more active endeavors. Deciding what constitutes "fun" relates to finding out who you are now. Some people love lunch and shopping, and others consider them torture. Please yourself. Maybe a weekend alone at a B&B reading a mystery does it for you. Or a bubble bath with the phone off the hook. Or running a ten-mile race. Even a simple movie. Ask that "new" person, "Hey, what sounds like fun to you?"

Maintain Your Boundaries

A single parent, especially one without an ex-spouse in the picture, risks "enmeshment" with his children, confusing his needs with theirs. Having no life of your own, you fulfill your dreams through your child, and in inappropriate ways—like shooting your daughter's cheerleading competitor or forcing your scrawny son to play football.

Being overly absorbed in your child's life discourages him from dissenting or asserting independence. He won't learn how to be in a relationship and still maintain his own identity. Since you project the message that others come first, he might even start putting your needs above his own.

Keep your boundaries intact: Remember that you and your child are two separate people with different lives, needs, feelings, bodies, tastes, talents, rights, goals, and opinions. Keep those differences alive.

Sacrificing yourself on the altar of your child benefits no one. You have enough love for both him and yourself. Make sure you get your share.

Let Others Nurture You

Although you are a single parent, you can't parent single-handedly. There's no point in trying to do everything alone. It brings no glory. No one will even notice, much less give you a gold medal.

Accepting Help

Is it harder to nurture yourself or to accept nurturance from others? For most of us, neither comes easily. Understanding subconsciously that my parents couldn't provide guidance or help, I always figured out for myself what I wanted and how to get it. My competence and independence became sources of pride, allowing little room for accepting assistance. Offers raised suspicions of ulterior motives. Actual help created perceived obligations to reciprocate and feelings of losing control. This mentality isolated me from the emotional sustenance of others' kindnesses.

After Tony died, help arrived from many sources. I say "help" rather than "offers of help" because people just gave without waiting for permission or instructions. I didn't have a chance to insist I could tough this out on my own. Not that I could have done so anyway. I was, for once in my life, overwhelmed. Looking back, I realize I needed an occurrence this big to learn how to "receive" graciously and wholeheartedly. As a result, I had some major realizations about giving and receiving:

- First, and perhaps most important, *letting people help you is a gift to them*. People want to assist. They refrain because of uncertainty or fear of intruding. Accepting their help allows them to feel good about their actions, and it brings you closer to them. Learn to say one simple word: "Yes."
- Second, you only have to accept, not reciprocate or even wonder how you could. I will never be able to "repay" the friends who stood by me during my difficult times. But as I am able, I can help *others* in need. That's one reason for writing this book. You'll have

your turn to give—maybe not to the person who gave to you, but to someone. The "repayment" need not be in kind.

Asking for Help

Unfortunately, our society, unlike some others, doesn't build in aid to single parents. You have to ask for it.

Single dads feel particular constraints against asking. In our society, men traditionally don't ask for emotional support—or even admit to needing it. Males often fend for themselves, hide problems and vulnerabilities, and fail to communicate.

People who have helped you during a crisis eventually drift back to their own lives. They still care though, and they will respond to requests. The catch is, you have to *make* those requests—not an easy task. You imagine you will overwhelm them with your "neediness" or they'll tell you to get lost or offer transparent excuses.

Besides other single parents, very few people recognize on their own that you need help, and they certainly don't know what kind. Sometimes friends marvel that I seem so calm and capable. Unless I speak up, they don't know about the mess percolating inside. They have no idea that if I don't get a break from playing trains with Christopher, for example, I'm going to derail completely. (A few, like my dear friend Staci, know my needs *better* than I. Besides providing unbelievable post-crisis support, she spent three years of alternate Tuesday afternoons with Christopher. Not only did I get a break, but they developed a special, independent, and loving relationship of their own.)

> "No, you never get any fun
> Out of the things you
> haven't done."
> OGDEN NASH (1902–1971)

If you have trouble asking, practice. Rehearse the question. *Don't apologize.* Start with something small. Ask to drop your kids off with a neighbor for an hour, for example. Or borrow last year's Halloween costume from an older child so you don't have to make or buy one. Ask a few people to bring food to your kid's birthday party. Whatever would help. Starting small gets you over that sense of incurring an obligation you don't have the energy to repay.

If you ever feel really ready to lose it, seek help through parental stress hot lines and temporary care agencies. You may just need a telephonic word of sympathy or advice, someone who understands.

In other cases, temporary care providers will find a family nearby to take your child for a few hours so you can cool off or collapse.

Be Resourceful and Creative in Getting Help

Get help however and whenever you can. Rely on your resourcefulness and creativity.

Hire Help

Okay, so you can't bring yourself to ask your best friend to clean your house. Maybe someday. Meanwhile, the kitchen floor reeks of spilled milk, toys cover every horizontal surface, and the bathrooms come straight from a deserted gas station. This is one of those days you think, "You couldn't pay anyone to do what I do!" You're wrong! You can pay someone to accomplish even the most odious tasks.

Hire out the chores you hate most. Cleaning, washing the car, grocery shopping, laundry. Pay someone to cook a meal once a week, with leftovers for another night.

Obviously, you have to get help for two-person jobs or those requiring skills you don't have, whether physical, legal, financial, or psychological.

Certainly, you can't afford to pay someone to do *everything*. You can't hire a full-time housekeeper, chauffeur, and cook, but you can occasionally treat yourself to a housecleaning service, join a carpool, and eat out once in a while.

Be creative. You don't have to hire professionals. Consider neighborhood teens. They'll do just about anything, and at a reasonable price. Even preteens can be "mother's helpers" for small children. Buy yourself an inexpensive weekend afternoon reading or working in the garden while a "big boy" plays with your youngsters nearby. Treat yourself. Take it out of your vacation budget!

Go on, make a call, no permanent commitments required. Consider it an "unbirthday gift." You'll thank yourself a hundred times over. That's an idea—write yourself a thank-you note!

Barter or Trade for Help

Payment for services needn't be in cash. Barter one of your skills as an ongoing proposition or a one-shot deal. Baby-sitting exchanges are the most obvious example. Some co-ops develop complicated systems to keep track of hours owed and earned. During my first year as a single mom, I participated in a simple trade: I took my friend Maddy's son on Tuesday mornings, and she took mine on Wednesdays.

Chores you hate are fertile ground for trades. I guarantee that for every person who detests cooking, there's another who breezes through meal preparation and would eagerly make a double batch for your freezer. In exchange you might spend a meditative time washing her car or installing her new house numbers with your electric screwdriver. A request for "fix-it" chits is always at the top of my Christmas wish list.

Other single parents are a great resource. We face the same problems and share many of the same needs. A single parent doesn't require much explanation when called upon for help. Traveling, camping, or day-trips run smoothly with another single parent and child along. One person can stay with the kids while the other goes to the bathroom or checks out the ticket line. That's a pure luxury, one that married parents simply don't appreciate.

Despite different ages, histories, and lifestyles, the four single moms on my little street bonded as close friends. Once a month, we meet for dinner with our kids, who range in age from five to sixteen. We rotate houses, and the hostess of the month cooks, serves, and cleans up. The other three women do . . . absolutely nothing! Except eat and relax—guilt-free. Depending on the venue, the kids dine separately or at the grown-up table—with good manners expected. They finish early and play while we talk. The rotation also includes a quiet, candle-lit, take-out meal at one house while the teen baby-sits the younger kids at another.

Sometimes a couple of us get together for yard work. We pull weeds for an hour at each house while our kids play together in sight. Each yard gets two "woman-hours" of work, the same as if we'd each worked our own properties twice as long. We have a sociable time; the children stay happy; we have extra muscle for heavy loads; and the time flies by. More often than not we throw together a meal after admiring two jobs well done.

We watch one another's cats during vacations, trade advice, celebrate some holidays, stuff articles in each other's mailboxes, trade photographs, give referrals for home repairers, and baby-sit. We're all on one another's school emergency lists. You needn't live on the same street to cultivate a similar support system among your single-parent friends.

Don't wait around for these kinds of arrangements to "happen" to you. It's up to you—and each of us—to forge societal structures that work for single parents.

Keep Your Antennae Tuned

Being resourceful means making contacts and cultivating sources of help. Let people know your needs. When you make new single-parent acquaintances, exchange phone numbers and suggest ways of helping one another. Offer to let your childless friends borrow your kid for a trip to the zoo. Explore hiring a common sitter with other working parents during school vacation times. Make note of community resources. Take responsibility for following up on contacts and cementing relationships.

By nurturing yourself in any of these ways, you provide a wonderful role model for your children, you become a more capable, centered parent, and you value yourself. And oh yes . . . you feel much better, too. Those massages come straight from the gods.

ORGANIZATIONS

Gay and Lesbian Parents Coalition, International (GLPCI): Newsletter. Box 50360, Washington, D.C. 20091; 202-583-8029.

Parents Without Partners: Local support groups. Publishes *Single Parent* magazine. 401 N. Michigan Ave., Chicago, IL 60611; 312-644-6610.

BOOKS LISTING RETREATS

U.S./Worldwide Guide to Retreat Center Guest Houses, John and Mary Jensen (Newport Beach, CA: CTS (direct mail publishing company), 1995. Lists 850 U.S. and international abbeys, missions, and sanctuaries that furnish room and sometimes board in restful settings. For further information, call 714-720-3729.

Sanctuaries: The West Coast and Southwest, Jack and Marcia Kelly (New York: Crown Publishing Group, 1992). Lists and describes spiritual centers and retreats around the country.

Chapter 5

Parenting Skills That Work

What's different about parenting skills for single parents as opposed to two-parent teams? Nothing—except you have to do everything alone. The skills are the same, but you have no backup to step in if you falter. When frustrated and exhausted, no partner "takes over." You have no live-in sounding board for difficult decisions, and sometimes you have to undo bad habits your children pick up at their "other house."

Divorce doesn't lead to deviance. Ineffective parenting does. That's good news, since you can *learn* to be an effective parent. So, instead of obsessing over the idea that splitting up the family irreparably "ruined" your kid, work on your parenting skills.

It pays off a thousandfold. Kids of all ages score higher in academic achievement and positive psycho-social behavior when effectively parented. When your parenting is working right, your relationship with your children improves and your home runs more smoothly. Your kids develop self-esteem and internal controls.

With luck, you and your ex-spouse see eye-to-eye on parenting. Agreement on child-rearing highly influences a child's successful recovery from divorce. If you can't agree, however, at least you can do *your* part.

Effective Parenting Must Be Learned

Because most of us had poor role models, skillful parenting doesn't come naturally. This is not said to denigrate your parents—they did their best—but to help you understand the origins of your own style. All else being equal, you tend to parent precisely like your father and mother—or sometimes exactly the opposite. They taught you their version of right and wrong, and those beliefs unconsciously influence your present perceptions of your kids' behavior. Instead of making conscious choices, you tend to react from these old attitudes without even realizing it. Because the way you were reared seems so normal, you've been blinded to different modes of parenting.

However, effective parenting *can* be learned with conscious effort and practice.

While Learning New Skills . . .

While learning new parenting skills, keep in mind that:

- Learning new parenting skills takes time and repetition. Have patience with your learning curve and faith in your ability. I purloined this note from Jane's refrigerator as a reminder: "Brahma said: 'Well, after ten thousand explanations, a fool is no wiser. But an intelligent person needs only two thousand five hundred.' " (From the *Mahabharata*.)

  Don't give up because the new ways feel awkward at first. Familiarity brings comfort and ease. Cliff uses a simple illustration in my support group: Interlace your fingers and notice which thumb is on top. Now switch the position of all your fingers so the other thumb falls on top. How odd this feels . . . but if you try the new way a few times, it begins to seem normal. That's how learning new parenting skills works.
- You can't be super-parent, so don't even try. Instead, love your kids by modeling a real person who sees mistakes as opportunities to learn.
- Read this book and one or two others that focus strictly on parenting skills. Even just a page a day while brushing your teeth or waiting for your coffee to heat helps. Practice the exercises and

incorporate them into your life. Don't be afraid to consult the books in front of your children until the skills become natural.

- Look for support groups and parenting classes at churches, schools, hospitals, government agencies, and child-rearing organizations. The S.T.E.P. programs (Systematic Training for Effective Parenting) have a national reputation for teaching successful parenting.

Types of Parenting Styles

- *Permissive* parents create a chaotic home atmosphere—freedom without order. They exert very little control over their children and make few demands when it comes to impulse control or mature behavior. The individual child's wants always come first, and he exhibits out-of-bounds behavior—and insecurity.
- *Authoritarian* moms and dads demand obedience to high, absolute standards in a rigid home atmosphere—order without freedom. Their needs always prevail. Work, tradition, and authority rank high on the list of values. Punishments include withdrawal of love and affection from the child. Negotiation and leeway for individual situations never occur. The parent is absolute boss, and the child has few choices about how to run his life. "Because I say so" could be the family motto. In response, the child becomes excessively compliant or rebellious.
- *Authoritative* or *effective* parents operate between the two extremes mentioned above, in a comfortable, balanced atmosphere. They encourage self-reliance, independence, responsibility, and individuality while enforcing clear rules and standards—freedom with order. They expect mature behavior and rely on "logical consequences" rather than punishment. Because the child has choices within limits, power struggles disappear. Open discussion in the household encourages give-and-take and the recognition of every family member's rights and individual differences.

The following sections highlight some parenting skills that aim to engender cooperation, reduce conflict, and solve problems. While all parents benefit from these skills, they play an especially important role for those of us consumed by the demands of raising children on our own.

Deal with Your Own Emotional Baggage

Until you unpack your emotional baggage, you can't detach well enough to parent effectively. Your buttons will get pushed, automatic pilot will take over, and you'll overreact. Later, you'll come to regret your reaction, but at the time, you'll seem to have no choice. Your own psychological issues will cloud your ability to recognize and tend to your child's needs.

Use Overreactions to Identify Your Hot Spots

If your child causes an earthquake in the range of two-point-five, and you bring down the house with a ten on the Richter scale, either you're under tremendous stress, or you hit an old emotional trigger. Once you've cooled off, review what happened.

Overreactions result from projecting your own psychological issues onto your child. When he requests ten bucks for the basketball game, for example, you scream that he shouldn't have wasted his allowance on video arcades. He calls you a miser and insists his weekly pittance doesn't even keep him in bubble gum. You have a fight over money on your hands—probably not for the first time.

Instead of screaming at your son, close your eyes and breathe. Could your reaction be fueled by resentment that *you* never even *got* an allowance as a youth? Maybe? Are you really angry at your dad instead of your son? Recognizing something like that takes the charge off the interaction with your kid. You don't have to fork over the ten dollars, and you can still say "no," but in a nicer way. Recognizing your own emotional stumbling blocks allows you to work out solutions to current problems, rather than reacting to issues left over from childhood or your marriage.

An overreaction can involve any emotion, not just anger. Your kid's refusal to try out for the school play might upset you, for instance. He *should* participate; what's *wrong* with him? Consider your own childhood. Did your parents ostracize you for being shy? Do you still feel the shame of not speaking up? This is your issue, not your child's.

Hurt feelings also cause overreactions. You want your child's approval as much as he wants yours. When he dislikes a gift or passes up an opportunity to be with you, you feel hurt. This wound brings up others you've suffered in life. Personal growth helps you express the hurt without the knee-jerk desire to wound back.

Overreactions can result from control issues. If you think you govern every aspect of your child's life, you'll feel lost and angry when you learn you don't. Once you stop trying to have the last say on everything, you'll stay cool when your kid asserts his independence. Overreactions may represent displaced anger. You've been batted around the whole day at work by people who will eat you for lunch if you say what you're really thinking. Frustration follows you home, and you "kick the cat"—or the kid, as the case may be. Nothing feels better just then than exploding at someone who can't kick back.

Lack of confidence often underlies another "button." Single parents, especially, feel judged by others. If you already doubt your ability to get through this experience in one piece, you'll be that much more vulnerable when your kid "makes you" look inadequate. When he whines loudly for fifteen minutes in the checkout line, you want to blast back at him. Of course, if you habitually act like a screaming idiot in retaliation, you really *are* inadequate, and you'll feel even worse later. Developing your own self-esteem and detaching from your child's behavior interrupts this cycle.

Preventing Overreactions

You can stop overreacting to your emotional triggers. To begin:

- Sit with your overreactions and get in contact with the underlying emotion. You might find, for example, resentment that your parents didn't provide you with the love, attention, and understanding that your child gets from you. Going even deeper, sadness underlies that resentment; you can't go back for another crack at childhood. You can, however, find love and understanding *now*—from friends or relatives. And from yourself.
- Work to create a moment of space between event and response so you can wedge in something besides your usual reaction. Count to three before speaking. Take a breath. Splash some water on your face. Just that can make room for other responses. Find a momentary distraction that works for you. Think of yourself in the *role* of detached parent, not as a human being with a vested interest. You don't have to take anything *personally*.

  Evading the reaction trap becomes easier with each attempt. You may still get angry, but you express your feelings with words rather than fireworks.
- However you address your emotional issues, make sure it's not with your child. He's not your confidant. Don't burden him with your

emotions about adult matters. He may assume your upset is *his* fault or feel compelled to fix the situation, which, of course, he cannot do. Let him be a kid. Leave him to concerns that are appropriate for his age. Find another adult with whom you can vent. A counselor brings a helpful objectivity to the process by identifying why certain events "set you off."

Take into Account Your Child's Developmental Stage, Physical Being, Temperament, Sensitivity, Birth Order, and Relationships with Siblings When He "Misbehaves"

Your kid usually wants to please you, but he may not yet have developed the capacity to understand or do as you ask. Likewise, he's human, and variations in his physical condition and environment affect his behavior. His individual temperament also controls his actions and attitudes. Having an explanation for your child's behavior lets you detach and refrain from taking it personally. Instead of deciding that your kid is "out to get" you, consider these factors:

Developmental Stage

> "Train up a child in the way he should go, and when he is old, he will not depart from it."
> PROVERBS 22:6

Some irritating new behavior comes along, and you want your child to *stop*. You try everything, and nothing works. What are you doing *wrong*? Then someone tells you, "It's developmental. All ten-year-olds do that." Your whole attitude changes. Your kid is doing what kids do. If they all go through this stage at ten, then, irritating as he is, rejoice that he's normal!

You can't get mad at a cat for being a cat, and you can't blame a child for being a child. Experiments, messes, wildness, stabs at independence, and myriad other behaviors are his *job*. He needs to do them to grow up. Like a butterfly changing from caterpillar to cocoon to beautiful-winged adult, your child must progress through each developmental task before moving on to the next. If you force the caterpillar from the cocoon before it finishes metamorphosis, it won't survive. Your job is to be in the background gently guiding the changes. You adjust, discuss, and let him learn through mistakes.

That "adjusting" should be appropriate to your child's developmental stage:

- A toddler, concrete and preverbal, learns best by action: Set him in "Time-Out," distract him, take away the spoon and pan he's using as a drum.
- Preschoolers are developing empathy, and they can begin to learn from simple statements about how their behavior affects others. More verbal, they also learn indirect lessons from reading stories or "overhearing" you talk about acceptable behavior.
- Elementary-age kids love rules and fairness, so use explanations focusing on equity. They also relate to stories that convey a lesson through *other* kids' behavior.
- For teens and preteens, control and independence are primary issues. They need areas in which to make their own decisions about their lives. Allow them to assert their independence within ultimate boundaries you establish (see Chapter 7).

Once I learned that "poo-poo" and "pee-pee" top the list of four-year-old humor, I didn't waste too much energy trying to stop Christopher's bathroom talk. (I did draw the line at being called "poo-poo head" though—I have my dignity.) I told him the rules, set limits, and ignored some transgressions. Developmental behavior eventually fades on its own if you don't make it into a power struggle.

Physical Factors

Always consider whether misbehavior might relate to illness, hunger, or fatigue (or, with teenagers, hormones). Children often don't realize they're hungry or tired until it's too late. My usually mellow Christopher becomes obstinate and cranky a week before showing any other symptom of illness. We had several tempestuous experiences before I finally put two and two together. Now I suspect an approaching virus and take steps to make him feel better before his nose starts to drip.

It's the same with hunger. I recognize a certain look that says, "Feed me or I'll make you miserable." It's a statement of fact, not a threat. I feed him.

Temperament

Some kids naturally exhibit high activity levels, and others move slowly. Many have the attention span of a gnat, while others make the Sphinx look overactive. Yours may throw projects across the room in frustration, and others persist until they succeed. Each of these kids reacts differently to limits and requests, so take temperament into account when forming your rules and expectations. You can't realistically ask an energetic school-age kid to sit all the way through *Henry IV, Part I*, though a more sedate one might be able to.

All personality types contain an upside and a downside. You may reasonably expect a persistent child to follow through on a chore once started, for example, but he also may argue longer before agreeing to do it. A slow-to-warm child feels uncomfortable in new surroundings but can also form deep friendships one-on-one.

Children also go through negative periods unrelated to anything in particular. You just have to wait these out. Defer trying to teach new behaviors during this time. Choose your battles.

Sensitivity

Some children really *care* about their surroundings, especially items that come into contact with their bodies. Their clothes have to feel just right (no tags, no "hard pants," zippers rather than buttons, and so on). Music must be neither too low nor too loud. Food has to be the right temperature, the right brand, the right color.

Do you really want to fight about these? Save yourself a lot of grief and buy what your kid likes.

Problems often arise if your temperament or sensitivity level doesn't match your child's. He's boisterous, and you're retiring. You deal in concepts, and he likes details. Or vice versa. Recognize, work around, and celebrate your differences.

Birth Order

Where were you in the birth order? Your place in the family and your relationship with sibs affect how you parent. Consider hidden assumptions you make—such as who attacked first, who won't share, and so on. You may unconsciously see situations from the viewpoint of the child who shares your birth order.

The oldest child in the family typically becomes "parentalized." He likes rules and tries to do as you want. When he acts out, it's often against something he won't let himself desire—it's against the rules, and he doesn't want the guilt. These kids tend to be perfectionists. To loosen them up, put them in situations where they aren't the oldest or the most knowledgeable.

The second child often adopts a role opposite the firstborn. Perhaps he excels in sports or academics. Appreciate his talents and never compare him to the older sibling.

The youngest often claims innocence or ignorance. He may be the family "clown." Give him chances to show responsibility.

Siblings

Some divorces or deaths occur just after birth of another child. Siblings can experience anger, competitiveness, and envy. A very young firstborn often sees a new baby as competition for his parents' affections, particularly amid the turmoil of divorce. He still needs to be "baby," but another one shows up instead.

In two-parent families, the father and young, firstborn child spend more time together when a second child arrives, strengthening their bond. This dynamic doesn't occur in single-parent families. If there is no father, Mom divides her attention as best she can. When Dad still participates after the divorce, both parents should spend special alone-time with the firstborn. Each should help him express any jealousy and anger without translating them into actions against the newcomer. In general:

- Don't pressure your oldest child to act more mature than his age, especially since divorce often causes regressive behaviors anyway. Instead, remind him that he gets extra privileges because he can do more.
- When resolving disputes with one child, keep the other out of it. If he gloats, remind him clearly that you're the parent. "This isn't your business."
- A kid older than five understands that babies need more attention. As long as he gets his share, too, he accepts this.
- Having siblings benefits children in the long run. They socialize earlier and accept not being the center of attention in every group. When divorce or other major events occur, the sibs provide comfort to one another, while an only-child copes alone.

Developing a Healthy Parent-Child Relationship

The sturdier a structure, the better it survives storms. A strong parent-child relationship remains intact in the face of the tornadoes that inevitably sweep through every family. Developing a firm foundation in an atmosphere of mutual trust and respect keeps thunderheads at bay and eases the way to recovery when lightning does strike.

Treat Your Child with Respect

I hear parents on the street talking to children in a tone of voice they wouldn't use with a rabid dog. People forget that kids hear, comprehend, feel, and react. Treat your children with as much courtesy and respect as a friend. Use the same tone of voice as you would with another child whose parent is present.

- Express your anger calmly and appropriately: "I'm very angry about this." Don't lecture. Wait until you've cooled off and then use your problem-solving skills to reach a solution.
- Never withdraw your love or threaten to abandon your child if he doesn't comply.
- Don't hesitate to apologize to your child or to others. Your kid needs to hear what an apology sounds like, even if the offense was accidental.

  Did your parents apologize during your childhood? Mine never did. Apologies undo a tremendous amount of damage. By example, they also show a child that mistakes are all right, and they demonstrate how to make up for them.

  Caution: Part of being sorry is not repeating the behavior. You can't resort to yelling every day and expect continual apologies to get you off the hook. Eventually an apology means nothing if the behavior doesn't change. Get some help if you can't manage this on your own.
- Acknowledge you don't know who your kid really is. Don't make assumptions, but ask questions in order to understand him.
- Tell him, "I'll never intentionally hurt you. If I do hurt you, you have to let me know."
- Keep commitments—no excuses. Don't make promises lightly. Live up to your words, even if doing so causes far more trouble than you ever imagined. If you say you'll pick your daughter up at six o'clock, make *sure* you do. Leave work extra early to avoid possible traffic

jams. She doesn't care about the accident on the bridge. All she knows is that you didn't show up on time. Your kids must be able to count on you, no matter what. If you don't come through on the small potatoes, they won't trust you on the biggies.

- Operate in an atmosphere of trust. Keeping a hawk-eye on a kid only encourages him to sneak around. Give him something to live up to. Talk with him about how broken trust is hard to repair.

> "Respect the child. Be not too much his parent. Trespass not on his solitude."
> RALPH WALDO EMERSON
> (1803–1882)

Grant Permission to Talk about Anything

Using this Life Preserver allows your child to criticize you without reprisal or tell you what you don't want to hear. He doesn't fear or protect you.

- Tell him directly that he can talk with you about anything.
- Show him by example that no topic is taboo. Bring up difficult subjects, such as sex, drugs, or hurt feelings.
- When the subject hurts or embarrasses you, say so—and then do your best. Commenting on your reaction validates your child's perception. "Sometimes it's hard to talk about Daddy." If he asks why, say, "Sometimes I get sad." The "sometimes" is so he won't feel responsible for making you unhappy by broaching the subject. If you're too emotional to talk at all, ask to put off discussion until a certain date so you can figure out the best way to talk about it. Follow up.
- If you find it hard to talk about something, it's probably a good indication that you need to do just that. Tell your kids the truth, though it need not always be the whole truth. Remember the parent who went into embarrassed detail about sex in answer to her young daughter's question about where she came from. At the conclusion, the little girl said, "Oh. Well, Sam came from Denver." Try to gauge your child's intent by asking, for example, "What makes you ask that?" If she tells you about Sam's geographic point of origin, you can let her know she came from Berkeley and save the biological details for later.
- If your child says something negative about you, first say, "Thank you for telling me." Then address the content of his criticism.

- Never dismiss a topic as trivial or shameful or too adult. There's always a way to discuss a subject at your child's level.
- If faced with a "case of first impression" that you simply don't know how to handle, tell the truth (what a concept!), or at least an edited version of it. It seems odd to need a reminder, but think of your own childhood. Parents of the last generation kept children ignorant of everything from adoption to sex. You don't have to follow suit. Tell the truth, tailored to your child's age and understanding.

Love Means Paying Attention

Your kid wants your energy. If you don't give him positive attention, he'll settle for negative—and misbehave to get it. When he provokes your anger, notice what you were doing just before. Were you distracted? In a hurry? Focusing on other kids? Zoned out? Was he trying to tell you, "Hey, I'm here"?

Short-circuit any bids for negative attention with daily doses of positive attention on your child's terms, with the intention of learning from him. If you have more than one child, schedule an inviolate "alone-time" with each, even just five minutes at bedtime.

You must be sincere. A kid easily picks up on pretense and inattention. Let go of your world fully during his time. Forget work or your Friday night date. Just be with your kid, playing trains or Monopoly or discussing the origin of the universe.

We often err in assumptions about what makes people feel loved. When I'm sick, for example, I want to be coddled and fed, but Tony always bundled up incommunicado with the shades drawn. When one of us caught a bug, the other did what he would have wanted for himself. I plied Tony with attention, and he left me alone for hours on end. I felt rejected when he shooed me away, and he resented my complaints at being left bedridden and starving while he cleaned the roof gutters "for" me. Despite high investment of energy on both sides, neither of us supplied the sickroom with what the other recognized as "love." A little communication would have gone a long way.

Ask your child, "What makes you feel loved?" Then your offerings will be right on target, even if you can't do everything. He will appreciate your asking and doing what you can.

His responses may surprise you. One teen replied to a caring mom, "Don't ask so many questions all the time." The mother had thought her "interest" would please him, and at one point it may have. Ask again at various ages, as the answers change.

Your attention need not be lengthy or elaborate—just consistent. Find small ways of showing your kid he reigns supreme in your life. Some suggestions:

- When you return from work, pay immediate, if brief, attention to your child before doing anything else, such as listening to phone messages, reading the mail, or starting dinner. Greet him enthusiastically. Hug him. Exchange a few words. Then nurture yourself, too (see Chapter 4).
- Sometimes give your child what he wants *before* he asks for it. A gracious offer changes the dynamic from, "I want," to, "Here, this is for you."
- Ignoring the phone when you're with your child says he's more important than a ringing bell. Let your answering machine do its work. If you must take an especially important call, warn him ahead of time that you'll have to interrupt your activities briefly.
- Leave a note or treat in his lunch box or another place he'll find it.
- Mail him a letter to your address. Send him a postcard from work.
- Set aside regular game evenings to play whatever he chooses. Dinner that night should be simple: hot dogs or mac-and-cheese maybe.
- Leave a message for him on the answering machine.
- Take a short trip on a train, bus, or subway, enjoy a meal out or a picnic together, and return.
- Write your child thank-you cards for small favors.
- Put a little gift on his pillow: a flower, a piece of candy, a miniature car for his collection.
- When you notice something positive about him, *say it*.
- Pack a picnic breakfast with a thermos of hot cocoa. Wake before dawn and watch the sun come up from a scenic spot.
- Take a midnight snack outside of town to look at the stars.
- At least once or twice a year, make a special "date" with each child. Pick him up at school early and go for dinner. Or go to a baseball game. Or visit the amusement park.
- Sit together at a coffee house for an hour.
- Buy something he wants "just because I love you."
- Make small dates: a trip to the ice cream store, a few minutes window shopping.
- Take your kid to a grown-up event. Lower your expectations and prepare your child for what will happen. Be ready to leave if his behavior disturbs others, but let him enjoy the experience for what it means to him.

- When he's sick, treat him like a king. Bring food on a tray with a flower. Rent videos. Read to him. Play his favorite music. Provide his favorite liquids, even if you don't allow them at other times.
- Dance with your child to the music of his choice.
- Look up the answers to his questions together.
- Get silly with him.
- Give unexpected hugs.
- Interview your child as though he were a "celebrity" in town for an award. Acting as a reporter, ask "serious" questions about his favorite foods, friends, travel plans, talents, dreams.
- Have a "birth-iversary" privilege each month on the date corresponding to your kid's birthday. Christopher was born on September 21. On the twenty-first day of other months, he chooses something special: a favorite meal, time in the park, a visit to the library.
- Make it a ritual to say what you like about each other at dinner.
- If you come from a definitive cultural heritage, have "family culture" times to teach your child his ancestry. Make Norwegian lefsa or Salvadoran pupusas.
- Draw a family tree to show your child his position. Show pictures of family, past and present.
- Take your child to visit the hospital where he was born. Tell him about the day of his birth and how much you love being his parent. Show him the nursery full of new babies.
- Measure your kid's growth on a chart. Take foot- and handprints with paint on butcher paper every birthday.
- Help your child host a "formal" dinner party. He chooses the guests and the menu and helps with preparations. While having fun, he'll learn how to play the host.
- Make personalized place mats together. Use magazine pictures, dried flowers from the garden, or bright fall leaves, whatever your kids find meaningful. Christopher's featured . . . trains, what else? We cut out pictures and made more train images on the computer. Cover the mats with transparent Contac paper to make them waterproof.
- Say it in his lingo: "I totally love you."
- Celebrate milestones, large and small. A candle at dinner or a favorite activity pleasantly marks an accomplishment. After filling out Christopher's baby book with "first tooth" and "first step," I kept going with a notebook of other "firsts," the sillier the better: first time on a Ferris wheel, first garage sale, first Halloween costume . . .
- Share fantasies. Take trips in your imaginations. Visualize what you'd like to happen.

- A child becomes very suggestible just before nodding off or when waking up. Take advantage of this hypnotic state with hugs and reminders of your love.

Keep Boundaries Intact

Enjoy closeness with your child without making him a friend, confidant, psychiatrist, or equal partner. He needs a parent. Keep your psychological issues separate from his. Take every opportunity to reinforce the notion that you're separate people.

- Grant your child freedom to have his own thoughts, likes, dislikes, and emotions, especially concerning your ex. Constantly emphasize that you each have your own feelings about everything (see Chapter 9). Avoid saying "we" feel, "we" like, "we" want, and so on.
- Never imply that your kid is responsible for your feelings—or those of your ex-spouse. Make it clear that he has no obligation to fix either of you when you're hurt or sad (see Chapter 1).
- Maintain physical as well as psychological boundaries. If your door is shut, for example, your child has to knock before entering. He should also have his own "space" in the house.
- Beware of "fuzzy" boundaries, especially between a single parent and an only-child:
  - –An only-child benefits from all your attention and resources, but doing *everything* together as "buddies" satisfies some need in you. It's unfair and unhealthy for your kid. If he's always with grown-ups and treated as a "little adult," he'll relate poorly to other kids. Logic and charm work wonders with the older generation, but peers demand their own social conventions. Break up your twosome frequently by adding his friends to activities. Ensure sufficient, independent time with other kids, including overnight visits. Encourage his playfulness and his silly side.
  - –You may understand an only-child too well. Always anticipating his needs, however, keeps him from having to learn communication and assertiveness. Require him to *ask* for what he wants, and show him acceptable ways for doing so. Without this skill, he will have trouble getting what he wants from future relationships.
  - –Make sure your exclusive focus on a single child doesn't lead you to unrealistic expectations.
  - –Finally, especially after traumatic times, an only-child may fixate on getting your approval or taking care of *your* emotional needs. He may feel responsible for your feelings. Make it clear by words and actions that this isn't in his job description (see Chapter 1).

Learning to Communicate

Communication involves effectively presenting your views and needs. It also involves attentive listening. Unless you can converse effectively with your children, your kids won't even know what you want, much less feel like giving it to you.

Communication becomes just a part of "how life is" for your children if you start young. And those early years give *you* practice at skills you'll need to keep the lines open later.

Conversely, it's never too late to start practicing good communication. New communication habits will seem strange to older children, but persist. Talk about what you're doing and why—even if they don't buy into the new ways immediately.

> "Sweet childish days, that were as long as twenty days are now."
> WILLIAM WORDSWORTH
> (1770–1850)

What Doesn't Work

- Nagging. This amounts to talking without acting—not being in charge. It leaves expectations and consequences unclear. Your kid knows you don't "mean it." Get your child's attention. Snap off the TV, look him in the eye, and tell him, "We have a problem to solve."
- Yelling. Either your kid will ignore you and internalize his anger or scream back. Get in the habit of pausing to consider an alternative response before raising your voice. Try whispering or singing your message instead. The surprise element gets his attention.
- Name-calling, sarcasm, criticism, and put-downs. "Who put you in charge?" "Haven't you learned anything yet?" "You're so lazy." These only hurt your kid's self-esteem and damage your relationship.
- Guilt trips. All you'll do is make your child feel he's responsible for your life.
- Demanding *immediate* action. Consider how *you* like to be bossed. Don't you respond better to choices and respect? Allow your child some control over the "when" and "how."
- Ordering, commanding. "You have to . . ." "Do it . . ."
- Threats and warning. "If you don't, then . . ."
- Punishment, as opposed to logical consequences (see *Enforcing the Rules: "Logical Consequences,"* which follows later in this chapter). Threats and physical force, including spanking, simply don't work. They teach hostility, aggression, and the use of violence against others.

- Lecturing, preaching, moralizing, and extended explanations. Kids stop listening.
- Advising, providing ready answers. "You should . . ." "What I would do is . . ."
- Evaluating, judging, blaming, disapproving, psychoanalyzing. "If you weren't so lazy . . ." "You don't have your head screwed on right . . ." "You're just trying to get attention."
- Denying the emotions or problems, dismissing the importance. "It's really nothing . . ." "Don't let it worry you." "It's not so bad . . ." "Let's don't talk about anything unpleasant . . ."

Effective Communication

Hone your communication skills. Do what works:

- Make sure your child is in a receptive mood before you try to talk. Neither of you should be stressed, distracted, highly emotional, or involved in something else. If he doesn't seem willing at the moment, ask *him* to designate a good time within an outer limit you set: "We have to resolve this by the weekend. You let me know when you're ready to talk before then. Otherwise, we'll have to do it Friday night."
- If your child approaches you at an inconvenient moment, tell him, "That sounds important. Let's talk about it later when we have more time." If you're too angry or upset to pay close attention, be honest with him—without going into detail about specific reasons. Adjust the timing but not the willingness. Say, "I'm upset now. I'll let you know when I can hear what you have to say." A younger kid will understand a simple, "I need a Time-Out." Suggest that for now he tell the dog or Barbie or Thomas the Tank Engine.

  Perhaps it's just the wrong time. Your casserole's burning and the doorbell rings. Try saying, "That sounds really important. I want to hear all about it at dinner." Or write down a "listening date" on the calendar. Kids can wait, but they like to know for sure when the talk is coming.

  Follow up on your own initiative even if he doesn't raise the subject again. He may be testing to see if you *will*.

  If you have a teenager, however, turn off the burners, ignore the visitor, sit down, and talk right now!
- Model the use of "I" messages. This technique has been around for a long time because it works. Even if your children don't cognitively

understand it, they'll unconsciously pick it up when you consistently adopt it.

"I" messages convey, "I have a problem." In contrast, "you" messages say there's something wrong with the other person. He's to blame. It's his fault. Hearing a barrage of "you" messages tells a child he's a problem. Sometimes he'll prove you right. He becomes defensive and retaliates with his own blaming, acting out, or withdrawing. Communication doesn't have a chance.

Using "I" messages takes practice, practice, practice. At first this device feels awkward and contrived, but it sounds honest and respectful to the recipient, regardless of content. Incorporate four points in your "I" statement:

–The emotion you feel
–A description of the behavior
–How the behavior affects you practically
–A clear description of how to improve or what you need

Instead of, "How many times have I told you to wipe your feet!" try:

–"I feel so frustrated
–when you leave your dirty clothes on the bathroom floor
–because then I have to pick them up or ask you to do it.
–I would like you to remember to put them in the hamper for me to wash."

I know, you think your kid will ignore you or laugh you right off the planet. Try adopting "I" statements anyway. If he doesn't respond, add a statement of logical consequences (see *Enforcing the Rules: "Logical Consequences"* later in this chapter) for non-cooperation: "From now on, whenever I have to pick up your clothes, I'll put them in a box, and you can launder them yourself." A series of mild consequences over time changes behavior far better than anger and yelling.

Also, don't disguise "you" messages as "I" messages: "I get frustrated when you're so careless."

- Use an "eraser" to restart badly begun exchanges. If, for whatever reason, you broach a topic in the wrong way or use an unpleasant tone of voice, just smile and say, "Erase that. I want to start over." When your child begins with a whine or a scream, asking, "Do you want to erase that?" gives him a fresh start without losing face.
- When a difficulty arises, try "I would understand if you felt. . ." This tells him you're ready to listen if he wants to talk, now or later.

- Try using the third person. This sometimes loosens youngsters' tongues, especially on touchy subjects. Direct inquiry about your child's feelings often feels threatening to him. With the third person, he answers without explicitly revealing his feelings about an uncomfortable matter.

  If you think your child has an unasked question, say: "A boy might wonder . . ." Ask, "I wonder how a ten-year-old would feel if . . ." Or, "I need your help. I met a just-divorced woman with an eight-year-old son. She wonders what he's going through and how to help him. Do you have any idea what I should tell her? If not now, tell me if you think of something later." Try, "When a daddy moves out of the house, some little boys feel he doesn't love them anymore."

  Keep the conversation in the third person unless your child switches to a more personal mode.
- Take the pressure off by making conversation a part of some other activity. Use chore-time to broach difficult subjects casually. Busy hands ease reluctance or anxiety. Try talking while riding bikes, painting the bathroom, or hammering nails. Sitting side-by-side in a vehicle feels less threatening than facing one another across the kitchen table. Besides, you have a captive audience in the car!

  Get a younger child to talk while drawing, coloring, or painting. Ask him to draw an innocuous-sounding subject, such as "going to the swimming pool," and talk about how he shows the family. Or ask him directly to represent how he feels about the divorce or some aspect of it.
- For young kids, act out a scenario with puppets, stuffed animals, trucks, or trains. Show the intact family and the separation and any other issues that arise.
- Encourage older children to write stories or journals that they can share with you at their option.
- Don't jump on your kids right away for a report of their day. When kids won't tell you what went on until much after the fact, they're probably saying, "I'll tell you, but on my terms."
- Ask questions that encourage meaningful answers. Instead of, "How was school?" ask, "What were the best and worst things that happened to you today?"
- Don't reserve "communication" for crises. Chat with your kid. Laugh together. Get to know him as you would a new acquaintance. After all, he's not the same person at twelve that he was at two.

- Read to your child, whatever his age. Reading together builds a sense of family and provides common experiences for reference. Talk about new words, new ideas, and the meaning of stories.
- Discuss issues that arise from watching your child's videos and television programs together.
- Be open to later discussion and reexamination. As a process, communication doesn't necessarily end when a conversation concludes.

Develop Active Listening Skills

Kids don't necessarily want answers. They want a listener. The more you listen—really listen—the more your child will open up.

What's the big deal about listening, right? You've done it all your life. Not so. While another person talks, you typically focus on yourself—formulating your next comment, passing judgment, thinking about your schedule, daydreaming, or wishing you were elsewhere. Your mind has time to wander about like this because you listen at about twice the speed the average person talks.

"Active" or "reflective" listening shifts attention to the speaker. Shut off your inner yak, pay attention, and reflect comprehension and concern. Turn off your defenses. This skill requires a good deal of—guess what?—practice. Ask a friend to spend five or ten minutes with you on a regular basis just talking so you can listen actively. Then trade roles so your friend can practice, too.

- Start active listening with your child as soon as he becomes verbal. Use those early years to perfect your listening skills under fairly forgiving circumstances. Besides, even little kids convey important matters.
- Give your child special listening time every day, no matter how limited. Put aside all thoughts of chores, worries, and work.
- Get rid of distractions, such as TV, radio, or music.
- Choose a setting comfortable for both of you. A familiar place keeps attention on the conversation rather than the surroundings.
- Look at your child. Use eye contact, tone of voice, facial expression, posture, and other body language to indicate you're paying attention.
- Listen with the intent to learn about your kid. Demonstrate your interest in how he sees life. Check back frequently on various topics, as his views change over time.

- Don't interrupt, advise, question, educate, correct, lecture, give opinions, or suggest solutions. Just . . . listen. Note his inflections, speed, emphasis, hesitations.
- Limit your responses: "Oh," "I see," "Uh huh," "I understand," and "go on." Minimize questions, and when you do ask them, never interrupt. Stay non-judgmental.
- Repeat what you heard him say—or say it back in different words—so he knows you understood. Nod. Reflect the feeling beneath the words. "That must have made you sad."
- Allow silences. Don't let discomfort tempt you to start blabbing. Never assume the conversation has ended. Tell your child that if he has anything else, you're still listening. If you let the silences be, he'll eventually share more deeply, but you have to let him proceed at his own pace.
- If he wants advice, let him *ask* for it. Then, instead of unloading your opinions, ask for his solutions. "What do you think you could do . . . ?"
- Listen without defending your side of the story when he criticizes you.
- Some parents don't want to hear about their kids' problems because they distrust their own ability to solve them. You don't have to fix anything. Just listen. Your child will often find a solution for himself just by expressing the difficulty.
- Listen even if your kid's words bring up your own old pain. Remember, do your own psychological work, and keep the focus on him, not you.
- Whatever your child's age, never just pretend to listen. Nothing will shut him up more quickly.
- Enlist the aid of teachers, teachers' aids, or other adults with whom your child has a relationship. Don't ask them to betray confidences, but tell them you would appreciate any appropriate insights that might help your child talk about problematic issues.
- Active listening works with adults, too, especially in difficult situations like death or divorce. You don't have to fix, advise, or deny the other's pain. Changing the subject, a purely defensive move on your part, deprives the other person of an opportunity to talk. Instead, ask, "How is that for you?" or "Do you want to talk about it?" Or even admit, "I don't know what to say."
- Remember: Despite all of the above, you *don't* have to listen to whining or yelling from a kid of any age. If he's young, make sure he

knows what whining is. Act it out for him. Next time he yells or whines, acknowledge that you've heard him, but say, for example, "That hurts my ears. When you use that voice, I won't listen. Use a regular voice." Leave the room if you like. Ask him to leave until he can speak more pleasantly.

Oh and yes, make sure *you* don't whine or yell, either.

Create Environments That Encourage Desirable Behavior

Insofar as possible, create environments that provide your child with the best chance of behaving well. Instead of constantly limiting him and having to say "no," eliminate conflicts by removing a problem element from the scene.

A child-friendly environment requires minimal supervision, contains nothing breakable, and has places to jump and run. When you visit Aunt Minnie, get those Ming vases off the coffee table and let the kids romp outside in her fenced yard. Be prepared to leave a place that can't be made child-friendly.

Look at the series of events that leads up to a recurrent misbehavior or conflict. Can you modify the environment to short-circuit it?

Consider the Kid's Point of View

Before you drag your child off somewhere, ask yourself what it will be like from his perspective. Wherever we drove on vacation, my dad looked up old army buddies he hadn't seen in twenty years. He expected the rest of us to sit quietly for a couple of hours in an unfamiliar living room while he and the other vet got reacquainted. I quickly reintroduced my dad to the concept of war—close-up. Instead of forcing your kid to endure your agenda, make plans for him elsewhere, or at least bring along something interesting (from *his* point of view) for him to do.

> "Children's playings are not sports and should be deemed as their most serious actions."
>
> MONTAIGNE (1533–1592)

Change the Physical Environment

Remove whatever objects cause problems, or change the way you do things. Homes with toddlers have no knickknacks. Dangerous corners sport plastic bumpers. Stairs and fireplaces lie beyond gates. Since you can't keep the toddler away from potential catastrophe, you keep the catastrophe away from him. The same principle applies to older kids. If your child throws toys or clothes all over the room when angry, just put out a few at a time and store the rest out of reach. If your teen always leaves soda-can rings on the end table, cover it or stop buying soda.

Be Flexible on the "Time Environment"

Does your kid habitually push your buttons at certain times of day? Maybe he needs a snack or a rest then. Or perhaps the problem isn't *his* behavior but *your* susceptibility to stress at those times. Plan activities with these vulnerabilities in mind.

Also, don't force your kid to eat or not eat at certain times. Let your child eat when he's hungry rather than force-feeding him by the clock. Likewise, if he needs to sleep in, pay it no mind unless it directly affects you.

Lastly, allow extra time for getting places.

Keep Your Expectations Reasonable

Remember to take development, physical factors, temperament, and sensitivity into account when forming expectations for your child's behavior. In addition:

- Don't expect overnight changes. Remember how hard it is to alter habits. Motivate him with positive feedback.
- Pick your battles. Like a good sports coach, you see *all* the problems, but focus on one at a time. Devote a week or a month to helping your child make a change. Get his input. Ask him, "What will help you remember to. . . ?"

  Leave other issues temporarily in the background, but don't give the impression your child is free to break the rules. You might pretend you didn't see him so he won't think you ignored a transgression. Or simply explain that the rule stands, but for whatever reason (you're tired, sick, or rushed) you *choose* not to impose consequences this once.
- Work on one thing at a time. Incidentally, while you're busy working on your child's behavior, assign yourself a task, too. Perhaps you could work on patience.

- Don't start anything you aren't willing to follow through on, and if you get into the middle of something you wish you hadn't begun, play it out if you can.

  On the other hand, if your normally cooperative kid seems particularly outraged, you can give in occasionally. Maybe you didn't realize this would matter to him. Say, "I need to rethink this. I didn't know you cared so much. Let's talk this over." If you do give in, make it clear that *you* made the choice for your own reasons, not because your child whined or complained.

  Giving in once in a while won't work with a child who throws a fit at everything. You'll have to allow time for his antics.
- "Reasonable" means not too high or too *low*. Low expectations tell your kid you don't think much of his capabilities. Provide challenges.
- When a generally cooperative child suddenly begins resisting everything, your expectations are probably too high or too low. Perhaps your rules are too numerous or unclear.

Assess the Clarity and Importance of Your Rules

State rules clearly, both verbally and through consistent enforcement. You can't fault a kid for not obeying an ambiguous requirement. As a parent, you get to make the rules, but you have the responsibility to make them *clear*.

Explain step-by-step what you want. "Clean your room" may include making the bed and doing the laundry to you, but unless you tell them, your kids will throw everything from the floor into a closet and wonder why you're never satisfied.

Pediatric nurse-practitioner Meg Zweiback provides a wonderful "traffic light" metaphor for judging the importance of rules and limits:

- Your kid knows you mean business on "red-light rules," which come in two varieties: Ones everyone follows—seat belts in cars, helmets on bikes, no drinking and driving—and ones peculiar to your family. These could include busing dishes to the sink after meals or no eating in the car.
- "Green-light" means your family has no rules or restrictions, though others may—including your ex. You don't require your kid to put away one game before he gets out another, for example.

- "Yellow-light rules" cause all the problems. You've really let go of them but won't admit it. Your child decides on the spot whether he can get away with breaking them each time. You enforce them intermittently, and whenever you do, your kid tests and resists, ignores you and becomes "uncooperative." As long as you're consistent, your kid will tend to observe limits. But if you allow him to overstep two or three times without comment, and then blow up the next time he transgresses, he'll become confused about where the boundary *is* and test to find out.

Change those yellows to green or red.

Don't waste energy enforcing a rule that doesn't matter to you. Step back and ask yourself if you really care. Is this *your* rule or your mom's? Does enforcing it take priority over peace and quiet? Does it make life easier, preserve your child's safety, or teach him a value? If not, let it go.

Encouraging Cooperation

Conflict-resolution techniques are wonderful—but so is never needing them! Encouragement can take you very far down the road to cooperation.

How to Encourage Cooperation

By making your child feel loved and capable, positive reinforcement increases his desire to cooperate and perform well. Just realizing you see him—which he might not know unless he misbehaves—raises his self-esteem. Although perfectly obvious to you, your kid doesn't always understand what's so "good" about a behavior. Use approving comments to inform him how it helps you.

Notice how often you point out negative behavior: "Stop that." "Get off there." "Don't sass me." "Now why did you drop that?" These comments escape your lips without thought. They're habits, probably inherited from your own parents. Unfortunately, they breed dispute.

- Notice *and comment* on what you like. Shower your kid with positive statements all day. Direct your comments to whatever you want to reinforce. You don't need to lavish praise. Quietly comment to show you noticed and liked what you saw: "I noticed that you . . . ," "I like the way you . . . " For a younger kid, it can be as simple as noticing he remembered to wash his hands or say thank you. Older children could hear your approval for doing their homework without urging or doing a kindness for a neighbor.

- Find a positive way to say almost everything. "Don't bang on the piano" can become "Play me one of those quiet songs instead." As a reminder, set yourself a goal at first. Give at least three positive statements to your child daily. Or make five positive remarks for every critical one that slips out.
- Tell your kid what he *may* do, rather than what he may not. "I have a meeting Friday evening, but you may borrow the car Saturday."
- Encourage rather than criticize. Convey the messages, "I know you can do it" and "I have faith in you."
- Find a way to say yes to requests. Instead of, "You can't go to Sarah's house because you didn't clean your room," or "No, not until you make the bed," try, "Sure, you can go to Sarah's as soon as you clean up." Remember those words: *as soon as* . . . AS SOON AS . . .
- Say thank you often, especially when your kid does something just to please you.
- Use the "eraser" if you catch yourself in a negative: "Don't do that—Erase, erase. I want to start over . . ." Offer this device to your child, too. It lets him try again without your having criticized him. "Do you want to erase that?"
- Don't say "don't" (!). Once you become aware of this word, you'll be amazed how often you use it.
- Avoid other red-flag words: Using "you" often just blames. "If you don't . . . " can threaten. "Why" accuses and diverts attention from the problem. (Besides which, your kid often doesn't *know* why or have the ability to articulate reasons.)

Give Choices, Not Commands

In the classic example, you ask your preschooler whether he wants to wear his red pants or his blue ones instead of telling him to "get dressed." Giving choices within stated boundaries encourages cooperation, builds self-esteem, and, most importantly, develops the ability to make important decisions later on between alternatives like drinking alcohol or soda.

- Set very firm limits about *whether,* but show compassion and lenience about *which, how,* and *when.* "Do you want to wash the car before or after soccer practice?"
- If necessary, state an outside limit on time. "You have to take that old couch to the dump this weekend. Do you want to do it Saturday or Sunday?"
- Always propose specific alternatives rather than asking open-ended questions. Try, "Do you want pizza or hot dogs?" If you ask, "What would you like for dinner?" you'd better pray he's never heard of lobster soufflé and floating island.
- Don't present any choice that will be unacceptable to you. A statement such as, "We can either stay at the concert without complaining or go home," could find you missing out on the best blues you ever (would have) heard.
- Don't offer a selection that will cause you more work than you're willing to do. Breakfast can be Rice Chex or Special K, but not cereal or eggs Benedict. Your kid will pick the eggs every time.
- Two choices suffice for young children. Offer more to older ones.
- If your child refuses to choose, give him the ultimate alternative: "Either you choose, or I'll choose for you." Follow through without nagging or lecturing.

Find Other Ways to Say No

- Use distraction. Give your child something else to do, especially in adult environments like stores, when you need to finish as quickly as possible. Grab a magazine off the rack for him. If he's older, send him off to choose the breakfast cereal.
- Suggest another specific activity to replace what he's doing. This works best with a smaller child. If he's making a mess cooking, give him a bowl of something tidier to stir. Don't overuse this device. Kids get wise and trap you into spending a lot of time finding alternatives.
- Set up a reward *ahead of time* so you maintain control. For example, don't give in to your kid's whining by giving him what he wants if he'll just *quiet down*. That gives him the upper hand and teaches him that whining works. Instead, before you go into the store, say, "I know you hate to wait while I try on shoes. If you sit patiently until I'm finished, I'll treat you to a frozen yogurt." Or, "I know you like having friends overnight, and if you do the dishes all week without complaining, you may invite them on Saturday."

- Talk less and act more. Sometimes you say "no-no-no" from across the room, but your voice and actions indicate you don't really mean it. Make your statement effectively the first time. Approach your child, bend to his level, look in his eye, state your point once, and have him repeat back what you said.

  Make a deal with yourself that you won't say anything unless you get up, go over to your kid, and physically touch him or stop his misbehavior. You'll become aware of how often you utter that gutless "no" without following through. Stooping to a small child's eye level by itself doubles his response rate. This may seem too intrusive to kids over seven, but you can still get close and make physical contact.

  Realize that sometimes kids act up just because they don't feel connected for some reason. A few hugs—some attention and some touching—may be all they need.
- Vary your tone of voice. Kids of all ages respond to your vocal delivery. Too much hysteria on minor matters makes you into the parent who cries "wolf." Soft cajoling for larger offenses doesn't make your point. In either case, the kids ignore you.

Set Limits

Kids want limits in order to feel safe and secure. Set limits on behaviors but not emotions.

Kids Need and Want Limits

In two-parent families, one parent often offers nurturance, leniency, and sympathy, while the other imposes authority by enforcing rules, pushing kids to do their best, teaching community awareness, and engendering self-discipline.

As a single parent, you must fulfill *both* roles, but you may hesitate to set limits. "He's been through so much already, suffering the trauma of divorce," you might think, "Why not give him free rein to make up for the pain?"

It might help ease your guilt a little, too, knowing he's getting what he wants for a change. In "competition" with your ex-spouse, you don't want to be the bad guy. Moreover, you're already overwhelmed. Saying no or taking charge means putting up with the fallout of your kid's anger and disappointment.

Especially after a divorce, however, kids need security. They force you to prove you know what you're doing so they'll feel safe. Children don't really want unlimited freedom. Ironically, unhappy or aggressive behavior often represents a desire for *more* rules! Not knowing who's in charge produces anxiety in kids. They wonder if you expect them to fend for themselves—a terrifying burden for a child of any age. If you're afraid to be in charge, they will be, and they don't know how!

Setting limits proves you care and reassures your kids you love them. They want someone to say no, someone to be the parent so they can be kids.

Of course, they'll never tell you any of this. When they're screaming at you for being "the meanest parent in the universe," just take it as their own sweet way of saying "thanks."

Validate and Accept All Emotions; Limit Only Behavior

Most actions have both emotional and behavioral aspects. Separate the two when interacting with your child. *Allow* and validate *feelings*, but firmly and consistently *limit behavior*. Many parents do just the opposite: They disallow emotions for various reasons and fail to regulate behavior.

> "Children have neither past nor future; they enjoy the present, which very few of us do."
>
> La Bruyère (1645–1696)

Nothing could be easier than accepting your child's love, joy, elation, and pleasure, but his anger, anxiety, aggression, and jealousy are hard to swallow, especially when directed at you. Nevertheless, let him have his negative emotions without limiting, forbidding, or denying them. Accepting a kid's feelings means accepting him.

Sometimes you have to get past your own agenda before you can address and accept his feelings. It's easy to accept Christopher's emotions when I have nothing at stake. I simply affirm what he must be feeling. "Michael hurt your feelings when he wouldn't let you play with him." When his upset threatens *my* sphere, however, I forget everything I know. Recently he accidentally marked up a new book and tearfully demanded we immediately return to the store for another one. Forget it! We'd been out all day, and I was tired. At first I tried to convince him the mark was barely visible. He only cried harder. I argued about the late hour and the need to start dinner. I did not want to go to the store. None of my logic reached him, and the incident escalated. But then suddenly, I just got it! He felt bad. I said, "Oh, honey, you must be so disappointed that your brand-new book has a mark."

The effect was astounding. He ran to me and cried in an entirely different way. My understanding his anguish over ruining a pristine page was all he wanted. He never mentioned replacing the book again and sat contentedly with it a couple of minutes later.

Sometimes you diminish your kid's feelings because *you* hurt when he's in pain. When you shut off his emotions, remember yourself at his age. Chances are you had trouble with your own parents at that point in your development. Imagining your child going through the same pain now stirs up your old hurts. (Also see Chapter 1.) Other times, though, it's the power struggles that tempt you to exert control over your child's emotions as well as his behavior. "Who does he think he *is* to feel like that!?"

To validate and accept your child's emotions:

- Help him *explore* his emotions. As part of his bedtime ritual, ask, "What made you happiest today?" "Saddest?" "Angriest?"

  Warmth and acceptance encourage him to cry and release intense feelings. With practice, you'll cut through angry statements and respond just to the emotional dimension. Don't try to explain why he *shouldn't* hate you, but agree it must feel rotten when you keep him home against his will. The more understood he feels, the more he'll reveal. Make clear your willingness to hear negative feelings—even about yourself—by keeping your responses neutral and accepting.
- Help him rephrase accurately. Kids' ultimate statements often really refer to some smaller complaint. After all, their communication skills are still under construction. When he says, "I hate you," say, for example, "That hurts my feelings. Is it that you hate me telling you to stay home Friday night? It's better to say it that way."
- Suggest innocuous ways to work off aggressive feelings. "You can hit pillows, but not other children." Get him a punching bag or a dart board. Use art.
- Model appropriate emotional expression for your child, especially anger. Rather than raging, say calmly, "I'm angry you got home so late," and talk about the consequences. Show him how other emo-

tions underlie anger. "I feel really angry about that, but under the anger, I'm feeling scared."

- When fireworks occur, stay detached. Afterwards, validate your kid's emotions and assure him of your love: "That was hard. You were really angry. I love you." When it's over, it's really over, and you're there for him.

Enforcing the Rules: "Logical Consequences"

To your parents, enforcing rules probably meant punishment for transgressions. Often you didn't know in advance what the punishment would be, but you had a vague notion you'd "get it" if you were "bad." Modern parenting methods eliminate "punishment," substituting the concepts of choice, education or "discipline," and "logical consequences." Rather than punishing *past* behavior, you mold *future* actions. You instill positive values and self-control instead of forcing obedience.

Punishment attacks the *person*. Logical consequences focus on the *behavior*. Punishment makes your child feel bad—guilty, humiliated, or fearful. Logical consequences seek to educate and develop self-responsibility.

Children generally want to please their parents, and misbehavior signals something else going on underneath. Convey to your child, through words and action, the message, "I'm on your side. How can I help you?" Ask, "What do you and I need to learn from this experience?"

The technique of logical consequences works like this:

- In a calm, authoritative voice, explain the desired behavior or describe the problem without blaming or shaming your child. Don't call him names or insult, accuse, or lecture him. After loaning him the car for a ball game the previous night, for example, say simply, "There was almost no gas in the car this morning."

  Try using the phrase, "I've noticed that . . ." or "Have you noticed that . . . ?" Perhaps your child is just unaware of the problem, not inconsiderate. "Have you noticed that you often forget to fill the tank after a long drive?"

  Set up a "code" reminder to give him a second chance or help him remember. "Gas," you say, as he leaves the house.
- Give information about why the behavior presents a problem for you: "I don't want to run out of gas on the way to work."

- State the consequences. As it stands, *you* have the problem—a habitually empty fuel tank. Now get your kid to buy in. Figure out a way to make it his problem, too—he won't get what he wants unless he complies. "If you return the car with less than half a tank, I won't let you borrow it for a week." Now he's motivated. He either gasses up or "chooses" seven days without wheels.

  The consequences should, if possible, ameliorate the misbehavior in some way. They should be "logical"—related to the misbehavior—and "reasonable"—proportionate to the offense. Taking the car away forever would have been too much, for example.

  Some consequences flow naturally. Your son's failure to set his alarm made him miss the ski trip bus. No need to pile something else on top.

  Don't get trapped into discussions and negotiation once you've explained the rule and the consequences. "If you help with the grocery shopping, I'll buy you one special thing." If your child makes a play for more, you can add, "And if you argue about it, you'll get nothing."
- As your kids grow, involve them in deciding and negotiating appropriate consequences (see Chapter 7).
- Constant warnings before acting on a consequence only train children not to pay attention the first time—often until you're furious. If your kid needs advance notice to make transitions more easily, make sure you phrase it as notice. "We have five more minutes before we have to leave." Then clearly announce the expiration of the time and leave.

  I give a very short warning. I count "one-two-three" and then act. My consistency through the years leaves no doubt that I'll follow through if I get to three. I often don't make it past one. Whenever I'm tired or lazy and lapse into nagging, Christopher ignores me, but when I say "one," he moves. One-two-three is my parenting "open sesame."
- To impose consequences, go into "robot parent" mode and unemotionally, determinedly carry them out without lecturing or I-told-you-so. This lets your kid know he'll gain nothing by whining, discussion, or tantrums. Too much talking and explaining implies that you're ambivalent and give him hope of reprieve. Just say, "Sorry, try again next time." If he does whine, state another consequence: "If you bring it up again, you'll have to wait *two* weeks."

- Consistent follow-through is important, but you don't have to stick with something that isn't working just because you started with it. Get creative and try another way.

I'm grateful I began learning effective parenting when Christopher was so young. We had a fairly clean slate, few bad habits to undo, no ruts to escape. Making changes is harder with older kids who are used to other ways. Stick with it. It's worth the trouble!

Discipline

The word "discipline" sometimes has a harsh connotation that implies control and enforced obedience, and maybe that's what you expected under this heading. But that's "punishment," which derives from the Indo-European for "avenge."

Like "disciple," "discipline" comes from the Latin for "learning." If you've taught your child according to these parenting techniques, you *have* disciplined him.

Problem Solving and Conflict Resolution: Family Meetings

Some people think acknowledging conflict is admitting failure. Don't compare yourselves to other families who never seem to disagree. You're only seeing the façade. Every family has conflict. Healthy ones acknowledge it and work on solutions. They learn from it.

Consider how your family of origin handled disputes. You may have battled loudly or pretended there *was* no conflict. Either way, unresolved issues probably *still* inhabit the family.

Parents often handle misbehavior without addressing underlying motivations and feelings, which then emerge, magnified, elsewhere. The actions of an oppositional or manipulative child frequently stem from feeling he has no control. Making you crazy at least allows him to govern the emotional atmosphere. Effective conflict resolution addresses the root of the problem by giving him a say in how his life runs.

Instead of "conflict," think in terms of differences and preferences among family members. Functional families allow each person to think and feel for himself. Clashes are inevitable. Conflict resolution doesn't assign blame, determine who's right and wrong, or pick winners and losers. Instead, it presents an opportunity to discuss how family members feel, to process events, and to reach agreeable solutions. The bottom line is respect, not just power (though your power as the parent is certainly a part of it).

"The Time of Conflict Is Not the Time of Resolution"

I've heard Liz and Cliff repeat this phrase dozens of times at support group meetings. Don't seek permanent solutions to problems and conflicts when emotions run high. Cool off. Talk about what happened later when you're all calm. Nothing is ever solved in the heat of battle.

Family Meetings

The best conflict-resolution tool I know is Jane Nelsen's "family meeting" as explained in her series of *Positive Discipline* books. Read them for detailed discussions, instructions, and applications. Meanwhile, here's my thumbnail summary:

> "Backward, turn
> backward, O Time,
> in thy flight;
> Make me a child again,
> just for tonight."
> ELIZABETH AKERS ALLEN
> (1832–1911)

Based on mutual respect, family meetings do more than solve problems—they enhance the sense of belonging. As a mini-society, the family cooperatively establishes rules and work assignments, plans entertainment, and relieves the parent from being cop, judge, jury, and executioner all at once. Together with your children, you find a solution that helps them work on making changes. Family meetings honor kids' needs and their ability to figure things out.

It's never too late, but if possible, start the meetings when your children are young and most open to new ideas.

Two people make a family, so if it's just you and your kid, you *can* have a family meeting!

- Keep an "agenda" on the fridge. As problems arise during the week, the aggrieved person notes them on the agenda, along with the "offender's" name. This both allows a cooling-off period ("the time of conflict is not the time of resolution") and assures that you will, in fact, address the problem. From the time he was four, one of Christopher's responses to adversity was, "Write that on the agenda."

Squelch your urge to nag. Put your beef on the agenda instead. Own the problem by describing its effect on you. "I have more work when Jerry leaves his shoes on the living-room floor."

No problem is too minor for a family meeting. Any desired change or improvement qualifies.

- Meet once a week at an inviolate, agreed time. Everyone must consider this a sacred commitment. Sunday night after dinner works for many families. Set a time limit. Even if you don't get through the entire agenda, five or six items in one sitting is plenty.
- Sit around a cleared table—no lounging. Conduct this like a business meeting.
- Begin with each person paying all the others a compliment about accomplishments, behavior, helpfulness, and so on—never about anything purchased, like "nice sweater." As openers, try:
  –"You were thoughtful to . . ."
  –"It was helpful when you . . ."
  –"I'm impressed/proud that you . . ."
  –"I liked/enjoyed/loved/appreciated/noticed how you . . ."

  The person receiving the compliment acknowledges it and says, "Thank you," without arguing whether it's justified.

  Whenever you see positive behavior during the week, point it out to others as a possible source of compliments for the coming meeting.
- Address the first agenda item. (Attack them in chronological order to obviate disputes over importance.) Keep a straight face for seemingly silly complaints. They wouldn't be there if someone didn't take them seriously. *Never* refuse to discuss a problem because there's no possible solution. This shows disrespect for the offended person's feelings and invalidates the process.
  –Ask for possible solutions (or logical consequences), as many as possible. Write them *all* down, non-judgmentally, even if they're ridiculous or intended as a joke. Your job is to guide the kids to a good solution. So no evaluating. No correcting or rejecting the kid's ideas. Even the most off-the-wall suggestions may lead to something else or at least elicit a laugh.
  –Often the conflicts resolve themselves before the meeting. In some cases the "offender" didn't know his behavior was a problem,

and he'll simply agree to change after someone mentions it. Sometimes just airing feelings resolves a difficulty.

–Don't use meetings as a platform to lecture or moralize. Put your statements in the form of questions: "Do you think there might be a better time to solve this?" rather than, "We're getting nowhere."

- Vote by consensus. *Everyone* has to agree in order to settle an issue. Otherwise, table the item for another time and go on to the next one. Whatever the solution, it applies to *everybody* in the family. *Everyone's* shoes left on the living-room floor go into a box for a week, regardless of inconvenience or "need."

  Stick to the solutions until the next meeting, even if painful. If they don't work, put the problem back on the agenda for further discussion. You may have to deal with it week after week. Don't worry if solutions fail. The process is more important.
- Review next week's schedule.
- Plan family fun for the coming week. Schedule one pleasurable activity as a family and one for each family member individually.
- End on a pleasant note by playing a game or serving dessert. At first Christopher's sole motivation was getting the treat, but he soon learned that family meetings bring him much more than that.

Effective parenting skills go a long way toward eliminating conflict. Family members have differences and preferences, and some dispute is normal and inevitable. Rather than shaming or blaming others, aim to negotiate, help one another, and learn from every problem.

BOOKS AND MAGAZINES FOR PARENTS

Full-Time Dads, The Journal for Caring Fathers, newsletter for men who are primary caregivers. POB 577, Cumberland, ME 04021; 207-829-5260.

How to Talk So Kids Will Listen and Listen So Kids Will Talk, Adele Faber and Elaine Mazlish (New York: Avon, 1982).

Parent Effectiveness Training (P.E.T.): The Tested New Way to Raise Responsible Children, Thomas Gordon (New York: McKay, 1970). For information about the training, write 531 Stevens Ave., Solana Beach, CA 92075, or call 619-481-8121.

Positive Discipline, Jane Nelsen (New York: Ballantine, 1987).

Positive Discipline for Preschoolers: For Their Early Years–Raising Children Who Are Responsible, Respectful, and Resourceful, Jane Nelsen, Cheryl Erwin, and Roslyn Duffy (Rocklin, CA: Prima Publishing, 1994).

Positive Discipline for Single Parents: A Practical Guide to Raising Children Who Are Responsible, Respectful, and Resourceful, Jane Nelsen, Cheryl Erwin, and Carol Delzer (Rocklin, CA: Prima Publishing, 1994).

Siblings without Rivalry, Adele Faber and Elaine Mazlish (New York: Avon, 1988).

BOOKS FOR KIDS

Communication, Aliki (New York: Greenwillow, 1993).

Chapter 6

Running a Single-Parent Household

About a year after my initiation into single-parenthood, my friend Ann invited me and Christopher to visit a couple at their new home in Marin County, a stunning "villa" atop a hill. Stepping inside, I thought I'd reached nirvana—and not because the television disappeared into the wall by remote control, the kitchen featured everything but a built-in chef, and the swimming pool summoned memories of the Mediterranean. What ignited my fervent yearning was the utter *emptiness* of the place. Recently remodeled and awaiting a decorator, this vast, child-free house contained little more than a kitchen table, a grandfather clock, a couch, and a bed. Marble and hardwood floors stretched to the horizons unobstructed by a single toy! No scattered socks. No half-eaten bagels. No fingerprints on the walls. No mashed crayons. No puzzle parts. No confetti from paper snowflakes. No peanut butter on the chairs.

God, I wanted this!

Of course, I went home to real life, wading through all of the above on my way to the dirty dishes piled in the sink because I'd had no time to empty the dishwasher. The laundry threatened to mildew in the washing machine, and dinner . . . maybe leftover mac-and-cheese for the boy.

My household didn't always operate like this, but entropy—the tendency of disorder to increase and energy to decrease in a closed system—clearly ruled the premises now. As chaos increased, *my* energy decreased, and the two hours of cleaning always undone in five minutes left me in tears. Still, some crazy urge forced me to persist, especially when I expected company.

I based my standards on the pristine homes of child-free acquaintances. It didn't matter that certain other friends let *their* houses go. They accepted the layer of jam smeared on the couch as a permanent part of the decor. Fine. But I noticed, and others would judge *my* house. Besides, I *liked* order and cleanliness.

Despite good intentions, however, my idea of what constitutes a clean house or an acceptable meal changed when I became a single parent—even more than it had when I first became a parent. My standards "slipped" imperceptibly but steadily. I just couldn't do it all. I slowly let go of the need for a perfectly clean, uncluttered house. Today I can, for example, allow friends to enter without first mopping the kitchen floor. Progress. Still, I suffered a lot of angst before getting to that point. I wish someone had clued me in sooner to the realities of running a single-parent household. But lucky for you, this chapter is filled with suggestions that have helped others.

Lower Your Standards

My first lesson can be yours, too. Forget perfection. You'll only make yourself crazy trying to achieve it. Think "Good Enough" for housekeeping, meals, yard work, laundry, shopping, and all the rest. Betty Crocker isn't coming your way with a blue ribbon anyway, so relax. Save that energy for nurturing yourself and your kids.

Break the Rules

This is the only rule you aren't allowed to break!

Be flexible with household requirements! Resist doing a chore out of habit or just because everyone does it a certain way. Be creative. Spray the kitchen floor with cleaner and "skate" away the spots with a layer of paper towel under your shoes: It saves getting out the bucket and mop. If you run out of storage space, keep toys in the bathroom vanity and park extra jars of pasta sauce in the linen closet. Keep your car vacuum cleaner hooked up to the cigarette lighter and dust up your auto interior at long red lights.

Let the sheets go an extra week. Scrub the bathtub or tile walls while you're in the shower. Bag pre-measured amounts of ingredients for food you make frequently. (I do this for my pasta machine so I have one big flour mess every few months instead of each time I make pasta.) Try freezing anything. Do the same with microwaving. If you take many pills, count out daily rations in an ice tray. Launder the colors and whites together, as long as you accept the risk of pink underwear.

> "Humor is the great thing, the saving thing after all; the minute it crops up, all our hardnesses yield, all our irritations and resentments slip away and a sunny spirit takes their place."
>
> MARK TWAIN (1835–1910)

Burned out by her job and frustrated by her daughter's finicky preferences, Elena prepared the same meal every night *for months.* Chicken, broccoli, and mashed potatoes. A healthy meal, if not exactly gourmet. She didn't care. During a difficult period in her life, Elena needed *easy.* Recognizing her priorities and limitations, she breezed through the shopping and switched on automatic pilot every night.

Some of these sound pretty silly, but each one actually eased the life of a single parent. Take your own break from the ordinary. You never have to tell anyone!

Double Up

I love the story about the Zen Master Seung Sahn, who taught his American students the traditional Zen concept, "When you eat, just eat; when you walk, just walk; when you sit, just sit." One day the students came upon him eating breakfast *and* reading the morning paper at the same time. Upset, they asked, "How can you do this!? You tell us to eat when you eat, walk when you walk, and here you are eating *and* reading!" He responded, laughing, "When you eat and read, just eat and read."

Don't go crazy trying to do everything at once. Sometimes, though, doubling up makes sense:

- Do (quiet) chores while talking on a cordless phone. Sort the laundry. Pick up the floors. Dust. Unload the dishwasher. Scrub the sink. Clean a mirror.
- Take chores with you for "downtime" while waiting alone. Do something useful at the doctor's office, for example, instead of reading a six-month-old issue of People Magazine. These portable chores can include making lists, balancing your checkbook, cleaning out your purse, writing letters or thank-you notes, addressing envelopes, paying bills, working on your budget, updating your calendar, and planning meals.
- Use driving time constructively. When alone, listen to a book or instruction on tape. Practice singing. Rehearse the presentation you'll give next week. Improve your Spanish. If you have a car phone, catch up on social calls. Or turn everything off and breathe deeply.

  With your child along, make driving part of your "together time," a learning experience. Relax and look around. Identify the plants by the side of the road. Point out interesting aspects of billboards. Summarize weather patterns. Discuss your day. Present a good model for handling traffic jams. Stay calm and courteous. Talk about why backups occur, why there are so many cars, what trucks carry. Christopher loves vehicles and can't understand why anyone hates being stuck in traffic. I join him on the lookout for automobile-carriers and tank trucks. Why, just the other day we saw a Caddy convertible pulling a hot-air balloon basket on a trailer.
- Do your sit-ups while watching a video.
- Cook two meals at once and freeze one for another time.
- Clean off your desk while on hold on the telephone.

Enjoy the Process

You can't get out of the big job of running your household, so make it as enjoyable as possible. You can alter your attitude even though you can't change what you have to do. After all, you ask your children to do precisely that when you want them to help "without complaining." Show them how. Even faking it helps. If you resist moaning about it, you often find you don't really hate a chore as much as you thought.

Laugh at Yourself; Use Humor

Some of my single-parent friends and I recognized and named a disease: "Single Parent's Syndrome." Symptoms include having your brain shut down—before it fries under the pressure of having too much to do. You often can't see the object of a search when you're looking right at it. And you put things in highly inappropriate places, like a shoe in the refrigerator. Your vocabulary shrinks to one word—NO.

We laughingly blame our bizarre behaviors on "SPS." To do yard work at my house one day, Sandra and I donned big work-gloves and hauled eucalyptus leaves for an hour. Looking at her wrist to check the time, she moaned, "Oh, no, I've lost my watch." We retraced our steps up and down my back hill and down to the street before concluding the dainty little timekeeper had forever disappeared in a pile of dead leaves. Promising to keep my eyes open for it nevertheless, I looked at *my* wrist for the time. Unbelievable! *My* watch had dropped off, too! Sandra and I commiserated for a few minutes and peeled off our work-gloves in frustration. It's always something! But wait—both watches appeared magically on our wrists! The glove cuffs had covered them. We hadn't even considered that obvious possibility!

SPS.

Laugh at yourself in the midst of crazy misery. What a great role model you will be for teaching your kids to deal with adversity! Lighten up. Breathe. Go on from there.

Simplify, Simply, Simplify

Get rid of extra possessions. Reduce clutter. You'll have less to trip over, pick up, and clean. The eye rests more easily on uncluttered space, and your whole life feels less chaotic.

You don't have to give away or sell valuable, meaningful, or beautiful belongings as long as you really want them and have a place to store them. My house used to display souvenirs from law-practice vacations all over the world. I loved them all, but combined with Christopher's growing toy collection, they became just clutter. I stowed them.

Think consciously about why you've hung onto your belongings. Question everything. It might be time to let go. The experience can be liberating. For twenty years, I'd dragged boxes from house to house without ever really going through them. In finally doing so, I had to own up to irrational reasons for keeping certain items. For example, an ancient, barely functional mixer, which I never used, represented pleasant, childhood baking times with my mother. Imagine being sentimentally attached to a Mix-Master! I finally decided that I could remember cooking with Mom by whipping up a batch of chocolate-chip cookies. Now I don't have to lug around a heavy, decrepit machine for the rest of my life.

> "A person without a sense of humor is like a wagon without springs—jolted by every pebble in the road."
>
> HENRY WARD BEECHER (1813–1887)

- Take it step by step. The kitchen is a shambles, but start with one drawer. You'll feel you've accomplished something, and next week you can do another.
- Get rid of anything whose purpose you can't identify. Many kitchen gadgets will fit here. Dump things you never use, even if beloved Aunt Celeste gave them to you.
- Buy bins or baskets for kids' clothes and toys. Picking up goes faster if you don't have to arrange things in drawers or on shelves.
- Rotate toys in and out of sight periodically. Fewer toys in circulation mean fewer to pick up. Besides, toys your kid overlooked in a pile of others suddenly become "new" and interesting again when you do this.
- Limit magazine subscriptions and toss out one issue as soon as the next arrives, even if you haven't read it. Be merciless. It's okay to tear out one article to read, but only if really necessary.
- Take pictures and get rid of the real items. Friends added to your cow collection at every opportunity? Gather it around you on the living-room floor and have someone memorialize the collection on film. Then *immediately* call Salvation Army.
- Establish a basket for loose parts to toys, puzzles, sports equipment, hobbies, and games. When you find a stray, drop it in the basket rather than taking the time to look for its home. Whenever a piece turns up missing, everyone knows where to find it quickly.
- If you have to change or replace something, consider not doing so. Do you really need a potted plant where that dead begonia sat? Maybe the kitchen would be brighter without replacing those

stained curtains. Did your cat tear that chair to shreds? Make a more spacious living room with just the couch and rocker.

- When you do replace, buy easy-care products. Never put light-colored tile or grout in your kitchen or bathroom. Trust me on that one. Buy low-maintenance furniture. Cloth dining chairs, for example, make little sense with pint-sized diners. Ornate carving requires tedious dusting.
- Give Goodwill any clothes you haven't worn for a year. If they're of good quality, consider selling them through a consignment shop—but ask that any unsold items go directly to charity. Otherwise you'll put them back in the closet "just in case."
- Get rid of all the jars, boxes, designer shopping bags with handles, and plastic bags you keep for unexpected hauling or storage duties. Okay, you can keep a few, say five. You'll never use them, but go ahead if it makes you feel secure. Just don't add more!

Consider Moving to a Smaller Place

Many divorcing parents go to great lengths to keep the house, thinking it provides stability for the kids. On the other hand, a large single-family house loses its appeal when you're the only one around to take care of it. Many housing experts believe that because of economy, safety, and convenience, condominiums and townhouses gain acceptance after divorce. Likewise, the divorce rate increases the rental apartment market. Consider your options.

Remember to Look behind Your Anger

Anger naturally flares on bad days when everything falls apart. Left alone to pick up the pieces, you're irate at your ex for sticking you with this situation, resentful at your children for not caring, and disgusted at society for not supporting single parents.

This anger is natural and justifiable, and you have every right to it, but it doesn't change a thing. You still have to see about the car insurance and repair the leaky roof.

Consider what other emotions your anger masks. While that doesn't change the circumstances either, it provides insight and understanding, which are the first steps toward personal growth.

Find a source of pride amidst the mess. A year after Tony died, I learned my house had long-standing, extensive dry rot. Preventing this problem had been *his* job, and now I had to get it fixed—and pay for it alone. Angry, I did the repairs, but eventually I started thinking about all I had accomplished by myself since Tony's death. I gave myself credit. In this case, anger led to an appreciation of myself.

Take the Time to Train Your Kids

Studies show that children from single-parent families do fewer chores than those in two-parent families! True, just doing the work often seems easier and faster than training a child, especially if he objects. Also, as a single parent, you suffer more guilt and face competition with your ex for the child's affections. You resist becoming the "bad parent" who requires too much.

Let go of the guilt. Families share the benefits *and* the obligations of making a home.

Training does take longer at first, but it's like sharpening the shears—it pays off in the long run for you *and* your child. Refer to his chores as a "contribution" to the family. He might not adopt your terminology, but calling his work a "contribution" subtly instills the feeling that you need him and that he belongs.

Requiring his help also models the message that you count. You're no martyr. You deserve a break, and teamwork is how you get it.

> "If you are too busy to laugh, you are too busy."
> ANONYMOUS

- Begin when your child is young. Start him on good habits before bad ones form so he believes "that's just the way things are."
- A preschooler enjoys helping—at least until the novelty wears off. When enthusiasm over the first chore wanes, let it go for a while and give him another.

  Kids this young love to surprise you. Set it up so they can by "subtly" letting them know how. Sigh deeply, "I just hope one day you'll pick up all your toys before I tell you." When he does it, get really excited. Pretend to faint. Make a big deal. Get silly. He'll love the positive reinforcement.
- Get child-sized tools: rakes, brooms, and work-gloves for example.

- Act as though you simply expect compliance. When Christopher was four, I started saying matter-of-factly after meals, "Please put the milk away," or "Don't forget your plate." Now he helps clear the table automatically. He sets his own place and gets out his own breakfast cereal, which I moved to an accessible cabinet. Sometimes he even makes his own school lunch. His shouldering these small chores lessens my feelings of being stuck doing everything as a single parent.
- Ask your child how he'll remind himself to do the chore so you don't have to nag. He can use a note, checklist, chart, notation on the family calendar, or string around his finger—make him responsible for figuring it out. Charts work well until age seven or so. Post them on the fridge and give stars for good—not perfect—performance. Making the bed six out of seven days qualifies. Draw pictures on the chart to show non-readers what to do.
- Provide incentives: "We'll have time to read a whole chapter of *Alice in Wonderland* if you put all this away in five minutes."
- Build certain cleanup elements into other routines. Clothes go straight into the hamper when the pj's go on. Shoes go "home" to their place on the shelf when removed. Making the bed is part of getting up. Being excused from the table means taking dishes to the sink.
- Be creative. I'm amazed at how well kids love to make work into a game. See who can pick up the most toys. Challenge your child to get the dishes in the dishwasher in two minutes. When Christopher was learning to count, I challenged him to pick up thirteen toys, then fifteen, then nineteen. It worked every time. A young kid won't initiate playtime cleanup. Give him a five- or ten-minute warning, using a timer if you like, and then help him wind down his play and start picking up. Once cleanup starts, no playing with toys found along the way.
- "Retraining" older kids is harder but still possible. Use logical consequences (see Chapter 5) to get them to buy into the system. Put something at stake *for them*. Cleanliness for the sake of cleanliness just doesn't cut it for teens.
- Have clear consequences for nonperformance. Anything left on the bathroom floor goes in a bag for a week. (Different rules apply to teenagers' own rooms, however; see *Getting Your Kid to Clean His Room.*) Maybe you could offer the option of retrieving the item early by paying in cash or doing extra work.

- Link responsibilities and privileges in your child's mind. He gets more independence as he grows, but he also assumes more obligation. Every birthday, for example, decide together on a new privilege and a new chore.
- Keep your expectations low. Your child won't perform perfectly, and that's okay. He will learn and improve.
- Give explicit instructions. Explain the how and why for each chore. Even willing kids don't know what you expect unless you educate them. Assume no knowledge whatsoever. Break chores into the smallest learning units and teach your kid how to perform them. Give him a system.

  Lucy complained that when her teenage daughter Kylie "did the dishes," she never wiped the counters, cleaned the table, or sponged off the stove. Strictly speaking, however, Kylie *did the dishes.* Because it seemed so obvious to Lucy, she had never bothered to tell her daughter what else that phrase implied. Chastising your child for not performing as you want isn't fair if you haven't outlined precisely what that is.
- Supervise and help at first. Offer suggestions and hints. Don't just turn over the job with a long explanation and expect it all to sink in immediately.
- Encourage kids to suggest and try alternative ways to accomplish a job.
- Seeing you redo any of your kid's work discourages him. Instead, call him back and respectfully make constructive comments. Suggest ways to avoid problems in the future.
- Allowances shouldn't depend on performing regular chores (see Chapter 16). Household chores are simply part of life. You can pay for extra jobs, however. Add complexity to the arrangement: If he hasn't accomplished the promised work within a stated time, *he* has to pay you or a third person to do it for him.
- Be liberal with praise and thanks for your child's contribution to the family. Gratitude is just as important for required tasks as for special ones.
- Delve below any lack of cooperation with communication. Use family meetings. Perhaps recalcitrance with chores indicates unhappiness about some other area. It may be a way to get attention. Ask, "How can we make this situation better for both of us?" Solving other problems increases overall cooperation around the house.

- Be a good role model. The smallest child knows cleaning the bathroom is no fun. How? By watching you grumble and mope through the job. You don't have to pretend scrubbing the toilet fills you with joy, but try not to complain. If you attack household chores with a light, enthusiastic attitude, your child will take the cue. Since actions speak louder than words, telling him to pick up when you leave your own clothes on the bedroom floor won't get you much compliance.
- Decide with your children during a family meeting how to mete out chores. Some families draw small cards with job descriptions from jars. Others assign regular jobs. Still others allow weekly choices from a list.

  Meredith's family members make their "contributions" together on Saturday mornings. They design combinations of chores that require about an hour each. The kids must participate, but they're free to choose their attitudes. Grumpy or cooperative, they can't leave until finished. They usually work steadily and without complaint.

> "To be happy at home is the ultimate result of all ambition, the end to which every enterprise and labor tends, and of which every desire prompts the prosecution."
>
> SAMUEL JOHNSON (1709–1784)

- Don't automatically suggest your child take over your ex's former responsibilities. Don't create a "little man" or "little woman" to replace the departed adult. If your ex-husband mowed the lawn, for example, you assume that job and let your son water the flowers.
- Ultimately, you should have to do nothing for your child that he can do for himself.

Buy Extra Essentials

Having extra essentials on hand saves you from disasters or just makes the day go easily. At the least, you'll avoid those annoying trips to the store for just one forgotten item. The definition of "essential" varies from person to person but will no doubt include the following:

- Extra keys. Leave them in different places. No longer can you simply phone your spouse when you lock yourself out of the car or house.

Losing my keys is a foolproof indicator that I'm not functioning well. Especially around holidays or the anniversary of Tony's suicide, I get "Single Parent Syndrome." Spacey and vague, I won't see my key chain right under my nose. I can't comply with the advice to "put the keys in one place where you can always find them." I drove myself crazy with lost keys so often that I finally made multiple sets. I kept three for everyday use and can usually manage to put my fingers on one of them. Two sets went to good friends. Two to neighbors. Another for my glove compartment, with a spare key to the car itself hidden on the exterior. I tucked away one set in a secret place outside the house (*not* under the mat or above the front door). Another hangs on a ring in my separate utility building. Maybe I've gone overboard here, but I don't stress out about keys anymore. I know "lost" sets turn up sooner or later, and in the meantime, I just use another one.

- Extra milk. With milk, you and the kids have breakfast of some sort. Without it, your morning routine breaks down, and you'll be late for school and work. Keep an emergency supply of canned or unrefrigerated, boxed milk.
- Extra medications, both over-the-counter and prescription drugs anyone takes regularly. Include painkillers, cough medicines, burn and insect-bite ointments, and so on. Avoid driving to the pharmacy with poison oak blossoming on your bottom. Stash calamine at home.
- Spare toilet paper, for obvious reasons. Paper towels, too, if you use them.
- A backlog of quick, nonperishable foods your kids will eat. Pasta and sauce in jars. Macaroni and cheese. Crackers. Dried fruit. Tortillas, cheese, and cooked, canned beans (tortillas and cheese both freeze well). Cereal. Popcorn. Applesauce. Canned goods. Whatever lets you throw together a snack or meal when you haven't had time to shop.

Shopping and Services

Shopping occupies a large portion of your nonworking hours unless you impose some organization. If you don't enjoy weekend parking and retail cashier lines, make shopping as efficient as possible. Likewise, organize visits to doctors, beauty salons, and other services to minimize driving and waiting.

- Consider appointments within walking distance of your work, rather than near your home. With your dentist, doctor, hairdresser, optometrist, and dry cleaner just a few steps away, you'll take off less time from work. Schedule visits at a late lunch or on the way to and from your job. As the time of your appointment nears, call to make sure the office is running on schedule.
- Decide whether convenience or savings takes priority. Sometimes it pays to pick up an item where convenient, even if it costs more.
- Consolidate errands in the same parts of town, but don't overdo it by expecting to accomplish too much in one trip.

> "Keep the home fires burning,
> While your hearts are yearning,
> Though your lads are far away
> They dream of home."
> LENA GUILBERT FORD

- Organize shopping. How many times have you stood in front of a store trying to remember what size thing-a-ma-jig you needed to buy? Keep a list of items you need at various types of stores. If you happen by, say, a hardware store, you'll know to pick up a broom handle and a pound of nails.
- Create a master grocery list of items you often purchase, organized by aisles in your regular store. Make multiple copies for several weeks ahead. Each week, circle what you need and write in any additional, occasional purchases. At the store, zip down the aisles gathering what you need with no backtracking for overlooked items.
- Separate perishable from nonperishable groceries on the checkout belt and ask that they be bagged separately. At home, you have the option to leave the nonperishable goods in your car for later. Living up a flight of stairs, I'm thankful not having to lug everything in at once.
- Buying ahead saves trips to the store. Keep a supply of greeting cards on hand for birthdays, graduations, and other occasions. Purchase items suitable for birthday gifts whenever you run across them, especially if they're on sale.
- Make a "transport bag" to carry things back and forth from your car on every trip. I use a cloth tote to haul my daily load of artwork, library books, jackets, shoes, mail, newspapers, and whatever else shakes loose from the car.

- Let the products and services come to you. More and more retailers deliver: Pizza, home videos, gourmet meals, car-washers, some grocers, and windshield repairers, to name a few.

Clothes and Laundry

A mother recently told me she irons everything, even her three kids' tee-shirts! She's married, but that still seems extreme to me!

- I don't see the point of ironing most clothes even if you have the time. Washing them is chore enough. I confess I've let the laundry go so long that piles of unsorted clean clothes got mixed up with baskets of dirty ones, and I couldn't tell them apart. Now instead of multiple loads on weekends, I do the wash every few days. Because my laundry room has only an outside entrance, I take a basket on the way out and put it in the dryer when I get home. Iron tee-shirts? Not a chance.
- You don't have to fold, either. Little kids cover themselves with dirt in five minutes, so a few wrinkles don't matter for everyday clothes. Christopher occasionally threw his neatly folded clothes from the shelves all over his room anyway. Finally I gave up. I toss pants, shirts, and underwear into separate bins. Why bother folding if everything ends up on the floor? Older kids can sort and fold their own clothes.
- Have you ever noticed that your daughter has outgrown a shirt, and then when you're sorting the laundry, you can't remember which one? Instead of putting it back into a drawer to repeat that cycle, mark the too-small garment when it goes in the hamper. I attach an old diaper pin. It's easy to identify and reroute these marked clothes to the Goodwill bag as I remove them from the dryer.
- Buy only easy-care clothes. Unless you really want to spend your time washing by hand or ironing, don't buy garments that require it, either for you or the kids.
- Consider sending laundry out instead of doing it yourself. Pick it up as you come home from work.
- Buy more of whatever drives your laundry. If you always do the wash because you're out of underwear, buy more underwear.
- Don't wash anything your kids don't put in the hamper. Why spend your time gathering up their clothes? They'll learn quickly when

that particular pair of jeans they *have* to wear tonight still languishes, dirty, under the bed.

Meals

Getting food on the table is a necessary fact of life. Meals are more than just physical sustenance—they can also provide occasions for family togetherness.

Preparing Meals

I don't know many single parents who relish cooking dinner after a hard day's work. Make it as easy on yourself as you can:

- Use some convenience foods. The name says it all. Yes, they cost more than a meal from scratch, and your dog might turn up his nose at them. Still, some are fairly healthful and tasty. Read the labels and write down which products meet with your approval so you don't have to read the packages at the store every time.
- Use the stock of nonperishable standby foods listed previously.
- On each shopping trip, automatically buy the ingredients for at least one simple, healthful meal you can make in your sleep. Many rely heavily on pasta. Top with pre-made sauce or microwaved veggies. For a slightly more upscale meal, I sauté chicken breasts in water, fresh lemon juice, and capers. Quick and delicious.
- Buy salad mixes and precut vegetables. They're worth the higher price in terms of convenience. Cook them or drop some raw into everyone's lunch box. Special bags keep them crisp longer than fresh, uncut produce.
- Have Thursday night hot dogs or cereal every Wednesday evening.
- On major shopping days, pick up a meal at the store's deli.
- Make some meals special. Get out the good china and light candles, even if you're having hamburgers. Eat at the coffee table before a fall fire. Sit outside on a warm summer evening. Have a living-room-floor picnic in the dead of winter.
- Eat together often, but don't be fanatical about it.
- Give everyone a way to participate in preparation or cleanup. Get the kids to help. Young ones can wash veggies, set the table, measure, and stir. Make occasional meal preparation part of your quality time together. Enjoy the process.

- Invest in a rice maker, which turns out perfect rice while you do something else. Rice and anything make a meal.
- Buy pizza crusts and top them with whatever you have left over from other meals.
- Make your own additions to a healthful canned soup.
- Prepare several meals at once. I'm happiest when I cook once or twice a week. I might make a pizza, a pasta sauce, a casserole, and a chicken dish. This sounds like work, but it only takes about an hour and a half with the economies of scale. Using the food processor for multiple tasks means less washing. I freeze half of each dish for later and supplement with microwaved veggies.
- Eat out occasionally. Ethnic restaurants usually welcome kids, charge little, and serve enough different foods to please the whole family. Chinese, Thai, Japanese, Mexican, and Indonesian get rave reviews around here. Use these excursions to foreign "lands" as teaching opportunities about different cultures.

  Take along toys, books, drawing paper, or whatever will keep your child occupied before and after the meal (kids always finish first!) Order bread or an appetizer right away to keep children busy and patient. Place your order quickly and tell the waiter you need the food promptly.

  Go early to minimize waiting. More relaxed servers better accommodate special needs at less crowded times. With fewer other diners, you feel less uptight about your kid disrupting the ambiance.
- Invite company for dinner, but keep it simple. Sponsor potluck meals where everyone contributes something and no one feels overworked.
- Start a single parents' cooking group. Either get together once a month as my single moms' group does, with the host doing all the cooking and cleanup, or arrange a schedule for preparing a double batch with half going to another family.

> "Set Thine house in order."
>
> ISAIAH 38:1

Getting Children to Eat

The closest my son comes to greens is the color of his face when exposed to vegetables. He adores sugar in every form. He likes milk and juice but still scavenges the last swallow of soda from discarded cans.

Cereal and milk would suit him three times a day indefinitely. Should I worry? No.

The main message about getting children to eat is *lighten up!* Single parent Tori constantly fusses over her daughter's diet—eat this, try that, just one more bite, you have to have vegetables before dessert. Sometimes *I* want to tell her to back off. Unlike some parents, from the first I avoided obsession about what goes into my kid's belly and spared myself much angst. Nagging sets children up for a negative association with food.

- Make healthful food available and teach about nutrition, but don't force kids to eat any particular amount. No one wins in parent-child power struggles over food. Refusals to eat sometimes represent a kid's way of exerting control over his body. Don't argue or allow him to manipulate you. If your kid doesn't want to eat, excuse him from the table.

  Allowing kids to decide when and how much they eat teaches them how to control their food intake. A recent study concluded that children learn to stop eating when they feel full if left on their own. When parents exert more control, such as by insisting on "clean plates," kids don't learn to pay attention to that sense of fullness, and they may overeat and gain weight.
- Eating disputes can also express anger over another issue. Perhaps your child feels upset at a certain discipline or feels unloved because his sibling gets "all the attention." He may refuse food or overeat in an attempt to provide comfort or compensation. Explore the possibilities by talking with him. Give him a little extra attention.
- Don't force your child to eat particular foods. When Christopher began eating solids, I read about studies showing that children naturally balance their own diets over time, so that what they eat on a particular day doesn't matter. When I mentioned the veggie phobia to the pediatrician, he let me off the hook: Christopher gets all the necessary vitamins and protein from the fruit, milk, cheese, and fortified cereals he likes. I stopped pushing vegetables entirely, though I do make them available on his plate in tiny amounts "just in case" he wants to try them.
- Have your child list what he'll eat this week before you go shopping. Kids' preferences change often, and suddenly that English muffin pizza he's scarfed down for a week goes untouched.
- On the other hand, don't be a short-order cook if your child constantly demands food different from what you've prepared. You're

a parent, not a slave. You count, too. Instead, always have a backup meal that is cheap, nutritious, and quick: Cereal and milk, bread and milk, something microwaveable, peanut butter sandwiches, raw veggies and dip. I recently experienced a two-week period when all Christopher wanted was macaroni and cheese ("the box kind") twice a day. I made large batches at once and heated individual portions in the microwave. Unappetizing as this sounds to an adult palate, he couldn't have been happier.

- Set a good example by eating a healthy diet yourself.
- Avoid arguments over sweets and junk foods by not keeping them around the house. (This will help *your* waistline, too.) Provide interesting but nutritious snacks. Make some of them yourself with your child. Structure your life so that your kids don't expect sugar and fat as regular rewards for "good behavior" or as everyday occurrences.

  I allow Christopher occasional sugar treats on the theory that he might otherwise feel so deprived he would overdose at every opportunity. I'd rather let him have cake and ice cream at a birthday party, however, than dessert every night at home. We make an excursion of going out for frozen yogurt rather than keeping a carton in the freezer. A couple of marshmallows or one chocolate kiss in his lunch makes his day. I'm often appalled at the amount of sugar consumed by other kids. It seems to be a matter of habit for both the children and the adults. I ask other parents to go easy on sugar snacks when Christopher plays with their children, and they willingly comply.

Make Mealtimes Pleasant

Make mealtime an oasis in a hectic day. Aim for a regular dinnertime so everyone can plan around it. Eating together engenders a feeling of belonging. Involve the kids in the ritual of setting the table, serving, lighting candles. Teach and require good manners, even from the smallest children. How else will they learn?

Turn off the TV. Talk. Kids who participate in dinnertime discussions develop verbal skills. Use your communication skills to elicit conversation (see Chapter 5). Ask everyone to describe one positive occurrence during the day. Give everyone a chance to talk; keep little ones from being drowned out or ignored. Encourage but don't require the kids to stay seated at the table until everyone has finished.

Cooking with Kids

Helping with meals gives children a learning experience and you a relief.

- Amaze kids by demonstrating that not everything comes pre-made from the grocery. Cook together to discover how to make noodles, for example, or spaghetti sauce.
- Bring home exotic fruits and vegetables from a farmers' market and look up how to use them.
- Provide child-size pot holders (one source recommends converting those useless shoulder pads from blouses and jackets!) and utensils the kids can use easily.

Kids Alone in the Kitchen

If your kids arrive home before you, make it easy for them to start dinner or prepare a snack. Adults who were barred from the kitchen as children eat out frequently because they don't know how to cook.

- Check the library for children's cookbooks. Make new recipes with your child before he tries them alone.
- Help him develop his own book of suitable recipes. Make photocopies or just note the book and page where he can find the recipe.
- Have a clear understanding about cleanup duty.
- Before you trust your children alone in the kitchen, make sure they are old enough and wise enough to use all appliances and utensils safely.

Cleaning

Though we vary in our standards and enthusiasm, cleaning is a factor in every single parent's life.

Your Cleaning Responsibilities

I've already touched on housecleaning under several headings. Other hints include:

- Practice preventive housekeeping to decrease the need to clean. Make and enforce rules about where your kids can eat and drink—only outside or at the kitchen table, for example. The same goes for "messes," such as painting, bean mosaics, chemistry experiments, and building projects. I forbid eating in my car. Christopher accepts this rule willingly since he's always known it. To be fair, I observe it, too, and enforce it on passengers. Other kids don't protest, even if they're used to backseat goodies on demand. We enjoy stopping for stretches and snacks on long drives rather than munching constantly in the car.

- Clean from top to bottom. A simple concept, but one people must learn. If you start at the bottom, whatever you loosen from subsequent efforts at the top will resettle lower, causing you to *redo* the bottom. Pure wasted effort.
- Don't let cleaning rule your life. Avoid scrubbing the kitchen floor during that one hour available for your kid. Beverly sets the timer for ten minutes and cleans like mad. When the bell rings, she's off the hook and free to play with her daughter. *If* she wants to, she can reset for another ten minutes.

> The Clean Team hot line answers housecleaning questions based on its trademarked "speed cleaning" system—which purports to cut cleaning time in half.
> 800-717-2532, 5 A.M. to 7 P.M. Pacific Time, Monday through Friday; and 7 A.M. to 3 P.M. on weekends.

Getting Your Kid to Clean His Room

This is one area in which you definitely have to abandon any expectations of perfection. Nevertheless, you needn't give up.

- Again, start at an early age and use logical consequences: "Tomorrow is vacuum day. Anything on the floor goes away for a week."
- Give clear instructions, breaking the job into discrete steps: "Clean your room" has very different meanings for an adult and a kid. Be explicit: "To clean your room, you put dirty clothes in the hamper, store toys in the bins, make the bed, dust the window sills, and sweep the floor." If necessary, further define "making the bed" and "sweeping the floor." If you don't spell out every step in detail, your child will rely on his own definitions—and they won't match your standards.

- Getting a teenager to keep a clean room is a losing battle. Save your energy to elicit teen cleanliness in common areas. A messy teen room represents more than a lack of interest in neatness. It's an assertion of independence and separate identity, requirements of his developmental stage. Treating a teen as you would a younger child interferes with it. Just ask him to keep his door closed. Don't worry, his tendency toward sloth isn't necessarily permanent.
- Provide bins, drawers, or shelves for storage, but don't require any particular organization within them.

Do Preventive Maintenance

Routine maintenance seems bothersome until you realize it prevents major headaches down the road. I've learned this lesson the hard way several times, sometimes on possessions I didn't even realize *required* maintenance. Frankly, I hate bothering with this sort of work—it seems like "fixing something that ain't broke"—but I hate paying the consequences more. I force myself to enjoy the process, but I make the jobs as easy and automatic as possible.

Keep a notebook divided into sections for the car, the house, and anything else that needs regular upkeep. Write the maintenance schedule from the manual at the beginning of each section (so you don't constantly have to look it up) and note the dates on your calendar for the year. As you take care of the work, write in the notebook what you did and when you did it.

Car

Consult your owner's manual for recommended frequency of oil changes, lubrication, tune-ups, tire-rotation, and the like. Check the tire pressure regularly. Not only will you keep your auto humming, but you and your kids will be safer riding in it.

House

If you rent, the landlord performs maintenance, but you should report any problems promptly to him. Beyond that, taking good care of the property under your control ensures return of your security deposit and earns you good references for future rentals.

If you own a home, good maintenance keeps it weatherproof and preserves its value and safety. Unless you really enjoy puttering around with a hammer and paint, hire someone else and:

- Have chimneys and flues professionally inspected annually for cracks, defects, soot, and any dangerous conditions that you cannot easily see otherwise. Crumbling mortar and loose or cracked bricks constitute fire hazards. Loose flashing causes rain leakage.
- Repair dangerous cracks in outdoor walks and patios.
- Keep handrails sturdy and stairs tightly nailed and free of slippery or worn treads.
- Paint the interior and exterior every few years, as needed. Outdoor painting helps to prevent damage to wood.
- Check the attic or upper-story ceilings for evidence of roof leaks.
- Search out signs of leaks and cracks in basements.
- Repair any malfunctioning electrical switches, outlets, connections, or wiring. Look for frayed wires on appliances, lamps, and other electrical items.
- Clean the kitchen ventilator fan to remove accumulated dust and grease, a fire hazard.
- Clean the furnace filter every year.
- Clear the sewer line periodically. In my tree-filled neighborhood, annual clearing prevents growth of roots through the pipes.
- Clean roof gutters at least twice a year, after spring and before winter. In wooded areas, check more often, as pine needles, leaves and twigs quickly clog gutters. If not cleaned, water backs up during a rain and rots underlying wood or overflows and washes away topsoil and plants below.
- Order a pest inspection every couple of years to check for termites, carpenter ants, and beetles. Insects do much damage if, like many people, you defer this inspection over the years until you want to sell your house. You'll face a hefty repair job at that point.

> "If a disease were killing our children in the proportions that accidents are, people would be outraged and demand that this killer be stopped."
>
> C. EVERETT KOOP, M.D., SC.D., FORMER U.S. SURGEON GENERAL

Also, store firewood away from the sides of the house. Be alert for signs of infestation in foundations, fences, trellises, and decks.
- Replace wood affected by dry rot or other damage before it spreads to structural components of the house.

Yourself

You need regular maintenance and nurturing yourself (see Chapter 4).

Consider Hiring Help

If you can't afford ongoing household help, consider it on an occasional basis or as a treat (see Chapter 4).

Pay Attention to Safety

Home should be safe in every sense of the word. Skimp on anything but safety measures. Take precautions against fire, falls, water accidents, traffic and bicycle injuries, poisoning, choking, and any other hazards you can think of.

While your household may often seem out of control, you really can influence a great deal of what happens there. Concentrate on methods to make home life run smoothly and safely. Use some of these suggestions or come up with your own. Involve your kids and keep a positive attitude. Don't forget to laugh.

BOOKS FOR KIDS

Pretend Soup, and Other Real Recipes, Mollie Katzen (Berkeley: Tricycle, 1994).

365 Foods Kids Love to Eat: Nutritious and Kid-Tested, Sheila Ellison and Judith Gray (Trabuco Canyon, CA: Sourcebooks, 1995).

Betty Crocker's Cooking with Kids (Old Tappan, NJ: Macmillan, 1995).

Chapter 7

Preteens and Teens

A friend with teenagers told me that one of Christopher's difficult phases was "just a preview of his adolescence." I laughed, but having talked with other parents in researching this book, I now agree. When the teens arrive, the good news is that you've been there before. Dust off the tools for dealing with the "terrible twos," and you're ready for the "terrible teens" (and preteens, which I lump in here because it's so hard to tell the difference anymore). The parenting skills discussed previously form a firm foundation for life with teenagers. A few refinements, and you're on your way.

The bad news? Despite your best efforts, teens will still drive you crazy.

Beneath the difficult behaviors of both preschoolers and teens lies a major internal conflict—separation, independence, and control versus retreat to safety and dependence. The kid is developmentally hard-wired to leap away from you at these ages, but doing so scares him, and he returns for reassurance until he feels secure enough to try another step outward by himself. Your setting limits provides that security and reassurance that you will protect him from himself. Then he stretches forward again. Many of the battles with your teen or preschooler involve his instinct toward separation and his tests to see who's in charge.

Let's answer that question immediately. You are. Your house, your money, your rules. In fact, your child wants you to be stable and in charge. You're his sounding board, the solid wall he bounces off in trying various ways of seeing the world and determining what fits.

Of course, teens *aren't* tots, and the context of the power struggles differs greatly. Your teen is no longer cuddly at the end of the day. His focus lies outside the family. Still, you'll recognize many of the same tools you used on your toddler.

Much in this book applies to kids of all ages, including teens. But since adolescents look more to peers than to family for support, they resist more. They consider your attempts to enter their world intrusive. Continuing to make efforts even when they turn you down shows your willingness and availability to bridge the gap when they're ready.

A Teen's "Job"

Your teen has a twenty-four-hour job—becoming an adult. Practically everything he does relates to developing identity, independence, and separate sexuality.

He fulfills the first two tasks—defining his separate identity and independence—primarily by showing he's different from you. (This explains the green hair!) He *needs* to prove he is absolutely nothing like you:

- Appearance. Hair, clothes, nails, and colors you hate can figure largely here.
- Slang. Jargon not only separates you from him, but marks him as part of a particular subculture or clique.
- Space. His room, his decor, his mess—just the way he likes it and you hate it.

> "Don't laugh at a youth for his affectations; he's only trying on one face after another till he finds his own."
> LOGAN PEARSALL SMITH

Take heed: if any of this doesn't drive you nuts, then it's not fulfilling its purpose. Let your teen know it all bugs you in the extreme so he won't have to escalate. (If something makes you crazier than you can bear, maybe you should suggest that you rather like it. "Gee, Blackboard Fingernails is the best band I've heard in a long time." He'll trash that CD in a hurry. Don't overuse this tactic, though. He's no dummy.)

- For more on identity and independence, see Chapter 9.
- For sexuality, see Chapter 8.

Your "Jobs" As the Parent of a Teen

Listen and Communicate

Teens don't confide much to parents, but when they do, drop everything. The average parent spends eleven minutes a day with his teen, and much of that is spent in argument. Rise above the average. Utilize the time together for listening, using the communication skills you've developed through the years.

Raise difficult topics for explicit discussion. Speak up when something bothers you. Comment on the dynamics between you and your teen. Mention how hard it is to get him to converse with you. Sometimes teens find talking about themselves threatening. Instead, try discussing "friends." You both know it's a fiction, but it can lower his feeling of vulnerability. Remind him you're ready to listen whenever he wants to talk.

As discussed in Chapter 5, active listening is a learned skill that requires practice. If you haven't mastered it, consider joint counseling with a therapist to ensure both you and your teen hear each other.

Keep Boundaries Intact

Single parents often become over- or under-involved with their children, especially teens. Friends take top priority with them. Your teenager's interests do and should lie outside the house now, a fact which may make you feel shortchanged. This a psychological issue for you to address yourself.

- Resist the temptation to keep him too close for too long. Don't continually require his presence or plan too many activities together. Avoid playing upon his guilt or seeming so needy that he feels obligated to care for you and put your needs above his. Never treat him as a confidant. Keep those boundaries separate. Get a life for yourself so you're not so absorbed in his (see Chapters 1 and 4).
- Be a parent first. You're still his friend, but *first* you're his parent. You will make some unpopular decisions, so prepare yourself for

the fallout. If you're too concerned about being a friend, you'll relent, and the wall will crumble.

- Respect your teen's privacy, and see that he respects yours. A closed door requires a knock. Never snoop among his possessions, listen in on his phone conversations, or open his mail—even "by accident"—or his sense of trust will vanish, perhaps permanently. On the other hand, his right of privacy has limits, and if he steps outside them, you are by definition involved. He does not, for example, have the right to use drugs "privately."
- Conversely, a teen also needs the opportunity to come to you for security. Don't become so caught up in your own drama about divorce or other matters that you effectively shut him out when he seeks reassurance. Expelling him into the world too soon—making him truly cope alone—amounts to abandonment and interferes with his developmental needs.
- When the inevitable conflict arises, look for other emotions that your anger masks, such as fear for the safety and well-being of your teenager or sadness at his growing independence from you.

  Sit with those feelings. Don't feel guilty for his rebellion or missteps. He *is* becoming an independent person day by day. Granting him responsibility for his own actions is the ultimate goal of parenting. Realize that you cannot influence everything in his life, and try to give up wanting to. The time is fast approaching when you have to abandon all claim to authority over him.

  Your fledgling is learning to fly and doesn't need you as he did before. Accept this. Ask for what you want from your teen, but realize you may not get it.

> "All adolescents are, in a sense, psychotic."
> FANITA ENGLISH

Respect Your Teen

- Speak politely. Use a neutral tone of voice when angry. Treat your kid as you would a friend, student, or teacher. Give his opinions credence. Show your respect for different aspects of his prowess: physical, mental, moral.
- Respect his struggles, too. Never intimate that his problems seem childish or trivial.
- Recognize the importance of his schedule. Adolescents can become completely unsettled by alterations in plans when they have no con-

trol or warning. Minimize unexpected or last-minute disruptions of his agenda. Give forewarning of potential, unavoidable changes.

Notice the Positive

Don't let your teen's thoughtful, considerate, and loving gestures go without remark in the midst of adolescent angst. Comment on them. Show how good they make you feel. Reciprocate.

> "Experience is a hard teacher because she gives the test first, the lesson afterwards."
>
> VERNON LAW

Keep Setting Limits

The garden in which your teen "plays" has grown large, but you are still the garden wall for him to lean on when he needs to.

Developmentally, he's seeking to arrive at a consistent value system and point of view. He needs you as his anchor. A recent national survey showed that sixty-five percent of preteens from ten to thirteen worry that their parents might die before they grow up. At a basic, unconscious level, your youngster fears you can't keep it together well enough to see him through to adulthood. As reassurance, he wants you to set and stand by your limits.

Now more than ever, he needs limits. If they don't exist, he'll unconsciously provoke them through negative behavior. He'll experiment in unsafe ways until he locates the limits, often at the hands of the police or school authorities. He'll push until you can no longer ignore him—pregnancy, drug addiction, crime, disease. Often this method works just fine for him. He goes to a special school or a drug rehab center. She gets pregnant and brings home a baby. Special attention!

Take it as a given: If your teen gets in trouble, he's sending you a message.

- Base the limits of behavior on your values. Teens deserve reasons, which don't generally include "because I said so." Discuss the values behind reasons.
- Think about what your *actions* say, as well as your words. For example, letting your teen take a mixed-gender, overnight ski trip with minimal adult supervision conveys the message, "Do what you want; whatever happens is okay with me." Instead, your actions should reinforce the message, "Yes, I trust you, but these are my values, and my number-one value is caring about you."

- Choose your battles. Work on one behavior at a time, perhaps week by week. Overlook minor transgressions in one area while focusing on another. Don't start anything you aren't willing to finish.

With teens, logical consequences often flow without your input. Skipping homework affects grades, for example. Missing soccer practice means not starting in the game. You don't need to add anything on top. As Mark Twain said, "Good judgment comes from experience with bad judgment."

Your ultimate parental responsibility is to send a capable, independent being into the world without you. Save your intransigence for health and safety issues and consider everything else somewhat negotiable. Let your teen practice his independent tightrope act with a safety net before he ventures out completely on his own. You're his "spotter," the one who guides him and restores his balance when he falters, just as you did years ago when he first walked on terra firma. But you don't walk *for* him. Think how you can *influence* him rather than *control* him.

Negotiate

Giving him a say in decisions affecting his life teaches independence and decision making (see Chapter 9). It encourages him to think about consequences in advance. Lack of control over his life breeds anger and rebellion.

- Discuss "scenarios" that may come up. Ask "What would be the consequence if you . . . ?" Often he'll devise something stricter than you would have suggested.
- Negotiate consequences—and requests for certain things—when you are both calm. Give yourself time to reflect on his suggestions and requests. This not only lets you make a more tempered decision, but it teaches your teen to plan and avoid asking at the last minute.
- Communicate your willingness to negotiate. Ask your teen what he thinks is a reasonable solution. Kids often come up with very workable ideas. He may joke or make an off-the-wall proposal. Go from there.
- State your concerns calmly and respectfully. Arrive at an appropriate middle ground. As we said in law, a good compromise gives both parties something and leaves them each feeling cheated.

Let Your Teen Be a Teen

Don't arbitrarily deny your teen the normal accouterments of adolescence. Do what you can, within the limits of your resources and capabilities, to let him be a "normal" teen. You don't have to eat beans for three years to buy him a car, but don't unreasonably deny him use of yours. Negotiate something that works for both of you. Allow him his extensive phone needs (perhaps sharing the expense of a second line) and a certain autonomy over comings and goings.

I spent my adolescent years fighting for what belongs to teenagers almost by definition—dating, clothes, use of the car, telephone privileges—and I guarantee that arbitrary refusals only produce rebellion and resentment.

- Accept a teen's self-absorption as part of the deal. The family may think he cares about nothing and no one else, but that's not exactly true. He cares about other people—it's just that he cares *so much* about himself!
- Likewise, turmoil is part of being the parent of a teenager. Rolling eyes and grimaces and emotional ups and downs go with the territory. You signed on for this back when that eight-pounds-fifteen-ounces breathed his first!
- Realize you can't control everything. At a certain point, you have to let go and trust that your teen's internal guidelines will hold up.

> "Young men are apt to think themselves wise enough, as drunken men are apt to think themselves sober enough."
> LORD CHESTERFIELD

Remember Developmental Issues and Don't Take Your Teen's Actions Personally

When you and your teen lock horns, realize you're probably fighting about the underlying developmental battle rather than the surface issue. If he lied about his whereabouts, impose your consequences, but also remember that being sneaky is an adolescent's "job."

Be open to his struggles. His feelings are intense and changeable—remember how it was? His moodiness and anger aim at your behavior, not at you. Stay relatively undefensive and avoid taking his challenges personally, just as you did when your four-year-old said, "I hate you" in mid-tantrum. Detach if you feel insulted, defensive, or outraged. Give yourself time to cool off. Breathe and think about your reaction before speaking or acting. To repeat Cliff and Liz's mantra, "The time of conflict is not the time of resolution." Explore solutions later at a family meeting.

Take Care of Yourself

This Life Preserver goes double when raising teens. You cope better, and your teen respects you more, if you nurture yourself. Consider *both* your needs when setting limits and negotiating. With curfew, for example, the issue isn't just whether you trust your teen. You can trust him completely but still worry about accidents. *You* have the right to go to bed at a reasonable hour and not wake up every thirty minutes wondering if your kid's body lies bleeding on the freeway. Balance your own needs and legitimate concerns against his, check into curfews set by peers' parents, and negotiate a compromise.

This goes even if your teen still lives at home after hitting that "magical" age of eighteen. When he's on his own, his hours are his, but until then . . . when his late nights cause *you* insomnia in your own home, the curfew stays.

Don't Compensate for Your Former Spouse's Laxity or Rigidity

If you can communicate with your ex-spouse, do so. Arrive at similar outside limits for your teen's behavior. If you can't, just do the best parenting you can without regard to your ex. Imposing excessively strict rules won't make up for his permissiveness. Nor can you even things out by removing restrictions when your ex-spouse never gives an inch. At least ensure that your teen gets the reasonable, firm boundaries that he needs from you.

Realize When It's Time for a Change

When asked about the most surprising aspect of single-parenting, Greta responded, "I was always late to realize that old safeguards weren't needed anymore." As a single parent, child care consumes half your life—finding it, getting it, and keeping it. Automatic pilot keeps you moving down that runway continuously—but it does eventually end. At some point, your child can stay home alone safely without a sitter. He can use the stove or power saw. He can go away camping for the weekend.

Recognize and honor his increasing capabilities. Encourage responsible independence by letting him stretch. Negotiate the next

> "Growing is not the easy, plain sailing business that it is commonly supposed to be: It is hard work—harder than any but a growing boy can understand: It requires attention, and you are not strong enough to attend to your bodily growth and to your lessons too."
>
> SAMUEL BUTLER (1835–1902)

step and evaluate how he handles it. If he's ready, make this change permanent and brace yourself for the next one.

Smooth the Way through Growth and Physical Maturation

While your teen is acutely aware of bodily changes, he doesn't necessarily know what to do with them. His hands and feet reach adult size long before the rest of him, resulting in awkwardness and lack of coordination. Height increases, hair grows in new places, curves form, periods start, voices crack, sweat glands work overtime, girls tower over boys, dreams become "wet," and skin erupts.

You can't—and wouldn't—change any of this. Assure your child that it's all normal and everything settles down eventually. Encourage him to eat a healthy diet and exercise. Get good medical advice about acne, which, contrary to what you were told, isn't caused by chocolate, greasy foods, failure to wash, or impure thoughts. Pimples result from bacteria and oil-clogged pores beneath the skin's surface.

Talk with your teenager about hygiene. If you don't, no one will. Non-judgmentally explain the need for a daily shower, clean clothes and hair, and deodorant for those newly active sweat glands.

Be sensitive to requirements for bras, menstruation supplies (include tampon package inserts about toxic shock syndrome), jock straps, shaving kits, and the like, all of which may embarrass your teen. Again, be matter-of-fact. Just say that as the body changes, so do requirements for its care. For discussion of teen sexuality, see Chapter 8.

Help with Peers

Cliques are a part of teen life. Whether your teen is "in" or "out," give him the message he doesn't have to like everyone, but he does have to show everyone respect.

For more on peer pressure, see Chapter 10.

- While recognizing the negative impact of peer pressure, don't forget the value of friendships. As a single parent, you know the importance of friends at practical, emotional, and psychological levels. Help your child receive similar benefits from his peers.
- Get to know your kid's friends. Learn these teens' personalities and styles. Watch to see who influences whom.
- Make your home a place kids enjoy visiting. If this means giving in to the latest junk food, so be it. Don't be intrusive, but occasionally take them out for activities or have them assist with interesting projects at home. During Tony's brief career as a sculptor, his teen sons and their friends helped him construct a twelve-foot "shoe tree" of discarded footwear and a giant "flea" from skis and crutches. Years later, they still reminisce about these experiences.
- If you find your kid's friends obnoxious or incomprehensible and can't imagine why he likes them, take a second look. Ask what he gets from the friendship. Maybe that passive girl who never says anything provides your daughter with an opportunity to lead, for example.
- If your kid's friend mistreats you or disregards the rules of your house, speak up. This, more than any discussion, demonstrates how to stand up for oneself and one's principles. "I don't like being talked to like that."
- Your child's friends can be allies. If your son seems lethargic and depressed but won't talk, perhaps a buddy can confirm whether he's the same at school. The friend has probably worried, too, and may welcome the opportunity to share his concern. Having your perceptions validated by your kid's peer gives you confidence to take action.

Let Your Teen Sleep

Teens stay up late and require resurrection rituals the next morning. Their sleep habits wreak havoc with school and work schedules. Cajoling and fighting have little effect, and for good reason: The latest studies reveal that adolescent biological clocks naturally program these sleep patterns. Since teens need at least nine-and-a-half hours of sleep, getting enough shut-eye poses a problem on school days.

Realizing the biological basis for droopy eyes and slow-motion mornings will give you a more understanding attitude. This is another developmental behavior, not a veiled attempt to ruin your life. Of course, you still have to get everyone out of the house on time, but maybe you can do so with less resentment. And on weekends, let your teen follow his own biological imperative.

Let Him Drive

When your adolescent gets his driver's license, his world suddenly expands, and your concerns increase. Traffic accidents and highway carnage terrify you, but having another driver in a single-parent family certainly makes life easier. You can't hold out on this privilege.

While you have less control, you still have the right to set limits, even if your teen has his own car. Make it clear that driving privileges come with a new set of responsibilities. Spell them out clearly before turning over the keys. The American Automobile Association advises parents to enter into a written contract with teens to formalize the rules.

Drugs

While drug use may often begin in the teens or preteens, preventive measures begin in preschool (see Chapter 10).

Stay Connected to Other Parents

- Keep in touch with other parents about limits and consequences on all issues, not just substance abuse. A quick call now and then keeps the lines open. Share information on undesirable behavior or influences. As much as teens protest, they feel comforted knowing their parents care. Knowing you talk with other parents inhibits your kid's misrepresentations about, say, whether a party at another house will be chaperoned.
- If your teen experiences a particular difficulty, consider filling other parents in so they can discreetly advise their own kids. They

might explain, for example, that your daughter hasn't really been unfriendly lately, just sad about her parents' breakup.

A Bleak View of the Future

What occupies the minds of older kids? While prior generations worried primarily about amorphous, external threats (the Bomb and polio), modern kids' concerns also reflect anxiety about abandonment and inability to cope with personal challenges. Among the fears listed in a recent survey were:

- Getting AIDS 54%
- Being kidnapped 50%
- Being physically or sexually abused 45%
- Having a baby out of wedlock 42%
- Using drugs 41%
- Using alcohol 40%
- Smoking cigarettes 38%

> The overall U.S. homicide rate declined by 6.8% in 1994, to 9.7 per 100,000 people. But the rate was 37 per 100,000 young men, ages fifteen to twenty-four.[1]

Forty-three percent of the kids surveyed could name no role model! Parents topped the list of those who could name one, but a basketball star, Michael Jordan, came in first among "nonfamilial heroes."

Parents need to give their kids clear, positive leadership so they feel secure, loved, valued, and capable of responding to negative pressures. Be a hero to yourself and point out other heros in the arts, science, business, exploration, literature, and other areas of life. Help your kid find role models for the type of person you want him to be.

Depression and Suicide in Teens

I don't like thinking about this topic, but I must, since suicide in the family, even by distant relatives, constitutes a primary risk factor for a child's suicide. I'll spend a lifetime countering Tony's message that killing yourself is a good way to solve problems. Perhaps I'm lucky in a way. My awareness heightens my sensitivity to the risk and allows me to emphasize other ways of resolving difficulties. In so many cases, parents, friends, and teachers alike puzzle over a sudden teen suicide, wondering what they failed or refused to see and how they could have helped.

Suicide is the second leading cause of adolescent death. Each year more than five thousand kids from ages fifteen to twenty-four kill themselves. The rate of suicide for this age group has nearly tripled in the past twenty years.

Research indicates that adolescent suicide attempts stem from long-standing problems coupled with a triggering event. Teens may regard death as a temporary means of escaping a troubling reality. Biological and chemical body changes may be associated with suicide. The stresses of adolescence—peer and parental expectations, sexual development and identity, fears of intellectual and physical inadequacy—can't be overstated. Suicide attempts are cries for help.

Trust your instincts. If you have even an inkling that your child is depressed or contemplating suicide, *act*. Don't wait for more signs to confirm your suspicions. Don't worry about breaking confidences or creating embarrassment. Saving a life justifies all these.

Suicide Risk Factors

In addition to prior suicide in the family, other important risk factors for teen suicide include:

- Giving away possessions
- Changes in behavior such as eating, sleeping, or favorite activities
- "Insurmountable" problems at school, which may seem insignificant to you
- Engaging in riskier behavior than usual
- Writing a will
- Writing or talking about death; obsession with death in art or music
- Recent major losses, including, of course, divorce and death of a parent; also a move, loss of a friend or lover, or a death
- Isolation and avoidance of friends and normal social activities
- Reduced communication with parents
- Increased rebellion
- Substance abuse
- Threats of or prior attempts at suicide
- Depression, or coming out of depression (which seems to provide energy to carry out the act)

Symptoms of Depression in Teens

An estimated five percent of children and adolescents in the general population suffer significant depression. Teen depression sometimes resists diagnosis because many of the symptoms look like normal teen behavior. In addition, because the kid may not seem *sad,* parents and teachers may not realize that misbehavior is signaling depression. Teens don't understand or express feelings well. They may not even be aware of the concept of depression and therefore don't seek help.

> The overall American suicide rate rose by 3.8% in 1994. Males fifteen to twenty-four committed 26 suicides per 100,000 in that age group. Females fifteen to twenty-four committed 3.2 per 100,000.[2]

Kids under stress, those who experience loss (again including divorce and parental death) or who have attention, learning, or conduct disorders, are at higher risk for depression. Symptoms include:

- Loss of interest and difficulty in interpersonal communication
- Aggressiveness, acting out, angry outbursts, "getting in trouble," sexual promiscuity, truancy, self-destructive behavior
- Brooding, sadness, feelings of emptiness, hopelessness, loneliness, guilt
- Fluctuation between apathy and talkativeness
- Overreaction to criticism
- Death wishes
- Grouchiness, frequent crying, touchiness
- Weight changes and/or change of appetite or sleep patterns
- Desire to run or actual running away from home
- Withdrawal
- Poor self-esteem, loss of self-confidence
- Feelings of helplessness and emptiness in life, pessimism
- Rebellion, refusal to cooperate in school or at home
- Feelings of inability to satisfy ideals and expectations
- Marked personality change
- Frequent fatigue, low energy, or physical complaints such as headaches and stomach aches
- Persistent boredom, poor concentration
- Irrational, bizarre behavior

- Overwhelming sense of guilt or shame
- Substance abuse

Talk about It!

If you see the signs of depression or potential suicide in your adolescent, *talk about it right away,* and be specific. Don't let denial delay you. Ask, "Are you thinking about killing yourself?" *Talking about suicide does not make someone kill himself.* To the contrary, it saves lives. Ask if he's thought about how to do it. Does he have a plan? The more detailed and available the means he mentions, the greater the danger he'll act.

- Let your child know you care and that you will get help. Listen. Don't lecture.
- Tell him that suicide is a permanent solution to a temporary problem. Amazingly, potential suicides, especially young ones, seem to overlook the permanency of death. They develop a sort of tunnel vision and think only of their despair. No other solution occurs to them.
- Open up that tunnel vision. A suicidal person is often ambivalent. Part of him wants to die, part to live. Help tilt the balance toward life.
- Tell your child that suicide is neither glamorous nor romantic. It's *messy.* Remind him that someone will find him, and he'll look awful. Finding him and realizing what he's done will cause deep trauma for others. At the same time, underscore that having *thoughts* of suicide doesn't make him bad or strange.
- Don't try to convince your teen that his problems aren't worth dying for or that "everything will be okay." He won't believe you, and he'll only feel more misunderstood.
- Get other adults involved—teachers he admires, mental health professionals, police. Suicide hot lines provide tremendous help just by talking and breaking the focus on death. Enlist your local Mental Health Association to find relevant resources for helping your suicidal teen.
- The belief that anyone who talks about suicide won't ever commit it is a myth. Four out of five people who kill themselves give prior clues of their intentions. Tony talked about it intermittently for years. Take suicide threats and death wishes seriously. Don't be afraid to speak up.

No one ever said that the teen years are easy for parents or teens themselves. For single parents, this stage is even harder. You have no one to back you up, no one to whom you can pass a particularly difficult issue. You continue as you have before, however, doing your best.

ORGANIZATIONS

International Youth Council: Activities and support for teens living in single-parent families, sponsored by Parents Without Partners. 401 N. Michigan Ave., Chicago, IL 60611; 312-644-6610.

BOOKS FOR PARENTS

Positive Discipline for Teenagers: Resolving Conflict with Your Teenage Son or Daughter, Jane Nelsen and Lynn Lott (Rocklin, CA: Prima Publishing, 1994).

BOOKS FOR PRETEENS/TEENS

Bringing Up Parents: The Teenager's Handbook, Alex J. Packer, Ph.D. (Minneapolis, MN: Free Spirit Publishing, Inc., 1993) (ages 13 and up); 612-338-2068.

Teens and Self-Esteem: A Teenager's Guide to Surviving Stress, National Mental Health Association, 800-969-6642.

The What's Happening to My Body? Book for Girls: A Growing Up Guide for Parents and Daughters, Lynda Madaras, et al. (New York: Newmarket Press, 1987) (ages 9 to 16).

The What's Happening to My Body? Book for Boys: A Growing Up Guide for Parents and Sons, Lynda Madaras, et al. (New York: Newmarket Press, 1991) (ages 9 to 16).

Chapter 8

Kids and Sexuality

My son knows more about the "birds and the bees" at five than I did at fifteen. The whole of my sexual education was a girls-only movie in the fourth grade showing a colorful animated egg sliding down a cartoon fallopian tube (with a hint that my own body housed something similar) and the one occasion when my mom said that it was time I knew babies came from "little seeds." Oh yes, she also later whispered that boys only wanted "one thing" (whatever it was . . . shhh), and I shouldn't "give in." Everything else I pieced together later through inference and experience. I met with many dead ends and wrong turns on my road to sexuality.

Sex blatantly permeates our public lives through every form of media, and yet, ironically, when brought down to the personal level, it causes embarrassment and shame.

Christopher will not travel the same route I did. Given my mother's belated, oblique "explanation," I marvel at my ease in providing Christopher with direct information. The secret, I believe, is starting young and being matter-of-fact, but it's never too late to begin.

Like other modern parents, I want my child to understand his biology, communicate freely, love and respect himself and his body, and know that sexuality is natural but private. These are the most effective means I have for helping him make conscious, healthy, responsible choices about sex when the time comes.

Prepare Yourself for Your Child's Sex Education

Imparting sexual values and facts comes as a hard task to some parents. Preparation eases the way:

- Children take their attitudes about sexuality from their parents. Examine your views carefully to ensure they're what you want to convey—some of them probably belong to *your* mother and father! Either consciously adopt them as your own or abandon them for attitudes that better fit your identity now. Talk with other adults to help clarify your own values.
- Whatever the content of your messages, stay relaxed when discussing sex. After all, you teach your child every day, and sexuality is just one more topic, right? True, but it comes with baggage. Some people have no problem with fallopian tubes but fall apart at explaining intercourse. Rehearse alone to get comfortable saying the words out loud. If the subject embarrasses you, say so. Just admitting it puts you more at ease.

  If you stumble with your child, admit, "It's hard for me to talk about this, but I'll do my best." Maybe reading a book together or renting a sex education video will get you off the hook more easily. Find out what, if anything, he learns on the subject at school and use it as a conversation starter.
- Experts recommend that you discuss and agree upon sexual issues with your spouse and present a unified approach. As a single parent, you may not have that option. With luck, your ex will cooperate. If not, just do your part.

> "Oh what a tangled web do parents weave When they think that their children are naïve."
> ODGEN NASH

- Think about what you will say on various subjects before they arise. Consult books both for parents alone and for reading with children. Practice how you will discuss the topic. Of course, you'll never outguess a kid's inquisitiveness, but you won't be completely in the dark about how to answer an off-the-wall question.
- Give questions and actions a developmental context so you will best understand them (see following sections). Even though a child's sexuality sometimes looks like adult behavior, reference it to his age and development to interpret it correctly. Knowing your

four-year-old's "bathroom talk" is normal, for example, reassures you. You still have to deal with it, but it's not a sign your kid will major in scatology at college.

Sexuality is a touchy subject (no pun intended) and you may already hold strong views and opinions. By all means, trust your own instincts and follow your own path. Go ahead and read this chapter anyway. Some points may fit into your approach.

Stages of Sexual Development in Children

Parents often don't understand that kids become sexual very early. Knowing the stages of sexual maturation helps you evaluate and accept behaviors that might otherwise alarm you.

- A preschooler learns about physical differences between the genders and finds other children's bodies fascinating. He's intrigued with bathroom talk and "bad" words. Being concrete, he explores differences by undressing with other kids, looking intently, touching, and masturbating. At this stage your child needs gentle, matter-of-fact reminders of acceptable behavior. Until age six or seven, he explores playfully but doesn't really engage in sexual activity or language.
- After this, during the "latency period," awareness of gender differences increases. Though he has little real knowledge, the child's developing conscience signals that sexuality is somehow private and personal. He begins to stake out privacy—covering himself, locking the bathroom, knocking before entering a closed door. Follow his lead and do the same. Respecting the boundaries he establishes confirms that he is master of his body. Feel free to talk about these changes, don't resist them, and don't be intrusive. Avoid nudity with him and take special care that he not be exposed to others' sexual activity at this time or any other.

  During latency, kids struggle to keep sexual impulses under control. They rechannel energy into sports, crushes on teachers, or other children. Out of natural curiosity, they may also "play doctor" with kids of both genders in sexually explicit ways that resemble adult behavior. While this is still play, it isn't desirable socially. Be ready for this stage so you don't ignore or overreact to it. Without shaming the children, simply say they shouldn't be touching each other and then redirect their energies. "Let's have a baseball game."

- The changes of prepuberty, from ages nine to twelve, bring awkwardness, modesty, self-consciousness, and anxiety about normalcy. Abundant sexual fantasies produce guilty feelings. Your child becomes exquisitely sensitive to media idols that define "handsome" and "beautiful." Kids of this age sometimes engage in exploratory same-sex play, which does not signal latent homosexuality.

  Help your child by tuning in to his anxiety. Ask how he feels about his body changing. Does developing too quickly or too slowly trouble him? Does he compare himself unfavorably to others? Tell him, "There's one right process, and that's yours."

  Give him positive messages about his body. Talk about how celebrities look much different in real life, minus the make-up and photographic manipulations. Assure him that fantasies are normal, that most people have them.

- Two words sum up teenage sexuality: Raging Hormones. Teens' hormones are so powerful that they literally have trouble controlling them. Acknowledge that.

> Sexual activity starts at younger and younger ages. Approximately 33% of fifteen-year-old boys and 27% of fifteen-year-old girls have had sex.[1]

Teaching Your Child about His Body

It's odd that we can be so ignorant about something so close to us—our bodies. You have a great influence on what your child learns about his body and how he feels about it.

Teach Healthy Attitudes

The body is programmed for pleasure from before birth. The mouth, genitals, and anus connect to pleasure pathways in the brain formed during gestation. Encourage an appreciation of the body as an asset to be respected and enjoyed.

- Start in the peekaboo stage by naming your child's body parts. "Where's your nose?" "Here's your belly button." Then, instead of skipping to the knees, include "This is your penis" or "This is your vulva." Omitting the genitals conveys the subtle message they are wrong or shameful. It creates a large, ominous, blank space on your kid's body like the great unknown areas on ancient maps marked "Here Lies Danger."

- Use correct terms from the beginning. Tell your child people also sometimes use slang words (which you don't have to enumerate). (Giving a child the vocabulary for his genitalia also ensures that he can accurately report any sexual abuse, and it contributes to his feeling he has permission to do so. See Chapter 10.)
- Help your kid experience and learn about touch. He will like some kinds and not others, and the choice is his. Massage him. Rub his back or his feet. Ask whether he likes a soft touch or a deep one.
- Encourage talk about his body in any context.
- Recovering from a divorce or death, your own interest in sex may be nil. At times you swear you'll have nothing to do with the opposite gender again. Still, as a model for your kids, try to maintain a healthy attitude toward your body and its capacity for giving you pleasure—even if that only amounts to a massage or a warm bath for now.

> Every twenty-one seconds a fifteen- to nineteen-year-old becomes sexually active for the first time.[2]

Masturbation

Masturbation starts in children as young as two or three. They have no idea it's a "sexual" activity. It just feels good. It won't make them blind, insane, oversexed, or anything else you heard growing up. In fact, researchers find self-touch beneficial because it:

- Promotes acceptance of sexuality and sexual identity.
- Substitutes for premature sexual encounters and provides a healthy way for relieving sexual tension.
- Avoids transmission of sexual diseases, including AIDS.
- Lessens resistance to use of condoms, which require self-touch.
- Creates awareness of the entire body's sensuality, as opposed to making intercourse the entire point. It helps people understand and later communicate what gives them pleasure.

Whatever your beliefs about masturbation, don't shame your child by overreacting or chastising. There's no reason to stop the behavior, but for the sake of socialization, limit *where* he does it. If he touches himself in public or with others, distract him with conversation or by showing him something. Don't make a big deal of it. Later, when you're alone with him, tell him matter-of-factly, "It's okay for you to touch yourself there, but only when you're by yourself." If you get this message across while he's young, you'll never have to deal with the issue again.

> Twenty percent of sexually active teens had their first sexual encounter at age sixteen, and only 6% at age seventeen. Of sexually active teens, 61% have had multiple partners.[3]

By the way, it's all right if *you* masturbate. Most people do, even married people. Feelings of shame still predominate, however, and people don't like to admit to it. One study reported that seventy-two percent of married men and sixty-nine percent of married women masturbate. However, ninety-two percent of husbands believed their wives didn't masturbate, and eight percent of the wives thought their husbands didn't. Perhaps more frank, open discussion about the subject could reduce shame and stigma. At any rate, if you're without a mate, feel free.

"Grown-Up" Experimentation

Your kids, particularly girls, will try "grown-up" activities before you're ready. Often these concern doing something to the body: make-up, tattoos, piercings, dieting, clothes, and so on. At ten, Denny's daughter Rebecca begged for make-up. Alarmed, he took it as a sign of growing up too fast, perhaps running with the wrong crowd. He adamantly refused her request at first. If confronted with a similar situation:

- Rely on your trusting relationship to encourage your child to listen and think about what you say. An authoritative approach only promotes rebellion. Make it clear your objections come from love, not a desire to control.
- If your reaction to the behavior is strong, talk with other parents first so you won't bring an emotional charge to conversations with your child.
- Get others' opinions of the activity in question and then trust your own intuition.

- Realize that such experimentation is normal.
- Communicate to determine the underlying purposes of the behavior. Make it your goal to have your kid feel all right about herself without make-up or a ring through her belly button.
- Allow experimentation, but set boundaries. Denny, for example, eventually decided Rebecca could use make-up at home but not elsewhere. With more permanent adornments, such as tattoos and eyebrow pierces, set a time in the future when you will consider the issue again. With any luck, whatever it is will be passé and forgotten by then, but if not, you must seriously deal with the question.
- Help your child undertake the activity appropriately. Show her how to use make-up, for example. If this is beyond a father's expertise, treat her to professional advice or ask a woman friend to help.

  Using a third party makes it easier for your child to buy into limitations she might not accept from you alone. Your telling her she looks like a clown in all that make-up won't go down nearly as well as an "expert" suggesting a subtler touch. (Be sure to communicate your goals and concerns to your helper privately, *before* she works with your kid.)

Talking about Reproduction and Sexuality with Your Child

Some parents don't know what to say about sex and reproduction—so they say nothing. You must overcome any reluctance to broach these subjects so your kids will have both information and healthy attitudes.

"It's Time for Us to Have a Little Talk"

> America surpasses all other western developed nations in teen pregnancy, abortion, and birth.[4]

In the Leave-It-To-Beaver days, parents had one awkward sit-down talk with their maturing children and told them about the birds and bees. Sometimes they never got around to the men-and-women aspects, but never mind. They'd done their duty, and thank God it was over.

In truth, however, one explanation doesn't suffice. You don't have just one birds-and-bees talk, but many, each building on the others as your growing child integrates the information in new ways. Expect him to ask the same question at different ages. Consider such repetition as a sign of success—he feels free to communicate and has normal curiosity.

Rather than doing what was done unto you, talk about sex in the way you *wish* you'd heard it. Stay relaxed. Respond to questions with an initial comment that welcomes inquiry: "I'm glad you asked about that." Be affectionate and relaxed. Then answer *all* questions—truthfully.

Young Children

As soon as your child shows an interest and can understand the subject, start communicating. This usually happens in early preschool, at which point *what* you say is less important than *how* you say it. Your kid will remember your attitude but not your facts. Take advantage of young children's eagerness to please and receptivity to begin passing along your views.

> In the United States, there are more than 1,000,000 adolescent pregnancies every year. Of these, 500,000 give birth. An increasing number of these choose to keep their babies. The other 500,000 abort or miscarry.[5]

- Give very young children simple, limited information. Take your cues from his questions and don't give him more than he requests. Make certain about what he's really asking before diving into a long explanation. If you aren't sure of his intent, ask, "What makes you ask?" or "Where did you hear that?" or "What did you hear?" His response gives you a context and an indication of what he wants to know. He may think about what you said and not ask more questions for months until he's fully absorbed what you told him.

  If you do go overboard with explanation, don't worry about it. What your kid doesn't understand just glides by. He concentrates on what he needs and asks for more later.

  Just a label often suffices for a young child: "It's a condom," might be just enough. If he wants more, "Sometimes grown-up men use them." Little kids have no need for information about

AIDS unless it affects them directly. Until age five or so, if they ask, tell them it's a serious disease they aren't likely to get. If you introduce sexuality early as a healthy, important part of life, your child won't panic later when he learns about HIV and other unhealthy aspects of sex.

- Experiences you have together often generate questions. Perhaps you see a pregnant woman in the grocery store. Maybe the goat at the petting zoo bulges at the sides or the cat next door produces a litter. Capitalize on the opportunity to impart truthful information that you can build on later without contradicting yourself: "Babies grow in a special place in the mommy called a uterus."
- Find out if you've answered satisfactorily: "Does that explain it for you?" If he says no, ask what he doesn't understand, and go from there.
- Correct your child's misconceptions positively. Never ridicule his belief, for example, that the daddy gives the mommy a seed to swallow to make a baby grow inside.
- When you don't know an answer, say so and tell him you'll try to find out. "I'll get the answer because I do want to talk with you about it." Be sure to follow through. Perhaps you can look it up in a book together.
- Kids of any age may be too confused, afraid, or embarrassed to ask questions. Casually raise the subject when opportunity arises—with the pregnant goat, for example. If your child doesn't take up the subject just then, he at least gets the message he can talk about it with you later. Keep your kid's style and personality in mind. A failure to verbalize may be nothing more than a natural tendency to keep his feelings to himself. Perhaps art or fantasy play can draw him out.

Menstruation

Given the increasingly younger ages at which girls start having periods, you should explain this part of reproduction early.

- Tell boys about it, too, in a matter-of-fact manner so they don't tease and invade the girls' privacy in a macho attempt to learn exactly what it is.
- Maintain a positive attitude. Even if you have difficult periods, your daughter won't necessarily have the same experience. Tell her about cramps, backache, and the irritability and bloating of PMS—

without any drama. She needs to know what might occur physically, but don't set her up for years of dread and anxiety. Emphasize that each person and each period are different.

- Relate menstruation to reproduction, explaining how and why it stops during pregnancy. Make sure your boys and girls know that, although rare, a female can become pregnant during her period.
- Show both boys and girls the sanitary supplies and explain how women use them. Then set up a supply for the time your girl needs them. Ask her to tell you when she starts.

Unexpected Questions

If a question catches you completely off-guard:

- Stay calm and matter-of-fact.
- Be positive. Even if you hate dealing with your period, add an upbeat spin when your son asks, "What's a Tampax?" Explain about the "wonderful change that happens in girls' bodies every month to prepare them for having families . . ."
- Answer every question, or your child will assume the worst. Answer even if the question seems intended to shock you. Don't put him off by saying, "I'll tell you when you're older." State the facts as accurately as you can at the moment. Responding builds his self-esteem. Follow up later if you think of more to say or a better way of putting it.
- If your kid asks embarrassing questions in public—"Mommy, why is that lady's tummy so fat?"—don't stumble around for an answer then and there. Instead, say, "That's a good question, and we can talk about it when we get home." Make sure you do. If you shush him and then forget to answer later, he remembers and thinks there's something wrong with the question or with him for bringing it up. (This applies to any embarrassing question, not just sexual ones.)

> Every 32 seconds a fifteen-to-nineteen-year-old woman becomes pregnant.[6]

Older Children

An elementary school kid needs more information. Again, use his questions as guideposts to decide how much detail to provide. The more trust and values you build in now, the easier your work will be as your child faces later pressure for sexual activity.

- Continue your willingness to talk. Build on prior explanations, elaborating as necessary. Your school-age child should know that a virus causes AIDS, for example, but that, unlike colds, he won't get it from casual contact. (See the AIDS discussion in Chapter 17 for more facts.) If he asks more detailed questions, explain that sex or illegal drug use transmits AIDS, but people can prevent it. Assure him that neither you nor he is likely to get the disease.

> By age 18, one in four teen girls will have been pregnant at least once.[7]

- If you haven't discussed sex with your kid by the time he's nine or ten, he probably won't ask, and your job becomes harder. The burden is now on you to broach the subject. One way to talk about sexuality without being threateningly direct is to discuss it in the context of a movie, music video, or other "impersonal" context.
- As your kids grow, expand your focus. A middle-school child needs more explicit information about sex and AIDS and how to prevent it.
- By the teens, children have the biology down and need guidance on behavior. Abstinence would be great, but there are reality and Raging Hormones to consider. Unlike teens' bodies, their emotions and minds are far from mature. They still lack complete impulse control and the ability to think reasonably and project future consequences, especially when hormones tug so forcefully in the other direction.

    Puberty occurs these days sometime between the ages of nine and eighteen. Maturation occurs earlier and earlier, which some people attribute to the growth hormones added to milk and beef. Whatever the cause, some girls today start menstruating at age nine—meaning they can also become pregnant then! In past generations, sexual maturity occurred much closer to the customary age of marriage and childbearing. "Waiting until marriage" was more realistic for a girl who experienced menarche at sixteen and expected to marry at eighteen than for one who starts menstruating at eleven and delays marriage until her twenties or early thirties. The latter leaves a decade or more of unmarried sexual maturity. No matter how desirable abstinence may be, you have to question its probability over such a span.

You can't control, so communicate. Whatever personal, moral position you convey, your teen will take it more seriously if he respects and trusts you and feels free to talk.

The ultimate message to teens is "not now." You aren't saying "never." Unlike with drugs, zero tolerance for premarital sex is probably an unattainable goal. I'd rather have my kid knowledgeable and prepared when he becomes sexually active. I just want him to make a mature, conscious decision based on more than pure animal urge.

Obscenity

A kid may use obscene words to find out what they mean or to shock adults. Don't overreact. Repeat the word to show your lack of shock. Big deal.

Ask your child to tell you what he thinks the word means. Listen. If he's incorrect, define it for him. Tell him how you feel about the way he used it. Explain that some people take offense at such language or that it hurts their feelings. This conveys your values.

What's Love Got to Do with It?

Sex with love means more than physical pleasure or being "cool." Don't get so mired in the mechanical details that you forget the part about a couple's love and mutual commitment.

Separate Sex from Violence

Point out for your child—because no one else will—that sex and violence have absolutely nothing to do with one another. Look around at pop culture, however, and see just how frequently the two are linked. Without even realizing it, kids get the impression they go together, when they really flow from opposite ends of the human caring spectrum.

> Every 64 seconds an infant is born to a teenage mother.[8]

Link Sex and Consequences

Similarly, sex in the media seems to have no consequences at all. In the movies, no one uses protection. People don't think about AIDS unless the plot demands it, and even then the deaths are not long and excruciating. No one commits suicide as the result of pregnancy. Sometimes soap opera sex brings consequences, but they're glamorous and exciting, not realistic.

Rather than just condemning movies as "terrible," talk about real-world results of unconsidered sexuality.

Talk about "Bad Touching"

Tell your kid that if someone touches him in a way he doesn't like, he should tell you, no matter who it is. Once or twice a year ask matter-of-factly if anyone has touched him when he didn't want. Raising the subject like this assures him he can talk if something untoward happens. (For further discussion, see Chapter 10.)

You and Your Child of the Opposite Gender

Does the prospect of talking birds-and-bees to a child of the opposite sex make you squirm? Don't bring in another adult of the same sex, even a very close one, to act as your surrogate, as this renders the topic somehow shameful. Admit your discomfort but forge ahead. Your open channel of communication will get you through it.

> Unwed American girls under 15 are five times more likely to give birth than their counterparts in any other developed country.[9]

- Having an opposite-gender child does present challenges, however. Sexual identity results from interactions and bonding with appropriate role models. While males and females are equal, they aren't completely alike. At some level they don't understand how the other thinks, feels, or *is* in the world. Being one sex, they can't offer a model for the other. A time arrives, probably at around age eight or nine, when your son (or daughter) wants to be only with members of his own gender. He's ready for and needs some real male (or female) input.
- If your former spouse participates in parenting, your kid can take his role model from there—not that you'd be happy to have your child turn out like *that.* Try to see that other adults of his sex enter his life in a way that allows him to form bonds. Single parents with no ex in the picture, like me, must do the same. It's not easy. In

primitive villages, other men and women automatically continue fathering and mothering if a parent dies or disappears. In modern America, that won't happen. In Africa, they say, "It takes a village to raise a child." In our country, you have to recruit a "team" of parents for your child to fulfill what's missing. You have to *make* a village.

- Be creative and proactive in searching out same-sex role models. Look for relationships with some built-in longevity. When given a choice between male and female in any circumstance affecting your kid, opt for his same gender, all else being equal. Hire a male math tutor or teenager to play ball regularly with your boy. Male high-school kids baby-sit these days. If you're a man, choose the female piano teacher for your girl. Perhaps one of your female friends will agree to do "girl things" with her once a month. Dads often spend time with their sons on the weekends; see if your kid can join them. Consider organizations like Big Brothers and Big Sisters, although waiting lists are notoriously long. Constantly be on the lookout for a way to work good, same-sex models into your child's life.
- Sexual feelings for one's own child are common. Don't berate yourself or doubt your fitness for parenthood if you discover them. These feelings hit different people at different times. Fathers often feel them for pubescent daughters and pull away emotionally in horror, leaving the girls hurt and confused about what they've done to merit this withdrawal. Some mothers feel sexual stirrings while nursing or cuddling sons. Whenever the feelings arise, give yourself a break. They're normal. There's only one rule: Don't act on them.

> Each year 3,000,000 adolescents contract a sexually transmitted disease, including HIV.[10]

- Expect to feel separation anxiety as your child grows and spends time with peers instead of you. If he and you are of opposite gender, you feel jealous when he starts dating. Why does he need someone else when he has you, who have given him everything? These feelings, too, are normal. Focus on the fact that your job as parent is getting him to the point where he can leave you. Not that he'll ever really leave. You'll always be his parent. You both will move to a new rewarding stage of family life. A therapist can help you sort out these feelings.

Making Responsible Choices about Sex

If anything is certain in this world, it's that you won't be there when your child experiences opportunities for sexuality. Therefore, you have to exert your influence in advance by teaching him to make his own responsible choices about his body.

The Child Has Ultimate Control Over His Body

Responsible sexual behavior begins with a child believing he ultimately controls his body, knowing he has the last word on who touches him and when. Explain that he has the right to say no to any touch he doesn't like. Urge him to trust his instincts and not to let anyone force him into doing anything that makes him uncomfortable. To accomplish all this, your child needs healthy self-esteem (see Chapters 9 and 10).

> AIDS is now the fourth-leading killer of American women ages twenty-five to forty-four.[11]

- Allow him to control what his body experiences, even if you don't understand his preferences. Massage is nirvana to me, but Christopher absolutely *hates* it. At first I made the mistake of trying to convince him he should love it. Fortunately, he's an obstinate little guy. I finally got it. He doesn't want his back rubbed.

  Start this message early. If your kid says no tickling, stop immediately. An indiscriminately affectionate child does need to understand that we hug only people we like, not everyone, but conversely, don't force a reticent child to hug anyone, even Grandma or his best friend. Christopher hates hugs from anyone but me. He says they're all "too hot." I don't understand, but I respect his right to decide who touches him and how.

- Model this principle for your child if the opportunity arises. If someone touches you inappropriately in his sight, say so firmly and move away. (For more discussion see Chapter 10.)
- Everyone knows to teach girls to say no, but parents of boys also bear a responsibility. Boys need to realize that sexual excitement does not equal love. Let them hear from you emphatically that no means no and that pressuring or tricking girls into intercourse is irresponsible and immature. Pregnancy isn't just a girls' problem, nor is HIV.

Choosing Sexuality

No dummies, kids eventually realize that having control over their bodies means they *can* say yes as well as no. How can you stop them from choosing to become sexually active in their teens and preteen years? Truthfully, you can't, aside from putting them under twenty-four hour surveillance—and even that might not work. Nevertheless, you can *influence* your child to make the right choices:

> Between 1986 and 1992, when the incidence of HIV infection leveled off among older Americans, people aged eighteen-to-twenty-five experienced a rapid rise in HIV infections.[12]

- Agree with your teen that sex *is* a choice. Then turn the tables again—he can say yes, but that doesn't mean he *should.* Talk about peer pressure (see Chapter 10). Emphasize that, contrary to rumor, "everybody" isn't having sex. Some, especially boys, exaggerate or even lie to impress others, often because *they* feel insecure. Encourage your kid to explore friendships with people who are not sexually active.
- Your ultimate weapons against premature sexuality are his self-esteem (see Chapter 9) and the trusting relationship you've built through the years. He'll listen to you and consider your point of view because you've always been straight with him. State your opinion firmly and calmly and give reasons. Emphasize self-respect, a value you've pushed all his life. It involves avoiding actions he won't feel right about the next day.
- Keep communicating. Taking the discussion from abstract to painfully particular shouldn't change your mutual openness. If any-

thing, the need for discussion increases when your child becomes sexually mature.

- Emphasize the importance of not making irreversible choices. One night of passion permanently alters the course of many lives, usually for the worse, through pregnancy, AIDS, and other diseases.

  Talk knowledgeably about AIDS in particular (see Chapter 17). Cloaked in feelings of immortality, youngsters simply don't believe they're vulnerable. You probably felt the same way yourself. Inform your child that AIDS knows no boundaries of class, race, age, or sexual orientation. It's not who you *are* but what you *do!* There *are* teens with AIDS, and the numbers keep growing.

  Even without AIDS, sexually transmitted diseases like Chlamydia pose threats of severe illness and reproductive dysfunction.
- Let kids know that girls *can* become pregnant or get HIV "the first time" or during their periods.
- Teach safe sex. You hope your child will abstain, but if not, give him the means to stay safe. Giving kids knowledge doesn't give them permission to have sex. Ignorance doesn't guarantee abstinence. Even if I believed this logic, I wouldn't bet my son's life on it.

> For a complete list of the safest condoms, send $2 and a self-addressed, stamped envelope to Mariposa Foundation, 3123 Schweitzer Drive, Topanga, CA 90290.

- Teach birth control and safe sex to children of both genders before it becomes a relevant issue. Remind them that the pill, diaphragm, and other birth control methods don't protect against HIV.

  Don't just *talk* about condoms, either. Show children of both genders how they work and emphasize that they only protect if used correctly *every time* (see Chapter 17). Provide a supply, together with a spermicide containing nonoxynol-9.

Your boy needs a dress (undress?) rehearsal. If he can easily manipulate a condom, at least he won't toss it aside in frustration when he needs it most. Your girl can practice on her vegetable of choice. When the time comes, she'll have her own condom available if her partner "forgets" his.

- Talk with your kid about the irony of couples who link their bodies in the most intimate ways but can't talk about sex. Ideally, every couple discusses whether and when to have intercourse and how to protect themselves. Communicating fears and doubts brings people closer together.
- Be a good role model. Chapter 17 discusses your sexuality as a single parent, and your status does not condemn you to celibacy. Still, you have to keep in mind that actions speak louder than words. As a mature, experienced person, you can distinguish your respectful relationship with a potential mate from teenage sexual experimentation. But certainly, a lover-of-the-week shouldn't parade through your bedroom. Talk about the differences with your kids.

> CDC National HIV/AIDS Hotline, 800-342-AIDS (2437) available 24 hours a day.

Homosexuality

Questions about same-sex lovers may not arise until later years.

- Whenever they do, however, follow the same policy of age-appropriate honesty and matter-of-factness. "Some people fall in love with a person of their own gender and want to be a family together." Later, you can expand that to say these same-sex people have sexual relations, and you can discuss various theories about the source of homosexuality.
- Ask whether your kid fears or suspects he may be gay. Tell him that most people wonder about their sexual orientation at some time or other. He may or may not be gay, but if he is, you will still love and accept him.
- About thirty percent of teens who commit suicide are homosexual (see Chapter 7). Self-hatred, which society and parents often engender, may be a contributing cause. Accept your teen as he is, including his sexual orientation.

Pregnancy

If your daughter turns up pregnant or your son contributed the sperm to a pregnancy, you already know what the choices are. While the decision isn't yours, offer advice and help.

Try to stay calm. Show that you love your child despite the situation. He's already scared and upset. You all have to realize that what's happened has happened. You can't change it. Go forward from there.

Bringing the topics of sex and reproduction into the light of day removes the awkward clumsiness most of us inherited from our parents. Often inaccurate and incomplete, the explanations we received left us ignorant and ashamed of our bodies. I wish precisely the opposite for our children.

BOOKS FOR YOUNG KIDS

How Babies and Family Are Made: There Is More Than One Way, Patricia Schaffer (Palo Alto, CA: Tabor Sarah Books, 1988).

Where Do Babies Come From? Margaret Sheffield, et al. (New York: Knopf, 1973).

BOOKS FOR PRETEENS/TEENS

Changing Bodies, Changing Lives: A Book for Teens on Sex and Relationships, Ruth Bell (New York: Random House, 1988).

*What's Happening to Me?: (*a guide to puberty,*)* Peter Mayle (New York: Carol Publishing Group, 1975) (ages 9 to 12).

Chapter 9

Long-Range Parenting: Engendering Moral Values, Self-Esteem, Self-Reliance, and Responsibility

To give the world an independent, capable, compassionate, happy adult, keep long-range parenting in mind even when handling short-term child-rearing issues. Help your kid develop moral values, self-reliance, assertiveness, responsibility, and self-esteem.

You can't wait until your child's eighteenth birthday and mail him these important gifts, no assembly required. Instead, you must hand him a small piece every day from the beginning. Everything you do now should contribute to your kid's ability to function as a grown-up. The duty of instilling society's next generation with values falls on parents' shoulders. What a fearsome challenge for a single parent!

Building Moral Values

Kids don't pop from the womb knowing right from wrong. They need instruction. Some experts believe that youngsters who commit increasingly cold, heartless, juvenile crimes don't really understand that their actions are immoral.

Using "I messages" gives kids your strong feelings about what they do. They need to understand that their actions affect you and others. Expect a lot from your children in all areas, not just in academics. Teach and model positive social attitudes: courtesy, good humor, consideration, willingness to negotiate and compromise, friendliness, and high moral and ethical standards.

How Morals Develop

First you and then others teach your child by expressing pleasure or displeasure at his actions. How you react to "bad" behavior governs his moral development. Withdrawing affection when he makes mistakes or breaks rules leads him to reduce people and experiences to black-and-white, all-good or all-bad. If there is no way to undo the "harm" of a mistake, he lies about committing it, inflicts guilty self-punishment, or turns that guilt outward into anger.

Using "logical consequences," on the other hand, leads him to form less rigid perceptions about the world. This framework for discipline accepts *him* while disapproving his *behavior* (see Chapter 5). Consistent limits give your child an inner order. Allowing him to make reparations through a logical consequence encourages him to admit mistakes and seek ways of making up for them.

Tailor your lessons about values to your child's developmental stage by presenting information in ways he is capable of understanding.

> "Every new adjustment is a crisis in self-esteem."
> ERIC HOFFER (1902–1983)

- Although a preschooler has no moral sense, he understands that rules govern the world. He knows not to hit because that's the rule, not because it hurts Sammy.
- Rule infractions and "unfairness" begin to bother a child as he ages. At around six or seven (the traditional "age of reason"), a child finally understands that moral values exist and breaking them is wrong. He knows he shouldn't hit because it's not right to hurt others. The beginnings of a conscience produce internal signals when he acts inconsistently with what he knows is "right."
- After age seven, your child absorbs and internalizes your values as he tries to please and emulate you. Using those values, he structures

the world's complexity. He begins to act according to his own signals rather than adhering blindly to rules.

- By the preteens, kids have a good sense of right and wrong and a certain amount of impulse control.

Help Your Child Delay Gratification

Teaching kids to delay some gratification strengthens their ability to behave appropriately despite competing urges. You must find a comfortable place on the spectrum between "spoiling" your child and denying him entitlements. Where does a $200 pair of sneakers lie, for example, if he insists he needs them in order to fit in? What about a Christmas ski trip to the Alps with his rich friends? Teach kids to accept that they don't "need" everything they want, and they're not entitled just because you could afford to buy it.

- Negotiate. Find a way to give that involves some sacrifice by him. You chip in the amount for ordinary shoes, for example, and he adds his own money for the special ones. Or he gets one pair instead of the two you would normally buy.
- Watch for opportunities to encourage his ability to await satisfaction. As you negotiate with him, make timing a factor. You'll take him to the movie tonight, but if he waits until Friday, you'll rent two films and throw in popcorn and soda.
- Teach him about money, saving, and budgeting (see Chapter 16).
- Limit television. TV, with its sixty-minute solutions, leads kids to believe all problems resolve (or should resolve) in an hour. Hard work and discipline mean nothing, as everything comes easily to TV characters. Television paints an unrealistic picture of the world. Nevertheless, the average child watches three to five hours a day! The American Academy of Pediatrics recommends a maximum of one or two.

  Get rid of the TV if you dare. Otherwise, limit the time and the subject matter (and set similar boundaries for yourself as role model). Select programs that model positive behavior by caring, considerate people.

> In the summer of 1994, American men watched an average of 3.75 hours of television a day; women watched nearly 4.5 hours. Total daily TV use in the average home was almost 7 hours.[1]

> "Television: Chewing gum for the eyes."
> JOHN MASON BROWN
> (1900–1969)

Use the TV schedule to plan viewing. Involve your child in the program selection. Turn off the tube when the chosen show ends. Forbid channel surfing to find more instant gratification. All too often one show leads to another—TV's addictive quality rivals that of chocolate and paralyzes the thumb's ability to operate the off button on the remote control.

- Limit video games. Their instant gratification diminishes kids' ability to stick with activities, like writing or solving complex math problems, which require long-term efforts.

Model Moral Values for Your Child

Be scrupulously honest—no lying about your child's age to get the kiddy rate. No gossip. Speak the same way about people whether they're present or not. Return the extra change if a cashier gives too much. No sneaking freebies from the bulk bins at the grocery. Observing these "small" points of honor imparts a message far more effectively than any number of lectures to your kid.

Reject Violence As a Value

Again, limit television. You've heard the spiel hundreds of times. Violent TV programs lead to aggressive behavior. Heinous acts have few consequences. Your child numbs to television violence with repeated exposure. He begins to regard aggression as an acceptable means of conflict resolution.

Despite virtually universal agreement about its effects, many parents resort to TV as a baby-sitter or teen-tender. Let's face it, the tube gives you breathing room, some time to yourself, and respite from squabbling. Still, the price is too high unless you limit and monitor viewing.

Watch some programs you don't like with the kids and talk about what you find offensive. Discuss real-life problem solving versus television methods. Emphasize that TV-land isn't real life. Tell young children that the fights are choreographed so no one gets hurt. Make it your mission to teach kids to evaluate and think critically about what they see instead of just soaking it up.

Stand by your principles. Almost every parent I spoke with during the Power Rangers craze agreed that the program conveyed unhealthy messages to preschoolers. Yet hundreds of tots showed up on Halloween as their favorite Power Ranger. Obviously, these children were allowed to watch the show, which, in my view, taught them that mere lip service to moral values is enough.

Limit video games, too. How many hours a week do you want your children ripping out opponents' still-beating hearts, tearing skulls off enemies' bodies, or annihilating realistic-looking babies into bloody pools of quivering pulp? If your answer is "none," be prepared to do battle against intense peer pressure and enticing consumer advertising for video games.

Although manufacturers claim these games are for adults, the primary audience is seven- to fourteen-year-old boys. If you haven't experienced video games since "Pong" or "Pac Man" or even "Super Mario Bros.," you will be surprised at how grisly the current crop is.

While game companies insist there are no adverse effects, studies raise concerns about children's interactive play with ever-increasingly realistic violence. Children who play video games often become frustrated, angry, anxious, and aggressive. Video games are also unremittingly sexist. They ignore or stereotype females at best, make them passive victims of male abuse at worst.

Games are, admittedly, convenient baby-sitters. Left alone, kids play for hours. Even families who strictly limit television often have no rules about video-game play. Busy parents may be unaware of the content. They may assume games are better than TV because they develop hand-eye coordination and introduce children to technology. The latter claim is specious—a better choice is an entry-level computer with a keyboard and varied software.

Video games do promote hand-eye coordination, but other, more traditional activities such as ball playing, drawing, and fort-building serve as well—and they don't come in a violent wrapper.

You may decide to steer clear of games altogether, a formidable task that risks rendering your kids geeks in a world in which "everyone else" has the latest in carnage and slaughter. Still, if every parent would "just say no," manufacturers' incentives to produce more gore would diminish. Video games won't realize their educational potential as long as blood and guts score the largest profits.

If you don't have the fortitude to forbid the games entirely, at least aim for moderation to prevent your kid from being a video zombie. Allow him a limited time of play on weekends and even less, say, half an hour, on school days. Or, better yet, encourage self-reliance by giving a weekly time allotment to be used whenever he wants.

Educate yourself and select acceptable games. The worst are violent, sexist, or just plain boring. The manufacturers' voluntary rating system, in effect as of November 1994, isn't necessarily a reliable guide for *your* child.

Introduce Your Kids to Altruism

Begin at an early age to make charity a part of life by:

- Letting your children see your charitable acts, even if you only write a small check now and again.
- Talking about causes that you hold dear. Explain their importance. If you're an environmentalist, for example, mention why we pick up litter or point out how recycling differs from dumping trash in landfills.
- Devising charitable family activities. Participate in a walk-a-thon. Take a meal to a disabled person. Collect pennies in the neighborhood to donate to a worthy cause. Trick-or-treat for UNICEF.

Altruistic Organizations

- UNICEF: Free fund-raising guide and collection cartons (minimum 25 cartons). Community Programs Dept., U.S. Committee for UNICEF, 333 E. 38th St., New York, NY 10016; 800-252-KIDS (5437); 212-922-2643.
- National Helpers Network: Offers names of local organizations in your area of interest. 245 5th Ave., Ste. 17095, New York, NY 10016-8720; 212-6799-2482.
- National Arbor Day Foundation: Free seedlings for new trees with membership, $10. 100 Arbor Ave, Nebraska City, NE 68410; 402-474-5655.
- Rainforest Action Network (RAN): Helps kids raise money to protect rain forests; 800-989-RAIN (7246).
- Kids for a Clean Environment (Kids FACE): Ideas for environmental projects for children. POB 158254, Nashville, TN 37215; 800-952-FACE (3223).

Have "light-meal" days, and send the grocery money not spent to Oxfam for distant starving people. Donate usable toys and clothes to a shelter or thrift organization. Volunteer at a project with "Christmas in April," which repairs and refurbishes low-income homes one Saturday a year. Younger children don't understand altruism, but they enjoy helping, and something sinks in.

- Encourage your child to set aside a small portion of his weekly allowance for charity. The first nickel of every dollar Christopher gets goes into his pink piggy bank for altruistic purposes. At first he asked me every time we budgeted his allowance, "What's charity again?" One of my explanations involved poor people who don't have as much as we do, like computers, cars, or even homes. A few weeks later as we drove home, he spied a well-dressed woman standing in the street. "Is she poor?" he asked. Puzzled, I wondered why he would think so. "Because she doesn't have a car," he answered. The message isn't clear yet, obviously, but it's coming into focus like a developing photograph.

Creating Self-Esteem

Nothing influences learning, growth, and development more than a child's view of himself. He arrives at this self-appraisal primarily through his treatment by family and teachers. If they value him just as he is, without always trying to change him, he learns to value himself.

Early childhood is crucial. During the first five years of your child's life, you "program" whether his "hard drive" will view the world as safe, people as trustworthy, and himself as valuable.

Self-Esteem Is Self-Acceptance

Self-esteem is, simply, self-acceptance based on a child's *accurate* perception of himself—his mind, body, spirit, and creativity. He doesn't automatically regard himself as either the best or the worst and can set realistic expectations. A confident self-image allows a child to take risks and overcome the fear of making mistakes.

A child with self-esteem accepts who he *is,* what he *does,* and how he *looks.* Without doing anything to "earn" love, he knows he is lovable. Others' acceptance and affection don't depend on his having particular emotions or acting a certain way. He feels capable and confident about what he does and comfortable about how he looks.

Because he recognizes his differences and accepts them as good, he trusts his own perceptions, inner voice, judgment, and intuition. He expresses feelings without judging them "right" or "wrong." They're just "his."

Self-acceptance doesn't mean giving up on improvements. It's simply accepting what is, for now. This is who he is, where he lives, how he looks, what he can do. He can change any aspect, but until he does, it's all okay.

Low Self-Esteem

> "Self-confidence is the first requisite to great undertakings."
> SAMUEL JOHNSON (1709–1784)

If a child does not find acceptance at home, he reaches out for it elsewhere, often in unsavory places and in self-destructive ways. Poor self-esteem underlies substance abuse, violence and crime, child abuse, premature sexuality, and poor school performance. Signs of low self-esteem include:

- Perfectionism
- Unwillingness or fear of trying new activities
- Derogatory remarks about himself
- Inability to state preferences, perceptions, or feelings
- Preoccupation (and unhappiness) with looks
- Constant desire to please others
- Overachievement
- Acting out, drug and alcohol abuse, sexual promiscuity
- Self-mutilation
- Eating disorders

Improve Your Own Self-Esteem

Divorce commonly flattens self-esteem, as do difficult times before and after. So do death of a spouse, childhood traumas, and many other life experiences. Most of us learned young that accepting a compliment and feeling good about ourselves are "selfish, self-centered, and arrogant." But you can't raise a kid with self-esteem if you lack it yourself. You quash his positive feelings, and he learns to feel bad about himself.

Negative self-images don't undo easily, which is why being the first to break the generational chain takes such courage. Take on that burden yourself instead of passing it along to your child. The best contribution to his self-esteem is your own healthy self-acceptance.

Therapy is an invaluable tool for this task. Aside from that, to work on your self-esteem:

- Agree when you get a compliment! If you respond, "This old rag?" instead of "I know, I loved this dress immediately," you denigrate not only your own taste, but that of the person who paid the compliment! If you can't manage to agree out loud, think it silently and say, "Thank you," without apology.

  Compliments about you, personally, are even harder to accept than those about something you bought. Resist the urge to discount or argue. If someone says you're generous, don't deny it. Acknowledge the compliment positively. "Thank you. I'm glad I can do something for others."
- Practice "positive self-talk." Most negative self-views don't represent the real you and are learned habits. When you show positive feelings about yourself to others who lack self-esteem, they shoot you down to reduce you to their level. If they do this often enough, you internalize the negative feelings and believe them about yourself, particularly if the others are important figures in your life—like parents. Later, when other people put you down, your internal voice agrees. You buy into the negative without hesitation because it's what you've told yourself for years.

  Positive self-talk plants the possibility of another truth. Commit to making five positive statements about yourself a day. You don't have to believe them one hundred percent, but say them anyway. If you can't do even that, at least become aware of your inner voice whispering negatives. Someday you'll be able to talk back to it.
- Make a list of everything you accomplished in the last year. Break it into meaningful detail. Finalized divorce, worked out custody, got new job, checked out schools for kids, started an IRA. You did a lot! Congratulations!
- Stand naked in front of a full-length mirror and say, "This is my body. I accept it just as it is. I may choose to get it in better shape later, but for right now, it's okay."

Help Your Child Achieve Self-Esteem

As a parent, you're the mirror for your child. He takes his self-concept from the way he thinks you see him. Accepting your child lets him accept himself. You are a "god" to him, and he *believes* what you tell him about himself. Your view of him forms part of his self-image. In a very real sense, how you view him is what he becomes.

- You have to know him in order to accept him. Look into his soul to see who he really is; then foster his growth in that direction. You may hate computers and love music, and yet you may spawn a programming whiz rather than a piano player. So be it. In the single-parent support group, Liz Hannigan speaks of a child as an anonymous seed entrusted to you for care. When it sprouts, see what you have. If it's a redwood tree, don't force it to become a petunia. With the right care, it will grow into a magnificent redwood, but no matter what you do, it will make a lousy petunia. Rather than urging your child to become something else, let him be every inch of who he is.
  - To see who your child is, separate from him, detach from your own desires and ambitions. Beware of trying to fulfill your own lost dreams through him. His own dreams are just fine.
  - Likewise, look out for family "traditions" that steer your kid in a direction that he doesn't really want to travel. He may play professional accordion despite his family's ten generations of doctors.
  - Spend time watching your child. Showing interest in his activities says that they—and he—are worthy. How does he play? What makes him passionate? How does he relate to others? What talents does he demonstrate? Conversely, where are his weaknesses?
  - Pay attention to developmental stages. Knowing he's normal for his age helps you accept him. He's *supposed* to act this way now.
- Every effective "choice" your kid makes, as described in Chapter 5, heightens self-esteem.
- A willingness to negotiate says his concerns are important. Teach him how to compromise, to give up this in order to get that (see Chapter 7). Maybe he could earn extra TV time during the summer by doing math problems or reading a book. (One teen earned one hundred extra hours, but she became so engrossed in the alternative activities that she never bothered to use them!)

> "Trust thyself: every heart vibrates to that iron string."
> RALPH WALDO EMERSON
> (1803–1882)

Everyone else's food at school looks better than Christopher's. He begged me to buy the same products for his lunch box, and I agreed, until I read the labels. Since nutrition and the environment concern me, I don't want to provide sugar, sugar, sugar, and a teaspoon of "juice" in a pound of wax packaging. Still, Christopher wanted these so badly and had asked so politely. We negotiated. He has one "juice" each week, and he chooses which day. In one simple interaction, he asserted what he wanted, learned my values, felt heard and respected, and began to make daily choices about what goes into his body.

- Point out that people vary in looks, dress, speech, and abilities. This teaches that there is more than one way to be and one way to do, and that they're all valuable.
- Value differences. Describe your child's characteristics. Talk about how he differs from others, and let him know you enjoy or at least accept his uniqueness. Emphasize that everyone in the family can be different and have divergent but equally valid thoughts, feelings, and preferences.
- Talk about how families differ, too. Some have mommies and daddies, some just mommies, some just daddies, some two mommies or daddies, some step-everythings, and some a slew of other relatives living with them. Your family may be different, but it's just fine. A family is people who live together and lovingly take care of each other, no matter what its form.

> "If a man does not keep pace with his companions, perhaps it is because he hears a different drummer. Let him step to the music which he hears, however measured or far away."
>
> Henry David Thoreau (1817–1862)

- A sense of community—belonging to a larger group—engenders self-esteem. Remind your kid that you are members of various circles and talk about what you both contribute to them.
- Don't interrupt your child when he's talking. Listen actively (see Chapter 5). If he wants to interrupt you in a conversation with someone else, teach him to say "excuse me" and await his turn. This demonstrates that everyone is important.
- Encourage him to consider others' interests, points of view, likes, and dislikes. This helps him develop friendships and a sense of himself as a caring person. Having friends means others find value in him, which makes him feel good about himself.

- Forbidding television when your child's friends visit your house emphasizes the value of personal interactions. Staring silently at a screen together promotes no social skills whatsoever. Model the appropriate behavior: turn the darned thing off when *you* have company. Leaving it on tells your guests that they don't rate very highly. Ask others to pull the plug when you visit them, or do it yourself. I won't put up with eyes wandering back to the car commercials when I'm talking with someone. I say politely that I have trouble following a conversation with the television in the background. No one has ever protested or refused to switch it off. TVs often stay on from sheer habit.
- Celebrate the positive aspects of your kid. Be the president of his fan club, regardless of bad behavior. A kid needs to feel lovable as a person even if you hate what he does.
- Keep your expectations age-appropriate so your kid can experience success over and over. Help him set realistic goals.
- Counsel him not to compare his insides with someone else's outsides. The other's exterior probably conceals internal conflicts equal to his—or worse.
- Permit him to explore his capabilities and limitations and make mistakes in the process. View mistakes as opportunities to learn, fears as chances to grow. Encourage him to take risks—physically safe ones, of course. Trying out for a play, signing up for the volleyball team, or running for student council all stretch him. Keep your expectations reasonable—trying out, as opposed to getting the lead part—so he has a chance of meeting them and feeling good about himself.
- Allow and help your child to look like his peers, no matter how ridiculous he seems to you. Don't denigrate his fashion sense. From his point of view, he knows what it takes; you're the fashion dinosaur. Let him feel good about how he wants to look. Parents of teens especially take note. Buy the "right" hair mousse or jeans (insofar as you can afford them) so he feels positive about his appearance. Draw the line on health and safety issues, and if you just can't tolerate the green hair, at least negotiate about it (see Chapter 7).
- Encourage your kid to participate in groups with positive values. Whether associated with school, church, or community, he'll spend his time in ways that make him feel good. Support your teen if he gets a job, especially one that teaches skills. (It will also cut down on the available exposure to peer pressure and temptations.) Encourage participation in sports and physical activities. Exercise

reduces stress and raises self-esteem as your kid sees himself improving with practice and meeting new challenges.

- Show affection and love just because you notice and love him, not as a reward for anything he's done. See Chapter 5 for suggestions on little ways to say "I love you."
- Help negate gender bias in the classroom (see Chapter 12). Largely because of gender bias, the percentage of girls who agree "I'm happy the way I am" drops from sixty percent in elementary school to twenty-nine percent in high school. Boys, in contrast, go from sixty-seven percent to forty-six percent.
- A child who blames himself for the divorce (or death of a parent) feels bad about himself. Repeatedly assure him that nothing he did contributed to the situation.
- Praise appropriately, not indiscriminately. Contrary to popular belief, continuous praise doesn't necessarily produce healthy self-esteem. Artificial, insincere compliments actually undermine self-acceptance because they either give a child a false, grandiose view of himself or destroy your credibility as a discerning judge. He'll discount your constant praise until he doesn't hear it at all. Healthy self-esteem comes from giving a child an accurate view of himself, letting him see where he shines and where he needs work.
  - –Praise in descriptive, not value-laden terms. Instead of "good," "wonderful," or other vague expressions, concentrate on concrete, detailed statements that demonstrate you really paid attention. "Your use of perspective really gives that drawing depth."
  - –Describe the facts of what your child has done: "You made spaghetti for dinner!" Single out improvements even when the result isn't perfect. You don't have to mention that every dish in the house lies dirty in the sink. Focus on his effort. "It must have taken you a long time to cook for all of us."
  - –Describe his actions with a concrete adjective: "How creative to use those beads in your sculpture." Coming up with a fresh adjective on the spot can be a challenge. I made myself a refrigerator list for quick inspiration (see box).
  - –Comment positively on how his actions make you feel. "Calling to say you'd be late put my mind at ease."

Help Your Child Avoid "Roles" or "Labels"

Avoid labeling your child, negatively or positively, and keep others from doing so. Labels discourage him psychologically from trying new experiences and identities. They limit imagination and potential.

Refrigerator list of descriptive praise to use instead of "good"

Cooperative	Neat	Compassionate
Persistent	Organized	Calm
Ambitious	Involved	Energetic
Interested	Friendly	Interesting
Fun-loving	Amusing	Mellow
Humorous	Creative	Inventive
Considerate	Thoughtful	Artistic
Helpful	Clean	Healthy
Sweet	Loving	Agile
Coordinated	Athletic	Affectionate
Practical	Mechanical	Honest
Open	Joyful	Courageous
Observant	Intelligent	Unselfish
Caring	Polite	Attentive
Happy	Cheerful	Smart
Took concentration	Showed long memory	Resourceful

Or, "That makes me feel . . ."

Loved	Respected	Cared for
Relieved	Calm	Happy
Comfortable	Funny	Joyous
Cheerful	Amused	Thankful
Proud	Heard	

Positive labels, like "smart" or "athletic" sound great, but they imply you might not love your kid if he isn't *always* smart. To avoid the risk of looking dumb, he restricts himself to activities he performs well. He lacks confidence that he *can* do anything else. Your bookworm may have the makings of a terrific basketball player, but he'll never find out if he won't join that pickup game on Saturday mornings.

To avoid assigning roles and to release your child from any he's already adopted:

- Be wary of unconsciously labeling him by saying he "always" or "never" does this or that. He'll soon adopt your expectations and prove you right.

- Describe instead of labeling. "Joey wrote a thoughtful theme on hoboes in America" instead of "He's such a good student."
- Resist making comparisons with other children, especially siblings.
- Talk to your kid in ways that give him permission to break out of his roles. Tell him, "I love you just as you are. And I see that you're capable of changing."
- Emphasize that you love him, not his accomplishments. Tell him, "I love you, just because you're you." or "Of all the kids in the world, I was so lucky to get you." I tell my son, "I love you just because you're Christopher."
- Model willingness to change. You don't have to do anything drastic, but accept the changes that come to you. Take some small control however you can. You can't become a professional tennis player, but you can improve your game.

> "The gods help him who helps himself."
> EURIPIDES
> (5TH CENTURY B.C.)

- When others label your child, rephrase the statement in a more acceptable way. Labeling me "shy" as a child created a self-fulfilling prophesy. I studiously avoid that word to describe Christopher, but unfortunately, other people blurt out, "Oh, he's shy, isn't he?" As his advocate, I undo this label by saying, "No, but he likes to observe what's going on before deciding whether to join in," or "He likes to warm up slowly to new situations." I also tell him later that no one is "shy," but everyone feels shy sometimes.

  When you're not feeling judgmental, it's fine to describe your child's behavior to him: "I've noticed you like to observe before you join a group." Perhaps add a contrary suggestion: "It's okay to be cautious, but maybe you could just say hi first and then watch."
- Let him see himself succeeding in many different realms. Put him in situations where he can see himself differently. Take your boy-crazy preteen backpacking in the wilderness. Provide ski lessons to your studious daughter. Teach your D-student to play the piano.

  Point out times when your child acts "out of character" to illustrate he's not just one way. He'll start to notice it himself. Christopher told a friend recently, "I take a long time to warm up sometimes, but my mind is giving my mouth the power to talk sooner."

Self-Esteem-Building Techniques for Under-Fives

The first five years of a child's life are paramount in developing self-esteem. These younger, less verbal children benefit from some of the methods listed previously and from other techniques aimed specifically at their age group. For example:

- Let your child do what he *can* do within the house, garden, workshop, or car—if you have time, of course. Let him unlock the doors, help measure the two-by-four, pour the juice, wash the tires, pull the weeds, and so on. Get him child-size tools if possible. The sense of accomplishment he feels at doing grown-up chores boosts self-esteem.
- Let his incomplete or inaccurate attempts stand without correction (at least within his sight). Your redoing the task tells him his work didn't measure up.
- Focus on how he feels so he can recognize his own inner states: sad, mad, glad, scared. Read books that illustrate feelings. Tell him to listen to his body: is it hungry? thirsty? tired? in need of the potty?
- Play with him. Having you enter *his* world underlines its importance. Get down on the floor with him. Let him choose the play and set the tone. Later introduce him to simple "grown-up" games he can master.
- Clear off space on a shelf, drawer, or box for him to keep his special things. Compliment what he chooses to place there.
- Tell him the story of his day as a bedtime story each night. Relate all the important occurrences and "firsts" he experienced. I always start the same way, "Once upon a time there was a little boy named Christopher, whose mommy loved him so much that one day . . ."

  Starring in a story thrills him. As a bonus for me, he often fills in gaps or adds commentary, which opens a window into his thought process and informs me indirectly of events I didn't witness.
- Let your child navigate when you drive to familiar places. Follow his directions for turns and stops. Find positive ways to correct his mistakes: "Could it be left here? Remember how we always go by that gas station?"
- Help him give gifts or do favors for others and receive their thanks. Talk later about how the others appreciated him.
- Have him look in the mirror and say specifically what he likes about himself—not just that he's "cute" or "handsome."

- Watch his videos with him. Give them your full attention, and talk later about the stories.

Encourage Creativity As a Value

Creativity comes naturally to young kids, but many of them lose it on the path to adulthood. Your response to your child's creative impulses tells him whether the world approves of trying new ways. If you don't respond positively, or at least with acceptance, he'll begin to quash them.

> "The childhood shows the man as morning shows the day."
> JOHN MILTON (1608–1674)

- Creative play begins when you pretend with your infant in his crib or changing table. "There's a little spider climbing up your arm." "Here comes a buzzy bee looking for a belly button." A toddler creates as he shapes his unique world. His "art" includes those wonderful mashed-potato sculptures.
- With language come opportunities for rhyming and making up sounds. Fantasies follow, sometimes with imaginary friends that allow kids to "try on" different personalities. Preschoolers often formulate entirely new worlds, departing from some aspect of reality. Christopher saw a movie in which illustrated doors on trees opened into various scenes. For months afterward, his "picture doors" became springboards for elaborate made-up stories about what happened when he stepped through them.

  Preschoolers also express emotions through imaginative play, letting Teddy and train engines assume personalities. Kids begin to understand jokes and the concept of the unexpected as humorous—mismatched clothes and straws up the nose—which requires creativity. Once, I asked Christopher to go put on his underwear, and he emerged from his room wearing it—on his head!

  Preserve the message that creative experimentation is okay—at least up to a point. We laughed at Christopher's underwear and then found a more appropriate place for it. Let him wear his shoes on the wrong feet or his shirt inside out if that's what he wants. Give him the message that being different is fine. Leave him free to try the unconventional and unexpected. Encourage imagination and inventiveness. Don't try to talk him out of fantasies. Allow him his own perspective on the world.

- At the same time, it's okay to limit creativity that breaks important household or social rules. After studying insects at school, Christopher came home and enthusiastically made my red couch into a "lady bug" with black marker spots! I appreciate his creativity, but I didn't applaud its application to the couch. Like all freedoms, creativity has an outer limit, and you teach him where it is.
- A kid loses his easy access to imaginative thinking as he approaches middle childhood. His maturing brain turns to logic, and the ready ability to make believe disappears. Still, creativity exists in his life. Play lets him experiment with emotions and impulses. He tries out different identities by imagining what he wants to be when he grows up. New activities lead him to new skills and interests.

Give positive reinforcement to painting, creative writing, dance, music, and so on, but realize that creativity is more than "the arts." Help your child engage his creative urges in everything he does at every age. Encourage him with activities like cooking, carpentry, computer programming, or science experiments. Follow his lead, and support him by participating and being creative yourself.

Undoing Your Ex's Negative Messages

As a single parent, you may have to deal with your ex's destructive messages to your child. Although you can't control your former spouse, you can help repair the damage.

> "The child is father of the man."
> WILLIAM WORDSWORTH (1770–1850)

- Listen attentively if your child relates negative statements he received from your ex: "Dad says I'm selfish." Don't minimize the effect or make excuses for your former spouse, such as, "He was probably just tired when he said that. He really loves you." Instead, validate your child's feelings: "That must have felt unfair."
- Point out times your child *hasn't* matched his other parent's negative description. "Remember how you gave some of your toys to the homeless shelter last Christmas?" Tell him his dad doesn't

know all the facts, and give your kid permission to judge for himself. Emphasize that you're glad he talked to you about this and make it clear that he can always check out his perceptions with you.
- If safe and appropriate, suggest your kid express his feelings directly to his other parent. Consider talking with your former spouse alone or with your child, depending on the circumstances, your kid's preference, and your relationship with your ex.

Hurtful Behavior by Others

Use the same approach if a teacher, peer, or other person hurts your child's feelings: listen, validate his feelings, and don't make excuses. Encourage him to tell the other how he felt, and offer to go with him. Emphasize that there's nothing wrong with *him.* The *other* person was rude and hurtful.

Apologize If You *Lose It*

You owe your kid the same respect and care you'd give a friend—or a stranger! Still, you'll lose it sometimes. When *you* hurt your child's self-esteem by, for example, yelling, impatiently taking over a job, labeling, or perhaps calling him a name, apologize as soon as you can. See Chapter 5 for more on apologies.

Self-Reliance, Assertiveness, and Responsibility

Single parents find letting go especially hard. You'll never be ready. It *hurts* to feel your kid moving into the world, leaving you behind alone. Acknowledge that pain, but at the same time, teach him to fly alone.

Self-Reliance

Consider it your job as a parent to wind your kid's rubber band up tightly as though he were a plastic toy and then set him marching across the floor. If you twist enough of the right stuff into his fiber, he should get to the other side of the room without wrecking anything important or bashing the walls. Don't feel guilty about letting your child fend for himself when he's capable of doing so. That's how he learns in the long run.

Your job as parent is to make yourself unnecessary! Set safe, age-appropriate parameters in which your child can practice making his own decisions. Allow more and more independence as he grows. Build self-reliance and responsibility so he will check in with himself to govern his behavior. If he only acts because you said to, he'll be lost when you're no longer around on a daily basis. Here are some practical steps for encouraging self-reliance:

- When something happens to your kid, first ask how he feels about it. Validate his emotions surrounding the event. "I know it's hard to ask for a date."
- Give your child a chance to correct his own errors and find out that mistakes are learning opportunities. Trust that he can find an answer. "That's a problem. What do you think you can do about it?" Let him decide how to remedy the difficulty, but be available for advice and action, *if requested*. Tell him you'll be happy to help if he needs you, but don't just jump in and give information, directions, or fix-its.

  Ask how he's going to solve recurring challenges, such as going to bed on time, remembering to take lunch in the mornings, avoiding excessive eating, getting to school on time, and so on. Guide him into finding solutions for himself.

> "Oft-times nothing profits more
> Than self-esteem, grounded on just and right
> Well manag'd."
> JOHN MILTON (1608–1674)

- Praise the effort and the process, whatever the result.
- Expect ups and downs in your kid's social life. Don't overreact or rush to fix things up. Sympathize, but wait to see what happens.
- Confirm the accuracy of what he sees, feels, smells, tastes, and needs so he can depend on his inner perceptions in running his life. Allow him to make choices based on feedback from his own body. Let him eat when he's hungry. If he wants to sleep until noon on Saturday, fine. When he cries over a skinned knee, agree, "That must have hurt," instead of insisting, "Come on, it's just a little scratch." Don't make him hug Grandma when he's not in the mood. When you're angry or upset, admit it.
- Validate his emotions so he relies on his internal perceptions to judge the world. When his feelings are hurt, don't try to take the pain away. If

he loses an election at school, recognize his disappointment rather than telling him, "Oh well, you've got too much to do anyway." How confusing and disorienting to hear he's just fine when he feels the sting of a skinned knee or hurt feelings. Too much of that, and he'll start believing he really doesn't hurt. He'll stop paying attention to his inner voice, making him more vulnerable to peer pressure and less able to recognize a dangerous situation.

> "Nothing will be given to you without the asking and nothing will be given to you until you are ready to receive it, and then at that moment the Heavens themselves will be opened and everything will be placed into your hands."
>
> SAINT GERMAIN

See Chapter 5 on accepting all emotions, including the negative ones.

- Again, limit TV. Aside from content, the "watching" itself supplants opportunities to develop other skills, such as critical thinking, articulate discussion, and imagination. A child watching TV does not actively engage any of his faculties for creating internal images, as he does when reading or hearing stories. To learn to use words for symbolic thought, memory, and higher mental processes, he needs the ability to create an internal world.
- If your child asks, "Why . . . ," don't rush into an explanation. Ask him, "Why do you think?" This forces him to explore his own thoughts, and it gives you a glimpse into his thought processes.

Assertiveness

As Liz and Cliff often say in my single-parents support group, "If you want to G-E-T, you have to A-S-K." Let your kid know that people don't read minds. They won't know what he wants unless he tells them. People grant the most outrageous requests—if asked.

Start the lesson early. Given Christopher's reticence with new people, I seek opportunities that encourage him to speak up for himself. At a garage sale, for example, he finds a toy he's "just got to have." I sometimes protest that I don't like it and won't buy it for him, but he can spend his allowance as he wishes. Therefore, if he wants the toy, he has to ask the price and bargain with the seller. Because he's little and cute, he gets positive feedback for speaking up. Friendly smiles and freebies often accompany the deal, and he always gets the toy at a price he can afford. He becomes a little bolder each time.

Many people think "assertive" means "aggressive." An assertive person stays calmly centered and focused on his goal. He asks for what he needs and persists through distractions and defensiveness. Aggressive people act from emotion. They make a lot of noise, but they often don't make it clear what they want. And they often don't get it.

Responsibility

As your kid grows, increased freedom brings more responsibility. Accepting responsibility means being proactive—taking actions, volunteering reparations for mistakes, and taking precautions against repetition. Model this behavior in your own actions. Responsibility means more than talking. Just saying, "I take responsibility for what happened," is a cop-out.

- Model and encourage language that expresses responsibility rather than blaming or victimization: "I should" or "I can't" imply outside forces are in control. "I can't" really means, though, that you won't try, and you fulfill your own prophesy.

  When your child says, "I can't," ask if he means, "I won't" or "I don't want to." Replace "should" with "I choose to" or "I decided to." Let "I have to" become "I want to" or "I don't want to." You do have choices, and so does your kid.
- Remind him of logical consequences: "If you miss the bus, you'll have to walk to school."
- Role-play so your child can practice taking responsibility. Offer to act the part of the irate neighbor whose prize rose bush he trashed while playing catch. He can try out various approaches and suggestions for restitution until he feels relatively comfortable talking with the real neighbor. Don't worry if he refuses your offer. Maybe he'll rehearse alone. At any rate, in the future he'll know you're open to this type of assistance.
- For chores or events to remember, ask your child, "How are you going to remind yourself to do your homework?" Help him come up with solutions. "Do you still need me to remind you?"
- When he makes a request you can't grant, ask, "What would your answer be if you were in my place? And what are the reasons?"

- Discuss issues of responsibility as they arise in daily life. Focus on *what* happened, not *why* (a blaming word). Ask your child what he would do differently next time.
- Instead of, "I'm proud of you," sometimes say, "You should be proud of yourself."
- Expect mature behavior, and your kid won't rebel when teachers and others do the same later. Require help around the house (see Chapter 7). He feels worthless if you never ask him to make a contribution to the family. Requiring him to do something he doesn't want to do—even if it renders him grumpy—reflects the nature of life. We all have to do what we don't like—paying the IRS or waiting in line, for instance. Seeing him through the grumpiness is your gift to him.
- Delayed gratification teaches responsibility. Wanting something means working for it in one way or another.

> This above all—to thine own self
> be true,
> And it must follow, as the night
> the day,
> Thou canst not then be false to
> any man."
>
> WILLIAM SHAKESPEARE
> (1564–1616)

Watching your child suffer hurt or disappointment brings you pain, but you have to let him struggle on his own to learn how to depend on himself. Self-reliance, values, responsibility, and self-esteem develop at their own pace, but they won't form at all if you don't give your kid a chance to practice. Your job is to provide hands-off guidance and a healthy environment for his development.

ORGANIZATIONS

Center for Media Literacy: Quarterly newsletter with membership ($35 per year); free catalog; workshop kits that train parents and educators to teach critical thinking and recognizing content of media messages. 4727 Wilshire Blvd., Suite 403, Los Angeles, CA 90010; 800-226-9494; fax 310-559-9396.

Children of Lesbians and Gays Everywhere (COLAGE): Local kids' groups sponsored by the Gay and Lesbian Parents Coalition, International (GLPCI). Box 50360, Washington, D.C. 20091; 202-583-8029.

Children's Television Resource and Education Center: Educational materials about TV for parents, audiotape series for kids, materials on socialization and conflict resolution. 340 Townsend St., Ste. 431, San Francisco, CA 94107; 415-243-9943.

National Foundation to Improve Television: Advocacy and educational organization. 60 State St., Ste. 3400, Boston, MA 02109; 617-523-5520.

BOOKS FOR PARENTS

Celebrate Your Self: Enchancing Your Own Self-Esteem, Dorothy C. Briggs (New York: Doubleday, 1986) (enhancing your own self-esteem).

Raising Self-Reliant Children in a Self-Indulgent World: Seven Building Blocks for Developing Capable Young People, H. Stephen Glenn and Jane Nelson (Rocklin, CA: Prima Publishing, 1989).

Your Child's Self-Esteem: The Key to His Life: Step-by-Step Guidelines for Raising Responsible, Productive, Happy Children, Dorothy C. Briggs (New York: Dolphin Books, 1975).

BOOKS FOR KIDS

The Cat at the Door: And Other Stories to Live By, Anne D. Mather, et al. (San Francisco: Hazelden) (affirmations to read to kids ages 3 to 10).

Teens and Self-Esteem: A Teenager's Guide to Surviving Stress, National Mental Health Association; 800-969-6642. Also provides local referrals, directory of local associations, and information about 200 mental health topics.

Daddy's Roommate, Michael Willhoite (Boston: Alyson Publications, Inc., 1990).

Heather Has Two Mommies, Lesléa Newman (Boston: Alyson Publications, Inc., 1989).

Chapter 10

Dangers from Outside: Abduction, Violence, Abuse, and Drugs

Nationally, the crime rate has decreased slightly, but you wouldn't know that to listen to most Americans. Single parents fear harm by human forces they cannot anticipate or affect. Reports of crime and terrorism hit closer, and the acts seem more violent and random than ever before. The 1994 Oklahoma City bombing profoundly shook our sense of security. The deaths of the children in a day-care center there brought us face-to-face with our own kids' vulnerability.

A recent study based on government statistics shows that social conditions are worsening in our country, including:

- Child abuse
- Child poverty
- Drug abuse
- Homicide

Unchanged, but not improving from prior years are:

- The number of high-school dropouts
- Alcohol-related highway fatalities

We can't be with our children every minute, and even if we could, we couldn't always protect them. Besides, they would never learn to function as capable, self-reliant adults if we stood over them constantly. So we take what precautions we can. Then we reluctantly give our children to the world and pray that it treats them safely, if not always fairly.

Practice Crime Prevention

Over five percent of American schoolchildren carry a gun. More teenage boys die of gunshot wounds than all other causes of death combined. A 1994 Roper poll found that forty-one percent of Americans older than age twelve reported having been victims of a crime. A man rapes a woman every seven minutes in the United States.

Of course you would abolish all crime if you could, but since you can't, at least take steps to protect yourself and your own. That in itself is easier said than done, especially in an era where violence often has no rhyme or reason. Living a good, honest life guarantees nothing. You would need a crystal ball to foresee the wrong place and the wrong time. Still, you do what you can:

- Teach non-victim behavior (see Chapter 11 for "home alone" precautions).
- Institute a neighborhood watch. At-home residents keep an eye out for suspicious behaviors, and children know to contact designated neighbors in case of problems. Your local police department will cooperate in setting up a neighborhood watch.
- Lock car doors when driving.
- Avoid high-crime areas. Don't risk shortcuts, especially at night.
- Don't leave young children alone in a public place for even a second. This includes a sibling left in the car while you take your younger child to a sitter or school.
- Even older children shouldn't be out alone at night for any reason. Assure your child that you will pick him up at any place, any time, if he finds himself stuck without a ride. Make good on this promise.

Influence Your Child's Attitudes toward Violence and Conflict Resolution

While you can't eliminate violence in our society, you can influence your own child's attitude toward conflict resolution.

- Be a role model for resolving conflicts appropriately—including conflicts with your kids. You can't spank, yell, or shame them without endorsing these as acceptable ways to deal with disputes. Instead, use your parenting skills: family meetings, communication, and compromise. If you have a problem resolving conflicts without violence, see a counselor.

- Urge school authorities to teach conflict-resolution skills. Derived from family meetings, "class meetings" allow kids to settle their differences amicably with everyone's self-respect intact. The more children receiving this training now, the greater possibility for future conflict resolution with words instead of guns and knives.

> 59% of Americans older than twelve who'd reported being victims of crime took measures to make their homes more secure (special locks, alarm system, guard dog).[1]

- Teach your kids the values of nonviolence and care and respect for other people (see Chapter 9).
- Limit aggressive video games and television, particularly children's programs that show violence, whether cartoon or "real." In Christopher's age group, TV's superhero Power Rangers get what they want by force—not a message I want for my child (see Chapter 9).

Preventing Abduction: "Good Strangers" and "Bad Strangers"

The idea of kidnapping sends chills down every parent's spine. How do you impress safety rules upon your children without making them fear the whole world? How do you give them a basic trust of people without rendering them overly confident? Difficult as it is, you must talk with your children about "stranger danger."

- They have probably seen media stories about murder, kidnapping, and molestation. Help your children to put people's evil acts into perspective. Get your kids to talk, perhaps using news reports to stimulate discussion. Emphasize that these events happen rarely and that you will teach your children how to prevent their occurrence.
- The most effective means of prevention is boosting your child's confidence and ability to trust his own sense of feeling threatened or pressured. (See Chapter 9.)

- Start young. Give even small children rules for staying safe with strangers. Naturally, you don't intend to leave your kid unsupervised in unsafe places, but in reality you will sometimes lose track of him. As a single parent, you have only one set of eyes. Even a brief moment of inattention can leave your child to fend for himself against unscrupulous people. While older kids understand the concepts of bad intentions and danger, younger ones, no matter how intelligent, lack cognitive understanding that someone who appears "nice" may not be so. Giving a blanket warning—"Never talk to strangers"—backfires if your small child thinks he can't tell a store cashier or police officer that he's lost. Besides, it's confusing—he sees you talking to "strangers" all the time without apparent harm.

  Keep your explanations simple when talking with young children. Evil people don't necessarily look scary or "bad." Normal-looking individuals who casually know their child-victim commit seventy percent of abduction and sex abuse crimes. I like the "Berenstain Bears" book that compares strangers with apples. Most are good inside, but some are bad; you can't tell which is which from the outside. The same holds true for people, so your child shouldn't talk or go with *anyone* he doesn't know.
- Emphasize that he should stay with you or within your sight when you're out and about. If he goes somewhere with others, make sure he understands he must stay with them, too.
- The National Center for Missing and Exploited Children recommends warning against certain *situations* or *behaviors*, rather than types of *people:* Tell your child, "Unless I've specifically said it's okay, a grown-up should never . . ."

  –Ask directions of you.

  –Invite you into his car.

  –Say that your mom or dad sent him to pick you up. (Emphasize, "I would never send a stranger to get you without telling you ahead of time." Have a family password he can request if he has any question as to a person's identity.)

  –Ask you to help him find his lost pet or anything else.

  –Offer you anything to eat.

  –Volunteer to take you somewhere to buy you something, even something you *really* like.

  –Call you by name if you don't know him. He may have overheard someone call you or seen your name written somewhere. (For this reason, don't buy your kids clothing or bicycle "license plates" bearing their names!)

Give your child ongoing, explicit permission to leave these or any other situations in which he doesn't feel comfortable. "If anything like this happens, you always have a right to say no and walk away."

- Another approach focuses on what your child *may* do rather than on what he may not. "Only get in a car with Mommy, Daddy, Grandma, or Ben's parents unless I say it's okay to go with someone else."
- Ask your child to tell you if anything untoward happens or if he has any questions at all. Reassure him that you won't be upset if he expresses fear, worry, or anger. You won't blame him. Emphasize that you love and trust him and will believe him. Let him know he can tell you anything, especially something that doesn't feel right to him.

  If you notice your child in emotional turmoil, don't be afraid to inquire into the source. Rather than broad, open-ended questions, which may feel threatening, try to name the emotion. "You seem afraid of something."
- Instruct your kid what to do if a "no" doesn't work. Tell him to run if he can and head for a police officer, a store cashier, a neighbor, or someone he knows. If a grown-up grabs him, he should scream and make the biggest racket he can until help arrives. Tell him to use the word "help" and to yell—so bystanders won't think this is just a discipline problem—"This is not my Daddy (Mommy). This is a stranger."
- Periodically test your child's degree of comprehension with a "What-do-you-do? game." Ask, "What do you do if a stranger asks you to help find his puppy?" "What do you do if someone tells you to keep a secret from Mommy?"
- Despite all the warnings, teach your children that "bad guys" don't lurk behind every bush. Let kids focus on the positive aspects of the world and the many people who help.

Sexual Molestation

As a single parent, you want to do all you can to prevent sexual abuse, and, if the worst should occur, to recognize and deal with it in the best possible way.

Preventing Sexual Abuse

The fact that sexual abuse most often occurs where you feel safe—and with people you trust—lends it a particular horror. It usually happens right at home or in the neighborhood, and the molester is usually a male relative or family acquaintance. It could even be your ex.

Molestation excludes no age, class, gender, or race. Studies reveal that twenty-five percent of girls and ten percent of boys suffer sexual abuse by age eighteen. Adolescents suffer more abuse than younger children. Ninety percent of female prostitutes were sexually abused as children.

> 41 percent of Americans older than twelve have been victims of a crime. Of those, 28% said their experience affected their current thinking about keeping the family safe.[2]

If you found talking about kidnapping difficult, discussing sexual abuse will be even harder. What do you say about sexual molestation to a youngster who hasn't the faintest idea about what sex *is*? How can you communicate the dangers without destroying his overall trust in people and the world? How do you provide a positive attitude toward sex and physical affection if at the same time you're warning against their negative aspects? Again, the answer is to instill a healthy, self-confident attitude about your child's own judgments and body.

- Use language appropriate for your child's age. With young kids, talk about "good touches" and "bad touches." Tell your child his body is his business and no one except you and his doctor may touch it without his permission—not even people he loves. This applies to *all* touching. Never force him to hug and kiss anyone, and ask others to respect his wishes.
- Let your child have his own opinions about people. He needn't like Aunt Suzy just because you do. Respect his ways of relating to others. If he needs time to warm up, let him hide behind the couch until he feels comfortable. He'll establish his own emotional boundaries. He doesn't have to relate to people as you do or in any way that feels wrong to him. Your child is the final judge of how he feels.
- *In addition* to the warnings to avoid kidnapping, tell your kid that no adult, even a familiar one should:

–Touch him in any way he doesn't like
–Ask him to keep a special secret, especially from his parents
–Want to show him pictures
–Ask to take his picture, clothed or naked, without your permission
–Offer to or expose his private parts
–Ask him to touch an adult, especially on the genitals
–Ask to see his private parts

- Avoid conveying a sense of shame about the body. Explain that we love, care for, and enjoy our bodies, but people agree to certain rules about when and how we share them with others. Breaking these rules is not okay for kids or adults.
- Know where your kid is, what he's doing, and who is with him. Require him to phone you if he's going elsewhere. Get to know the adults and older children in regular contact with your child.
- Check out all sitters and day-care providers (see Chapter 11). Visit often and observe the interactions between adult and children. Do they seem fearful, overly obedient, or otherwise unnatural?
- Inquire into school abuse-prevention programs so you can review the materials and be ready to supplement it and answer questions your child asks.

If Your Parent Abused You . . .

If you suffered abuse at the hands of your mother or father, what do you do now that your parent is also your child's grandparent?

Protecting your child takes priority. Never expose him to abuse. How you ensure that requires careful thought, depending on your current relationship with your parents, whether you have confronted them with the past abuse, their reaction, your current geographic proximity, and what your parent otherwise has to offer your child. Get professional advice for your particular case. Depriving your children of grandparents represents a big decision, and there may be a middle ground, such as requiring all visits to be supervised.

As an abuse victim, make sure you don't imitate what you suffered as a child. Abused children often become child abusers. Get counseling if you have any question about your ability to escape this pattern. The bottom line is your child's well-being.

Identifying Sexual Abuse

Don't take it on faith that your child will tell you about sexual abuse. Kids respond differently depending on age and temperament.

They may seem confused or afraid, or they may exhibit little reaction at all. They may talk or isolate.

- Be alert to mentions of anything out of the ordinary during everyday conversations.
- Watch for nonverbal signals of possible problems, but if you see them, don't jump to conclusions. Many other causes exist for these behaviors. Possible signals are:
  –Nightmares and sleep disturbances
  –Fear of adults or of certain people or places
  –Unusual clinging to parent
  –Sophisticated or unusual sexual behavior or knowledge for the child's age
  –Acting out abuse with dolls, friends, or art
  –Excessive masturbation
  –Bedwetting
  –Unexplained behavioral changes at school or with friends
  –Loss of appetite
  –Regression to younger behavior
  –Withdrawal
  –Running away
- Most molestation involves neither violence nor physical injury, but if either has occurred, the most common physical symptoms are:
  –Vaginal or penile discharge
  –Discomfort sitting or walking
  –Injury, itching, pain, or bleeding in the genitals or anus
  –Appearance of a sexually transmitted disease

If Sexual Abuse Has Occurred . . .

Unfortunately, most sexual molestation remains unknown and unreported because the children fear no one will believe them. They imagine you will blame, punish, or reject them. The closer the relationship the child has with the abuser, the less likely that he will tell what happened. He'll be very reluctant to talk about any inappropriate actions by your ex, for example, especially if he already feels responsible for the divorce. Girls are more likely to report abuse than boys.

- If your child speaks of sexual molestation, *stay calm*. Your reaction plays a large part in how he recovers from the incident. Your kid doesn't need to see you overcome with horror, shock, anger, disbelief, revulsion, or panic. Whatever your reaction, let him know that your feelings are not aimed at him.

- Believe him! Children rarely make up stories about this subject.

  Reassure your child that you still love him, that the encounter wasn't his fault, and that he will be all right. Obtain specifics without suggesting facts to him. Try not to pressure him, but do let him talk if he's willing. Assure him you will protect him from further abuse. Tell him what you plan to do. Avoid further contact with the person. Report the incident to the proper authorities, which may be the police or child-protective agencies. If others might be at risk, seek guidance about informing them.
- Get medical attention if you know or suspect your child was molested. Though he may seem fine mentally and physically, he may have contracted a sexually transmitted disease or suffered internal injury.

Other Abuse

Physical or emotional abuse can come from anyone in contact with your child, be it a day-care provider, teacher, ex-spouse, or relative. Signs of physical abuse include unexplained bruises, welts, burns, fractures, and abrasions, as well as fearfulness. Children suffering emotional abuse exhibit slow development, passivity, aggressiveness, bedwetting, learning disabilities, speech disorders, nightmares, or inadequate peer relationships.

If you suspect abuse, check it out with the child, his doctor, or the child-protective agencies.

Drugs, Alcohol, and Tobacco

Recognize the pervasiveness and dangers of drugs, alcohol, and tobacco use and start combating them early.

Start Early—the Kids Do!

Begin talking about addictions as soon as your child becomes fully verbal. The federal government agrees that, "The best way to fight drug use is to begin prevention efforts before children start using drugs. Prevention efforts that focus on young children are the most effective means to fight drug use." Fifteen-year-old Mani confirms that her current ability to withstand peer pressure "started a long time ago, when I was really young."

Regarding the early years:

- Many parents postpone giving information on the theory that it only gives their children ideas. But the kids get those ideas anyway—earlier than you think. The average child first tries alcohol at age twelve! The earlier they start to experiment, the more likely they are to wind up with serious problems.
- Early alcohol and drug use correlates with later dependence, relationship problems, negative school performance, increased risk of unwanted pregnancy, involvement with other drugs, disease, and criminal behavior. Students who use drugs and alcohol are fifty percent more likely to start fights, three times more likely to be truant, and four times more likely to participate in vandalism.
- Nearly sixty percent of adult smokers started smoking between the ages of eleven and fourteen.

In a study by the Centers for Disease Control and Prevention, teens reported the following during the preceding month:

	AGE 12–13	AGE 14–17	AGE 18–21
Rode with drunk driver	10%+	20%+	35%+
Smoked cigarettes	8%±	20%+	35%+
Got drunk	3%±	18%±	40%+[3]

Appreciate the Pervasiveness and Acceptance Your Child Encounters about Drugs and Alcohol

Perhaps you think you don't have to worry about *your* child. Think again. According to the federal government, drug use among children is *ten times more prevalent than parents suspect!* The United States has the highest teenage drug-use rate of any industrialized nation. Junior and senior high kids drink thirty-five percent of all wine coolers sold in this country—plus about 1.1 billion bottles and cans of beer each year. Contrary to stereotype, drug use affects youngsters in all geographic areas and economic strata, from elementary to high school. Although boys currently use drugs in higher proportion than girls, the gap is narrowing. White high school seniors report more illegal drug use than blacks. In 1994, fifty percent of high school seniors had tried an illegal drug.

Teenage smoking is also on the rise, despite reduced tobacco use in the general American population. The country's leading preventable cause of death, smoking kills over 400,000 Americans a year. Every day, three thousand kids become smokers, and almost half of them will eventually die from smoking-related illness!

People increasingly regard marijuana as benign. It accounts for eighty-one percent of the drugs used in America. Only forty-two percent of teens regard it as a dangerous drug, as opposed to fifty percent two years ago. Although adults' overall drug use has leveled off, teens have doubled their use of marijuana since 1992, a reversal of thirteen years of prior decline. Some kids believe they can use any drugs without fear of repercussion. Our children experiment with alcohol, tobacco, marijuana, inhalants, cocaine, stimulants, depressants, narcotics, hallucinogens, glue and paint fumes, "designer drugs," and anabolic steroids.

Alcohol in some ways presents the most difficult issue, however, because it's such a part of our culture. Society sanctions moderate drinking, even glamorizes it. Wine with dinner signifies sophistication and elegance. A beer means fun and good friends. You're probably no teetotaler yourself.

> "O God, that men should put an enemy in their mouths to steal away their brains!"
>
> WILLIAM SHAKESPEARE (1564–1616)

Messages to use alcohol assault kids from every direction, primarily from TV and movies. If typical, by the time your child is eighteen, he will have seen 100,000 beer commercials. Peer pressure is the second-greatest influence toward alcohol use. A recent California survey concluded that advertising is the most influential means of creating lifelong tobacco users among the twelve to seventeen crowd, the ages most smokers begin the habit. Peer pressure and smokers in the family together exert secondary influences. You have some powerful adversaries in the battle to keep your children from substance abuse.

Preventing and Dealing with Substance Abuse

Given the widespread acceptance and pervasiveness of drugs, alcohol, and tobacco, how can we meet the challenge of keeping your kids away from them? There are no guarantees but the following steps point in the right direction.

Help Your Child to Build Self-Esteem

The most powerful weapon against substance abuse is your child's healthy self-esteem. If he has a positive self-image, he won't base his choices on the need to please someone else or change himself (see Chapter 9).

Set a Good Example

- Although not the number-one influence on children's drug and alcohol use, your behavior is an important factor. Avoid drugs. Don't smoke. Be conservative in your approach to over-the-counter medications and stress-relievers. Avoid giving the impression that external substances cure everything. Limit drinking. Wine with dinner is fine, but don't get drunk.
- If limiting your own alcohol or drug use seems impossible or difficult, honestly evaluate your own relationship with substances. Get counseling or check out the appropriate "12-Step" program. Alcoholics Anonymous is one such 12-Step program.
- What about the idea that since your child will experiment, it might as well be in your house, under your supervision? Many parents adopt this rationale, but it really makes no sense to me. First, it's illegal: do you want to model disregard of the law? Second, and more importantly, having booze at home *doesn't prevent* outside drinking. Rather, it may mislead your kid into thinking he can handle alcohol. Third, access and familiarity with alcohol encourage its use. Only forty-four percent of sixth graders even think of alcohol as a drug.

  Yes, you argue, but you won't allow drunkenness, just a glass of wine with dinner. After all, kids in other countries consume alcohol from birth. In France, for example, children think nothing of sipping *vin* with meals. True, but our culture is not French culture, and drinking doesn't mean the same thing here. It's very hard to import and incorporate only a *part* of another culture into ours.

Involve Your Former Spouse

Unity with your ex-spouse can be a potent weapon against your kids' drug use—especially when you agree about nothing else. Suzanne found a small amount of marijuana while her son Max was at his father's house. Despite extreme alienation from her ex-husband, Jon—partly the result of his own substance abuse—Suzanne immediately telephoned him and explained what she'd found. Acknowledging their mutual hostility, she calmly presented the case for backing each other up regarding drugs and alcohol. Jon responded by driving their son to Suzanne's house at once, where he affirmed that Max's welfare came first for both of his parents. He assured Max that his parents would communicate and stand together on drug issues. In near tears, Max stated his intention to avoid drugs and alcohol. The fact that his parents united over this one question brought home its importance, even though, unfortunately, Jon made no promises about his own behavior.

It needn't take a dramatic scene to create unity. If your former spouse cooperates, agree on your mutual approach and talk separately or together with your child.

Involve Other Parents

The older your kid, the less likely you will automatically connect with his friends' parents. No more chats with them at school drop-offs, no more hanging around at birthday parties. Moreover, adolescents actively resist parent-to-parent connections—for the same reasons you should seek them!

With your child's knowledge, take the initiative to form a support network with parents of his peer group. Parent groups share information on drugs and provide mutual emotional support. They lobby for action at school and in the community and collaborate in drug-prevention projects. They communicate with one another about social events and monitor their kids' activities. They lose their hesitation to "rat" on others' children, since that is, in effect, part of the agreement.

Just knowing parents are united curbs attempted deceptions by kids. If peer pressure is a reason for drug use, then stopping peers from using drugs relieves that pressure. United, parents overcome the negative influence of others who use drugs.

Having seen a son through a destructive period of drug use, Ceil believes in drawing other concerned adults together. "Your kids will hate you," she says, "but if you aren't talking with other parents, the kids will play you off one another. If you suspect drug use, inform parents and double-check the kids' stories with them. It's harsh, but it was the only way I found to help my son."

The National Institute on Drug Abuse reports the following annual deaths in the United States from substance abuse:

tobacco	364,000
alcohol	125,000
alcohol & drugs in combination	4,000
heroin/morphine	4,000
cocaine	2,000
marijuana	75[4]

Communicate

Like sex education, drug and alcohol awareness is an ongoing process that starts early with a simple foundation. Bring up the subject in context, starting with, say, seeing an intoxicated person or a syringe on the street. Stay casual, open, and relaxed.

Maintaining trust has more potential than spying or invading your child's privacy. You aren't a cop, and the more you try to be, the less you'll be a trusted parent. For that reason, many people reject the idea of sending samples of their kid's hair to drug-testing companies for an analysis of substance abuse. Communication is a more productive use of time and energy.

- Educate yourself so you can discuss the subject knowledgeably. Kids will obtain accurate information from you rather than questionable facts from peers.
- Start with preschoolers.
  –Build early awareness that your little one can't put just anything into his body.

–Because very young children think concretely, use real-world examples. Some foods help his body grow and stay healthy, and some, like sugar and fat in "junk foods," harm it. Introduce the concept of "poisons."
–Use illness to explain that "medicine" heals a sick body, and it comes in different forms, such as liquid, pills, and injections. Emphasize that he only take medicine from you, the nurses, his other parent, or the doctor (or anyone else who regularly cares for him, such as grandpa or the baby-sitter).
–Show him a syringe at the doctor's office or in a picture, and warn him never to touch one he finds lying around, as it might be "poison." Reassure him that the ones the doctor and nurses use are fine, but it's not okay for anyone else to touch him with a syringe.
–As you teach your child to care for his body, emphasize its value and the need to keep it healthy. Inform him that drugs can interfere with health. "Drugs change how your mind and body work. Some drugs are good, and some are bad. The good ones help you feel better when you're sick, and we call those 'medicine.' The bad ones hurt your body." Use the words for the harmful activities: "taking drugs."

- Tell your child that some adults foolishly take drugs even though they hurt their bodies, but that children should never do them. Introduce the concept of addiction as a disease that makes it very difficult for people to stop using unhealthy ingredients once they've started.
- As your kid grows, continue the lessons begun earlier about good versus bad substances for the body. Tell him that some seemingly innocuous products, like cough syrups, also contain substances harmful to children, so taking exactly the amount shown on the bottle is important. To learn which substances are safe to eat, drink, or touch, ask an adult.
- Rather than just saying drugs are "bad," talk about specific negative effects (see following sections). Emphasize how easily drugs become the center of life and destroy interest in other activities through physical and emotional dependence.
- Ask your child to tell you if anyone ever offers him drugs or alcohol. Assure him you will not be angry at him. And keep that promise!
- Reinforce warnings about drinking and driving (or being driven by a drunk driver). Assure your child that no matter what the time and

place, you will come pick him up, without anger, if he would otherwise have to occupy a vehicle with a drunk driver. "Intoxicated," by the way, doesn't mean falling-down drunk. Even in an adult, just one or two drinks can exceed the legal limit and impair driving abilities. Teens have even less physiological tolerance.

- Talk from time to time so the topic remains comfortable. Waiting to bring up the subject until your child faces peer pressure to use drugs and alcohol makes him feel threatened, conflicted, and less open. Ask, "Have you heard about anyone using drugs in your school?" Don't overreact if the answer is yes. Make it an occasion to explore your kid's feelings toward drugs and impart your own lessons.
- Handle cigarette smoking in the same manner as drug experimentation—because that's just what it is. Use any past experience to explain the downside.

  My former three-pack-a-day habit—which started with a few cigarettes in college to be "cool"—will provide the basis for discussions with Christopher. I found cutting down impossible and finally quit cold turkey, a miserable experience I never want to repeat. I'm not certain I *could* repeat it. Nicotine is such a powerful drug that now, almost twenty years after quitting, I still sometimes feel a wistful tug toward a cigarette. I know, however, that I'm only a puff away from three packs a day. The only way to avoid having to go through the agony of quitting is never starting.

> "First the man takes a drink, then the drink takes a drink, then the drink takes the man."
>
> JAPANESE PROVERB

- As an exercise, ask your child to give up a habit for a few days. Use the results to emphasize that breaking a bad habit is much harder than not starting it in the first place.
- Admit that drugs make people feel good—your child will hear this from others—but the effect is fleeting. A cocaine high lasts only fifteen or twenty minutes. Over a longer term, the negative effects far outweigh the brief "pleasures." Discuss finding true, lasting pleasures in life instead.
- Counter media influence. Limit TV commercials and programs and movies that portray drugs, alcohol, and cigarettes as glamorous. Don't treat drunkenness in movies or TV shows as humorous, even when it's so intended. Explore messages conveyed by ads. Separate

hype from reality. "Smoking doesn't make you sexy; it makes you smell bad."

Address Peer Pressure

- Peer pressure begins early.
  –Kids in *grades four through six* say they tried alcohol and marijuana "to fit in" and "feel older."
  –About twenty-four percent of California *fourth graders* say they feel pressure to try cocaine or crack!
  –Over thirty percent of *sixth graders* experience peer pressure to use marijuana and cocaine or crack.
- The best defense against peer pressure is your child's healthy self-esteem, a permanent goal of all parenting (see Chapter 9). Encourage sports and other physical activity, not only for health reasons but to reduce stress and increase self-regard. With healthy self-esteem, he'll trust his own judgment above anyone else's. If he loves and accepts himself, he'll be less likely to comply in order to find love and acceptance.
- Talk openly about peer pressure, emphasizing that "everyone" doesn't participate in anything. Admit that it's hard to be around kids who are using. In a recent survey, two-thirds of preteens admitted peer pressure might be enough to influence them to do something they otherwise would not do.
- The bottom line is each person's own right to refuse something that makes him uncomfortable (see Chapter 9). Emphasize that anyone who urges your kid to harm his mind and body isn't a friend. Someone inviting him to join in an illicit activity is probably just trying to justify his own misbehavior.
- Discuss kids giving in to friends' urging in order to feel "normal" and "with it."
- Talk about how people try unsuccessfully to feel better about themselves by putting substances in their bodies.
- Find stories about famous people who stood up for their beliefs despite opposition.

> Addiction to food, tobacco, or drugs occurs in four out of ten people in the United States. At least one in one hundred Americans (2.2 million) is a cocaine addict.[5]

- Give your child ways to say no under pressure. Refusals needn't be confrontations. He doesn't have to make speeches or try to convince anyone else. Do some role-playing. (Also review the discussion of saying no in Chapters 4 and 11.)
  - –If your child knows of drug hangouts or probable use at a party, ask him to stay away.
  - –"No, thanks" is a complete reason, no explanations required.
  - –Say "no" and leave.
  - –Suggest another activity instead.
  - –Have something else to do.
  - –Give a reason: "Drugs aren't good for me."
  - –Change the subject.
  - –"I don't feel like it."
  - –"I'm too busy now."
  - –"I'm not interested in drugs."
  - –"Sorry, I've got to go."
  - –Encourage him to make you the bad guy if he needs an excuse. "My dad won't let me." "My mom will ground me if I'm late again."
- Remind him that there are different types of pressure, and he can tailor his responses to them. Meet friendly or teasing pressure lightly. If it's threatening, leave. By refusing, your kid might even exert positive peer pressure and help someone else not use drugs.
- The least obvious pressure may be the most powerful because your kid feels he's making his own decisions—but he's not. For example, when a joint goes around at a party, he may feel pressured to join in, though no one says a word.
- You can't choose your child's friends, but you can subtly influence the choice. If you criticize a pal directly, you may tighten your child's bond to him. Instead, offer positive comments about friends of whom you approve.
- Suggest that your child participate in positive activities where he might find better companions (although you can never be certain! Even nerds become drug addicts . . .).

Preteens and Teens

Peers become paramount now. Keep building on the above messages.

- Educate your teen more specifically in the appearances and effects of various drugs on the body. Using facts rather than pure emotion lends credibility to your viewpoint. Simply denouncing drugs and alcohol as "bad" or "evil" may stimulate curiosity and rebellion. Emphasize reasons for not taking drugs.

Surprisingly, many parents and teens know nothing of some of the most insidious aspects of drug use:

–Prepubescent boys incur special risks from marijuana, which can repress testosterone production and inhibit development of secondary sexual characteristics!

–Formation of identity can freeze at the age a kid starts using drugs. He may not, therefore, go through the typical teen development of the ability to think critically. (Don't you know some adults who fit this picture?)

–It takes only six months for a teen to become an alcoholic, as opposed to years for adults! Experimentation can easily get out of hand. Your child may deny this, but plant the idea anyway.

–There are significant differences between adult and teen drinking. Youngsters absorb alcohol into their blood streams faster than adults and suffer more impairment for longer times because of their lower body weight.

–Alcohol's quick alteration of perceptions and judgment leads to dangerous risk-taking. Among people aged fifteen to twenty-four, alcohol-related highway accidents are the primary cause of death.

–Don't forget the risk of AIDS from shared needles.

> "Drunkenness is nothing but voluntary madness."
>
> SENECA
> (4 B.C.–65 A.D)

–Emphasizing the short-term effects of drugs and alcohol (changes in appearance, performance, and behavior) as well as long-term effects helps overcome kids' sense of invulnerability.

- Discuss addiction and refer to substance abuse as a disease that can overcome your child before he knows it. Tell him there are ways to get help for substance abuse problems. If a parent or close relative suffers from alcoholism, mention possible genetic aspects of the disease. Don't exaggerate or relate scare-stories, or your kid will distrust your honesty. He'll only come to you for facts and advice if you're straightforward and trustworthy.

"How Do You Know? Did You Ever Try Drugs?"

You have to answer this question honestly if only because someone might eventually prove you a liar. An old college buddy shows up and mentions that "great weed" you had on that backpack trip, for example. You've worked so hard to build your credibility. Don't risk losing it. Your kid's trust level will plummet on this *and* other issues.

But if you admit to having used drugs or abusing alcohol, how do you counter the inevitable question: "Well, you got to experiment; why shouldn't I?"

- Start by explaining that "way back then" people knew less about the long-term effects of drugs. Moreover, no one gave *you* the whole picture, as you're doing for your child. Perhaps no one cared as you care for him. Tell him you feel lucky you survived your drug experiments. Many people literally did not. If it's true, tell him you regret having used drugs.
- Perhaps most importantly, the drugs on the market today exceed the strength of those in years past, and new drugs with unknown effects constantly appear to satisfy increasing demand. Today's pot is *five to twenty-five times stronger* than that available just a decade ago and may contain from four to six percent THC, its major psychoactive ingredient. Just two percent can cause severe psychological damage, including paranoia and psychosis.

  PCP (phencyclidine), an animal tranquilizer, sometimes produces violent and unpredictable behavior. Some dealers sell "marijuana" that is really parsley laced with PCP. Some "designer drugs"—illicit drugs varied slightly in chemical formula to circumvent legal restrictions—have caused permanent brain damage with one dose!
- If you had a problem with substance abuse, be honest about its negative impact on your life and the difficulty overcoming it. If you're still in its grip, get help—for your kid's sake.

  If your spouse abuses substances, you won't be able to make him stop. Get help for your child in dealing with the situation, either through Al-a-Teen, Al-Anon, or professional counselors.

When Your Efforts Fail

Your kid may try drugs, cigarettes, and alcohol despite all your work. Although you can intercept drug use at any of its progressive stages, the more deeply involved the child, the more difficult the task. Signs of substance abuse include:

- Direct evidence of drug use
  - Possession of drugs (pills, white powder, crystalline rocks, seeds, leaves, model glue, aerosol cans for use as inhalants)

- –Disappearance of prescription pills from your supply
- –Possession of drug paraphernalia (pipes, rolling papers, eye droppers, small decongestant bottles, small glass vials, syringes, small butane torches, ampules)
- –Drug odors—or odor "masks" such as incense
- –Sunglasses at odd times to hide dilated pupils
- –Long-sleeved shirts at unexpected times and places to cover needle marks

- Identification with drug culture
  - –Collecting beer cans, drug-related magazines, stickers
  - –Drug slogans on clothing
  - –Frequent jokes and references to drugs
- Changes in mental and scholastic performance
  - –Poor school performance (increased tardiness; skipping classes; incomplete homework; marked decline in grades—including a drop from generally high to mediocre as well as from mediocre to failing)
  - –Memory lapses, difficulty concentrating, short attention span
- Physical changes
  - –Lessened physical coordination
  - –Slurred or incoherent speech
  - –Dilated pupils, bloodshot eyes
  - –Inattention to hygiene
  - –Change in appetite
- Psychological changes
  - –Secrecy
  - –Mood swings
  - –Depression (see Chapter 7)
  - –Remorse
  - –Impaired relationship with friends or family
  - –Anger, hostility
  - –Irritability
  - –Reduced self-esteem
- Changes in behavioral patterns
  - –A new set of (perhaps hidden) friends and reluctance to talk about them
  - –Decreased interest in hobbies or extracurricular activities
  - –Refusal to communicate
  - –Sudden resistance to discipline at home or school
  - –Denial

–Rationalization
–Ignoring curfews
–Chronic dishonesty, lying, or thievery; increased money borrowing from parents or friends; or unexplained disappearance of jewelry, cameras, electronics, and other valuables from the house
–Decreased self-discipline
–Wild schemes
–Unexplained possession of large amounts of money
–Preoccupation with getting drugs
–Trouble with the police

"Much drinking, little thinking."
JONATHON SWIFT
(1667–1745)

Don't Let Denial Paralyze You

If you find evidence of drug use, you'll experience anger, guilt, and denial. You may delay acting in hope that this is a "phase" that will go away. You may convince yourself that your child wouldn't use drugs, or that if he did, it's just "harmless experimentation" or "developmental." It's not. Work through your denial. Don't postpone action. The earlier you detect drug use, and the sooner you face the problem, the less difficult it is to overcome.

Confront Your Child Calmly

Talk to your child when he is sober. Discuss your suspicions calmly, straightforwardly, and objectively.

- Convey the reasons for your concern: physical, mental, and social problems. Remind him you have zero tolerance for drug and alcohol use and you intend to enforce that position. Be firm but understanding. "I know you're under pressure to use drugs, but I care about you and can't let you participate in dangerous activities." Be supportive. "I'll help you to find a way to say no and stop using."
- Avoid sarcasm, accusation, and guilt-tripping, all of which put your kid on the defensive. Don't call him names or label him.
- Arrive at a plan to remove your child from friends and locations where drug and alcohol use occurs. Engage the support of the school, professionals, and other parents (see above). Consider 12-Step programs for yourself and your child. Look in the phone book for hot lines that make referrals to local resources.

- Be aware that if your child uses drugs, he may also lie to you. With alcoholism in the family, teenaged Jerry consistently insisted he would never try drugs. One day, however, his mother, Karen, found drug paraphernalia in his room while cleaning. Confronted, Jerry insisted it belonged to a friend (as if that would put his mom's mind at ease!). Not knowing what to believe, Karen reiterated her feelings about drugs and told Jerry that from now on, she would presume that any drug- or alcohol-related items in their house were Jerry's, and Jerry would suffer the consequences. Karen still doesn't know the truth for certain, but her actions eliminated ambiguity for any similar incidents in the future.

Dangers from Cyberspace

Protect your child from taking a wrong turn on the information superhighway. The appeal of the Internet is its relatively inexpensive, virtually limitless access to worldwide information, and there lies the problem. The Info-bahn is as wild and woolly as the old frontier before Wyatt Earp. No one can enforce the few rules in existence, and any weirdo can insert his sick version of the world alongside fat-free recipes, bulletins from China, and every known fact about gila monsters.

Anyone with a modem can access violent and pornographic images and text, much of it definitely kinky. In one six-month period, Americans downloaded 900,000 porno files about six-and-a-half-million times. Estimates project that erotica will be a four- to five-billion-dollar business on the Internet by 2001.

Scarier yet, the National Center for Missing and Exploited Children reports incidents of pedophiles luring children into in-person encounters via kids' "chat rooms" and bulletin boards. Short of standing over your child's shoulder every time he boots up, what can you do to keep him in the slow lane? And, while you're at it, how do you keep little snoopers out of your computerized journal?

Because cyber-technology is so new and amorphous, no foolproof solutions exist. Some programs seek and destroy defined files, such as those labeled "sex" or "kill." Pending Congressional bills would impose punishment for offenders and requirements that online sleaze be scrambled. But none of these current proposals seems likely to solve the problem because the offensive material is extensive and no one really "owns" the Internet. No one "out there" is accountable. The demand for protections grows, however, and perhaps one day you will be able to assure safe driving on the info-roads. Meanwhile, you have to do what you can on the driveway at home:

- Communicate with your child about the problems and dangers in cyber-ville. Discuss the reasons for your concern, but don't scare him. Some school districts issue guidelines for helping parents talk to their kids about staying safe online.
- If you're not computer literate and your child has his own machine, get educated so you'll know what you're talking about. Take lessons from your kid or a community college.
- Check computer stores for software that blocks out pornographic pictures or "walls off" limited areas for kids' access. Of course, your computer-whiz youngsters may find a way around these before your check clears. Some companies offer programs that require a password to turn the computer on at all. This is fine if you want to deny your child the benefits of cyber-space completely or if you want to monitor every use closely.

For guidelines on Internet use by children on the World Wide Web, go to:

http://www.missingkids.org

or:

http://www.crc.ricoh.com/people/steve/warm-kids.html

- Inquire what controls your online service provides and consider using them. The major online Internet access services, such as America Online, Prodigy, and CompuServe, now require passwords and take other steps to protect kids. The services also have policies regulating online behavior and terms. America Online allows parents to block access to chat rooms and Internet news groups, and it plans to expand those controls to e-mail, software files, and message boards.
- Limit the amount of time your child sits at the computer, just as you do with TV and video games. Excessive late-night usage indicates a potential problem.

- Photocopy the following rules and post them by the computer as a reminder:
  –Never give your home address, phone number, school name, real name, or other identifying information, especially in chat rooms or bulletin boards.
  –People online aren't always who they say they are. Anyone can assume any identity on screen. A thirty-year-old man can "be" a fourteen-year-old girl, and there's no way to know.
  –Never give your online-service password to anyone except a parent. Not even a best friend.
  –Never arrange a face-to-face meeting with *anyone* you encounter online without a parent's permission. (If you do allow him to meet someone, go with him, and get together in a public place.)
  –Never respond to any message that makes you feel unsafe or uncomfortable. If you find pornographic, violent, or threatening messages online, immediately sign off and report to the online service (each one has a way to contact the people in charge of enforcing the rules). If more unsavory messages arrive, change your screen name.

Whether the danger is abuse, crime, substances, or crazies online, the key to prevention is your honesty and your child's knowledge, trust, and self-esteem.

ORGANIZATIONS

CHILDHELP U.S.A./I.O.F. Forester's National Child Abuse Hotline: Twenty-four-hour crisis help, information, and referral by trained counselors, for children and adults. 800-4-A-CHILD (422-4453).

Children of Alcoholics Foundation. 555 Madison Avenue, 20th Floor, New York, NY 10022; HelpLink Line (for information and referrals): 212-754-0656 or 800-359-2623.

- Cocaine Helpline: Round-the-clock information and referrals. 800-COCAINE (262-2463).

Johnson Institute: Information, publications, and videos. 7205 Ohms Lane, Minneapolis, MN 55439; 800-231-5165 or 612-831-1630.

National Association for Children of Alcoholics; 714-499-3889.

National Council on Alcoholism; 212-206-6770.

National Council on Alcoholism and Drug Dependence Hope Line: A national nonprofit organization that provides information about local affiliates and referrals. 1-800-NCA-CALL (622-2255).

National Drug and Alcohol Treatment Routing Service: Free materials, confidential information, and referrals to local treatment centers; 1-800-662-HELP (4357).

BOOKS FOR KIDS

Abuse and Neglect: (good answers to tough questions) Joy Berry (Dallas, TX: Word, Inc., 1989).

A Better Safe Than Sorry Book: A Family Guide for Sexual Assault Prevention, Sol Gordon, et al. (Buffalo, NY: Prometheus Books, 1992).

It's My Body, Lory Freeman (Seattle, WA: Parenting Press, 1983) (ages 3 to 9).

My Body Is Private, Linda Walvoord Girard (Morton Grove, IL: Albert Whitman & Co., 1984).

Please Tell! A Child's Story about Sexual Abuse, Jessie (Center City, MN: Hazelden, 1991) (ages 3 to 13).

What Would You Do If . . . ?, Marilyn Kile, et al. (Circle Pines, MN: Amer. Guidance, 1986) (younger kids).

Who Is a Stranger and What Should I Do?, Linda Walvoord Girard (Morton Grove, IL: Albert Whitman & Co., 1984).

About Substance Abuse: (good answers to tough questions) Joy Berry (Danbury, CT: Children's Press, 1990) (grades 3 and up).

Part 3

Family, Work, and Money

Chapter 11

Balancing Work, Career, and Family

Does your child experience your career as an unwelcome family member? *You* know you don't "like it better," but your kid may view your job as a sibling to whom you never say no. No matter what the issue, work always seems to take priority. It dictates the daily schedule, interferes unexpectedly with family activities, and determines your mood. No wonder your child sometimes feels "sibling rivalry" with it.

Perhaps you hate your job. It's a dead-end nine-to-fiver, and the pay stinks. Your boss keeps asking you to stay late even though he knows your child care charges a dollar for every minute you arrive after pickup time. You get more and more work and less and less respect. Given half a chance, you'd bag the job, but then who would come up with school lunch money?

Or maybe you love your work. It's stimulating and challenging enough to occupy you twenty-four hours a day. You studied long and hard for this career, and you're good at it. Working extra hours will get you to the top. You adore both your kids and your job, but they pull you in opposite directions. The constant tension between them cranks the stress level up another notch. No one likes the way you allocate your time—not your kids, your boss, or, least of all, you.

Raising a child shouldn't require giving up a cherished, hard-earned career, but subtle pressure to do just that is common. Some professions require long hours as a matter of course. Many law firms, for example, expect over sixty hours a week from their new lawyers, plus reading and socializing on the side.

Whether you love or hate your work, it claims an enormous chunk of your week. Many single parents work long hours just to make ends meet. Even if your paycheck generously covers material needs, commuting, stress, overtime, deadlines, and travel leave you exhausted, cranky, and just barely able to collapse on the couch after work. You don't have enough time or energy left for nurturing your children as you would like.

In addition, the quality of the time you do spend with them diminishes if you use it to unleash pent-up frustrations you can't express at work. Unfortunately, kids provide a "safe" (for you), convenient place to unload the pressures of the day. Energy and patience flag after a difficult work experience. Flexibility declines. A parent's job stress and long hours show up negatively in children's behavior and emotional well-being.

> The difficulty of balancing home and work is the number one issue American women say they confront, according to a recent Department of Labor study.[1]

How can you balance work and family life? Can you expect your kids to become happy, productive members of society if you either complain about your job all the time or become addicted to it? How do you overcome the guilt associated with pursuing your career at the expense of time with the kids? And then, on a more practical level, how do you get out of the house on time when your children won't even get up and put on their shoes?

Give Up All Pretense of "Doing It All"

Forget perfection. Don't even wish for it. The ideal parent and perfect employee don't exist, especially in combination. Accept that you will make mistakes at home and at work. Some areas of your life will be chaotic and disorganized. If you want a sense of control, choose for yourself a couple of areas in which you will impose one. Better yet, lower your expectations all around. What and how much you do is a *choice. Your* choice.

- Before you start any task, either at home or on the job, question its necessity. Consider the direst result if you just let it go. What if you did it monthly rather than weekly? Would anyone care? Would anyone even *notice?*

- Be especially aware of time-consuming but nonessential tasks you do at home or work simply because they make you feel comfortable and useful. Ditch them. I routinely entered financial information on my nifty computer software as monthly or quarterly statements arrived. I never did a darn thing with those figures, and the companies sent me an annual form for the IRS anyway. Aside from the temporary buzz I got from adding thirty-four cents' worth of interest to my account (a very exciting life I lead!), I had no reason to perform this time-burner, especially when it came at the expense of exercise, pampering myself, or spending time with Christopher.

  As a test, ask yourself whether this chore is important enough to justify hiring help. If you wouldn't pay someone else to do it, why do it at all? I certainly wouldn't have paid anyone to computerize my little earnings, so I stopped doing it myself.
- If a chore seems important enough that you *would* hire help for it, do so! Or get help some other way.
- Say no. Turning people down requires practice. Pause before responding to a request—maybe you never even think of no as a possible answer! Don't scream it or assert it bluntly when you feel the last straw descending. Say it early, confidently, and nicely. A firm, sincere "no" conveys more regard for the other person than a reluctant "yes." It's also much more likely to stick than a weaselly negative, which just encourages wheedling and persistent repetition.

> 32% of the female and 19% of the male managers and professionals surveyed at a major corporation had told their supervisors that they would not take a job that required extensive travel.[2]

  Be truthful and respectful to the other person *and* to yourself. Don't give a lengthy explanation. "Sorry, I promised that evening to my son." If it's true, express regret that you can't help, or, if you want, suggest possible availability at a later time. Perhaps adding a sincere compliment will soften the no. "You're so good at getting your friends together; why don't you round up a few of them to play catch until I make that call to the insurance broker?"

  You can also say no to your employer. "Won't that get you fired, or at least passed over for a raise?" you may ask. Admittedly, telling your boss no can be tricky. I won't guarantee anything, but having been both an employee and an employer, I'll bet you won't suffer for it. Trust your instincts, but at least consider no as a possible answer.

As my friend, Alex, said, "I know which of my employees I can ask for extras, and which ones I can't. After a while, you just ask certain ones because you know they'll help, and you don't bother with the others. I feel sort of guilty taking advantage of those people, but if they're willing . . ." Taking advantage! Maybe the "yes" helps get that raise, but I doubt saying no to extra work *prevents* you from getting it. Don't buy into the hidden assertion that you're no good if you don't do everything requested.

Saying no to an authority, such as a boss, terrifies someone not used to asserting his needs. Kathy's childless, workaholic supervisor used to show up regularly just before quitting time with emergency projects. Although Kathy, a single parent, usually obliged, she resented staying late, especially on nights she picked up her daughter after a visit with her dad. Explanations produced no results. It seemed the boss had to validate her own compulsive work habits by indirectly requiring the same of her employees.

Kathy felt increasingly trapped. Leaving early to dodge the requests wasn't feasible. Finally, she tried responding enthusiastically, "Oh, I'll be happy to do that—first thing in the morning." The supervisor acquiesced in surprised silence at first. The next time, however, she insisted on immediate action, and Kathy found the courage to say, "Sorry, I can't do it tonight. It's already after five." Even if she couldn't "train" her boss not to ask, she learned she can say no when she wants.

Other things that Kathy could still do? She could take the offensive by going in at four o'clock with pad in hand and asking what else the boss wants accomplished before quitting time. If the list is unrealistic, she could ask for priorities "in case I don't get to everything tonight."

People, especially employers, often overstate the importance or urgency of their requests. At great personal sacrifice, you go crazy getting something done, all for nothing. What would they have done if you'd already left on time when they burst from their offices full of requests? They would have waited until the next day.

I still seethe about the late nights I worked to meet a senior lawyer's stated deadlines for legal briefs, only to see them sit unread on his desk for a week. One day, I asked if he "really" needed a certain legal memorandum on the day he specified. "Of course," he assured me, but I didn't hear a word of objection when I turned it in late. I realized he gave artificial deadlines as a matter of course, and I never again broke my back to meet one of them. In this case I said no with my actions.

- Avoid taking work home if at all possible. Delegate it to someone else. Don't do it at all and see if anyone even misses it! Leave thoughts of work behind, too. Believe me, it will all be there in the morning, and nothing you do tonight will have much effect.

  If you habitually bring a home a briefcase, leave it at the job unless you truly have an emergency deadline. You won't be tempted to read that journal article or draft a letter when your kids want your attention. If you can't ever seem to catch up, consider taking a course on efficient work techniques.

Time Versus Money—Parenting Versus Career

Whatever your employment situation, balancing it with family life seems to be a choice between time and money. Less time at work means more with the kids—but less money. And vice versa.

Jeanette, who is now a single parent, makes a generous living in a job which requires substantial travel. While childless, she invested in a house, car, clothes, and other accouterments of a modern, prosperous life. When she found herself pregnant by a man she did not want to marry, she became a single mom. Her income was quite sufficient for raising her daughter, Julie, but the travel and at-home work she'd gladly done before became a nightmare. For business trips, she sometimes has to patch together child care for up to a week at a time. While satisfying her financial obligation to Julie, Jeanette confessed that "whether she gets the rest of what she needs is a matter of sheer luck."

> "When the night is beginning to lower,
> Comes a pause in the day's occupations,
> That is known as the Children's Hour."
>
> HENRY WADSWORTH LONGFELLOW (1807–1882)

Jeanette worries about Julie when she travels and about her job when she returns. The stress often leaves her short-tempered and unavailable. Her impatience grows with Julie's constant interruptions of her work at home. Out of guilt, she buys her daughter every toy invented, which fails to make up for her frequent absences. Julie's behavior sometimes reflects the insecurity and chaos of her life. Jeanette considers other jobs, but they might mean a substantially lowered standard of living. She still struggles to balance home-life with a very difficult employment situation.

> As many as 40% of employees in large companies surveyed in the western United States had considered leaving their jobs because of child care difficulties.[3]

Maggie, on the other hand, made the ultimate "time versus money" decision. After her divorce, she quit a good job and sold her house, in which she had substantial equity. "The house was my kid's childhood," she says. She stayed home with her son until he entered school, stretching each dollar to the limit. Then Maggie reentered the workforce, dead broke and with no retirement or college savings. For her, the gift of her presence in her child's early formative years outweighed future security.

My own decision was similar. Tony "didn't believe" in life insurance, but he did have separate assets that paid the estate's bills and then were split among five different heirs when he died. Fortunately, his most recent will made me one of the beneficiaries. (The estate lawyer told me later that Tony had added and deleted me regularly as our relationship waxed and waned. Learning that he sometimes actually considered leaving me alone with our baby and no "spousal support" gave me a true understanding of the plight of divorced women with no financial assistance.)

At any rate, I put my inheritance together with what was left of my own money and considered my options. Child care, managing the estate, selling the new house we'd bought, and fielding hassles fully occupied me. Now wasn't the time to explore career choices or seek employment. Though legal work offered the best compensation, I'd been away from it for several years and didn't want to practice again anyway. No other readily marketable skills came to mind. Mostly, I wanted to be with Christopher, at least while he was young, and I "paid myself" to do just that. No matter what my future holds, I will always have those years with him and feel that I got him off to a good start in life.

While most people won't take such drastic paths, everyone makes a choice of some sort between money and time with their children. It needn't be all-or-nothing.

Flex-Time

Consider "flex-time"—that is, breaking up the traditional nine-to-five workday into something that better suits your single-parent lifestyle and yet still satisfies your employer. Normally, flex-time makes good business sense. It increases worker satisfaction and productivity and decreases turnover, recruitment, and training. In 1994, a majority of sixty-six percent of major U.S. companies offered some kind of flexable hours and both men and women took advantage.

The precise arrangements for flex-time vary. You still work full-time, but during hours you choose. Perhaps, you put in a compressed work week, say four long days instead of five shorter ones. Or a split-day, perhaps mornings and early afternoons while the kids are in school and a few hours at night while they sleep. You shorten your lunch hour and take off early in the afternoons, or come in later after seeing your kids off to school. Telecommuting from home allows you to skip the commute, sometimes saving two or three hours a day.

Nontraditional work schedule alternatives, in order of popularity, among 1035 major U.S. companies in 1994:

Flexible work schedule	71%
Part-time work	65%
Job-sharing	34%
Compressed work week	21%
Telecommuting	16%[4]

Even if your company has no formal program, it might consider a case-by-case proposal. Do a little background investigation first to find out the results of any previous flexibility experiments. Ask long-time employees or human resource personnel. Then think through what you really want and how it would affect your job. Consider the downside, too. For example, can you really work ten-hour days? How will you stay informed without attending staff meetings? Then argue the case to your boss, emphasizing solutions to possible objections. If you meet resistance, ask for at least a trial period with frequent reviews for adjusting difficulties. Write the plan out so there's no misunderstanding.

Realize that occasionally you'll have to sacrifice flexibility to meet crises or deadlines. Knowing you'll do so willingly helps your employer accept your proposed alternative.

Unfortunately, flex-time usually extends only to those with white collars and higher salaries. Blue-collar, hourly, and service workers are fifty percent less likely to obtain flexible working schedules. Sometimes this results from Neanderthal management resistance, but some jobs don't easily allow flexibility because your availability to clients must remain stable. In the latter cases, you might stagger hours with another worker. Perhaps the last resort is switching to another, more flex-friendly job within the same company.

Give Up Guilt

I had planned to stay away from work until Christopher was at least in kindergarten, perhaps first grade. Then I got the opportunity to write this book, a project close to my heart. Fine, I thought, I'll work nights and mornings when Christopher attends preschool. Not so simple. The publisher gave me a deadline, a tight one. So I added the afternoon preschool session. Finally, getting a sense of how much time I *really* needed for the book, I enrolled Christopher in the full-time child-care program. Now instead of having a two-hour lunch together and picking him up at 4:30 P.M. for a fun activity, as I'd done the previous year, I dropped him off in early morning and retrieved him at 6 P.M., just in time for dinner.

> 60% of women with kids under age six and 76% of women with school-age kids are in the workforce.[5]

I needed every minute to work, but I missed him. I'd become one of those moms trying impossibly to "have it all" and felt guilty dumping him at school for all those hours. I wailed about the damage I must be doing him. My therapist, pointed out, however, that Christopher *loves* school. He leaves me cheerfully in the morning and often doesn't want to come home even at six o'clock. Far from experiencing these all-day sessions as deprivation, he enjoys friends and learning opportunities all day long. Kids are adaptable and resilient.

In fact, *I* felt deprived, and I'd let my boundaries blur by projecting my feelings onto him. The lesson? Avoid guilt unless you have something to feel guilty *about.* In this case, at least, I didn't, and I learned that it pays to check it out by talking with or observing your child before making assumptions. Then make the best of the time you *do* have with him.

Make Your Time Together Count

The once-popular concept that "quality time" makes up for lack of "quantity time" has fallen into disfavor. Still, reality is reality, and as a single parent, you have to work with whatever time you have. If it must be limited, at least make it good. It needn't be "play" time as long as you give attention and awareness. Make ordinary time with your kid into an enjoyable learning experience.

- Rather than changing work hours, perhaps you can simply readjust your attitude and improve how you spend the time you do have at home. Dave, for example, a partner in a successful computer software firm with sole custody of two small boys, has "the bucks to hire a small army of help" for all his hours away. A caring man at base, his schedule provides little daily contact with the children, and guilt prevents him from setting firm limits when they are together. He won't "sharpen the shears," insisting he has "no time" to learn parenting skills that would improve life in the long run—his partners already resent his family commitments. They subtly make it clear that remaining a full partner means acting like one. Dave's sons behave obnoxiously, whining for attention, intentionally destroying property, and calling everyone names. They run roughshod over Dave, who yells and pronounces unenforced (and ignored) ultimata. Those boys are begging for him to impose real limits as a sign that he cares.

  Does Dave have to choose between a career he loves (and one that provides his children with many material benefits) and personal attention to his children? Not even a "paid army" substitutes for parental interaction. Sometimes the answer isn't "either/or" but a reorganization of *how* you use time at home. Stress and chaos consume Dave's hours at home and keep him so scattered that he never applies his analytical abilities to his schedule. He could use the time he wastes shouting to learn parenting skills, enforce limits, and afford each boy regular, undivided attention.

- Use the drive to school or day care to talk, sing, and laugh.
- If you pick your child up from school, look at a classroom project or work in progress.
- Don't bring your job home. Take a deep breath and leave thoughts of work behind as you enter the front door. Consciously shift gears. This is your home, your refuge. Allocate some time, even just a few minutes, to your children and then to yourself before tackling the evening routine—and then make that routine a time of togetherness. Have older children help with dinner or other chores. Set small kids up with some activity near you—but not underfoot. Turn off the TV and enjoy dinner as a family.
- Consider giving each kid a weekly "late night" during which he may stay up an extra twenty or thirty minutes to be with you. Use the opportunity for reading, talking, planning, or doing a project together.

Provide for Last-Minute Schedule Changes

- If existing child care can't accommodate your child during unexpected delays or late work obligations, find a backup. You'll need someone who can pick him up as well as care for him until you arrive. For more on finding care for your child, see *Finding Child Care* below.
- As a sign of respect for your older child's plans and state-of-mind, promptly inform him of changes in your schedule, such as travel or a late work night. Forewarn him, even if just by calling a few hours earlier. At least he can plan around it.
- Keep the larder supplied with foods your older kids (or the caretaker for younger ones) can easily prepare. A favorite meal sometimes takes the sting out of your late arrival, and full tummies help with moods when you finally do make it home.

Stay Connected When You're Apart

Being apart doesn't necessarily mean being out of contact. Even small gestures remind your child that you think about him during the work day.

- Arrange a time for him to call you at work just to say hello. While short and superficial, the contact perks you both up.

- Put a note, card, drawing, or poem in your child's lunch box.
- Provide your day-care worker with a camera and ask him to snap occasional photos of your child at play.
- Even if your child experiences a "first" in your absence, celebrate when he repeats it as a "first" with you.
- Give younger children a photo of you to keep with them, and display theirs at work.

> Almost 53% of employed women have children under six; 61% have kids under eighteen.[6]

Communicate with Your Kids about Your Work

When I was a child, I more willingly accepted something I didn't like if I understood the reason for it, and this is true of most kids (and probably adults as well!). Explain to your kids what you do. They may know the label "lawyer" or "receptionist" or "mechanic," but do they really understand what you do all day?

What Do You Do and Why?

Describe a typical day. Talking about your work acquaints your kid with you *as a person.* He views you in a new context. Speak in terms he understands. What do you enjoy about your job? How did you get into this line of work? What else did you consider? Was this something you fell into, or was it a lifelong ambition? What else have you done? What skills does it require? Why are you good at it? Would he like work like this?

Take your child to your workplace. Most employers won't object. If you can't do so during a work day, try after hours or on a day off. Make it a family outing, complete with a meal out.

Whatever your circumstance, talking about your work helps your children understand your "devotion" to it.

Your Attitude

Remember that you're the role model for a future productive member of the workforce. Explain not only *what* you do, but *why* you do it. What good does your job do the world? How does it benefit others? Why do you have to do it? Why does it seem to take priority?

Taking your child into your confidence flatters him. If you view your job as important and beneficial to you and the world, he more willingly accepts it and his own later employment.

Complaining about your job or boss poisons your child's outlook on *all* work. Stay positive, or at least calm and respectful. Let him see you proactively work out solutions to problems. Show him how an employee goes about maturely asserting his rights. Demonstrate how to leave work at the office.

Illness

Balancing work and family obligations is difficult enough when everyone is healthy. Illness adds further complications.

Sick Days

Until I became a single parent, I never believed the tales of my Oklahoma great-grandmother working in the fields every day of her life, sick or not. The flu knocks me flat every winter for at least a week, and I couldn't imagine hoeing weeds in that condition. Now I believe it. Somebody must have surgically implanted Eveready batteries in single parents because they just "keep on going." They have to.

Illness presents dilemmas whether a bug trounces you alone, just your kid, or both of you. If everyone goes down, you're the one who has to bounce back up for liquids, meals, and vomit cleanups amidst your own collapses and emergency bathroom trips. Although you go to bed, you never completely rest, aware that a small voice may cry out for you at any moment. And the little ingrates have no inkling that you're sicker than they are!

Except for a very few with "sick rooms," schools and day cares bar ailing children. Some enlightened employers allow you to take sick days for your children's illnesses or even provide in-home care programs for them. Bravo! In the Bay Area a group of employers set up a pilot program to send a qualified child-care provider to the home of employees with sick children. Just by calling a 1-800 number with a few hours notice, the employee receives help for as long as necessary. Although the employers are primarily law firms and accountants, they offer the service to all their employees. Annual employer membership in the program costs several thousand dollars a year, and the hourly rates are high, though employees pay just a fraction of the latter.

In most employment situations, when you alone get sick, you go to work as long as you can remain vertical. You know the kids will succumb next. You have to use your sick days for *their* illnesses, not yours—without telling your boss, of course. This little sham guarantees your germs a comfy new home with all your co-workers. They'll drop like flies next week, but that's the penalty your employer pays for remaining in the Stone Age. You can count on missing four to eight workdays a year because of your child's illnesses.

Sometimes you *can't* stay home with a sick child, however. Plan for that eventuality. Don't make dozens of frantic phone calls when you're due at an important meeting in an hour. Instead, keep a list of people who can care for your son or daughter when the bug strikes. Ask in advance for a commitment from relatives, neighbors, and friends who don't work during the day. Because the obligation is contingent, occasional, and short-term, they may be willing. Be specific about what you need.

> The Bureau of National Affairs estimates that worker absenteeism, related to child care, costs U.S. businesses $3 billion a year.[7]

Check with baby-sitting services in advance about sick-child care. Use the sitters a few times before your kid gets ill so he knows them. Home nurses come to your house, but they're expensive, and your child won't know them. A few hospitals and communities have sick-child care centers for kids suffering from temporary, mild illness. Going to the hospital may frighten your child, but at least he will have care and entertainment.

Get as many names on your list as possible so you can come up with care when needed. Have someone look in on teens a couple of times a day. No matter how competent and trustworthy your child, if he's ill, he needs TLC.

Sometimes kids get "sick" just to have more time with a parent, especially if you've been preoccupied lately. Encourage your child to tell you directly that he needs your attention: "If you ever feel you need more time with me, let me know. Don't get sick instead."

Health Insurance

If your job doesn't provide health insurance, see that you have some on your own, even if only for catastrophic coverage. Make this a priority, no matter how difficult. Health insurance is ridiculously expensive, but without it, ten minutes of health care wipes you out financially—assuming you can even get treatment. Cover your children if your spouse's benefits don't extend to them. HMOs offer the least costly alternatives. Consider traditional plans with high deductibles.

Shop around for the best deals. Try to affiliate with a group that contracts for reduced-rate, group health insurance. Trade organizations often offer members access to insurance. Do some research. It may pay to join a group and pay annual dues just to take advantage of the insurance plan.

Disability Insurance

Disability insurance pays if you suffer injury or illness that precludes you from working. It adds a layer of security. You'll have to decide if you can afford it, taking into consideration the risks of your job, the premiums, your income, other sources of support, and your overall health.

Finding Child Care

In a 1994 survey, fifty-six percent of mothers with children age five and under identified "finding affordable child care" as a serious problem. Because our society pays so little attention to the needs of working parents, child care alternatives fall short. *Good* day care benefits your child in ways you can't. It provides peer socialization and additional adult input, points of view, and role models. It may offer exposure to grown-ups of your opposite gender. In reality, though, you may have to settle for "adequate" child care.

Or "none." Sometimes older children care for their younger siblings, occasionally with tragic results. In my area, a young child drowned in the bath while his working mother left him alone with his nine-year-old brother. My heart aches for the older boy, who will live forever with the guilt of having failed at a task he should never have been asked to assume.

> 25% of all working parents in a 1993 survey had suffered a breakdown in their usual child-care arrangements in the prior three months.[8]

Finding full- or part-time child care is a career in itself—an unpaid one. Married working parents also face the child care challenge, but as a single parent, you meet it alone with just your time and money. When you put out the money, it adds up to too much, but as a society, we woefully underpay our caregivers. I hired a woman who both baby-sat and cleaned houses for a living. I entrusted my child to her for $5 an hour, but turning over my house for cleaning cost $12, with a four-hour minimum. That rate structure seemed backward to me—I care much more for my child than my house—and yet I simply couldn't have paid the higher wage for child care.

Then, of course, when you finally have everything nailed down and operating smoothly—and your child has bonded with the kids and adults—something changes and you have to start over. Day-care personnel turn over at an alarming rate, so even keeping your kid in one place doesn't guarantee continuity. Nothing, especially a good child care situation, lasts forever. Children experiencing their parents' divorce benefit from constancy, but you can't count on that with child care—except for the constancy of change. You may be lucky and find a long-lasting solution. Don't expect to. Stay flexible and have possibilities for the next step in mind for when everything falls apart.

Precisely what type of care you want depends on your budget, your personal preferences, your child's age, local alternatives, and whether you want some housekeeping in addition to child care. Assess these realistically before you start looking. Naturally, you want a loving, safe, stimulating environment, a place where your child receives individual attention. You want reliability and a prevailing philosophy that is in tune with your child's temperament and your own notions of child-rearing.

Child Care Options

- Ideally, your employer provides on-premises child care so you can commute with your kids and see them at lunch. Perhaps they even visit at work occasionally. Some companies offer other support, such as care subsidies, paid leaves, or before- and after-school programs. Most employers don't see the need to do this, however. They should. It does the bottom line a favor. Incorporating child care into the business encourages earlier return to work after a birth and raises morale among working parents—which results in decreased turnover and a need for less training.

- Relatives, if they live reasonably close, provide care. Angie rode Bay Area Rapid Transit with her baby every morning, going a few stops beyond her office to hand him over to Grandma. Few single parents have relatives willing and able to take on child care, however. In these mobile times, aging parents either live at a distance or wish to move into retirement without further day-to-day child-care duties.
- If you commute, consider child care near your office, rather than your house. Use transit time to interact with your child. If you drive, unexpected traffic snarls don't threaten your timely pickup, and you're closer in case of emergency. On the other hand, maybe that commute is your sole opportunity for time alone each day. You run childless errands on the way home or just use the time for transition between job and family.
- Live-in help may be every single parents' dream, but affording it isn't everyone's reality. Still, in the long run, it may be cost effective if you have extra room where you live. Combining households with another single parent results in potential shared child care in the home.

  You can hire *au pairs*—young, non-resident-alien caregivers—on a twelve-month cultural exchange visa through government-approved organizations. In exchange for airfare, room and board, and weekly fees totaling about $200, you receive up to forty-five hours of live-in child care per week. The program screens applicants for experience, language, character, and health. Since the visa lasts only a year, you will have to start over with someone else after twelve months, but you are guaranteed that period of time.

  > The child care industry averages a 41% annual turnover rate.[9]

  Hiring outside the programs is illegal and could result in deportation for the *au pair* and a fine as great as $10,000 for you. In any event, since a non-program person makes no enforceable commitment to stay for any particular period of time, he can suddenly leave you high and dry.
- If the caregiver works in your home, don't forget the complicated requirements for reporting and withholding taxes. Failure to observe these requirements can haunt you years later (witness Zoë Baird) when, for example, your former employee applies for Social Security benefits or unemployment compensation. You may need a

tax advisor to guide you through this morass. (See IRS Publication 926, Employment Taxes for Household Employers.)

You aren't supposed to hire *illegal* aliens, and it's your legal duty to check eligibility. Get a copy of the Immigration and Naturalization Service *Handbook for Employers* for details on how to verify status and fill out the required forms.

- Finding an individual "nanny" consumes enormous amounts of time, and you may decide to use an employment agency that specializes in caregivers. You pay a hefty placement fee, usually equal to a month's salary, and the hourly charges tend toward the high end—perhaps ten to twelve dollars—but the agency does all the background work, and you get someone qualified and suited to your needs without much hassle.
- Legal daytime sitters in your home come at a premium hourly rate, but your child remains in his familiar environment and gets individual attention. Unless you share or have multiple children, however, your child receives no peer socialization.
- Licensed family day care (six or twelve kids in California, depending on whether an assistant is available) or child-care centers (usually larger groups of more than fifteen) provide less costly alternatives. As one of a number of "employers," however, you have less say in the daily routine and acceptable activities. If you're satisfied overall, you'll have to be somewhat flexible in how the details are handled. Some providers take only certain ages, while others handle a mixed-age group. Handling six kids alone sounds inconceivable to me, but some family day-care providers are masters at organization and routine. Others are not. Visit and observe.

  Because of the small group size, many family day-care providers accommodate unusual hours and special requests. Day-care centers tend to be less flexible. By the way, licensing doesn't assure quality, but it does make certain the facility meets health and safety requirements.

> Child-care workers' earnings fall within the lowest tenth of all wage-earners and they often receive no benefits.[10]

- Work on your child's schedule. Consider employment that allows you to work when your child doesn't need you. When I'm not on deadline, I write while Christopher sleeps. Being a night owl, I prefer this schedule. Teachers share holiday breaks with their kids. Real estate agents have a fair degree of control over their hours. Other single parents work from their homes as consultants, cottage-industry manufacturers, typists, and whatever their imaginations create.

- Take your baby to work. Babies present a special child-care problem, especially if you breast-feed. Pumping milk for the freezer is time-consuming, unsatisfying, and sometimes painful. The national Family and Medical Leave Bill requires twelve weeks of unpaid leave for childbirth, adoption, or caring for a sick child. That's insufficient compared to the benefits afforded in other industrialized countries, which normally allow months of *paid* leave.

  Is there a way to take your infant with you to work? I can't imagine doing this myself, but it might be fine under certain conditions that allow you to do your job and meet your baby's needs.
- Consider hiring a driver. When the kids grow older, perhaps all you need is a chauffeur to get them to and from school and activities while you work. A college student or parent of a classmate may fit the bill. I've seen several recent ads for "kid taxis," minivans that transport children for a fee on a regular or one-time basis.

Checking Out Child-Care Providers

The newspapers exploit horrifying stories of danger and molestation at well-respected day-care centers. Seemingly wonderful sitters do loathsome things to kids. It may not happen frequently, but once is too often. And you don't want it to be *your* kid. How can you protect him?

- Eliminate anyone who won't participate in a thorough background check.
- Prepare questions in advance. Focus both on who the person really is and how he would handle child care. For the latter, pose hypotheticals: How would he deal with temper tantrums, thrown food, sass, fire?
- Require a full employment history with explanations for gaps. How much child care has the applicant done, and for what age children?
- Has the applicant had any training? Sometimes caregivers without much practical experience take courses in child development, CPR, or first aid to gain credibility. "Nanny colleges" also train people interested in starting new careers in child care.

- Have your child meet the applicant or visit the facility and observe the reactions and interactions.
- Check references, and lots of them, both before and after your interview with the applicant or facility. Ask references piercing questions that don't call for yes-or-no answers: What did you find least commendable about this person or facility? Were you ever surprised by anything you saw when dropping in? How does the person compare with other caregivers?
- Ask for a driving record. In California, you can't obtain a report on another person, but the applicant can get a copy of his own record. Review it for the number and type of traffic violations so you don't unknowingly turn your child over to a speed-demon, drunk driver, or crash enthusiast.
- Check any child-care registry available in your state. In California, the legislature created "TrustLine" to list applicants without criminal convictions or child-abuse reports. While registration is voluntary, you could require submitting to it as a condition of employment.

Safety and Other Standards

A licensed facility must pass a safety inspection, but more informal family day cares and share-cares at another home do not. Licensing requires certain standards in discipline, snacks, cleanliness, ventilation and heating, emergency plans and information, and illness policies. Address similar concerns yourself in any private setting where your child spends his time. Don't be shy—your child's safety depends on you.

- Drop in unexpectedly at different times of the day. Observe children's reactions to the setting and the adults. Watch how the grown-ups interact with kids. Are they respectful? Do they seem harried? Caring? Is the feeling soothing and calm or chaotic? Does television provide the main entertainment? Do the adults have time for more than just feeding and cleaning the kids? Do any children appear ill? Is hygiene stressed? Is the atmosphere too lax? Too rigid? Chaotic? Are kids allowed to follow their own interests? Do they fight? How is discipline handled?
- Obtain a roster of other parents so you can compare notes and share concerns.
- Get to know everyone involved in the facility, whether employees, family, neighbors, or interns.

- Never sign "blanket" permission slips for field trips, and make certain your provider never takes your child off the premises without your knowledge and express permission. Provide a list of people authorized to pick your child up, and abide by it yourself by giving advance notice of any changes. If your ex is not authorized, tell the caregiver specifically that your child should never be released to him.
- Listen to your child; observe his reactions. If he rebels at going or seems unhappy, delve into the source of his discomfort. Is it merely the separation from you, or is he neglected or abused in your absence? Making that distinction can be so difficult, especially with young children. Give it some time. If the behavior persists, talk to the caregiver and listen to your instincts. Increase the frequency of your drop-ins for a while.
- Check out any concerns with the caregiver, but realize that occasional bumps and bruises are normal, as is sexual curiosity among young children.
- Report unresolved concerns to the licensing body or other appropriate authorities. In some instances, you may make anonymous reports.
- Trust your instincts. You know your child best. Pay attention to uneasiness, even if you can't pinpoint the cause. Don't let reluctance to move your child again keep you from acting on your inner alarms. If you suspect abuse of any sort, see Chapter 10.

> Almost 87% of single parents are women. But they earn 30 to 50% less than men in equivalent jobs.[11]

Before- and After-School Solutions

Like most working parents, you go to your job earlier and return later than your child's normal school hours. What does he do during that extra time?

When reviewing your options, don't forget to consider transportation, schedule, cost, and available activities. If the site isn't at school, how will he get there? Who could take him? Kid taxis? Is walking safe? How will he learn the way? Can he be trusted in traffic? What about bad weather? Is care available during school holidays? Will he just hang out or have something interesting to do? Is there opportunity to suit both quiet and active moods? Is outside physical activity available? Will he be able to do homework there? With help? How many other kids will be there, and will they be separated by age? Among your choices are:

Average incomes for single-parent families in 1991 were:

	SINGLE MOTHERS	SINGLE FATHERS
Caucasian	$20,000	$32,000
Hispanic	15,000	23,500
African-American	14,000	23,000 [12]

- School programs. Fortunately, educators in the last decade recognized that working parents need safe before- and after-school care for their children. Inquire about the local school program, which usually offers nonacademic activities.
- Other organizations. Groups like the YMCA sometimes provide care nearby or on the school site. Some transport children in vans (make sure they're insured!) from various schools to a central location. The schedules usually revolve around school holidays.
- At-home sitters. Because you need two short "shifts," before and after school, finding in-home sitters for school-age kids is difficult. Consider neighbors and college students who drive and maintain irregular hours.

  Perhaps an all-day, in-home sitter for a younger child can also handle transport duties for the older one.
- Some schools have lists of retired people willing to take and pick up children at school. They usually live nearby and have flexible hours. They feed your kid and supervise homework. Consider nonworking neighbors who might take on transportation and a few hours of child care.
- Share-care. A local sitter working for another family might take your child on a part-time basis, with the other family's permission.
- Family day care. These providers sometimes take school-age kids, and they often don't mind irregular hours. Older children can walk to a nearby home, or a provider may drive them to and from school.
- Enlist your teenager. Don't deprive your teen of his own extracurricular interests, but perhaps he could work for you part-time.

Before going this route, think about his level of responsibility, relationship with the younger kid, and desire to take over this job.

Home Alone

Older kids who lack or refuse to attend after-school programs may come home alone. Nobody recommends this as a first choice, but America has many as 15 million kids on their own while parents work. While latch-key kids used to be poor, more middle-class children now come home to empty houses, especially those in single-parent families. This solution teaches responsibility and self-reliance, but some kids give in to excessive TV or experience loneliness and stress. Children as young as eight or nine stay by themselves, but the experience frightens them. Can your child handle the latch-key alternative?

- Take his age, maturity, willingness, and personality into account. Will he panic in an emergency? Can he keep track of a house key? Will your employer allow daily phone calls when he arrives home?
- Check his knowledge about what to do if a stranger calls or rings the door bell. Regardless of age, your kid should never open the door to *anyone* he doesn't know, even an injured person or Ed McMahon with that million bucks you've won. He should never let anyone know he's alone. He can screen calls by answering machine, and if he should answer a call for you, instruct him to say you are "not available right now" rather than "not home." Have him keep doors and street-accessible windows locked.
- Line up neighbors to help out should a problem arise.
- Leave extra keys with a neighbor or in a secure hiding place in case of a lock-out.
- Communicate. Your child can't *possibly* do what you want if you don't make clear what that is. Simplify your requirements, however, or your kid will feel overwhelmed and resentful of "picky" rules.
- Devise projects together for your kid's time alone. Include the structured chores you expect, like weeding the garden, cleaning, or cooking dinner. Limit the amount and type of TV. He can do his chores or exercise. If he likes to cook, let him start dinner. Create a "message center" where he looks every day for special instructions.
- Require him to call you if he goes to someone else's house, and have a clear understanding about how long he can stay and how he'll get home.

- Have an understanding about who can come to the house in your absence, and how many can come at once. Make clear what activities are and are not allowed.
- If your kid can't get through to you at work when he needs you, have him leave a message and call another person who has agreed to be your backup. Other parents should be happy to share such standby duty.
- Don't assume your children know what to do in case of earthquake, fire, or other crisis. Make and review emergency plans periodically.
- Nowadays some teens wear a beeper so their parents can reach them by phone wherever they are. In any event, let the kids know that you will call at random and occasionally, even show up unexpectedly, "to make sure they're okay." The thought of your possible sudden appearance might be enough to dampen the more outrageous plans.
- Make sure your child understands safety rules. Don't be afraid to state the obvious:
  - –Wash hands before preparing food.
  - –Be wary of getting burned: Conventional stoves, whether gas or electric, present burn dangers. Also, electric burners remain very hot for a time after being turned off, and some give no visual indication of heat.
  - –Increasing numbers of burns result from microwaves. The National Safety Council recommends supervising children with microwaves until age twelve. Unevenly heated food causes burns. Cheese in a burrito, for example, heats faster than the tortilla. Though the outside feels just warm, the cheese can get mouth-burning hot. Hot food or liquid can spill on hands reaching up to remove a dish. Hot steam escapes from beneath plastic wrap or lids.
  - –Small hands should never use adult oven mitts. They're too awkward to manipulate.
  - –Picking up a hot item with a damp pot holder forms instant steam that can seriously burn a hand.

> The average employed American man spends the annual equivalent of two-and-one-half *extra* weeks on the job compared with 20 years ago. Women average an additional *seven*-and-one-half weeks![13]

–Be careful not to get cut. Emergency rooms report an increased rate of "bagel-related" injuries. Holding a bagel vertically like a wheel and cutting down often causes it to "jump away," leaving a knife slicing through a hand. Buy a gizmo that holds the bagel for slicing. Or, rather than standing the bagel on end so it rests on a rounded, unstable surface, lay it flat on the counter and saw sideways with one hand on top (keep the fingers out of the way!) Cut at least halfway through before turning it vertical.

–Be aware of fire hazards. Turn off the oven and stove-top burners before cleaning up and leaving the kitchen.

- Some cities have hot lines for latch-key kids to call for reassurance, often staffed by retired people. To find one in your area, inquire at your child's school or the United Way.
- Consider hiring a local college student for cooking or chores around the house when your older kid is alone. Whether or not you require your child to assist, the student's presence provides companionship and supervision for him. If you don't let on, he may never guess your ulterior motive!

Child Care for Special-Needs Kids

The 1992 Americans with Disabilities Act requires providers to accommodate *all* children, including those with special needs due to disability. Special-needs kids' physical, mental, or emotional disabilities range from mild to terminal, but they're still kids. They are more *like* than different from other children.

Decide first whether you want just care or special education. Does the disability require care by someone with training? Are you willing to train someone?

The alternatives are:

- In-home baby-sitters. Check applicants out just as you would for any child, and add questions about experience and willingness to deal with special needs. Start with a trial period.
- Shared sitters. You might find a family to share a special-needs sitter in your homes. Inquire at offices where your child gets therapy or medical care.
- Family day care. Some providers have training or experience in this area, either with their own kids or others'. Small size and flexibility make family day care a good choice.

- Some licensed centers either serve special-needs kids exclusively or mainstream them into regular programs.

Make sure you meet the director *and* the staff who will actually care for your child. Be honest about your child's condition and what care and medication he requires. Discuss your child's mobility and any idiosyncratic means of communication. Whatever alternative you consider, carefully evaluate the caregiver's experience and attitudes toward your kid and his disability. Ask yourself:

> Women around the world work longer hours than men—both at home and on the job. The Population Council reports that in seventeen less-developed countries, women's work exceeded men's by 30%. In twelve industrialized countries, formally employed women worked about 20% longer hours than employed men.[14]

- Does the caregiver seem to treat your child "normally," in a friendly, supportive way, without constantly making a point of the disability? Is he hesitant or overly protective?
- How will your child's special physical needs be handled—assistance in the bathroom, for example?
- Does the program include any other special-needs kids? Seek references from their parents.
- Will your child be able to participate in activities he especially enjoys? What will happen when he finds an activity very difficult?

Remember to provide written instructions to aid the memory of the caregiver you select.

Finding Night Care

The difficulty of finding adequate child care for the nine-to-five crowd pales in comparison to the 14 million Americans working nonstandard hours—nights, early mornings, and weekends. They represent nearly one in five full-time workers. The number of male and female employees working nonstandard hours grows as we trend toward a twenty-four-hour, service-based economy; increased overtime; and longer work weeks. Service jobs include many of those traditionally held by women. In 1990, 7.2 million women with 11.7 million children under age fifteen worked full- or part-time nonstandard hours. Seventy-one percent of these moms did so as a job requirement.

The single-parent night worker has few alternatives. Child care at work, while ideal, rarely exists. Very few child-care centers stay open past early evening. Relatives may live at a distance or work odd hours themselves.

> "Work consists of whatever a body is obliged to do and play consists of whatever a body is not obliged to do."
> MARK TWAIN (1835–1910)

Desperate needs create desperate solutions. Some night workers at a round-the-clock food processing plant created their own form of "care" by allowing kids to sleep unattended in their cars in the factory parking lot! Others accept inadequate or doubtful care situations.

Fortunately, the issue has received some attention in the media. A few centers exist in scattered areas, run by single employers, consortia of employers in an industry or geographic area, or community interests. This admirable first step needs to be cloned nationwide.

Keeping Good Child Care

Remember that your caregiver is human and therefore needs consideration, respect, and good communication.

Getting Out of the House on Time

You might expect to find this topic in the chapter about running a household, but getting out of the house only really matters when you have to be somewhere—usually work—at a particular time. The secrets to a smooth morning departure are (1) preparing the night before and (2) establishing a routine. The more you do ahead, the less you must squeeze into those limited morning minutes, and the more routine, the less chance of forgetting something important.

Do As Much As Possible the Night Before

- Set out everything that goes with everyone for the next morning—books, briefcases, dry cleaning, notes to the teacher. Designate a

convenient spot—a table, a certain shelf, the floor by the front door. Share locations or choose separate ones. Leave yourself a note in that spot for anything out of the ordinary you must remember, such as a dentist appointment. If you or the kids pack a lunch, set out the lunch box with the nonperishables inside and the lid open, which reminds you to grab the rest of the food from the fridge.
- Select your clothing for the next day and have your kids do the same. If your child is young, offer a choice between two outfits. If he won't choose at night, lay out the alternatives for quick morning selection. If he doesn't choose then, you do it.
- Set the breakfast table after dinner to have it ready for action when people roll out of bed.
- Make lunches. Older kids prepare their own from a selection of requested ingredients you buy every week.

Establish a Routine

If everyone does everything the same way each morning, you get out the door even if still half asleep—an especially handy tool for those hard-to-rouse teens.

- Orchestrate the mornings. Have the kids make their beds by quickly pulling up the covers, even if the results look like . . . well, an unmade bed. If you have just one bathroom, establish an order and time limits for use. Assign tasks. Someone clears the breakfast table; perhaps another checks the calendar for everyone's schedule. Make adjustments when the school term ends or begins or other changes occur in your lives.
- Put clocks in every room, including bathrooms, so everyone knows the time. Furnish every bedroom with an alarm clock that each kid sets for the time he needs to get up. For those who can't drag themselves out of bed, set the clock across the room—and make it electric, one that won't wind down and let the drowsy ones slip back to dreamland.
- Give periodic warnings of time before departure.
- Screen morning telephone calls and take only the most urgent.
- Incorporate time as a part of a young child's routine. Use a timer. Allow, say fifteen minutes for him to dress, after which you take over. Permit playtime or television only after he is completely ready for the road. This includes shoes on feet. Someone suggested that if the kid isn't dressed when the timer goes off, he has to wear what he has on at that point.

Travel

Whether your work requires constant travel, like Jeanette's, or rare business trips, ensure the well-being of your children when you hit the road without them.

Physical Care

In your absence, someone has to feed the kids, get them to and from school, discipline them, and keep them safe.

- Perhaps you're lucky enough to have family or friends who can care for your child for a few days. You're fortunate if your ex will take over when you leave town. Flexibility in rearranging your normal schedules is a real blessing, and, of course, it requires reciprocity.
- If you arrange care in your home, find a sitter you trust who can be available at the hours required to get your child to and from school and his other activities. Make the schedule very clear, written out on a day-by-day basis. Arrange for your child to have time with friends. Keep his life as "normal" as possible during your absence.

All major, commercial, online services, such as AOL, CompuServe, and Prodigy, offer employment-search services and Internet access.

- On the World Wide Web:
  –Go to http://www.yahoo.com for a list of popular Web sites. In the menu, click Business, then Employment, and then Jobs to get a list of sites that offer job listings, career advice, résumé postings, and other services.
- Online Careeer Center: http://www.occ.com
- America's Job Bank: http://ajb.dni.us
- JobWeb: http://www.jobweb.org

- Forge relationships with the stay-at-home parents and parents of your child's classmates at school. Since their kid is on the same schedule as yours, they can chauffeur your kid to school and after-school care along with theirs. Arrange overnights at his friends' houses while you're gone. (Don't make this your child's *first* overnight, however. For that one, you must be available for a mid-night run in case he panics in a strange house without you.)

Emotional Care

With an infant, the best approach is "out of sight, out of mind." He won't understand any explanations anyway, and he'll be content as long as he has a loving caretaker. Ideally, that person should be someone he already knows.

Older kids miss you. Make your presence felt even at a distance:

- Before you leave, explain where you're going and show the location on a map. Talk about how far it is, how many hours you'll travel, and what you'll do once you're there.
- Discuss the length of your trip. Small children have little sense of time, so relate the absence to something they'll understand. "I'll be back when you've gone to nursery school five times."

  Leave a calendar showing the days until you come home, and have the sitter help mark them off. Paste a small picture of yourself or a special sticker on the date you return.
- Assure your child you will call him, and do so often. Set prearranged times for calls, if possible, and then follow through.
- Leave pictures of yourself where your child will see them. Or provide a box of photos of the two of you.
- Leave letters behind for the sitter to read to him each day or every few days, depending on the length of your trip.
- Send postcards.
- Write short notes for the sitter to put where he'll find them.
- Make a recording or videotape of yourself for him to enjoy while you're gone. Read his favorite stories on tape.
- Leave a collection of small "surprises" from you for the baby-sitter to dole out daily.
- Plan a special activity when you return home. In your phone calls, remind your child of how much you're looking forward to it.

Taking Your Child with You on Business Trips

Consider taking your kid along when you go on business trips. Use a post-work weekend as a mini-vacation. Take your child's age and personality into consideration. Some kids adapt well to new situations, and others dissolve into nervous wrecks.

Warning: This alternative exhausts you. Make sure you're up to it.

- Use accumulated frequent flier miles to pay for your child's ticket. At least one airline offers a companions-fly-free fare, and hotels normally charge nothing extra for children in your room.

- Locate child-care facilities at your destination:
  - –Network among co-workers in the area.
  - –Let your child visit any nearby friends or relatives while you work.
  - –Some hotels either provide child care or arrange it with local, screened sitters. They're costly but convenient.
  - –Depending on your older children's maturity, leave them alone for a few hours at the hotel with prearranged phone check-ins.
  - –Rethink your accommodations. On a business trip to Chicago, Margaret passed up a local hotel to stay in Madison, Wisconsin, with relatives who watched her daughter during the day. Contact with family and the ability to see her at night made up for the inconvenience of commuting to Chicago every day.
  - –Bring along a retired or unemployed friend to baby-sit during the day. Someone otherwise unable to afford trips will jump at the opportunity.

None of these travel solutions are perfect, but, as Jeanette put it: "My situation isn't what I would prefer, but it's what I have." She goes from there, as we all must.

> "In order that people may be happy in their work, these three things are needed: They must be fit for it. They must not do too much of it. And they must have a sense of success in it."
>
> JOHN RUSKIN (1819–1900)

Single parents must fulfill their obligations to pay for their children's material needs, but parenting requires more. Your children need *you*.

Our society gives little support to the demands of working parents in general, and even less to working single parents. Until it does, you do your best on your own.

ORGANIZATIONS

Child Care Aware, National Association of Child Care Resource and Referral Agencies: Provides referrals to local resource centers specializing in finding child care; information packets. 800-424-2246.

Child Care Action Campaign. 330 7th Ave., 17th Floor, New York, NY 10001-5010; 212-239-0138.

National Organization of Downsized Employees: $25 annual membership and newsletter. 914-266-3556.

National Parenting Association (NPA): Nonprofit organization whose goal is building a society that cherishes children. Works on political issues such as family-friendly work environments and violence. Membership, $10 for two years, including insurance rates and direct-mail pharmacy. NPA, 65 Central Park West, New York, NY 10023.

Child-Care Organizations for Night and Other Nonstandard Hours

Palcare: A nonprofit group formed by unions, employers, community groups and local government. Operates a center seven days a week, 20 hours a day. 945 California Dr., Burlingame, CA; 415-340-1289.

Toyota Motor Manufacturing of Georgetown, KY: Maintains a twenty-four hour child-care center for 230 kids, ages six weeks to thirteen years.

Close to Home: A consortium of Phoenix employers. Recruits and trains child-care providers willing to provide services for nonstandard hours.

Children's Inn of Atlanta: A twenty-four-hour facility sponsored by the Atlanta Marriott Marquis, Marriott Suites Midtown, the Omni Hotel, and the Hyatt Regency. It provides child care for hourly employees of the hospitality industry.

BOOKS FOR PARENTS

Be Your Own Headhunter Online, Pam Dickson, et al. (New York: Random House, 1995).

Finding a Job on the Internet, Alfred and Emily Glossbrenner (New York: McGraw-Hill Computing, 1995).

Hook Up, Get Hired! The Internet Job Search Revolution, Joyce L. Kennedy (New York: Wiley, 1995).

The 100 Best Companies to Work for in America, Robert Levering and Milton Moskowitz (New York: Doubleday, 1993).

"The 100 Best Companies for Working Mothers," *Working Mother* magazine, Milton Moskowitz and Carol Townsend (annual survey).

Working Mother subscriptions. Customer Service Manager, POB 5239, Harlan, IA 51593-0739.

BOOKS FOR KIDS

Alone at Home, Barbara Hazen (New York: Atheneum, 1992) (grades 2–4).

Chapter 12

School and Learning: Getting Your Kids a Decent Education

When I was young, my mom bought me a new coat every September and shoved me off to school without much angst. It never crossed her mind that her daughter could be knifed or gunned down in the halls. While high-schoolers guzzled a little beer, no one dealt crack cocaine to sixth graders. Teachers performed with varying degrees of competence, but most students could at least read their diplomas after twelve years. Mothers and fathers deferred to school authorities to decide what was "best" for the children. Most moms didn't work and greeted the kids after school each day. Relatively rare, divorces produced few single-parent families. My parents' generation confronted few of the dilemmas and difficult decisions we face in getting our kids a decent education.

Perhaps I'm idealizing my own school years, but today's parents and media demonstrate strong reservations about educational quality and school safety. As a mother in one of the lowest-ranked states academically, I'm one of them. Before Tony died, I planned to home-school Christopher, but that's not an option for me as a single mom. Now I'm learning that making the school system work to my advantage requires time and energy—assets at a premium for single parents. But it's worth the investment. In fact, there's no other choice.

Much of this chapter applies to married as well as single parents, except if you're single, you have to do it *all.* As a single parent, you may face an additional disadvantage—a difficult ex who cares more about pulling your chain than ensuring your child's educational well-being.

How do we educate our kids in the midst of all this? We play the hand we're dealt, concentrating on what we *can* influence. As my friend Ann said, "It helped me a lot to live near the school; from my kitchen window I could watch my children walk across the street and in the big blue door. I didn't work more than a couple of miles away, either, when they were little. Perhaps these were ideal conditions, but I carefully chose them."

School Resources for Single Parents

Some schools, recognizing the high rate of divorce, offer support for single parents and their children. Ann attended a six-week group led by a guidance counselor. The members found it so useful they continued on independently. Consult your school's counselor or principal about the availability of similar programs.

If informed, school counselors help mitigate the effects of death or divorce on your child. Ask if the school could sponsor a support group for children of divorce (see Chapter 1).

School and the Difficult Ex-Spouse

If you get along with your ex, negotiation and compromise aid in educating your children. However, your job becomes much, much harder if a spiteful ex thwarts your efforts. He appears at school with criticism and orders for everyone, threatening careful alliances you've forged. Perhaps he demands a mid-year change of schools or teachers. He paints you as nefarious, stupid, and uncaring.

- Work around a hostile former spouse as best you can. If he doesn't send you a copy of the school calendar, get one for yourself. Ask the school for copies of all relevant papers your ex submits to make sure he puts you on the emergency list *and* provides the correct name, address, and phone numbers. Double check from time to time to make certain he hasn't removed you.

  As Ann says, "One wishes that everybody could get a grip when they show up in the school arena, rallying round the embassy flag as it were, but some people constantly seek votes in an imagined competition for best parent, often by defaming the competitor. I guess the only thing you can say is that at least they care."

- Perhaps your ex's failure to cooperate arises from neglect rather than bad intentions. You share custody, and your child travels back and forth during the week. Your ex doesn't monitor homework. He forgets permission slips. He never mentions messages from the teachers. He sends your kid to school dirty or without lunch.

  These things will drive you crazy if you let them. Just take care of your side of the street. You will not change your ex's behavior by nagging, screaming, or pleading. You never have, right? Do what you can to protect your child. Help with homework, double-check for messages, give him emergency lunch money. And then let go.

Getting the School Year Off to a Good Start

A successful school experience requires action long before September rolls around. As a single parent, the burden falls on you alone.

Get the School You Want

> "Real education consists in drawing the best out of yourself. What better book can there be than the book of humanity."
> GANDHI (1869–1948)

Parents' determination to enroll their children in schools with high "test scores" can be fierce. The efforts start months before that first September school day.

- For those who can afford it—and for many who really can't—private schools offer the answer. Even scrimping everywhere else, most single parents find it impossible to dish out multiple thousands every year for private-school tuition. Some, like Tia, spend what would otherwise be college money for private primary and secondary schools, and hope for university scholarships later. Public-school advocates argue that irresponsible flight to private schools causes further deterioration of local programs—public schools would vastly improve if only the parents who care would stick around. I agree, and at the same time, I understand not sacrificing your own child's education on the altar of abstract principle.
- Some people contemplate moving across the country for improved educational opportunities. Many relocate a few miles away to take advantage of another district's better schools. Real estate prices directly reflect school quality, however. You might as well opt for private school, although a higher mortgage is at least tax-deductible.

- For other people, inter-district transfer among city schools provides the solution. State laws vary on whether and on what grounds they allow transfers. Acceptable reasons might include distance from home or after-school care, racial imbalance, special interests or needs, or readiness for more advanced work. Even without a law, local school officials can often authorize transfers. Start with a letter or phone call.

  In my town, test scores range from "pretty good" in the hill areas to "horrible" elsewhere. With California's inflated housing costs, even two incomes often can't afford the better districts. Families compete each year to fill the few vacant seats in the best out-of-district schools. Selection by lottery eliminates most.

Some parents resort to "borrowing" an address from friends in the right district. While not legitimate, this practice attracts even otherwise strictly principled people, and some say that authorities at their current in-district schools helped and encouraged them. Likewise, the transferee schools turn a blind eye, not bothering to confirm student addresses. I don't advocate this solution or approve of the values it teaches children; but I understand the desperation these parents face.

Make your school selection if you can. Then work the system to your child's best advantage. Start with choice of teacher.

Get the Teacher You Want

Schools always insist that requests for particular teachers won't be granted. Of course they say that. But the fact is, everyone I know who expressed a preference got the teacher he wanted.

How do you *know* which one you want? Perhaps you have first-hand experience with your older children at that school. If not:

- Talk to other parents.
- Schools usually sponsor open houses in early spring. Attend one for the grade your child will enter next fall and check out the teachers. Consider what the room tells you. Is it so neat and clean you wonder if the teacher discourages creativity? Or so chaotic he has no control? Inspect the quality of the student work exhibited. Are desks arranged in rows or groups or circles? What does this say about teaching methods? Form some tentative impressions.
- Talk with the teachers. Test the conclusions you drew from the rooms themselves. Get a sense of methods, educational philosophy,

homework, and attitudes toward strengths and weaknesses of your child. If necessary, make an appointment for further discussion.

Mention how you volunteered in your child's previous classrooms. Say what you hope to contribute in the coming year. Any educator wants a kid who brings along a helpful parent as a bonus. Don't, however, exaggerate beyond your ability to follow through; you'll ruin your credibility for following years.

- Once you have a teacher preference, express it—at pre-registration or in a private call to the principal, for example. Tell the teacher directly that he's your choice, and why.

Set Aside September

Reserve September entirely for school-related matters. Try to postpone business trips and deadlines during that month. A good start at school pays off all year long. Take time to sharpen the shears now. Ensuring a smooth transition is especially critical if the school is a new one for your child.

- Exactly what to do in September depends on your kid's age. A five-year-old entering kindergarten with little prior school experience needs more hand-holding than a sixth grader, but a freshman entering high school also faces many unknowns—whether he'll discuss his insecurities with you is another question. Talk about your own "ancient" experiences to convey information or food for thought without seeming to interfere or condescend.
- Help your kid anticipate the new experience. Emphasize familiar elements as bridges to the unfamiliar world. "You'll still have time to run around outside, except now it's called P.E. instead of recess."
- Remind your child that others will be in exactly the same situation and won't know what to do—teachers expect that, and they'll state the rules and procedures.
- Convey any information about class routine, expectations, or homework that you gleaned from discussions with the teacher earlier in the year. Don't be afraid to say you don't know something. Suggest ways your child can find out, and ask him to let you know the answer. He can watch to see how older children operate, for example.
- If the school and your kid approve, go in with him the first day. (At a certain age, your child will blanch at the thought, though.) Reintroduce yourself to the teacher.
- When the first week's chaos dies down, volunteer something right away. One dad, a naturalist, starts every year by lecturing about a

tarantula he captures for the class. *Most* teachers consider this a positive contribution—at least if he takes his hairy friend home after school!

- Iron out glitches and establish a routine rather than "putting out fires" every day for months. Devote a week of September to one of the four major aspects of attending school: getting out the door in the morning, handling after-school time, making and remembering lunches, and doing homework (see Chapters 5, 9, and 11 for specific suggestions). Figure out any transportation problems. Agree on chores expected. Explain any before- and after-school program to your child. Urge your kid to let you know what, if anything, doesn't work as the month progresses. Think of the first weeks of school as a shake-out cruise.
- Attend fall "back-to-school night" for exposure to the personalities your child may mention at home. Unfortunately, parent attendance at these events plummets in higher grades, which is precisely when they may most be needed.
- Maintain strong family connections during this time of change. Save September weekends for activities together.
- Discourage your kid from spending all his time with one friend. The more styles and personalities he experiences, the better.
- Encourage him to make new friends at the beginning of the year. Friendships influence academic success, and making them is easier before cliques and alliances solidify. One mother promises to take her daughter somewhere special as soon as she makes two *new* friends to ask along.

  You may have to explain how to make friends: Smile. Take the risk of speaking first. Show interest and curiosity. Avoid negative snap judgments. Ask someone for help. Make someone feel needed or special. Don't take rejection personally (let's all learn that one!). When someone mistreats you, assume the cause is not you but some problem in *his* life. Show (or, if you have trouble believing it, pretend) that you care about yourself, that you're worthy of being liked.

You Are Your Child's Only Advocate: Be a "Presence"

You know how great your child is, but to the teacher he's one of thirty-five staring faces. Even if the instructor spent every minute of a six-hour day giving them each individual attention, he'd have only ten minutes with your kid. Add instruction and discipline, and those minutes melt away to nothing. How can you ensure that the teacher notices your child, especially if he's quiet?

Be an ongoing "presence" in the life of the class. Subtly plant a favorable view of yourself in the teacher's consciousness. You've already laid the groundwork with your open house and back-to-school chats. Knowing you preferred him as the teacher flattered his ego. Your involvement buoys him. It lightens his load, focuses him on your child, and it demonstrates your caring, giving nature. He'll remember this when you request something of him. Your physical presence encourages casual remarks that he wouldn't think merited a special phone call.

Ask the teacher when and how you can touch bases with him just to make sure everything is going smoothly. Establish a regular schedule to exchange a few words. Ask if you can drop in on Tuesdays as you pick up your daughter, or as you leave her in the morning. Maybe the teacher prefers a phone call at night. Whatever the details, knowing you'll be checking in motivates him subtly to notice your child so he'll have something to tell you.

If you *really* can't swing the time, go in at least once and tell the teacher that you won't be able to see him often, but if he needs something you can provide, he should call. Then tell him expressly what you *can* offer.

> American students consistently rank near the bottom in international comparisons of academic achievement. In one study, Americans ranked fourteenth out of 20 nations in math and science.[1]

- Level with the teacher about your divorce if you expect it to affect your child at school. Telling him you're having difficulties with your ex may make your kid stand out as someone who needs a bit of extra attention.

  I enlist Christopher's teachers and administrators to reinforce what I tell him about our family. Not ready to expose him to the typical adult discomfort at the mention of death, I bring the subject up myself. Better that they overcome their uneasiness with me than with Christopher. I emphasize that talking about Tony's death is normal and acceptable and tell them *how* to discuss the subject when it arises (see Chapter 2).

For the most part, this approach works well. Once, however, I spoke with a prospective preschool teacher, who then introduced me to the school's director as the mother of a son with "emotional problems"! Needless to say, this assumption outraged me. I learned from this experience that disclosing personal circumstances runs the risk of having your child characterized wrongly or labeled negatively. This difficult choice ultimately rests upon your intuition about how much to reveal and to whom.

- Build connections with teachers' aides and classroom helpers, who have fewer specific duties and more available time than teachers.
- Show appreciation to teachers and teachers' aides. Say thank you, give compliments when due, recognize their efforts, deliver croissants, donate persimmons from your tree, or even bring an occasional bouquet of flowers. These seem simple, but they work very well because so few parents bother to do them!
- Get into the classroom occasionally, even if you have to take a day off work. This is not "interfering" or "being nosy." It's your responsibility. (Keep in mind, however, that teens would rather see you dead than in their school, much less in their classrooms. Opt for a more behind-the-scenes approach with their teachers.)
- Volunteer as much as possible—in class, as a driver on field trips, or whatever you can do to help the school. Volunteer work needn't be a second career. Think of contributions geared to your time and talents. As a caterer, Amy provides food for class parties and regularly drops off leftovers from other jobs for the teachers' lounge. Teachers can't wait for her kids to reach their grades.

  Like Amy, be creative in contributing without making your schedule crazier than it already is. Don't pass an opportunity to do something you can do just because you can't do it *all the time*. Make instructional materials, help with paperwork, demonstrate a science experiment, speak about your profession, do clerical work like filing attendance forms. Perhaps you can use the photocopier at work, make a presentation about your industry, or get a special deal on hot dogs for the school picnic. All of these free the teacher to plan, devise new teaching strategies, and work directly with the kids.

  In recalling her experience as the single mom of two elementary-school kids, Ann put it well: "I was always a very active parent—on the after-school program board, in the PTA, inviting teachers to dinner, fixing the single ones up with my brother, building alliances, and lobbying for my kids. It seemed obvious to me that the kids with active, likable parents got the most attention;

teachers wanted these kids in their class. It's probably the only time in my life I was diplomatic; I could tell that the teachers resented the bossy parents, and I didn't blame them. My kids always got the teachers I selected. I guess I believe in the old truism, 'Ninety percent of everything is just showing up.' But single parents have to show up twice as often and have twice as strong a band of friends."

Parent visibility also gives your child a popularity "edge," at least until the teen years. He gains importance in the eyes of his peers when his parent gets involved. Mary found that: "Parents who do volunteer work at the school really pave the way for their kids. They are visible, all the kids and teachers know whose parents they are, and the teachers feel indebted to them."

As Ann said, "Parents are fundamentally ambassadors for their children in the world of adults. It's more than being an advocate; it's a diplomatic mission that calls for many social skills. It helps kids when their parents are well-liked. On the other hand, it definitely hurts them if a parent does anything embarrassing. When I was in grade school my mother got a popular bus driver fired for not closing the bus door as he pulled away from the stop. Riding the bus was hell for me from then on because the kids hated me. This was not diplomatic, ambassador-quality mothering!"

Yes, I know that whatever your child gets will be at another's expense. As sad as that is, you can't single-handedly alter the school system. You can, however, ensure that *your* child benefits from it. If you don't, no one will. You're his only advocate, the only person looking out for him. Maybe his academic brilliance or athletic prowess will bring him forth into the limelight, but don't count on it. Use whatever means you can to direct that extra bit of positive attention to him—but do so nicely. You'll enjoy the process more yourself by staying on good terms with important figures in your child's academic life. Call this manipulation if you must, but it's far more effective than adversarial demands.

Encouraging Success in School

Don't imagine that education stops at the final bell. That's why this chapter is called "School *and* Learning." A child's home life greatly affects his success in school, and your efforts pay off. Most of them take little extra time if incorporated into the minutes you spend with your son or daughter anyway, and you may find them entertaining yourself. I list many suggestions—don't think you must do them all or all at once. Pick and choose over time according to interests and ages.

Don't fret about whether your ex does anything at home to enhance your kid's education. It's great if he does, and if not, your child will benefit from *your* efforts to:

- Actively show that *you* are still a learner
- Help your child develop self-esteem
- Establish good family work habits
- Approach learning as its own reward
- Help your child understand how schoolwork applies to his life
- Be supportive about homework
- Reinforce learning with stimulating activities and skill development at home

> The top U.S. students are the worst of the best.
> - When compared to the top 1% of other countries, *our* top 1% ends up *last.*
> - In math, our *top* 5% are about equal to *average* Asian students.[2]

Actively Show That You *Are Still a Learner*

Once again, modeling influences behavior more than anything else. Let your kids see you in educational or enriching pursuits. Read and discuss books. If you must watch television, make it educational. Attend lectures. Discuss ideas on social, scientific, political, and aesthetic topics. Play educational games. Take up an art. Go to the library often. Enroll in occasional courses yourself, perhaps computer graphics to enhance your employment or stained glass art just because it's fun. If your children see you practicing what you preach, they'll view learning as a fun, lifelong, fascinating activity.

Help Your Child Develop Self-Esteem

A child who feels worthy and confident easily tackles school's challenges. He considers himself a problem-solver and creative thinker. He knows he can learn and speaks up when he doesn't understand. A child with self-esteem participates in class and doesn't fear mistakes. He learns from failure instead of giving up in despair.

Self-esteem underlies all learning, even that which seems to require special talent. My own art-class teacher insists that "art is entirely a matter of self-esteem. You need someone to say what you're doing right and show you techniques for improving the rest." Even a little validation goes a long way.

- Get to know your child's strengths and weaknesses. Explaining his learning style to teachers helps them exploit it and avoid misinterpreting his behavior. Christopher, for example, is intelligent but has his own ideas about how and when to approach new experiences. He focuses very intently on what interests him and ignores anything else. If bored, he gets goofy and won't pay attention. A teacher who understands the meaning of his behaviors can respect his style and temperament, which makes him feel capable and successful.
- Help with self-esteem by keeping your own issues and feelings separate from your child's. A father who pursues his football dreams by forcing his unathletic son to go out for the team has his own interests at heart, not his son's. The boy's failure to please Dad can severely damage the youngster's self-esteem. Trying to change your child's nature signals that something is wrong with him never alleviates *your* old pain, anyway. For more on self-esteem and boundaries, see Chapters 5 and 9.

Establish Good Family Work Habits

Interestingly enough, healthy family routines favorably affect a child's school performance. Skills from home transfer to the classroom, and feeling rested and unstressed gives your kid the energy for learning.

- Through observing a structured household routine, your child learns the satisfaction and effectiveness of planning and following through. He sees that, like regular meals, bedtimes, and morning departures, school's routines make life run smoothly.
- Set up a family calendar that everyone updates together once a week, perhaps at the family meeting (see Chapter 5). Include all deadlines and events: doctor's appointments, homework due-dates, allowance days, lessons, soccer games, family meetings, exams, team practice, vacations, and family activities. This instills an ability to plan.
- Include the children in planning, shopping for, and preparing some dinners. Do this perhaps weekly or monthly. Sitting down to a meal they engineered is a reward in itself.
- Being punctual and relying on others' punctuality encourages dependability and discourages tardiness at school (see the section on getting out the door in Chapter 11.)
- Requiring work before play teaches children to set priorities. Getting chores and homework out of the way ensures enough time

for those must-do items and leaves no looming obligations to spoil playtime later.

- Requiring chores at an early age creates skills such as folding laundry and wiping up spills. It instills a sense of belonging, usefulness, and responsibility. Even a very young child can have household jobs. When first introduced to, say, sorting the silverware, he'll think it's more fun than mashed potatoes in a wide-open mouth. Of course, the novelty wears off after a few times, so substitute a new job. Try feeding the pets, setting the table, emptying the trash, sorting laundry, watering the garden, vacuuming, or carrying light bags of groceries from the car. For your own sanity, remember, at least with a young kid, that this is primarily a teaching tool for him and only secondarily a work-saver for you. Initially, you'll have to prod and remind until he finally knows you really *mean* he's supposed to do the job. Your effort will pay off later. (For more on chores, see Chapter 6.)

Approach Learning As Its Own Reward

Twenty years ago, the average high school student graduated with twice as many C's as A's on his record, a result consistent with a normal distribution of grades. Today, however, the high-school grad pulls more A's than C's, creating a false sense of accomplishment that encourages coasting. Both public- and private-school teachers experience administrative pressure to give B's to any student who "tries." Parents want high grades to improve chances of college acceptance and scholarships.

A recent international study asked students, parents, and teachers, "What factor best produces academic success?" Asians responded with "hard work." Americans named "intelligence." The American response implied, by and large, that if you're not smart, don't bother trying. And that if you're intelligent, you don't have to work because you'll just naturally get good grades.

- Avoid giving rewards for good marks. With this rampant grade inflation, even A's mean little.
- More importantly, studies find that punishments and rewards simply don't improve grade performance. Instead, a parent's encouragement to learn for the pleasure of learning correlates highly with success in school by creating internal motivation. Other kids who do not receive this kind of reinforcement tend to lack autonomy and look for external controls.

Moreover, if you start rewarding a child for grades when he's already eager to learn, his interest will *shift* to the reward, and he'll begin believing that's why he studies. Rewards *destroy* internal motivation.

- Show pride in your child's learning and reasoning abilities, not just in his grades. Acknowledge his efforts. "I like the way you tackled such a hard subject in that report." Let him feel good about learning every day, rather than waiting for report cards to be issued.

  If your child exhibits difficulties in school, maintain your expectation that he can learn effectively. Remind him that problems are puzzles to be solved. Work with him.
- Encourage your child to take challenging courses instead of "Micks," or "easy-A's." Although I love science, I avoided most formal courses from fear of ruining my GPA. I wish I'd had someone to tell me that learning matters more than grades. Anyway, I might have aced physics—I'll never know.

  Of course, grades do count in many ways, especially for college entrance. I'm not recommending that you disregard them. But interior motivation, not reward-and-punishment, is the most effective route *to* them.

Help Your Child Understand How Schoolwork Applies to His Life

"Why do I have to learn geometry? I'm going to be a sports announcer!" Sometimes school seems so irrelevant. Inform your kid that knowledge from all areas crops up in surprising ways, that exposure to many disciplines helps in social interactions.

- Speak positively about your own school experiences. Don't lie or minimize problems, but do talk about how you solved them. Generally let your child know that education is a valuable pursuit.
- Find out who your child's heroes are, and why. Discuss what it took for them to achieve success. Even if the heroes are all nonacademic baseball players, remind him of a playing career's limited duration. Emphasize that athletes fare much better after their playing days if they have an education. Find out together how geometry *does* apply to the science of baseball.
- Explore possible careers your child might pursue. Research occupations at the library. Encourage him to look into careers that don't seem obvious for him. A junior scientist with little interest in English class could end up writing science articles for *Newsweek,* for example. See if he can interview someone in the field.

Take your kid to your job and those of friends or relatives to get a feel for real world employment. Discuss what educational preparation these jobs require.

Be Supportive about Homework

Homework is a frequent battleground between parent and child. It doesn't have to be.

> The average American student reads only a total of 12 pages a day at school and home.[3]

Why Homework?

When Julie, a single-parent teacher, mentioned that she gave homework to her kindergartners, I didn't believe her at first. Homework for *five-year-olds?* What were they supposed to do—scribble themes on summer in the sandbox? I'll rebel, I thought. My young son won't waste *his* time on homework. Don't we pay teachers to educate the children in class?

Julie patiently explained that homework develops healthy study habits in very young children. *How* your child does the assignments ranks far above getting right answers. A good start in the early years correlates with academic success in high school and college. The main lesson for kindergarteners is just remembering to take the paper home and return it.

For older students, homework informs parents of class content and subject difficulty. It highlights problem areas and provides conversation openers for communication. It supplements what the teacher conveys in limited class time.

Good homework skills will serve your child well for the rest of his life. Many adult tasks—such as purchasing a car or home, or investing in the stock market—require the ability to research, analyze, and use information. The initiative and responsibility your kid learns by consistently turning in his homework translate into positive skills for the job market. Whatever path he chooses in later life, his success will depend to some extent on knowing how to "do his homework."

Be positive about homework. Don't label it cruel drudgery. Bring lightness to it.

How Much Homework?

Naturally, the amount of homework your child must do varies with teachers. As a general rule, third graders and younger children should have to do twenty to thirty minutes a day. Fourth to sixth graders get as much as forty minutes, and the amount increases from there.

If you feel your child has too much or too little homework, talk with the teacher.

A Good Environment for Doing Homework

- Supply the proper tools. Provide a comfortable, well-lit "homework area." Ideally, set up a desk in your child's room where he can escape family interruptions during study time. If space limitations require use of the dining room, make it clean and quiet. Find a nearby shelf to keep all reference materials and supplies in one place. Get a good dictionary.
- Many experts recommend against allowing television, music, or other background distractions.
- Involving your child in creating a study schedule will make him more likely to accept it. Help him set aside a realistic amount of time. Studying at the same time every day forms an easy-to-remember habit. Make study time early so your child isn't too tired to work well.
- Ask his teachers what you can best do to help.
- Try doing *your* "homework" during your kid's study time. Pay your bills, answer letters, update your address book—or do quiet chores like dusting or laundry. You'll get a lot done without interruptions, and your kid won't feel he's the only one doomed to evening work.

Helping with Homework

Everyone agrees that parents should not *do* their children's homework. It's a learning tool, not an end in itself. A study confirmed, however, that parents of good students usually show genuine interest in homework, make certain the children complete it, and provide some degree of help and review.

Beyond this, experts differ on how and how much you should assist with homework. Some encourage you to work closely with your kid: Make sure he understands the directions. Work the first few problems with him. Suggest ways to find answers. Go to the library and help research. Check the finished assignment for accuracy and completeness.

Other experts recommend you review homework only after grading by the teacher, on the theory that kids should learn to think for themselves and learn from mistakes.

I like the middle road:

- Let your child know you are available for help. If you're at work during his study time, either allow him to call you or keep a list of questions for your return.

- If he runs into difficulty on a large project, work with him to set goals and break it into separate steps. Then let *him* take the steps.
- Emphasize that homework is for understanding. Suggest that he first get the main ideas by reading introductions, summaries, and study questions, then go back and read carefully.
- Share other homework tips that worked for you, but don't require them.
- Review graded work, concentrating first on what your child did correctly and then offering extra help on problem areas.
- Praise his accomplishments without implying that you require perfection—or that you're surprised he could do so well.
- The ultimate goals are helping your child get to know himself as a worker and establishing routines that work for him. Set it up so that he is responsible for finishing and returning assignments. "How are you going to remind yourself to do your homework?" Help him come up with solutions. "Do you still need me to remind you?"
- When homework problems arise, don't fight, issue orders, or make threats. Describe what you see happening. "It seems you're leaving your book report until the last minute. Remember how you had to stay up late to finish the one you did last month?"

  Alternatively, ask him what *he* sees happening. "Can you see any pattern in how you handle book reports?"

"I Don't Have Any Homework"

We've all either used this excuse or seen it used. You hate to accuse little Molly of lying, but is it possible that her teachers assign so little? Does your child not consider the report due next week as tonight's homework? You want him to learn independent responsibility, but what if you suspect he's abusing your trust? Share your concerns with him and evaluate his response. Perhaps suggesting a talk with the teacher about assigning more homework will jog his memory!

At least one local school instituted a recorded homework-assignment line for parents. Some teachers provide assignment lists or homework-completion forms. One parent dealt with the problem by enforcing a "homework hour" even when his daughter insisted she had nothing to do. She hated sitting at her desk, alone and bored. Finally the books came out, and she gave up the excuse.

Keeping up your informal relationship with the teacher and aides is the best answer to this homework problem.

Reinforce School with Learning at Home

A stimulating home environment enhances school education. You are your child's first teacher. No, I don't expect single parents to dissect frogs on the dining room table, but you can consider times with your kid as potential learning experiences.

- Everyday activities offer myriad opportunities, and your child won't even know he's "learning." I see many single parents rushing to get something done with a youngster waiting and complaining in the background. Get him involved. Explain some weird facet of your task. Ask him to propose a solution.
- Set up special at-home learning experiences, especially ones where you learn, too. Christopher and I have done "science experiments" since he was three. Okay, I admit they're mostly for me, but I never would have done them alone. He loves mixing ingredients and seeing "science magic" right before his eyes. One day in science class he'll remember the quarter dancing on top of the soda jar or the copper-plated nails and think, "Oh yeah, I know about that."

A list of possible activities appears in the next section, just to give you some ideas. None of them requires much, if any, advance preparation:

Provide Stimulating Activities at Home

Kids *love* learning about new things, and opportunities exist everywhere around your house and neighborhood.

- For small children, just talk. Name objects, body parts, shapes, and colors. Explain what you're doing to his fingernails. Show him how the dishwasher works. Don't worry that he won't understand the vocabulary. Some of it sinks in.
- Play simple games with tots, such as peekaboo. Encourage movement to develop muscles.
- Provide opportunities for a young kid to socialize with others his age.
- Allow a preschooler to do whatever real-life activities he can—dressing, sorting, pouring, setting the table, helping with meal preparation.
- Play pretend and fantasy games with young kids.
- Play identification games—spot all the VW Beetles.
- Make up rhyming songs and word games.
- Help your child with hobbies, or at least show genuine interest in them. Ask questions and participate when you can.

- Encourage your child's passions, whether or not they're related to school. Research in reference books or on the Internet, just for fun. Approach the subject from many angles: In pursuit of Christopher's train obsession, we've rented movies, taken trips, subscribed to magazines, read innumerable books about history, diesel mechanics, track construction, and railroad lore. We've written stories. We've downloaded photos and train games from cyber-space. Christopher has learned to classify engines by the number and order of wheels, and his train drawings have become detailed and accurate.

  A single subject leads in many directions.
- Play board, card, or word games once a week, possibly after family meetings.
- Explore the "Neighborhood Wilderness." Talk about directions and learn to use a compass. Explain how to use a map. Get different kinds of maps of your area—topographical, road, geological, and so on—and compare their differences and uses.
- At home, blindly trace a route on a street map. Then walk or drive it and notice changes in neighborhoods along the way. Consider whether the map showed directly or through hints what you might see. A lake on the map, for example, indicates the possibility of ducks.
- Take a "Looking Tour" or go on a "Treasure Hunt." Choose a route and select a few things to inspect in detail. Bring a magnifying glass. Take turns identifying interesting aspects. Take the items apart. Open a seed pod. Examine how the parts of a bird feather attach. Take your specimens home for further investigation. Plant them. Drop them in water. Dye them.
- Keep a world map or globe accessible and pinpoint places with which you have even a tenuous connection. Christopher may be the only five-year-old who can confidently point to Kuwait, simply because our friends moved there.
- Ask your child to play teacher and introduce you or a younger sibling to something he learned.
- Teach your child to ask questions. Visit a small bakery when it's not busy, and ask to see how they make the bread. When grocery shopping with a small kid, use posted prices to teach him numbers. As he begins to read, let him hold the list and mark off items you put in the cart. If your sewer backs up, explain how sewer lines go beneath streets, to the water-treatment plant, and so on. Check into tours of fire stations, factories, artists' studios, and construction sites.
- Explore new portions of parks you already know.

- Go on a "Transportation Picnic." Consult maps and schedules and take the subway, bus, train, or car to a place where you can eat lunch. Talk about what you see on the way.
- Limit video games, which are passive and ultimately stultifying. Although they are interactive, the *type* of interaction is limited. Some experts believe the fatuous repetition impedes cognitive development by getting the brain stuck in a "groove" and "shutting it down" during the early years when thinking skills should be forming.

  Even if video games are not, in themselves, harmful, the hours spent playing them are at the expense of other activities such as reading, music, sports, conversation, and social interaction. (For more on TV and video games, see Chapter 9.)
- Limit television. Remind your children of the alternatives: games, cards, art, reading, hobbies, music, sports. "Too boring!" they protest? Boredom is valuable—it stimulates creativity.

  When you allow TV, use it to inspire reading and discussion. Talk about the news, plot and character in dramas, and what makes a comedy funny. Discuss canned laughter and why formulaic sitcoms are so common.

  If you watch commercial TV, tape programs and fast-forward through the ads. Occasionally, watch a few commercials and discuss why they are or are not effective. Left alone, kids don't know ads from programs until age six or eight, but they learn earlier if you teach them. Ask how a particular commercial works: What is it really saying? Does it sell products or feelings? Dissect sales talk and slogans. What do they *mean?*
- Having said all this, let me suggest that you also take time to appreciate nature's simple, quiet beauty with your child. One of my favorite cartoons shows a young boy saying something like, "Look how beautiful the moon is," and the father jumps in with a lecture about the moon's phases, its effect on the tides, the distance from earth, the rate of orbit, and so on. In this age of information overload, let your kids' naive eyes guide you back to the awesomeness of this planet.

Encourage Speech and Language Development at Home

Facility with language underlies almost every aspect of education, even the hard sciences. Obtaining and sharing information requires verbal and writing skills, both of which begin at home. You're not "teaching" so much as engendering a respect for communication, learning, and books. Some suggestions:

- Talk, talk, talk. Provide a role model for good communication. Set aside a regular time for discussions. Dinner, perhaps, or Sunday brunch. Take turns choosing topics. Discuss school matters, sports, a book, or politics. Anything of interest. Demonstrate that opinions may differ as long as everyone shows respect and politeness. Model for your kid how to analyze and respond to another's point. Show how to ask for information.
- Ask open-ended questions that invite a response in full sentences rather than yes-or-no answers.
- Speak to your children as you hope they will learn to speak, since they will imitate you. Use adult vocabulary. I don't believe in talking down to babies, and it's amazing how easily small children learn sophisticated words and phrases. Why limit them? Christopher constantly comes out with statements like, "That baby's crying annoys me," or, "Excuse me, may I have a word with you?" (He also blasted me with a "Damn it" the other day, and I swear I haven't said that in front of him more than once. Parents are powerful role models!)
- When new words surface during your activities, look them up together and try to incorporate them into conversations.

> Aristotle was asked how much educated men were superior to the uneducated: "As much," said he, "as the living are to the dead."
>
> DIOGENES LAERTIUS (412–323 B.C.)

Help Develop Reading and Pre-Reading Skills

- Read to your kids from an early age. They'll come to associate reading with pleasant times together, learn concepts from what they hear and see, and value books as sources of pleasure and information. Caring about characters in books also engenders empathy. Reading opens up other ways of life.
- Choose a variety of books including those dealing with difficult subjects such as anger, death, jealousy, and fear. Books not only teach but validate a child's inner experience and let him accept all aspects of himself. They allow children to see themselves in new contexts. Reading provides a mechanism for safely confronting fears of monsters, evil people, and abandonment.
- As much as I dislike television, a little of the right programming won't hurt and may even help preschoolers read earlier and score higher on verbal and numerical tests.

Christopher woke at 5:30 A.M. every day for about two years after Tony died. As a night owl, I simply couldn't start the day that early. Even Barney and Sesame Street came on much later. I finally videotaped previous days' shows and let my son watch them in my bedroom while I burrowed back under the pillows. I had to maintain some level of consciousness in case he needed me, but at least I didn't have to get up in the dark. At the age of two, Christopher completely surprised me by naming the letters on his new Denver Broncos pajamas. He read at four. As a bonus, he's a master at working the TV and VCR.

- Establish a time for reading to your child every day, whatever fits your schedule. After dinner, before bed, after school. Make this time inviolate, and ignore interruptions. Turn off the TV and stereo. Let the answering machine get the phone. Jumping up for even a brief conversation conveys the message that the bell and the voice on the wire rank higher with you than your child does.
- Make going to the library a weekly or biweekly routine. Get your kid his own library card. Our library issues them at age five.
- Read to your children even after they can read for themselves. Maintain that closeness you've enjoyed while lost in a book together. Take turns reading to one another. Read the classics aloud as your children grow. The pleasure of being read to overcomes any reluctance to tackle "old-fashioned," long books.
- Discuss what you've read. Answer any questions along the way, but don't interrupt a good story with long discussions. Afterward, ask open-ended questions. Don't make your kid feel as though he's taking a pop quiz. There are no "right" answers. Give your opinions and ask for his. Let imaginations spin off other stories or possible endings. Keep the process enjoyable.
- Model an appreciation for reading by letting your kid see you engrossed in your own books.
- Treat books as cherished treasures. Give them as birthday gifts to both your friends and his. Handle them with care.
- Keep a variety of reading materials around the house. Valuable information comes in many forms: books, newspapers, magazines, pamphlets. Consider magazine subscriptions as gifts.
- If you have a computer and modem, let your kid browse in the Internet encyclopedias. The median age of Internet users is now twenty-six and will probably drop to fifteen within the next five years.

Help Develop Listening Skills

- Check out books-on-tape from the library for car trips, sickbeds, or nighttime listening.
- Make up serial stories, where one person adds to what another says.
- Introduce your child to different kinds of music and instruments.
- Play verbal memory games.

Help Develop Writing Skills

- Encourage your child to tell and write stories. Have a younger kid "dictate" to you. Let him illustrate the pages later, and staple them into a book. Give these as gifts to grandparents.
- Supply stamps, envelopes, and writing paper for correspondence with relatives, distant friends, or a pen-pal.
- Help your kid develop persuasive writing and reasoning skills by forming an opinion, garnering facts and reasons in support, and taking opposing viewpoints into account. Fewer than two percent of American students can perform this invaluable skill!

  This isn't just for lawyer-wanna-be's. Writing persuasively gets you ahead in business, commercial transactions, political causes, and personal interactions. Provide real-world practice for your child by having him present a written argument in favor of something he wants, expressly countering your anticipated objections.

Help Develop Reasoning Skills

- Focus on the art of asking the right questions as well as knowing where to get the answers. Don't rush to provide information. When a new topic arises, explore what questions might lead you to an answer.
- Play word games like Twenty Questions or Botticelli while driving in the car or relaxing together.

Help Develop Math and Science Skills

- Do simple science experiments. Find books in the library that list the household materials required, explain the procedures, and decipher the results.
- Start an ant farm.
- Plant a garden—in a window box if necessary—to observe the cycle of life.
- Compost your organic waste with earthworms.
- Sneak in math concepts during everyday activities. When your young kid sets the dinner table, talk about the number of knives,

forks, and spoons needed. What if someone didn't show up for dinner? What if you had three guests?

Buy place mats imprinted with addition/subtraction and multiplication/division tables.

- Take your child to science museums and talk—at his level—about what you see.
- Cook together and comment on the properties of ingredients: What happens if you mix oil and vinegar? If you apply heat? If you mix yeast, sugar, water, and flour and leave it for an hour? If you cook an egg in the shell, unbroken in a pan, mixed in a pan? Pick wild blackberries and make a pie. Eat beans from your garden.

  Experiment with weight, solubility, density, and reactions. Mix vinegar and baking soda to make a "volcano."
- Read your child a science magazine. *National Geographic* works very well because the stunning photographs carry detailed captions. I read the descriptions and translate them to Christopher's level of understanding. We treasure our once-a-month sessions learning together.
- Give even small children an allowance in various coins and introduce them to the idea of budgeting (see Chapter 16).
- Teach your kid to negotiate at garage sales. Hold your own sale and let him sell muffins and lemonade to customers. Christopher raked in a child-sized fortune this way—and practiced with money, addition, subtraction, and speaking up for himself.
- Introduce increasingly sophisticated math through everyday activities. Sorting, counting, addition (two crackers plus two crackers), fractions (half a melon, quarters, eighths), percentages (twenty percent-off sales, tax, or tips to waiters), and so on.

Gender Bias in the Classroom: Educating Girls

Studies confirm that teachers treat boys and girls differently in the classroom, and guess which gender suffers. Right. At every grade level, teachers call on girls less frequently. Boys call out answers eight times more often than their sisters, and the teachers respond to the *content* of their comments. Conversely, when assertive girls do venture spontaneous answers, teachers tell them to raise their hands or wait their turns.

Praise for girls centers on demeanor and neatness, while boys receive accolades for intellectual achievement. Boys receive more meaningful feedback and encouragement on how to correct wrong answers. Girls, on the other hand, often find the teacher simply redoing their work for them, especially in math and science. As a result, the girls don't learn strategies for self-correction and thinking through solutions. Classroom interactions convey subtle messages that girls' opinions don't count and that females aren't worth the teacher's time.

The effect on female self-esteem is profound. Many children suffer a drop in self-acceptance as they progress from lower grades to high school, but this decrease is much more pronounced in girls. A national study concluded that those having confidence in their own abilities maintain higher self-esteem. It is just this confidence that classroom experience fails to engender in girls.

Most teachers are frighteningly unaware of the different treatment they give girls and boys. Despite good intentions, they subtly perpetuate stereotypes that harm female self-esteem and discourage girls from entering technical fields.

What can you do for your girl student?

- Approach the teacher in a nonconfrontational way to confirm that he knows about the research on gender bias in the classroom. With luck, he will already be addressing the issue in his methods. If not, tell him you've read about it and, as the parent of a girl, you want to nurture confidence in her abilities.
- Work with the teacher to provide positive role models for the girls. Volunteer to line up skilled working women for a series of monthly classroom talks. Since you're one yourself, perhaps you'll be the first speaker!
- Beyond this, bolster self-esteem at home (see Chapter 9). Give praise beyond looks and "good" behavior. Engage your daughter (and your son) in discussions that require taking and defending positions.
- Boys' parents have a special responsibility to keep their sons from uncritically adopting stereotypes as truth. Whether or not you have girls, curb any of your own stereotypical statements about, say, women having trouble with math.

Learning Styles and Special Needs

Not everyone learns in the same way, and some children need more or less challenge in certain areas. How do—and should—schools address the differences?

Learning Styles

In 1994, 86% of eighteen-to-twenty-four-year-old Americans had graduated from high school, or had an equivalent degree.[4]

Most curricula still target kids who learn in traditional ways—by mastering facts and understanding relationships. These are the scholarship winners and the honor-roll students. They learn by practice, drill, analysis, organizing, explaining, and testing.

Research confirms, however, that a large number of people best absorb information through other learning styles. For example:

- Some excel in "cooperative learning" situations in which small groups work on projects together. These students learn best through role-play, group interactions, discussion, and relating personally to subject content.
- In the "synthesis" learning style, the child learns by creating and using imagination through writing or drama, pursuing independent interests, and making connections between seemingly unrelated facts.

Some teachers recognize these different styles and address them in the classroom by, for example, giving alternative assignments, tests, and projects. Traditional teachers, who themselves learned in standard ways, often overlook opportunities to encourage students with other learning styles. Educators mark these kids as "failures" even though they simply have a different way of seeing, absorbing knowledge, and responding. I once saw a cartoon on learning styles: A child stood at the front of the class pointing to the east. The teacher impatiently said, "No, point to Africa on the *globe.*" This is amusing but tragic. She could have commended his completely accurate, real-world approach and *then* gone to the globe.

As a parent, your goals should be, first, to become aware of your kid's learning style so that you know what to promote for him and how to encourage him, and second, to support teachers in using a variety of teaching styles in the classroom. Educators know of the research on learning styles, but they need parental encouragement. They need to know you don't care about drills and exercises if your child is learning better through some other style. If kids don't learn the way we teach, why not teach the way they learn?

If your child has trouble academically, observe a class or two and pay attention to learning style. The difficulty could be in the presentation, not the kid. From your own interactions with him, you probably have good instincts about how he learns and what motivates him. Engage the teacher as a partner in exploring methods that will fit his learning style. He's probably not alone; other similar learners in the class will benefit as well. As Plato said, "Do not then train youth to learning by force and harshness, but direct them to what amuses their minds, so that you may be better able to discover with accuracy the peculiar genius of each."

Some experts believe that half the jobs today's kindergarteners will take as adults don't exist yet! Christopher may work in some field that society has yet to invent. We can't hope to prepare kids for such unknowns. So in this respect, we should also do what we can to stretch our kids a bit from their dominant ways of learning and to give them different ways of thinking so they can adapt to their futures.

Gifted Children

Having a "gifted" child, however defined, isn't necessarily a "gift." As public schools suffer reduced budgets, money for enrichment programs disappears. Art and music programs go the way of the buffalo.

Many schools these days have eliminated "tracking," or separating children by perceived intelligence, so gifted kids often end up mainstreamed with everyone else. Research favors this approach for *slower* children, but not necessarily for *gifted* ones. Gifted kids bore easily. They feel alienated without others who share their advanced interests.

Giftedness manifests several behavior types:

- Ideally, a gifted child accepts himself and the fact that he is different. He is self-motivated and satisfied to do well but doesn't require perfection. Too commonly, however, gifted kids become overachievers or underachievers. Usually quite sensitive, they have a high rate of substance abuse and suicide due to feelings of powerlessness to meet expectations, define their life's work among so many choices, and change an unjust world.
- They may rebel. Feeling they can't measure up to others' high expectations, they refuse to play the game at all. They become isolated or domineering. Gang leaders are often gifted, and our prisons house many highly intelligent but rebellious criminals.
- Alternatively, gifted kids may simply withdraw from competition, "dumb down," reduce emotional risks, and disappear into the safety of being average.
- Finally, they may "conform," accepting the high expectations and meeting them at any cost. They're insecure, and fear of failure represses creativity and risk-taking. They overachieve and live for

the external rewards. The conformist may look like the ideal, self-motivated kid, but he's really unhappy and subject to depression.

To feel satisfied at school, gifted kids need complex activities and interaction with intellectual peers. This may mean taking some classes at higher levels. At a minimum, it means "clustering" gifted children within mainstream classes so they can interact daily with others of similar level and interests. Additional "wrinkles" on assignments challenge these kids.

- If you realize your child needs more than he's getting, suggest that the teacher add extra challenges to his work. Perhaps your kid can spend time on independent study while the class learns material already familiar to him. Maybe an advanced class is appropriate. Or individualized work on the computer. Or extra reading.
- Go in as a partner, not a critic. You're not asking for a *better* education for your child, but one that is more appropriate for his abilities. The teacher may have a completely different perspective on your child, but he's doing his best and wants to help him. Your child may act very differently at home than at school in a group. His boredom in class may result in clowning, rebelliousness, or irritation. Do further brainstorming with the teacher. If he's reluctant to try something, ask for an experimental trial period so no one feels trapped in a new situation that may not work out. Offer whatever help and resources you can. Stay in touch with the teacher and your child for feedback and advice.
- Most importantly, teach your child to advocate for himself (see Chapter 9). Often teachers simply don't realize that a child is gifted. The kid may sit at his desk doing nothing and looking uninterested, when in reality he's bored out of his mind. Give him permission to verbalize his needs. Encourage him to tell the teacher he needs more stimulation and to make suggestions for other activities and projects. One parent described his agony as a gifted youngster in a regular class: The classroom wall sported an old clock that ticked away time by the second, and as a child, this man felt the space between each tick as an eternity—and there are 3600 of them in an hour!
- Never criticize a teacher at home. Let your child know you will work for him, but don't suggest the teacher is incapable or unwilling.
- Value the whole child, not just his intelligence. Expect effort in every area of life. Teach him to respect less-gifted people. Help him find a peer group. Don't push academics too early. Let him learn for his sake, not yours. Give him a sense of belonging within

the family. More than anything else, warm support helps gifted kids live up to their potential.

Special Education

The current educational philosophy favors mainstreaming special-ed children or kids with learning disabilities. For their parents, the issues parallel those of parents of gifted children. First, make certain the identification is accurate and that your child's problem isn't just a difference in learning style. Consult with your child's educators to come up with a school program that will work for him.

Then aim for self-acceptance and self-esteem. Recognize effort. Work as a partner with the school and teachers. Envelop your child in a warm, loving environment that takes him on his own terms.

Getting Your Kid to Talk about School

"What happened at school today?" "Nothing." "Who'd you see there?" "Nobody." These answers stump parents, especially those of preteens and teens. Kids of all ages dislike being "interrogated," even if *you* thought of it as "expressing interest." Happy to see your kids after a long day, you try to engage them in a friendly way, and all you get is rejection and withdrawal.

- Don't take it personally. Stop asking those particular questions. Realize that teens especially, often feel a keen need for privacy. Granted, you didn't ask for any state secrets, but respect your teenager's struggle to gain independence and separation from you. He's entitled to keep a portion of his life to himself and to feel he controls it. By backing off, you allow him to exercise power over when, where, and how he discusses feelings and events. Often you'll find that if you wait a while, a few facts slip out.
- Even a normally talkative kid may not reveal important facts, especially if they involve wounds to his pride or ego. He might not

> The average French student spends twice as much class time studying core subjects (math, science, history, geography) as does the average American student.
>
> The average German student spends two-and-a-half times as much time studying as his American counterpart.[5]

admit, for example, that a big guy bullied him or he tripped in front of the class and suffered merciless laughter and teasing.

- Don't drill your kid. Let him set the pace for transition from school to home. Instead of asking questions, tell him about your day. He'll open up more easily if not pressured.
- Ask casually about school while you're relaxed and absorbed in other activities together. While playing a game or doing the dishes, for example, he won't feel the interrogator's bright light. When he's no longer the center of attention, resistance decreases. This by-the-way approach lessens the feeling that you're grilling him.
- Try varying your questions: Ask him to teach you what he's learning in a certain subject. "What did you find out that surprised you today?" or "Did you learn anything that changed any of your beliefs today?" or "Did you have any unanswered questions?" or "What was the oddest thing you learned?"
- Ask specific questions based on what you already know—his unit on *Beowulf* or the chorus's new song, for example. Maybe one of those chats with the teacher clued you in to coming tryouts for the school play.

  Attend activities at school—open houses, carnivals, conferences, plays, or garage sales. Anytime you're there, notice posters on the walls, scheduled events, and extreme fashions. All fodder for conversation.
- Make questions open-ended rather than calling for a yes-or-no answer. Not, "Do you like *Beowulf?*" but "What do you think Grendel symbolizes?" Try "Tell me about . . ." Ask him to explain an assignment.
- *Important:* once he does speak, be sure you *listen actively* (see Chapter 5).
- If you have a specific topic you must discuss, such as that toilet paper in the principal's trees, let your kid choose when to talk—within a deadline. He decides "when" but not "whether." "We have to talk about this by the end of the weekend. Let me know when you're ready." Don't be surprised if he starts talking right away to dispel the black cloud of anticipation hanging over his weekend.

None of this is guaranteed to work, of course, but you can't do any worse than "Nothing" and "Nobody."

Parent-Teacher Conferences

Never pass up a parent-teacher conference, both to obtain information about your child's performance and to convey your questions and concerns to the teacher. A short conversation can spot small problems before they grow large.

Separate Conferences for Divorced Parents

If you and your ex can't sit in the same room together, request separate conferences. Teachers commonly encounter divorced parents, and seeing you one at a time presents no problem.

Even if you're on speaking terms with your former spouse, meet separately if you think he will dominate the conversation or intimidate you. You must feel safe to communicate your problems and questions freely. Some of those concerns may even involve your ex or the effect of his behavior on your child.

On the other hand, if you and your ex co-parent successfully, attending a conference together makes sense.

Go Prepared

To take advantage of your limited time with the teacher, organize beforehand:

- Ask your child if he wants you to discuss anything in particular with the teacher. Maybe he can't hear from the back of the room, or he feels called on too much or too little.
- Write out your points and questions so you won't forget them if you get nervous. List them in order of priority in case you run out of time.

At the Conference

Use your time well when you meet with the teacher:

- Leave your anxiety at home. Breathe. A conference is an information exchange, not a trial. Go with an open mind. Don't expect the worst. Try to relax so you can hear and use the information you receive.
- Don't take your child or younger children to the conference. Not only might they disrupt the discussion, but having siblings repeat what they hear is detrimental.
- Be on time. Even a few minutes' delay derails the tight schedule of these meetings. By the same token, stop after the allotted time. Let the teacher concentrate on you, not on how she'll fit in another six conferences before the lights go out. Make another appointment if you haven't finished.
- Consider academic and behavioral questions separately. Ask for specifics. If your kid has "problems reading," what are they? Does he fail to recognize letter sounds, skip lines, or what? If the teacher

uses jargon or terms you don't understand, ask questions until you do. Get detailed suggestions for ways to help at home.

- Stay objective. Your child is neither *always* at fault nor *never* at fault. Seek solutions rather than assigning blame. Don't feel disappointed if the teacher doesn't fully appreciate your kid's better side.
- If your child exhibits behavioral problems, now might be the time to let the teacher know about the divorce or death, if you haven't already. You don't have to let any family skeletons loose. If you don't feel comfortable giving details, just generally refer to the circumstances. Since you know your child best, offer specific suggestions for helping him cope at school.
- Maintain your boundaries. This conference is about your child, not you. You're not a bad person because he "egged" the history teacher's house. (Neither is he, even if his *behavior* was rotten.)
- Ask your questions; make your suggestions; relate problems your child mentioned. Ask about that "nonexistent" homework. Get details: How often should you expect assignments? How much time should they require? How should you help? How can you double-check homework assignments?
- Approach teachers about problems in a nonthreatening, constructive way. You'll find them more open if you are "one-down" in the conversation: "I was wondering if you had any thoughts about why Melissa's algebra grade is falling," rather than "She's not getting enough individual attention."

  Use "I statements" to describe difficulties (see Chapter 5). "I feel concerned that Joey never gets to be room monitor. He feels slighted." Not, "You always choose your favorites for special jobs." Focus on your child's needs, not the teacher's failures.

After the Conference

You may rejoice at the report you received, or you may boil with rage. Probably, you'll feel somewhere between these extremes.

- If you're angry, give yourself time to cool off, then evaluate what you heard. Confer with a friend. Does your anger mask another emotion? Are your boundaries intact? (See Chapters 4, 5, and 9.) Does the report confirm something you've resisted admitting?

  Did you and the teacher rile one another? Did he take offense at your suggestions? Try to be objective about what happened, remembering that teachers are human, too. Perhaps you misunderstood each other's statements or intent. Think seriously about

making another appointment to get everything back on track—for your kid's sake.
- Tell your child about the conference. Mention the teacher's positive statements first and constructively discuss any negatives. Again, seek solutions rather than blame. Relate the teacher's recommendations for work at home. Ask your child for suggestions. Explore the possibility of the two of you meeting with the teacher.
- If behavioral problems exist, find out more from your child. Factors not obvious to adults may reveal a solution.
- Don't expect immediate fixes, and keep communicating. Trade information with the teacher about the results of any experiments.
- You may need an outside opinion about physical, mental, or developmental questions. In my state, schools must provide an assessment of a child's need for special education if a parent requests one.

Solving Problems with Schools

Problems arise even in the best schools and with the most caring teachers. As your child's advocate, you have the responsibility to recognize difficulties and help find solutions. Whatever the specific problem, keep the principles discussed in the following sections in mind:

Trust Your Instincts

> "Only the educated are free."
>
> EPICTETUS (50–135 A.D.)

You are the ultimate authority when it comes to your kid. Don't let the gods of education intimidate you into doubting your own judgment. I planned to apply to a certain innovative school until the administrators discouraged parental input and classroom visits. "Parents don't know what they're seeing anyway," one insisted, "and they raise all the wrong issues." I *do* know my *son,* and if I can't see him in the environment where he will spend most of his day, I don't want him there, no matter how "right" the educational theory.

Be Assertive

Ask questions. Speak out—politely. Consider yourself in partnership with educators. Alienating them with anger and threats helps no one.

You do have the right to be fully informed. To get information and ask for what you want, you must often be persistent and assertive.

If this isn't your usual style, fake it for your kid's sake. Learn to squeak. You're the only voice your child has.

To advocate, you'll have to let go of caring what others will say or think about you. This includes your ex, your parents, your child, other parents, and the school authorities.

I don't mean to suggest that interactions with the school are or should be adversarial. Most education professionals would not be in the field if they didn't care about the welfare of children. They certainly aren't in it for the money. They're on your side from the beginning. Try to keep it that way. If problems arise, work with them rather than against them.

Get Help

Join with other parents to accomplish goals, get information, apply pressure, or solve common problems. Get both emotional and active support wherever you can.

Do Your Homework

When you need something from the school, plan your strategy in advance. Have relevant information at hand.

Know Your Bottom Line

Solutions require give and take, but there is a point beyond which you cannot go. Know what that is. Know where you won't compromise on your child's behalf.

Educating a child today takes much more than showing him the door to the school. Get him off to a good start in September, volunteer as much as you can, supplement his schooling with at-home learning, and work with teachers to make education an effective, pleasant experience.

PUBLICATION FOR PARENTS

"Making Science Make Sense: Parents' Survival Kit:" Helps you answer your kid's scientific questions, contains simple experiments to do together and tips on teaching science at home. Free from Bayer Corp., One Mellon Center, 500 Grant St, Pittsburgh, PA 15219-2507.

Chapter 13

Surviving the Holidays

Whatever holidays you observe, they won't be the same after you become a single parent. The first holidays after your marriage ends usually produce bouts of emotional upset, which may recur in later years. If you're a single parent by choice, you predict nothing but joy for the first holidays with your child. Even so, the added obligations and activities create additional stress in an already hectic life.

Take the initiative to ensure that your holidays as a single parent are happy ones. Because we celebrate Christmas, most of my examples relate to that holiday, but the following principles apply to Kwaanza, Hanukkah, birthdays, or anything else.

Deal with Grief (Both Yours and the Kids') Over Loss of Family and Traditions

Holidays highlight changes and stir up emotions. Even if you can't stand the sight of your former spouse, you will probably experience a new cycle of grief for the loss of your happily-ever-after (see Chapter 1 on grieving).

You may think you feel no sadness, only anger at having to prepare and celebrate without a partner. It's so much work, so much stress, so much money. Indeed, anger is understandable and appropriate. Take a moment to look further, however, and see if the anger isn't also masking sadness. If you don't let yourself express pain, it will stay with you a long time.

Although death or divorce probably represents the most tragic incident of a child's early life, some seem to handle it with no trauma at all—initially. Then, when they sense that you are okay, they experience a delayed reaction. The holidays may catalyze their feelings. (See Chapter 1 for helping kids deal with their grief.)

Grieving doesn't necessarily mean being gloomy. You can use humor to acknowledge the losses and difficulties of your present situation. Maybe your ex always lit the holiday fire, and your first attempts set off all the smoke alarms in the house. You can curse yourself and your ex, or you can bundle everyone up, throw open the doors and windows, and sing "Smokey the Snowman" with a cup of hot chocolate until the air clears.

Decide What Makes a "Happy Holiday," and Include Your Needs

What do I mean, "decide" what makes a holiday happy? Isn't it written in stone somewhere? Doesn't a Merry Christmas require sending cards and photos, decorating a tree, hanging lights from the house, throwing a party, choosing the perfect presents, caroling, hanging stockings, cooking turkey and trimmings, visiting relatives, attending the Sing-It-Yourself Messiah and the Nutcracker and Amahl and midnight church services, opening presents on Christmas morning, and . . . and . . . and. . . ? What about birthdays? Isn't there another long, rigid list of requirements for those?

No!

You decide what would make the holidays happy. Neither your childhood traditions nor last year's celebration controls what happens now. Likewise, don't be lured into believing you have to duplicate the mythological perfect holiday so often seen in the media.

- Ponder what "happy holiday" means to you. Excitement? Control? Perfection? The family as it used to be? If you define "happy holiday" in these ways, even subconsciously, you set yourself up for failure. Instead, redefine it as serene, relaxing, fun, and loving. Think of it as a process, not a goal, best efforts rather than perfection. If you're worn out and cranky trying to create a faultless experience, your very efforts defeat you.

Instead, wipe the slate clean and consider what would be pleasant for you. No matter how child-centered the holiday is, you count too. Give up any guilt associated with doing something for yourself. Many of us feel undeserving anyway, and divorce exacerbates that belief. You're entitled.

- Knowing you're providing a model for your children gives you permission to treat yourself with love and respect. It's easy to know what to do for your kids, but giving to yourself requires thought (see Chapter 4). Specifically for the holidays, ask what you enjoy, what makes you feel peaceful and relaxed—here you will probably want to list time alone, a rare commodity for single parents. How can you have fun? What draws you close to the family and friends you love? Only you can answer these questions. Be proactive. Don't wait for Santa to drop through the chimney with what you need.
- Do for yourself what you do for your children. Buy yourself a holiday gift. It can be meaningful or silly, expensive or cheap, useful or frivolous—something that would be right if you had a friend just like you. Wrap it up and open it with the other presents and tell your kids who it's from. Mail yourself a card saying what you like about yourself and read it every day through the holiday season.
- Communicate. Tell your friends and relatives how you want your holiday to be. Don't assume they know, especially if this is your first year as a single parent or if you've decided to make changes from last year. People may think that they should help you make everything resemble the celebrations of prior years, when what you really need is a complete change.
- If you don't have full-time custody of the children, you may be apart from them during the holidays, perhaps even on The Holiday itself. Prepare them for where they will be. Talk about how they—and you—will feel. Admit that you will be sad while they are away, but avoid expressing bitterness at your ex. Let them know you will be all right.

  If the custody arrangement leaves you childless during this vulnerable time, there's no point in sitting at home waiting for calls or wondering what's going on at the ex's house. Make plans while staying flexible. Arrange to be with people, but let them know ahead of time that you may feel like cutting the visit short or backing out at the last minute. You don't know how you'll feel when the day arrives. Maybe a long hike alone or serving turkey dinner at a soup kitchen will be what you really need.

While the kids are gone, consider getting away from home entirely, either alone or with friends. If a week in sunny Mexico isn't possible, how about a day or two at a nearby retreat? Maybe a ski weekend. A bed-and-breakfast in a restful setting. An overnight at a local fancy hotel with a spa.

- Perhaps you'll wait until the kids get back and take them, too. Most hotels have special prices for children, and some allow them to stay free in a parent's room. (If you should opt for a trip out of the country, your ex's written permission may be necessary. To avoid disappointment, check the requirements before you get to the border.) How about a trip to some popular attraction that is too crowded to visit during tourist season? Or maybe just a walk in the neighborhood together.

  You decide.

Make New Traditions

You've said good-bye and mourned the loss of old traditions, so don't try to replicate them. You and your children will only be disappointed. Do something completely different to celebrate your new life. Make it enjoyable. And be ready to adjust if it doesn't work out.

- Explain to your kids about establishing new traditions and get their input. Incorporating their ideas boosts their self-esteem. If your children are too young for an opinion, think of which traditions you would like to share with them in future years.
- Christopher and I established new traditions with friends. We invite three or four playmates over to help trim the tree and drink hot chocolate. We got together for activities with our special friends Staci and Randall until they moved out of the country. A week or two before Christmas we had Cookie Day with them, during which we cooked dinner, drank wine, baked, and decorated cookies. Christopher participated fully, making certain we had just the right gingerbread-person to leave for Santa on Christmas Eve. We also joined Staci and Randall for Christmas Day brunch. With them gone, we'll either change what we do or invite others to par-

ticipate. We always have Christmas dinner at the home of a superchef friend and her husband. It sounds like a lot of activity, but the gatherings are small, informal, and relaxing. And someone else does the cooking!

- Some regular activities acquire a Christmas flavor without much change in the usual routine. The four single-mother families on my street have a monthly dinner together. In December, we each bring $2 presents for the kids and a wrapped "white elephant" gift for the adults. The white elephant must be something we already have around the house (i.e., no shopping). It has to be something we hate but just haven't had the heart to throw away. We draw numbers for the packages and are stuck with the contents (*or at least the responsibility for getting rid of them!*). Last year I was the lucky recipient of three dainty and completely useless porcelain spoons painted with pastel flowers. The year before it was a light fixture and a can of pickled leeks. Treasures one and all!

Be creative in thinking of new traditions. Here are some more suggestions that others have tried:

- Invite an elderly friend or neighbor to attend your child's school concert with you. Older folks without grandkids nearby seldom get to experience the joy children bring to holidays. Taking them along isn't expensive, and both the senior and the kid feel honored.
- Sponsor a talent party during which each person's gift to the others is a performance of some kind. I've done this for adult birthdays, and the presents included stories, songs, a puppet show, games, magic tricks, fortune-telling, and drawing lessons. Some of the more imaginative presentations came from people who claimed a lack of creativity.
- Take a driving tour of Christmas decorations around town.
- Have an ornament-exchange party. In my favorite version of this activity, the guests bring a wrapped ornament that has some personal meaning for them—not an heirloom or a favorite, just something that relates to some memory or special aspect of their lives. A cat for a cat-lover, for example. A piano to represent a musical interest. The guest wraps a signed or anonymous note with each ornament describing its personal significance. Everyone chooses an ornament in a blind exchange and reads the note aloud.
- Get a group together for caroling at a senior home, hospital, or other institution.

- Create a "holiday time capsule." The container can be as simple as a shoe box. Let the children choose the contents, objects that are significant to them now. For perishable, indispensable, or outsized items, substitute photos, drawings, or written descriptions. Make tape recordings of songs, poems, or conversations. Set a date in the future for opening the capsule, perhaps two or three years from now. Seal the box and tuck it away somewhere. When the opening date arrives, reflect on how much you've all changed. Fill the box with a new selection for next time.
- Have a potluck open house. What could be easier than letting friends come to you—with food!
- For the New Year, the kids can present an original New Year's play. Find a ritual to formalize New Year's resolutions, like writing them on paper and burning them in fire. Or writing and burning what you want to get rid of in your life. Inhale and consciously let go as you exhale. Light candles. Plant seeds to represent what you want. Whenever you water the plants, think of them growing your fondest wishes.

Reduce Stress

I feel the pressure rising already as you consider adding new traditions to already existing obligations. The good news is that you're going to pare down those "shoulds." If your eyeballs are popping from stress, you won't be able to create a pleasant experience for your kids. Remember, your behavior during this time will model how a busy adult stays sane during a stressful time. Your duty as parent entails reducing the pressure and enjoying yourself.

Cling to the Life Preservers: Simplify. Get help. Get organized. Set limits. Communicate. Stay flexible and creative. Forget perfection and set priorities. Enjoy the process. Be proactive and concentrate on what you can control. Get in touch with your true emotions. Use the time to teach and learn. Practice good parenting skills. Use humor. Honor yourself and your instincts. Give up guilt. Breathe.

Consult your children. Ask what they would most like to do and what they disliked about past celebrations. Take their preferences into account, but in making your selections, remember that you'll be the one doing the work.

A Stress-Reducing Exercise

Read through this entire section first, and then come back for the following exercise that Liz Hannigan and Cliff Crain gave the single-parents support group:

- On a piece of paper write in large letters across the top: "What I Should Do for the Holidays." List everything you want to do or feel you must do. Pretty intimidating.
- Now replace "Should" in your heading with "Could." This subtle but meaningful change represents a positive step toward taking control over what you will—and won't—do. You have a choice.
- Start eliminating from the list of "coulds." Trust your own instincts and forget other people's demands and expectations for a moment. That's not easy, but ask yourself, "What is the worst that could happen if . . ." If you didn't decorate the house, for example, or if you served soup instead of turkey dinner. You may assume you have to meet others' expectations to gain their love or respect. Usually however, you'll realize on reflection that the real consequences are much less momentous.

  For each item, close your eyes and imagine how you will feel when you've accomplished it. If your reaction is, "Gee, that was fun," leave it on the list. If it's, "I'm glad that's over," mark it off, unless you come up with a way to make it enjoyable. Dragging a tree home, hauling it up the stairs, digging the stand out of the garage, fussing with the lights, and keeping the cats away from the ornaments can be a miserable chore. Inviting a few friends to help might make it fun. Or not. Maybe you'll just skip the tree. Or get a tiny one for the children. There's always next year.

  Some questions are close judgment calls. Must you have Christmas dinner at your mother's house if skipping it will hurt her feelings? Do you have to visit Santa at the mall to avoid disappointing your kids? For the moment, leave such items on the list.
- You've eliminated much, but many "want-to's" remain. Performances, school programs, parties, open houses, parades, Santa visits, exhibits, and special activities in every museum, park, and club for miles around. Even if each one is absolutely delightful, attending them all will lead to collapse from sheer overload. For every item remaining, write down whether you *need* to do it to have a happy holiday or would simply *prefer* to do it.

- Analyze your list. Assume you will do all the "needs." Star those. Now add a few items from the "preferred" activities, but only to the extent that you can accomplish them without feeling stressed. Double the time you imagine each one requires. Err on the side of adding too few.
- Voila, your Reduced-Stress Holiday Schedule is now complete. At the top of the page, substitute "Get To" for "Could." This proactive language orients you toward following through with proactive behavior. It puts you in control and changes the feeling from pressure-filled drudgery to positive accomplishment.
- Oh yes, about those duties you left on the list in deference to others' strong feelings and expectations. First, honestly assess your obligation and the likely result of your not meeting it. Your situation as a single parent is a great opportunity to dodge events you've always hated anyway. "I just can't manage that on my own this year" is enough. Somehow having a good excuse helps you get over the guilt of not doing something expected of you. You might even receive some sympathy.

  If you are unable to bow out completely, figure out how to honor the expectations in a more limited manner than usual. Can't stand spending the whole day with your parents? Don't. Stop by for dessert instead. Dread having those out-of-town relatives stay in your house? Tell them they'll be more comfortable in a motel this time. Next year say, "That worked so well last year, I think we'll do it again." There you have the birth of a new tradition, one that works for *you*.
- One last thing, by the way—this reevaluation of the holidays can serve as a wake-up call for the rest of your life. Once you begin consciously questioning your usual holiday activities, you'll be able to step back and find out how you really feel about, say, being with your relatives. You may finally admit that your mom never listens or your dad drinks too much or Uncle Jeb puts his hands where he shouldn't or Aunt Jill disapproves of your job. Consciousness and detachment break down denial and put you in touch with your real feelings and perceptions, and then you can make your decisions based on a more accurate picture of what's going on.

Making your reduced-stress list doesn't guarantee a perfect holiday. Take it as a given that things will go wrong. If something doesn't pan out, laugh and make the best of it.

Beverly, an MBA who knew how to "prioritize" before that was even a word, runs her life like clockwork. Her Christmas tree is always up early, decorated with ornaments collected with her young daughter, Heather. Still, Beverly is nothing if not flexible. Last December she contracted to have her home's long, steep front steps rebuilt. During construction, the only access to her house was through the blackberry thicket on one neighbor's property or across a wet, slippery incline from her other neighbor's house. Too late, she realized there was no way to get a tree into the house by either of these routes. Instead of cursing herself or the contractor, she explained the situation to Heather with a laugh at herself and moved on. No tree that year. Something different. The presents went on the piano.

More Holiday Stress-Busters

Here are some more stress-reducing suggestions:

- If you must work during your kids' school vacation, arrange child care well in advance. You may be lucky enough to have extended care at their schools. Otherwise, you'll have to patch together something for the younger children: neighborhood trades, babysitters, drop-in child care, relatives, play dates. Older kids may be used to being at home alone after school, but you'll have to decide whether they can manage on their own all day throughout the vacation (see Chapter 11).
- Don't travel if you don't feel like it. I've received a fair amount of family disapproval for not visiting my mother, who lives in a small Texas town a million miles from anywhere. Getting there means driving to the airport parking lot, shuttling to the terminal, bulldozing my luggage into the check-in, schlepping a bag of toys through security, hiking miles to the departure gate, and dragging a frightened little boy who needs to go potty onto the plane. And this is all before takeoff. In Dallas we have to run for a connection with a scary commuter airplane that might or might not be able to land on an icy runway after a nauseating flight. I made this trip once—and paid several hundred dollars for the privilege! It amazes me that everyone doesn't comprehend how stressful it is to manage all this alone with a small child, but I'd rather take any amount of flak than do it again anytime soon.
- Change dates and "deadlines." Celebrate when you can. If your kids are with the ex on Christmas Day, have your "Christmas" on

December 28, or whenever it works out best. You might even get a few bargains if you do your shopping at the after-Christmas sales.

Go to the Nutcracker or other holiday performances *after* Christmas. The week between Christmas and New Year's seems rather dull after what goes before. Take advantage of productions that offer discounts during this time.

Send your cards and letters late. I like to stay in touch with people I rarely see, but at Christmas it's more important for me to be with those nearby friends that I love. I have the whole year to write letters. Maybe I'll get them out by Valentine's Day.

- Give yourself an out. When you accept invitations, reserve the option of canceling. Explain that you would love to come but are afraid your holiday responsibilities as a single parent may prove too stressful and cause you to back out at the last minute. This will greatly reduce your guilt load if you don't make the event. If you're honest, people will usually sympathize and grant you this advance permission to flake out. If they can't, you may just have to decline the invitation with regrets.
- Change your expectations. For years I've attended a sing-along Messiah at the local university. Christopher joined me when he turned four. I knew we would probably have to leave early, even with the crayons I brought for him. The orchestra fascinated him, and he seemed to enjoy some of the singing, but he'd had enough by intermission. I took him to see the instruments up close, and then we left. Had I been committed to making it through the Hallelujah Chorus, the excursion would have been a failure. As it was, I congratulated us both for a rewarding experience and finished by singing along with the record later.
- Simplify cooking. Buy baked goods instead of making them. Many kids don't know the difference between homemade and store-bought goodies anyway. If you really need to impress someone, buy some of that scent that makes the kitchen smell like baking cookies!

Don't cook turkey dinner. Go out. Or take out. Some delicatessens and grocery stores sell complete holiday meals with all the fixings. If you stay in, have a potluck dinner with friends. Or prepare something easy. There's nothing wrong with lasagna for Christmas.

By all means, cook if you want. Involve the children. It's your choice. Just make sure food preparation doesn't lock you away in the kitchen when you'd rather be elsewhere.

- Stick to routines. While one point of the holidays is to escape routine, your family will stay saner if you maintain the basic schedule that grounds your daily life. Exciting, active festivities can mean physical and emotional overload. Younger kids in particular become confused, cranky, and sensitive with excessive change in mealtimes, bedtimes, and quiet times. As much as possible, plan activities around the regular routine.
- Limit the sweets and alcohol. Science has supposedly proven that sugar doesn't affect youngsters' behavior, but science obviously hasn't studied my son. Left alone, Christopher will gobble all the goodies in sight, bounce off the ceiling for several hours, and then crash. Nutritional questions aside, dealing with him after a major infusion of sucrose presents challenges. It's not easy to limit the intake unless you want to watch your kid every minute, but do what you can. At the very least, serve nutritious meals on days when sweets are in the offing. Watch your own sugar consumption, too. The aftermath of too many sweets leaves many people irritable and exhausted. I personally resist that first bite. Like an alcoholic, one taste, and I'll binge for days.
- Speaking of alcohol, keep the liquid spirits at a moderate level. If you think you're stressed now, just try doing everything with a hangover.
- Get silly at least once a day. Let humor lighten the mood. Sing, dance, stand on your head, tell a joke, hang an ornament from your ear. Young kids will join in. Do something silly even if all you get in return is blank stares from older children. Cutting loose a little will release some tension and make you feel better.

Pay Attention to Safety

The opportunity for accidents skyrockets during the hustle and excitement of the holidays. Busy with special activities, you're more likely to be careless and distracted. Take all the usual care—and then some.

- If you have small children, barricade the Christmas tree and burning candles. Guard electric cords, and keep small decorations out of reach.

Keep string, ribbons, and other strangulation hazards away from little ones. Ask women guests to stash their purses up high. Ingestion of cosmetics and medications, including aspirin, from unattended handbags is a leading cause of childhood poisoning. I've read that Christmas poinsettias are poisonous, and I've read that they're not. Play it safe and keep them out of chewing distance. Other holiday plants are toxic, including mistletoe berries.

- Observe safety recommendations for Christmas trees. Secure them from falling with wires or cord. Don't exceed allowable electrical loads for extension cords, and don't run cords under rugs. Refill the stand frequently with water. A five-foot tree takes a pint a day. Keep trees away from sources of flame and heat. A twelve-foot Christmas tree goes up in flame in eighteen seconds!
- Never burn wrapping paper in the fireplace, as this releases toxic fumes.
- Look for unsafe features on new toys.
- Renew your vigilance in the kitchen, as holiday preparations easily divert you from normal precautions.
- Keep all alcohol, including eggnog, vanilla, and almond extract, away from children
- Be on the alert for angry, agitated, or intoxicated drivers. Drive carefully in adverse weather, even if you arrive late. Always designate someone as the non-drinking driver.
- Spiff up the house if you must, but keep toxic cleaning materials out of small hands' reach.
- Watch out for flammable papers and cloth around portable heaters. It's not a bad time to check the batteries in your smoke detectors, too.

Make Gift Giving a Pleasure

Some holidays call for giving presents. The sense of obligation and the stress of shopping can be reduced. Another year you might feel differently, but if the thought of finding just the right thing for everyone on your list feels overwhelming, consider the suggestions in the following sections.

Give Fewer Gifts to Save Time and Money

- Take the initiative and propose to friends that you not exchange presents. Watch them sigh in relief, thankful for your suggestion. Alternatively, agree to cut back or set monetary limits. A group can draw names instead of buying for everyone. One year our extended family decided to skip "big" gifts in favor of five-dollar stocking-stuffers. The next year we each brought one gift with a higher price tag but with no particular person in mind. One of us chose a package and opened it. The following person had the option of unwrapping another gift or taking a previously opened one, and so on. Very amusing!
- Don't feel you have to give your kids the moon, especially if this impulse comes from guilt. Christmas is not a competition with your ex, and bigger presents don't mean more love. You can't do much about peer pressure, but try to short-circuit the kids' desperate "need" for the latest fads by limiting their exposure to media advertising (which whips into high speed soon after Halloween). Discuss the purpose of commercials and remind the children of any times when an advertised toy did not live up to the hype. Watch your own response to advertising as well and don't over-buy. A few simple gifts please small children. One of Christopher's favorite early presents was his own box of pop-up Kleenex to empty at will.
- Also, don't let guilt force you into buying your children gifts that you don't approve of, such as violent video games. Before buying, imagine how you'll feel after you've plunked down your plastic card. Good? Manipulated? Let that feeling guide your decision. Communicate with the kids about your reasons for refusing something on their wish lists. They may moan and groan, but they learn about your values and respect your ability to stick to them.
- Kids love opening packages, so even if you give just one "big" present, wrap some stocking-stuffers, too. Make them useful items you would buy anyway, like clothes, snacks, or a backpack for school.
- Try a new way of opening gifts. If you usually unwrap everything in a five-minute frenzy, open them one-by-one with everyone watching.

Shop Wisely

- Get organized. Plan so you can make as few shopping trips as possible. Last year I bought books for almost everyone on my list, and my shopping consumed about an hour and a half in a good bookstore. One place, one line! And I enjoyed browsing the shelves, a favorite pastime I hadn't indulged recently.

- Make a realistic budget and stay within it. Avoid the depression of facing the new year with a load of fresh debt. If money is short, talk with your kids honestly about why they won't get everything on their lists. If money is *really* short, sign up with a local agency to receive holiday donations of toys, clothing, or food. Eligibility criteria vary. Contact the agencies in early November, as they finalize their lists early. If you're on AFDC, call your eligibility worker for a referral.
- Shop when you're rested and alone. Arrange a child-care exchange or hire a baby-sitter so you don't have to hide purchases or contend with an onslaught of the "buy-me's." You'll finish faster and make much better decisions in a peaceful frame of mind.
- Buy early. I keep an eye open all year long for bargains on items I can give for Christmas or birthdays. Going to the "gift box" saves me many special, time-consuming trips downtown.
- Escaping the frustration of Christmas crowds makes up for the extra cost of ordering from catalogs, and you save wrapping and post-office time by shipping directly to out-of-town recipients.
- Consider making cards, decorations, and gifts with your children. Christopher and I created gift ornaments together. Mine were potpourri-filled lace with red and green ribbons. His were paper with glitter. His friend Johnnie made one of cardboard and Play-Doh, a valued, if lumpy, addition to our tree. Encourage the kids to make as many presents as they like, but don't succumb to the temptation to make all your gifts or you'll have time for nothing else.
- Explore new ways of giving. Write a poem for a friend or frame a favorite photo for him. Sing him a song. Help organize his storeroom. Our friend Staci wrote personalized story books in which Christopher appears in photos as the main character. These gifts from the heart are rare treasures.

Focus on People, Not Gifts

- Give your children the gift of time, which is more memorable than any other. Experiences rather than material presents stand out in your memory of your own childhood holidays. Reminisce about them with your kids. Instead of rushing out to buy something,

consider what talents you could offer as a gift. Teach your kid to play the guitar or to use a circular saw. Spend time just being together. During school breaks, take a day off from work to hang out at home.
- Also give your children the gift of communication. Let them know they can be honest with you (see Chapter 5). Allow them to tell you, without your defending or commenting or getting angry, what bugs them about you.
- Teach your kids about tolerance and the significance of the relevant holiday, culture, or religion. Respectfully ask friends if you can join some aspect of their observance of Hanukkah, Ramadan, Buddha's birthday, Chinese New Year, or Kwaanza. Whether you're part of the majority or minority, emphasize that no one should be ostracized because of the holidays he celebrates.
- Connect with friends honestly. Though I appreciate the time-savings of those photocopied holiday newsletters, I hate them. Not so much because they're impersonal, but because they often don't communicate the truth, which for me is the only basis for relationships. One year I received a cheery newsletter full of the youngsters' accomplishments, the family activities, the hobbies. But inked in at the bottom was, "It's been a rough year. Bill's brother died in a car wreck, and we learned my mom has Alzheimer's. I hate my job, but the economy here is dead, and I'd never find another one if I quit. Bill and I are having trouble. Sometimes I just want to cry." That brief note brought me closer to my friend than all the preceding paragraphs.
- Decorate a gingerbread cookie to represent each member of your family.
- Formalize the gift of good deeds. Require that one of the gifts each person gives be a chit for some service or chore. It can be specific, like, "taking out the garbage," or general, like, "an hour of my time." Draw names and do a secret good deed for whomever you draw. Wash his car or fix his wagon without ever revealing your identity.
- Surprise an overworked friend by taking her dinner complete with paper plates and napkins. The food needn't be homemade, of course.

Practice Charity for the Less Fortunate

Teach about social class, poverty, charitable organizations, and related subjects.

- Do some volunteer charitable work with the kids. Take them to buy toys to give to the less fortunate. Spend the portion of their allowance saved for charity on a worthy cause (also see Chapter 9).
- Take gifts to patients at a children's hospital. Marilyn's annual party invitation requests that each guest bring a toy to add to the contribution.
- Participate in a charitable group's project to be a needy child's mystery-Santa.
- Serve holiday dinner at a homeless shelter or meal program.
- Donate warm, outgrown clothing to the homeless.
- Donate blood.

Feed Your Soul

During the holiday crunch, find some quiet time to counteract the tense and harried atmosphere on the streets. Lock yourself in the bathroom if you must. Better yet, visit a museum, a church, a forest, or a seashore while everyone else is pushing, shoving, honking, and waiting in lines. Breathe.

BOOKS FOR PARENTS

Family Traditions, Celebrations for Holidays and Everyday, Elizabeth Berg (Reader's Digest, 1992).

Chapter 14

Surviving Summer Vacation

I was in such a fog the year after Tony's suicide that I didn't realize until the last minute that Christopher's preschool had no summer program. This was a serious oversight, since being with a toddler twenty-four hours a day exceeded my limited ability to cope. Together with late nights, those school-day mornings had been my only times for exercise, therapy, child-free errands, and work at my "job" as executor and general untangler of legal and fiscal knots. As much as I needed child care, however, I didn't want to shelve my son just anywhere for the summer months.

After a blitz search (just what I needed, another big job!), I found a good program at another preschool. Fortunately, there were openings; unfortunately, the session lasted only six weeks. I patched together visits from out-of-state grandmothers, generous friends, and paid baby-sitters for the remaining days. Although that summer worked out successfully, you can bet I gave much more advance thought to the next one.

In a sense, summers are easier to arrange for younger children than older ones. Our society at least recognizes that small children need somewhere to be during their parents' hours of employment. If you work, your established child care probably continues year-round. Grade schools often expand after-school care to full-day summer programs.

Many children of divorce go to the other parent's home for all or part of the summer. If this is the case with your children, you may just have to let go of controlling their activities. If you have a decent relationship with your ex, discuss rules and expectations. If not, hope for the best (see Chapter 1).

Keep in mind that while summer may seem endless, it's really only ten to eleven weeks long. Block these out in manageable week-long sections.

Build in Structure

The lack of routine during the summer tempts kids to push limits. Build in as much structure as you can so that you and your kids know where they are supposed to be and you have some ability to check on their whereabouts. Sit down with your children and consider camps, classes, jobs, volunteer work, and rules for hours at home alone.

Camps

Camps can be expensive, summer-long affairs or low-cost day camps associated with the local park system, the Y, the zoo, museums, school, Outward Bound, community centers, clubs, art schools, churches, or fraternal organizations. One advantage of sending your children to camp is that in later years, they more easily find employment there as counselors.

Your kid finds camp exciting but a little frightening the first time. He has to make new friends and learn a new routine. He may suffer homesickness. Talk with him about your own positive camp experiences. Appeal to his curiosity and sense of adventure and play down the scary aspects. Remind him of fun camp activities he doesn't get to do at school.

If he insists his camp experience is negative, get details. Perhaps he's being bullied or excluded, or the activities may be too challenging or simplistic. If he's in day camp, talk with the counselors. If he's away at camp, encourage him to try other activities or request a move to another group of kids.

Classes

I'm not advocating academic summer school (it *is* vacation, after all), but some kids need to repeat a class from the previous term. For others, enrolling in a class or two, especially in a subject *not* taught in school, awakens a new interest or develops an old one. If your son enjoyed last semester's gymnastics unit, maybe he'd like advanced instruction at a gym or karate at a dojo. Special interest programs abound for activities such as computers, music, or team sports. City park-and-recreation departments, Y's, and other organizations offer reasonably priced athletic, educational, and artistic programs. In my locale, kids can, among other things, learn to sail on a lake, take pre-college classes at art schools and colleges, enroll in a wide variety of community center classes, or study pond life at a nature museum.

Jobs

Having a job instills responsibility, and the money isn't bad either. Summer jobs for youngsters are difficult to come by, especially when the adult unemployment rate climbs, but they're not impossible to find with creativity and persistence. Brainstorm with your kids about what *is* available.

- Help your teen formulate a strategy to search for a job. Scour the want ads together. Consider this an opportunity for teaching your child what you know about the working world. Food service, swimming instruction, baby-sitting (sometimes involving traveling on vacation with the employer-family), yard work, car washing, dog-walking, and small retail sales work are traditional sources of youth employment.
- The availability of other jobs depends to some extent on where you live. As a teen in Colorado, I spent summers hoeing sugar beet fields and crating freshly picked corn in a farm shed, options clearly not available to urban kids. Golf caddying or coaching younger children in team sports may be a possibility. One teen's favorite job was as a car valet—where else could she drive a Porsche? Sometimes nonprofit organizations hire teens for door-to-door canvassing.
- Entrepreneurship may be the answer. One boy made a small fortune in the summer by selling knives to friends' parents. An eighth grader carted a lawn mower on a platform hooked to his bike, and by the time he could drive, he hired his friends to work for him all summer at his sizable lawn-care business.
- Help as much as you can, and that includes networking among your own acquaintances. Your call may alert someone to a need he didn't know he had. Call your lawyer, for example, to see if he could hire a summer "go-fer." We used such help when I practiced law, but only if someone called to request a job. (Otherwise, buried

in our writs and depositions, we barely noticed the season.) Your teenager may end up slaving over a hot photocopy machine, but he'll also get a worm's–eye view of a "foreign" culture.

Volunteer Work

While not financially rewarding, volunteer work develops skills and experience to parlay into paying jobs later. It also exposes kids to the "real" world and teaches the values of commitment and giving without expecting something in return. The desire to take on summer volunteers varies from organization to organization.

Letting your teen call for information develops his phone skills and ability to ask for what he wants. Don't limit contact to established charities, but also think of special programs and organizations where your child's natural talents and interests might be useful. If your daughter is a computer whiz, for example, perhaps she could organize a database of emergency volunteers for a disaster agency.

Leaving Older Kids Home Alone

What do you do during your workday with kids who are "too old" for a baby-sitter or day care? Or, as Ann put it, "What do adolescents do in the summer while the cat's away?—oh boy!"

Older children may do fine alone while you work, especially if they are used to being on their own for a few hours after school (see Chapter 11). Still, summer days provide a lot more hours to fill and many more temptations from television, video games, and footloose peers.

Everyone I talked to on this subject, single or married, groaned at the lack of a real solution and instead told me their horror stories. Kate, for example, arrived home unexpectedly one day to find her preteen son and his friends rolling barrels of water off the roof just to see the splash. This was not what she'd had in mind when asking him to water the lawn. Another mom, arriving home to her teenage son having sex with a girlfriend, could find her only consolation in the fact that they weren't in *her* bed.

Probably the best guarantee of your children's behavior and safety is an open and trusting relationship with them. This is, of course, a long-term goal you work toward from infancy. Though nothing is sure to "work," the following sections offer some suggestions from parents who have been through summers with their older children at home unattended.

Be Home As Much As You Can

Try not to leave your children with vast amounts of time on their own. Be around as much as possible. Go home after work. Stay home on weekends. Include the kids in your off-work activities.

Have Rules

For those times your older children are alone at home, you will, ideally, make the rules explicit, clear, and enforceable with stated consequences. Easier said than done. In any event, just stating the limits conveys that you care about them, and this is no small achievement in itself.

- Discuss your expectations for summer at a family meeting, even if you secretly suspect you have no effective means to enforce them. Set priorities and emphasize the rules that mean the most to you. You won't get perfect compliance, but your kids will be less likely to stray on the requirements you have imbued with importance.
- Once you've distilled the rules, write a contract that you all sign. Just the formality encourages compliance, and a copy on the refrigerator door serves as a reminder. Or maybe not. Ann told me, "I remember having lots of written rules and signed contracts that didn't work but made me feel better." See Chapter 11 for general home-alone rules.
- Restrict television, video games, and "surfing" the Internet according to whatever limits make you comfortable (see Chapter 9). Short of having a gizmo that limits use, however, this rule is hard to enforce while you're away. Encourage pleasure reading by helping your children develop a list of appropriate and enticing books. Perhaps you could reread favorite classics as you commute and hold literary discussions at the dinner table.
- Sometimes the problem isn't your kids, but their friends' parents. Some people have no qualms about leaving their kids alone for extended weekends or even weeks during the summer. Ann felt "that was probably harder on me than anything else, because the partying at those homes was insanely out of control. Eventually I got to calling and complaining to the absentee parents upon their re-

turn—even though it made my kids furious (they called me the 'town snoop'). But I formed a circle with other worried parents, and we backed each other up."

See Chapter 11 for additional rules.

Get Help

For Ann, getting help was the bottom line when her kids were teenagers: "Money helps, there's no doubt about it, but so does community. That's the key—making friends with other kids' parents, sharing the checking in and going away and overnights, having some adult agreement about rules and regulations."

- Get organized ahead of time. Work out arrangements with friends for rides, supervision, meals, and entertainment for your kids and theirs. Don't forget to include your married friends when asking for help.
- If you have family or nonworking friends nearby, ask them to schedule stops at your house. They can open their homes for meals or volunteer for activities such as shopping trips, museum visits, or afternoons at the public pool with the kids.
- Invite your geographically-distant relatives to visit when you most need to have someone around. Grandparents usually qualify for senior-citizen airline discounts. Instead, perhaps the children can spend a week at the homes of distant grandparents, aunts and uncles, or close family friends.

Family Vacations

Many working parents take their own vacations during the summer when the kids are out of school. Often this means travel away from home.

Brainstorm Possibilities

Discuss possibilities for family vacations at a family meeting.

- Kids' ideas blissfully disregard cost. If funds are limited, you can still acknowledge their desires. Make a fantasy list of what everyone, including yourself, would like to do. Write down every suggestion. Acknowledge every one you cannot manage with "I wish we could . . ." and briefly discuss what it would be like. Empathizing with your child's desire, even if the reality is unattainable, makes him feel heard.

- From the remaining suggestions, agree on what you can do. Perhaps two shorter vacations rather than one long one will satisfy more family members. The backpackers will put up with your time at the beach in exchange for a few days in the pines. A long weekend at a nearby bed-and-breakfast is relatively inexpensive. Perhaps you could rent a holiday house with another family or two.

  Christopher and I have enjoyed city- or university-sponsored mountain "family camps" that feature semi-rustic accommodations, three meals a day, and child care included in the modest price. Some clubs and other organizations maintain lodges with similar setups. We love hiking, skiing, or just sitting by the fire with friends or playing games. Aside from feeling wonderful, I model relaxation and silly adult fun for my son. Club Med, with children's and teen's clubs, are the same idea at a higher cost in more exotic locations.
- The mere presence of other responsive single parents takes the load off. We instinctively just pitch in, watch each other's kids, and wipe any little bottom that needs it. Consider a joint vacation with another single-parent family.
- Want a more active diversion? Consider a "volunteer vacation" during which you work at projects such as rebuilding trails or helping at archeological sites.

Making the Vacation Pleasant

There will always be some rough spots when traveling with the family, but advance thinking can minimize them.

- Perhaps not all teenagers are the same, but Ann swears hers "wouldn't move one step without their friends along." They hate being seen with parents. At the least, bringing your kids' friends along frees you from the role of entertainment director. If you're lucky, the friends' parents will invite your kids on *their* vacations in return, giving you some time for yourself at home.
- If you drive, prepare for backseat bickering, junk-food stops, and whines. A recent survey of kids between six and seventeen revealed that nearly half the children get bored on vacations. A full two-thirds

of teens thought family vacations were "little fun," and 40 percent described cross-country travel with the family as worse than cleaning their rooms or eating vegetables. The kids hated being cooped up with their sibs, the dog, or mom's boyfriend. Take sufficient breaks.
- Be sure the kids bring along activities for the car. Don't get sucked into thinking you're responsible for keeping them happy. Tell them boredom stimulates creativity and self-reliance. I've told Christopher from the beginning that the only person who can relieve his boredom is himself, and he's bought it. Most of the time he looks around and finds something of interest.

Protect Your Home from Prowlers While You're Away

There's no worse end to a vacation than finding your house ransacked when you return. Before you leave, take steps to foil burglars:

- Leave drapes and window shades open.
- Have someone care for the lawn so dead grass doesn't advertise your absence. Besides, who wants to come home to a patch of brown?
- Have a trusted neighbor pick up mail and newspapers every day.
- Leave a radio on to signal that someone is home.
- Turn down the volume on your phone bell and answering machine so a burglar won't know a call has gone unanswered.
- Set automatic timers to turn the lights on and off at different times in different rooms.
- Park a car in the driveway, or, if you take yours, ask if a neighbor will park there. Not only does this imply you're home, but it makes it impossible for someone to back a truck up the drive and load all your possessions.

Taking Care of Yourself

Wondering about your kids running free during the summer exacerbates the stress in your life. Be sure to take care of yourself, too. In your eagerness to keep your children safe and entertained, don't overlook your need for adult activities and quiet time alone. Do something extra-special for yourself at least once a week in the summers, even if it's just a long bath or a night reading a trashy novel.

If You're the Noncustodial Parent

If your kids spend only summers and holidays with you, prepare ahead.

- Take care of practical issues like child-proofing your house, locating a doctor, and—unless you take a vacation for the duration of the visit—arranging child care in advance. Dust off your list of nighttime baby-sitters. If you have a new partner or family, prepare them for the visit. Discuss adjustments in living space, chores, sleeping arrangements, and so on. If your child made friends in your area on previous visits, let them know when he will arrive.
- You should have been communicating with your kid throughout the year, even if you live at a distance. If not, catch up in advance on occurrences in your lives since you last met. Talk with your ex and your child on the phone or by e-mail. Exchange pictures so you'll each be ready for physical changes. Prepare your kid for any new people in your life, but make it clear that he can form his own opinions about liking them.
- Shift emotionally into "parent mode." Try not to build up your expectations, as transitions may be rocky. Acknowledge that both you and your child may need time to warm up and get back in sync. He may even exhibit reluctance to leave his other home and its familiar aspects. Confessing your own anxieties may free him to expose some of his, but don't pressure him. See Chapter 1 for further discussion of your child's visit to the noncustodial parent.

No matter how you spend the school vacation months, prepare for them and then relax. Use your parenting skills. Have some summer fun with your kid.

BOOKS FOR PARENTS

Peterson's Guide to Adventure Holidays (Princeton, NJ: Petersons Guides, 1995).

Where Should We Take the Kids? (New York: Fodor's Travel Publications, 1995) (state-by-state guides).

For "Volunteer Vacations," Consult:

Environmental Vacations: Volunteer Projects to Save the Planet, Stephanie Ocko (Santa Fe, NM: John Muir Publications, 1992); 800-888-7504.

Free Vacations & Bargain Adventures in the U.S.A., Evelyn Kaye (Boulder, CO: Blue Penguin Publications, 1995).

Volunteer Vacations: Short-Term Adventures That Will Benefit You and Others, Bill McMillon (Chicago: Chicago Review Press, 1995).

BOOKS FOR KIDS

Biz Kids Guide to Success: Money-Making Ideas for Young Entrepreneurs, Terri Thompson (Hauppauge, NY: Barrons Educational Series, Inc., 1992).

Directory of Overseas Summer Jobs '95 (Princeton, NJ: Petersons Guides, 1995).

Summer Jobs, Aidel Stein (Southfield, MI: Targum Press, 1995).

Summer Jobs USA 1995 (Princeton, NJ: Petersons Guides, 1995). ($15.95)

Chapter 15

Single Parents and Their Money

Money Troubles

A woman's standard of living drops an average of 27 percent when she divorces. Her ex-husband's, in comparison, *rises* 10 percent. Half of all single-mother families live below the poverty level, three times the rate for two-parent families. Men comprise 14 percent of custodial parents, and while less likely to collect child support, they are also less likely to be poor. This is not to deny that some men suffer financially after separation or that some women fare well. Financial hardship can arrive in various ways after you become single again:

- While kids are your most precious "assets," their upkeep definitely goes on the debit side of the money ledger. Court-mandated spousal and child support fail to approach your real costs of living. Though the formulas differ from state to state, the awards usually relate to the incomes of one or both parents, not to the actual amount required to raise a child.
- A significant proportion of noncustodial ex-spouses don't keep even these inadequate payments current. Less than half of absent parents pay child support. About 30 percent of the kids living with a parent who is owed child support live in households collecting welfare. In 1991, custodial mothers received $3011 in average annual child support, and custodial fathers received $2292.

  As of May 1995, the United States Congress was considering various initiatives to make it easier to establish paternity, locate noncustodial parents, and penalize those in arrears on child support payments. Various states already have such programs, but a federal law would set a national standard and allow collection by out-of-state enforcement. As it is now, about one-third of child-support cases involve parents who move out of state to foil collection.

The proposed national child-support reforms aim, in part, to reduce the welfare rolls by ensuring noncustodial parents' compliance with court orders for support. The new law would require employers to report new employees' names and Social Security numbers to aid in locating—and garnishing the wages of—deadbeat parents. It would also follow the lead of some twenty states that revoke or refuse driving, business, hobby, or professional licenses to those in arrears on child-support payments.

- The court splits marital debts between the partners, forcing you to start your new life in a financial hole.
- You reenter the job market with outdated skills. You lack money for retraining and related child care.
- You rejoin the workforce at a lower level of compensation than when you left to have children. Your time out of the ranks of the employed means small pensions and small Social Security benefits in later years.
- Your spouse handled all money questions, leaving you with little fiscal knowledge beyond how to balance the checkbook.

> Noncustodial parents owed $17.7 billion in 1991 but paid only 67% of that amount, or $11.9 billion.[1]

Even the formerly well-off can end up on Aid to Families with Dependent Children. Welfare, that is. The very words stigmatize you. People assume you're lazy, immoral, or permanently living off the fat of their hard-won earnings. In truth, your ex may be the lazy and immoral one, but no one wants to hear it. And you're hardly living fat. The tax dollars supporting AFDC are relatively modest compared to other government programs, and you'll be lucky to make rent and put some beans on the table. What's worse, even if you *want* to work and find a job, your pay reduces the amount of aid you receive. By the time you add in the cost of child care, transportation, and suitable clothing, you'd make less working than you'd get in aid. Why take a deal like that?

Still, as illogical, demeaning, and tangled in red tape as it is, AFDC can be a lifesaver in emergencies and can put you on your feet for the future.

If you were widowed, you may have some life insurance proceeds or social security benefits to bolster your savings. Perhaps these leave you set for life financially. Or maybe your salary is all you have. Like single parents by choice, you may share the following money-related difficulties with the divorced:

- You're the only support for your children. As a woman, you find that a man doing the same job pulls down more pay. While nearly 87 percent of single parents with sole custody are women, men earn higher wages for equivalent jobs.
- You stay in a job you hate in order to keep the benefits. Or you take the only employment you can find, and your family's health suffers because of inadequate or nonexistent insurance.
- You have to sacrifice your well-paying job or turn down a promotion because you can't meet the travel or other requirements now that you're on your own with children. Your employer expresses sympathy, but travel is still part of the job.
- You lost your limited funds in a "foolproof" investment, perhaps even one suggested by a trusted acquaintance.

> In a recent survey, the median assets in married households equaled four times those in divorced households.[2]

Almost without exception, every woman I asked replied that the hardest aspect of single-parenting was "the money." Money questions exist whatever your financial circumstances. Do you live within your means? Conversely, do miserly tendencies keep you from enjoying life? Do credit card and other debts make saving impossible? Where will you get money for a car? For down payment on a house? For your kid's college education? For your retirement? How should you invest retirement-plan money? When you accumulate more assets, how can you best make them work for you? Should you keep them in "safe" investments or take a risk in hope of reaping large returns? How much of a risk is acceptable? What do you do to find out what stocks, bonds, and mutual funds are—and which are good ones? This chapter starts you on the road to answering these questions. Get ready to become proactive and play the financial hand you were dealt.

The enthusiastic response to a financial planner's talk at my single-parents' group—and the members' surprising lack of basic knowledge—inspired me to include this chapter. Personal finance is not hard to understand. If you think it is, you've probably just never been taught. Even people at modest income levels vastly improve their financial health by learning money management.

If you've never approached personal finance in an organized way, take a breath. Think of this as sharpening the shears. Setting a responsible, low-maintenance financial course for the future ultimately simplifies your life.

Know Your Money Style

How you relate to money depends in part on your own psychological qualities and your parents' attitudes. Because you provide a role model for *your* children, you must demonstrate capable, healthy monetary habits yourself. How *do* you handle money? Assessing your money style identifies your strengths and weaknesses and provides clues for making improvements. Both under-spending and over-spending represent extremes on a continuum. You'll probably recognize yourself somewhere in the middle.

Under-Spenders

Most personal finance advice focuses on people who spend too much money. Because I fall toward the opposite end of the spectrum, however, I also recognize "under-spending" as detrimental.

At the extreme, call us "tightwads," "penny-pinchers," and "cheapskates." You know who you are. You love bargains, avoid retail, buy nothing you don't "need," and waste half a day in comparative research that ends up saving a nickel. Ads touting low monthly payments don't tempt you because the overall cost of buying on credit is a rip-off. Being "taken" weighs in as the Eighth Deadly Sin. You'll split a dinner check down to the penny, always hoping no one notices that you gave yourself that extra cent.

Ironically, you focus on the dimes and overlook the dollars. You balk at an overpriced $5 item but can't quite get a grip on the difference between, say, $16,000 and $18,000 for a car. You have experience with the $5. You *understand* the $5. Everything above a certain level, however, qualifies as "big money" with no meaning in practical terms. In my own case, suddenly having a lawyer's income after years of student living changed little for me—I just banked everything I didn't spend. I knew nothing about investing. As long as the principal stayed intact, I was happy.

Psychologically, I believe under-spending reflects low self-worth. You don't deserve to have it easy. You don't count. You can't buy anything just because you like it, and guilt assails you if you do. My deeply ingrained attitudes came straight from my Depression-era parents who saved their own nickels and didn't know enough about the big picture to teach me. They never changed. My mother recently announced her decision not to buy anymore half-price senior discount airline tickets because she had to pay a $12 departure tax at the airport. I suspect that fee applies to everyone, but in any case, she found it perfectly sensible to forfeit a $300 discount because it cost $12! With parental reasoning like this, no wonder I had odd ideas about money.

> "A man who both spends and saves money is the happiest man, because he has both enjoyments."
> SAMUEL JOHNSON (1709–1784)

Isn't saving prudent? Doesn't the environment benefit by avoiding indiscriminate consumption? Yes and yes, but you can overdo it. While married, I pulled the purse-strings even tighter in response to Tony's bursts of manic spending and his labeling me "parsimonious." "Hire somebody," he urged, "consider the value of your time." He multiplied by my hourly rate as a lawyer and demonstrated how much I'd "save" by hiring a typist, house-cleaner, or baby-sitter. The only problem was, I didn't work as a lawyer anymore. My time might have been worth that much, but nobody was paying for it! Strangely, whenever the mania passed, Tony pinched a lot of pennies himself, and I'd feel all the more justified.

After Tony died, I decided to live off my savings for "a while," and frugality seemed even more necessary. (As this strategy involved "big money," however, I played ostrich and never tried to figure out how long I could survive.) Soon, however, I realized I simply had no time or energy for my old habits, and I tipped a bit too far in the other direction. Comparison shopping gave way to convenience. When I needed a new (used) car, I literally bought the first one I saw—a luxury model I would never have considered previously. I felt guilty and sinful, and my anxiety meter hit the top. A few more moves like this, and I'd be broke, I knew. So I went straight back to being "parsimonious," where I felt comfortable.

My therapist assured me that freer spending, especially on myself, would make me a better parent. Not to own more "things," but to enjoy life a little and demonstrate for Christopher how to give to oneself. I had to be reminded that I count, too. He urged me to get knowledgeable financial help and pin down the realities of my financial situation. He was right. I *was* happier opening that tight fist a little. Seeing a professional money person helped both my pocketbook *and* my mental state. As I've repeatedly learned, taking a positive step—being proactive—relieves anxiety.

Over-Spenders

Debt happens. You overdraw bank accounts, carry huge credit card balances, and sport black marks on your credit report. You may spend more than you have. Some of you juggle sums from one account to another. If you want something, money is no object. The amount of monthly payment concerns you, not the overall cost. You commonly run out of money before payday, but you can't say where it all goes. Budgeting is too restrictive and bothersome. Whoever thought up the concept of saving obviously buzzed in from another planet.

Shopping elevates your mood. Buying counts as therapy. Having an outfit in your closet for every possible occasion makes you feel secure. So does buying a new one that is just right for tonight. You deserve a little something new after all you've been through lately.

If this describes you, you are an over-spender. The sections about debt, budgeting, and saving aim especially at you.

> The average annual child support payment received by mothers in 1991 was $3011, representing 17% of their incomes.[3]

Get Advice from a Knowledgeable Professional

A professional financial advisor can help you get out of debt, set up a budget, establish goals, recommend investments, translate the mumbo-jumbo of your job's retirement plan, and more. Someone who works daily in the financial field immediately points out what might take you days of study to see. Most advisors will also invest, monitor, and manage your entire portfolio if it's large enough.

On the other hand, if your divorce has left you impossibly debt-ridden, perhaps bankruptcy is the only answer. Certain attorneys specialize in this area and can best advise you.

Although my financial plan is now in place, I still consult my advisor at least annually for reality checks and new ideas. Oh yes, and for anxiety relief.

Finding Financial Advice

Lots of people will be happy to give you financial advice. Finding them isn't the problem; finding the right one is. Keep the following in mind:

- Each state has its own rules, but often there are no requirements whatsoever for someone calling himself a "financial planner" or "financial advisor." Certain training programs award certificates that entitle a person to add letters behind his name. "CFP" means "certified financial planner," for example. This indicates that the person has training, if not experience.
- Planners are either "fee only," which means you pay them by the hour, or commission-based, meaning the advice is free, but you pay them a commission on any investment you buy or sell. Advisors on commission are prone to frequent calls with recommendations.
- Stock brokers fit in the commission-based class. Brokerages employ analysts who constantly research market conditions and investments for their clients. Brokers advise you on individual stocks or on an overall investment plan. (So-called "discount brokers" execute transactions but offer no advice.)
- Forget "hot tips." Instead, concentrate on learning how personal finance works and what the basic jargon means. Consider taking classes at a community college. Planners sometimes give free seminars in hope of attracting clients. If the subject matter interests you, attend, but also get recommendations for good financial advisors from friends and acquaintances. Ask your divorce lawyer, your hairstylist, and your tax preparer. You might be surprised who uses a financial pro.
- Schedule an introductory appointment to test the "vibes" between you and the planner. Consulting a commission-based professional costs nothing unless you buy. Some fee-only planners offer a free,

limited initial consultation. Shop around until you're satisfied you've found someone knowledgeable, trustworthy, and able to speak your language. Make certain the person will take time to understand your *entire* financial picture and recommend only investments prudent for someone with your knowledge, background, and situation.

Paying for Advice

The question isn't "whether" but "how" you pay for advice. Get an answer right up front, and keep asking until you fully understand all potential charges. Perhaps you'll get a break. The planner who spoke to my support group halves her normal hourly rate for single parents, having once struggled as one herself!

In 1991, 75% of women due child support received some payments. 63% of men due child support payments received them.[4]

Because fee-only planners charge by the hour, they don't push you to buy and sell. Therefore, some people favor their recommendations over those of commission-based advisors. The latter may encourage frequent, perhaps unnecessary transactions to generate fees for themselves rather than to promote your best interests. At the extreme, "churning" your account costs you a bundle in commissions.

Fee-only planning is relatively straightforward—an hourly rate multiplied by the time expended on anything done in your behalf. Fee-only planners don't execute transactions for you, so take their advice to a "discount" or "deep discount broker" and buy or sell the securities at relatively low commissions. Or buy directly from mutual funds. Planners' fees average around $75–150 an hour. Yes, it can add up, but I consider my advisor's charges analogous to my mother's $12 departure fee.

You may have heard of "no-load" mutual funds, which require no fee to buy or sell shares. You *do,* however, pay an *annual* charge of 0.3 percent to over 2 percent (average 1.17 percent) of your investment for the advisors who choose securities for the fund. You may never really miss this fee because the fund subtracts it before reporting the share value, but you do still pay it. This is only right, as you benefit from their expert research and management decisions.

Beware, however, of funds that charge far in excess of the norm for similar funds. Every penny comes out of your returns. Also, mutual funds have begun charging for many shareholder services, such as redeeming shares by wire, exchanging funds within a fund family, providing copies of past statements, or maintaining your account below a minimum amount. Many impose a charge for *each* IRA account, which adds up if you have multiple accounts. Unfortunately, even the prospectuses don't mention some of these fees.

In short, you *will* pay for advice. There's nothing wrong with that. Just know what and how you are paying.

Using a Financial Planner

Get organized before you meet with a financial advisor. I don't mean bringing in your grocery receipts or even balancing your checkbook. Just do some homework to make your information accessible and understandable. If you use a fee-only planner, don't waste time with the meter running to scratch through a sheaf of unorganized documents. Take your last few tax returns, the financial papers from your divorce, the latest statements from all accounts, and any other summary of your assets and income. Call beforehand and ask your advisor what else he wants to see. And please, take it in something other than a shoe box (see Chapter 18).

> In the spring of 1992, 11.5 million families with kids had a parent living outside the home. 54%, or 6.2 million, had a decree or agreement for child support. Of those, 50% received the full amount, 25% partial payment, and 25% no payments.[5]

When you arrive, get to the point: Why are you here? What are your assets, debts, and income? What is your level of experience? What kind of help do you seek—particular investment advice or an overall plan? What do you want to accomplish? A budget? A savings plan? Aid with retirement investments? What are your money problems? Your goals? If you have money to invest, what level of risk can you accept?

If your children are old enough, consider taking them along to meetings with your planner. I believe in informing the kids about family finances and communicating honestly about money difficulties. Letting them hear professional advice underlines the seriousness of money matters and increases their understanding, especially if your own mastery of the subject still feels shaky. Your refusals to buy-buy-buy for them make more sense. Working out a financial plan creates a learning experience for both of you. Your seeking help also models responsible behavior.

I must admit that at first I had trouble communicating with my planner. She threw around numbers rounded off to the nearest thousand, and I'd flip through bank statements to prove the figure was really only $995. That same old five dollars again! Learning to ignore it in discussions with my advisor was my first lesson in getting the big picture.

Make sure you understand the answers to your questions. If not, ask again. Listen to the advice, and *take notes.* Everything sounds perfectly clear when your planner explains it, but just try remembering it all at home.

Take the Advice

I put this advice in a section of its own to emphasize that it's not enough to get information. You have to use it, too. Don't blindly follow every recommendation. Get a second opinion if you like. Let your planner educate you. But after you've decided the advice is sound, *act.*

Make a Budget

I'd never needed a budget—I always just spent as close to zero as possible—but the financial planner created one, in part I think, to set *minimums* for this under-spender. I choked when she penciled in the yearly figure for "vacations and entertainment," knowing I could never spend that much. It was helpful, however, to see where my money went and to know that every purchase wouldn't land me in bankruptcy. I gradually started spending more. I loosened up, hired baby-sitters for relief, even had nights out. Before therapy one day, I bought a new outfit I didn't "need" just because I liked it. Of course, I spent a good part of my therapeutic hour discussing whether I deserved it. I concluded, somewhat tentatively, that I did. This, for an under-spender, was progress.

A budget lists all your expenses by category on a monthly or yearly basis. Most people use budgets to figure out where they spend money, to get out of debt, to prevent the outgo from exceeding the income, to simplify money matters, and to start saving. While you can't affect the trade imbalance or abolish the national deficit, you *can* influence your personal spending.

Budgeting sets a good example for your children, too. So does refusing to wallow in guilt if you blow it. Just pick yourself up and carry on.

To create a budget:

- Go through your checkbooks and credit card statements for the last year to track expenditures. This ensures that you pick up large but infrequent items like insurance payments and car repairs. Avoid catchall categories like "car expenses" and "household costs." The point is to learn in detail where your money goes. Don't forget to include a category for saving!

  Here is a sample list of categories to get you started:

  auto: gas, maintenance, payments
  bank and safe-deposit box charges
  business expenses not reimbursed by employer
  charity contributions
  child care
  cleaners
  clothing: yours and the kids
  credit card: interest, finance charges, annual fees
  dental expenses
  eating out
  education expenses
  entertainment
  gifts
  groceries
  home: insurance, maintenance,
    mortgage or rent, taxes
  investment expenses
  life insurance
  loan interest
  medical
  memberships: associations, museums, organizations
  miscellaneous one-time expenses
  personal care
  retirement savings

> Half of custodial mothers without a child-support award lived below the poverty line in 1991.[6]

savings
taxes: local, state, federal, Social Security, unemployment, etc.
subscriptions: newspaper, magazines
travel
utilities: cable, garbage, gas and electric, telephone, water
vacations

- Next apply your take-home pay to basic, *necessary* categories. Your "needs" include: housing, food, insurance, transportation, utilities, clothes necessary for work, emergencies, and so on. This is the beginning of a new budget. Be realistic, based on your past requirements. Include a category for taking care of yourself in some special way. Keeping you in good working order is definitely a "necessity." Maybe a video every week is it for now, but include something.
- Now pencil in a figure for saving. Then spread leftover sums among discretionary items— your "wants": vacations, nonessential clothes, entertainment, hobbies, pets, memberships, and the like. The goal is to live within your means. It requires setting priorities and lowering expectations about your lifestyle. If you fall short, play with the categories until it all adds up, even if you have to switch poor Kitty over to dry food. Your planner can help with this, and most personal finance books outline the process in detail.

Making a budget is the easy part. Now follow it. For at least the first couple of months, write down everything you spend in each category so you know where you stand as the weeks go by. Watch for sinkholes you might not otherwise notice:

> The fastest increase in poverty between 1990 and 1991 was among female heads of households with kids.[7]

- Kids. A nickel here and a dollar there add up.
- Gifts. Do you spend too much out of obligation or a sense of having to repay others' gifts in like amounts? Substitute cards or send less costly presents (see Chapter 13). If you like garage sales, look for new, unopened items you can give as gifts. Don't expect to find what you need for next week's birthday, but accumulate presents for later. The same principle applies to sales.
- Insurance. Have you shopped for the lowest rates?
- Subscriptions. Do you pay for newspapers and magazines that you never get a chance to read anyway?

- Cash. Do you make too many trips to the ATM and lose track of where the money goes? Limit those withdrawals and pay by check.
- Impulse purchases.

Plan so you don't blow a category's entire allotment at one time, and accept that maxing out a budgeted amount means foregoing further expenditures there until next month. The Life Preserver about staying flexible and creative does *not* apply here. Enjoy the process, but be strict with yourself. You have a lot at stake.

Save More

If you're financially stretched already, you may wonder how you can increase your savings. There are three ways: save more, earn more, spend less.

> About 61% of all children of single parents live below the poverty line.[8]

Treat savings as a necessary and inviolate budget expenditure. Start *now*, and put away something every month, even if it's only $15 or $25. It will grow faster than you might imagine. For example, investing just $10 a month at 10 percent produces $7657 after twenty years. You needn't do anything fancy with the money at this level. Open a money market account or buy U.S. Savings Bonds. Steady contributions add up. Meanwhile, you learn a healthy new money habit.

The average Japanese saves 15 percent of his annual income, and the French save 12 percent. The average American weighs in with only 5.5 percent, down from 8 percent in 1984. Not much when you consider the cash required for car and housing down payments, college, retirement, and other lump-sum obligations. Are you above or below this average? As an interim goal, add another percentage point to what you already save. Then look for other ways to increase savings.

It's easier to save if you never see the money. You don't even think of it as yours. If possible, have savings deducted from your paycheck and deposited to a credit union, savings account, money market, or mutual fund. Some mutual funds waive the usual initial minimum investment amount (usually $500–3000) if you sign up for small, automatic deductions from a designated bank account each month. If this isn't possible, write a check to yourself first thing every payday and deposit it in your savings. Squirrel away your bonuses and raises in a separate account and pretend you never got them.

If you're "safe" with credit cards, get one that issues rebates and use it for every possible purchase. Make sure you'll use the incentive offered. Frequent-flier miles mean nothing to me because I rarely travel now. Instead, every purchase on my card earns free gasoline for driving Christopher to preschool. Pay off your entire balance every month to avoid incurring finance charges, which tend to be steep on these cards. Avoiding a credit card interest of 18 percent on a $100 balance is the same as tucking $18 into your savings account.

Earn More

Can you ask for a promotion or a raise? Change jobs? Add additional part-time work? Make money from a hobby? Get additional training? Relax, you don't *have* to do any of this. Don't even try until the fallout from your divorce or the death of your spouse settles. At some time in the future, though, you may think of these alternatives. Don't, however, make any changes that cost too much in time with your children.

Spend Less

Opportunities for spending less exist everywhere.

Reduce Budget Allowances

> The average annual child support received by fathers in 1991 was $2292, or 7% of their incomes.[9]

Go through your budget item-by-item and analyze where you could make do with less. Look first for areas that create the least sense of deprivation and sacrifice. These differ for everyone. Trim some expenditures, eliminate others. Cut back on the gift budget by agreeing not to exchange. Shrink your clothes allowance. Rent videos instead of seeing first-run movies. Buy food in bulk rather than in small packages that cost more per ounce. Get your kids to wash the car instead of putting out cash for it at the local automated car wash. Pulling back a little in various budget categories can add up to a significant amount.

Ask for Discounts

Except for car purchases and garage sales, bargaining isn't part of our culture, as it is in many other countries. Most Americans hesitate to ask for lower prices. Too bad, because many businesses will give them if you do! Naturally, any profit-making enterprise would like all customers to pay full freight, so don't expect to see these bargains advertised. Companies will knock off a few bucks to close a sale, however, and the flimsiest excuse may suffice.

- Most hotels and car rental agencies, for example, contract for lower rates with organizations such as businesses, professional organizations, or special-interest groups. Ask about a reduced rate for your associations, and you may get a discount without even producing proof of membership. Saying the magic words, "Do you have a lower rate?" or "What's the corporate rate?" or "Is there a group rate?" may be sufficient. In booking a niece and her friends into a hotel room, I asked about a reduced rate and mentioned the soccer tournament that accounted for their visit. The reservations clerk didn't need anything else. Hotels are especially eager to fill weekend vacancies and rooms still unsold late in the evening.
- In retail stores, if you're willing to take a floor model, ask for a discount. Request quantity discounts. Even two items can qualify as "quantity," depending on the circumstances. Just be sure you can really use two! Ask, "Is there a discount if I buy more than one of these whatzits today?" I buy bread for my freezer by the six-loaf case at a health food store and save 10 percent, but I had to ask for this concession. The local camera store offers a similar discount on film. Ten percent isn't a fortune, but it adds up. It more than pays the tax on my purchases.

  To make room for new versions, stores often mark down models going out of production. This is the classic buying scheme for last year's new car, and it worked for my sewing machine. The motivated seller even reduced the sales price further and threw in a carrying case—at my request, of course.

  Use any excuse to request a discount. That small scratch qualifies as an excuse for a price reduction. Tell the clerk you'll buy at this shop if she matches the price you saw across town. Ask if the store takes trade-ins.

- Request discounts on payments for services rendered. My neighbor Beverly, a single mom and busy executive, invites three or four bidders to her home *at the same time*. They know they're in a competitive situation and often even hear each other's bids. If the low bidder's references check out, she's saved substantial money. If not, she moves on to the second-lowest bid, and so on. Beverly uses this strategy for weed clearing, house remodeling, roof repairs, and even sewer backups. Until she told me, I had no idea that the sewer service rep who arrives with snake and plunger *could* charge less than the quoted rate. Like most people, I was always so eager to get the use of my bathroom back that I just called one service and paid whatever it wanted.

Don't feel odd about asking for bargains. You won't always get the answer you want, but sometimes you will. Even if you don't, the worst than can happen is a polite "no" or "sorry, we can't do that." No one will harass, arrest, or otherwise punish you for effrontery. Often the salesperson softens and tells you something about his business. The process itself is interesting and fulfilling. Even if you don't save money, you'll have a pleasant human interaction.

- The average 1991 income of a custodial mom *with* a support order was $18,144; average income of a custodial father *with* a support decree, $33,579.
- The average 1991 income of a custodial mom *without* a support decree was $10,226; average income of a custodial father *without* a support order, $27,578.[10]

Reduce Your Credit Card Debt Service

Next look at your debt service—the interest you pay for the privilege of borrowing. Hauling around a huge debt takes a toll on self-esteem. Retiring debt accumulated during your marriage aids recovery from the divorce. Debt, the last unpleasant remnant of life with your ex, traps you in the past. Pay it off and get on with your new life.

Credit cards are the worst offenders. Besides their convenience, letting the balance ride gets you through periods of low cash flow.

The interest rates are so high, however, that large debts quickly build up. Counting interest, you end up paying much more than the cash price for everything you charge. You risk staying in debt indefinitely. For example, by making only the minimum two-percent payment on a card with a $20 annual fee and interest accumulating annually at 19.8 percent, retiring a $2,000 debt will take *31 years!*

- Pay off existing credit card balances as quickly as you can. Use the proceeds from a home-equity loan if possible, as its interest rate will be much lower than those of your credit cards, *and* the interest may be tax deductible. Shop around for home-equity loan rates and fees, which vary significantly. Then repay the equity loan as fast as possible with regular payments. Don't even *think* of using any of the proceeds for a shopping spree or vacation!
- If you can't get a home-equity loan, request a lower interest rate on existing cards. Issuers sometimes agree in order to keep customers with good long-term records, but again, you have to ask. Forget it if you chronically pay late.

  In fact, if you haven't been the model cardholder, you'd better clean up your act. Credit card companies recently began adding punitive charges in the small print. A few late payments or an over-limit charge can result in multiple, significant penalties.
- Consolidate all balances into one card with the lowest rate you can find. Popular personal-finance publications like *Money Magazine* list these every month, with toll-free numbers. Close out your high-interest cards and have your balances transferred to the low-rate one.

To get copies of your credit report, contact:

• TRW	800-422-4879 (CA only)
• Equifax	800-685-1111
• Trans Union	316-636-6100

Again, watch out for the small print. With a few late payments, that low advertised rate can double. In addition, some issuers raise the rates on cardholders they consider high credit risks, based not only on your record with the company, but on your overall credit report.

Next, zero out your consolidated balance as quickly as you can. From then on, pay off the entire monthly balance in full and on time to avoid finance charges, late penalties, and over-limit charges entirely. Since you'll pay no interest, you won't care if the interest rate is sky-high, but the amount of annual fee still matters. Find a no-fee card by consulting the lists in those same money magazines. Perhaps your existing issuer will even waive its fee for you. It can't hurt to ask.

- Some people are truly "dangerous" (to themselves) with credit cards, and aside from creating financial tangles, they model perilous behavior for the kids. If you have trouble limiting credit purchases, consider canceling all your cards and relying on your checkbook to stay within budget. Unfortunately, without a credit card, you'll have trouble renting cars, making hotel reservations, or buying anything by phone.

  The answer is an "equity credit card," which looks just like an ordinary card. The credit limit, however, cannot exceed the amount you deposit with the card company, say $100 or $500, and purchases in excess will be denied. Use the card only for emergencies or as security for reservations. The equity card helps you break the "charge it" habit while preserving the other uses of credit cards.

Reduce Your Car Loan Debt Service

Some people take out another loan for a new (or used) car as soon as they pay off the old one. Instead, hang on to the old car *and* continue making those payments—to yourself. Have them deducted automatically from your bank account to a savings account or mutual fund to keep temptation at bay.

> The threat of license revocation works very well to encourage support payments. With its program, Maine collected from 60% of parents owing support.[11]

When you do borrow again for a car, use a home-equity loan instead of a bank loan, if possible. Take advantage of the lower rate and interest deductibility.

Reduce Your Home Mortgage Debt Service

If you're lucky enough to own a home, you probably also have a mortgage. In the early years of a mortgage, most of the monthly payment goes to paying interest rather than to reducing principal.

- If current interest rates sink significantly lower than your existing mortgage rate, consider refinancing or substituting a new loan at the lower rate. Whether this makes sense depends on the costs of refinancing, the difference in rates, how long you plan to stay in the house, and other factors. Personal finance books, computer programs such as Quicken, or your financial planner provide formulas for making the decision.
- Consult your financial advisor as to whether you should pay off additional principal with every mortgage payment (refinanced or not). Check for prepayment penalties first. Some advisors recommend even small prepayments because they reduce the overall amount of interest over the life of the loan. Should you run into an emergency later, you can get the cash back by taking out a home-equity loan. Paying half your monthly payment in biweekly installments instead of once a month accomplishes the same thing, and it's practically painless.

  The advisability of using your cash to prepay your mortgage instead of investing it depends on the financial climate, the loan terms, and your circumstances. Get individual advice.

Change Your Living Situation

You and your children have suffered enough change in your lives. If your situation is desperate, however, or if enough time has passed since the death or divorce, think about reducing expenses by altering your living situation. That doesn't necessarily mean moving.

- Consider a tenant or roommate, a traditional money-saving tactic. The student who took a room in Sonya's house not only paid rent but provided male role modeling for her son, Ben. Fortunately, her house accommodated a tenant without disrupting her life. Because I require quiet for my work at home, I don't want a roommate. I don't have the space anyway.

  Consider a roommate or tenant a *temporary* arrangement, and make this clear in a written agreement to avoid later misunderstanding. Plan to reevaluate after six to twelve months.

> There are 11.2 million low-income renters competing for 6.5 million low-rent units, leaving a shortage of 4.7 million.[12]

Finding a roommate to share rent is hard when you have children. Regular referral agencies for shared rentals cater primarily to single adults, who often balk at living with other people's kids. In my area, a new nonprofit business puts single parents together with others to form households. This agency even accepts some tenants with poor financial conditions and provides support for learning to live in a group.

- Some single parents enjoy living communally or semi-communally with others, either single parents or not. They feel the communal lifestyle exposes their children to other adults, models cooperation, affords informal child care, allows for living in a larger space than otherwise possible, and, due to reduced cooking and cleaning responsibilities, frees up time to be with the kids. You have to be ready to take on the responsibilities of living communally, however: less privacy, more personalities to please, and more compromises.

> Three out of five poor renters (defined as having incomes of $12,000 or less) pay at least 50% of their incomes on housing.[13]

- Some single parents find themselves in apartment buildings full of other kids, some with just one parent. They throw their doors open to all the children and find ready support and baby-sitting among neighbors.
- A housing concept from Scandinavia combines the best of separate and communal living and seems ideal for single parents. Gaining a slow but steady hold in the United States, "co-housing" features a common building with living, cooking, eating, and recreational facilities for general use. Families live separately in small houses nearby and participate in group functions only when they want. They choose whether to cook in their own kitchens or join a communal meal, for example. The community shares equipment such as laundry machines and major tools. Best of all, the groups value and provide for children. All have safe play areas visible from most of the homes. Child-centered activities abound, perhaps with schools or child-care centers on the property. Co-operative baby-sitting occurs naturally. Though co-housing groups value privacy, they become close and integrated.

Co-housing has its downside, and these negative factors have so far kept me from joining a group organized by some of my friends.

Everyone must agree on location—rural or urban, near schools or near business centers, and so on. Whatever the site, it usually requires substantial building or remodeling to conform to the co-housing idea, and members must contribute time and money long before they move in. The concept dictates unanimous agreement for group decisions, producing lengthy, tedious meetings. Personality conflicts can blow a group apart. Zoning authorities unfamiliar with co-housing pose bureaucratic obstacles. Ownership requires a fairly substantial income because of relatively high costs.

> Moving is a pain, but a common one: The average American makes 11.7 moves in a lifetime. While one in six Americans moves to a new residence during the year, most stay in the same county.[14]

Still, residents of established co-housing projects love their lifestyle. As the concept grows, resale units should become available to people who don't want to go through the building process. Costs should decrease. I don't have the time and energy to aid the creation of a co-housing group. If I could simply move into an existing one that met my needs, however, I would sign on the dotted line.

- Some single parents make another type of major housing change to save money—moving back in with their parents for the long or short term. This can be a positive, nurturing, intergenerational family experience, and grandparents can provide child care and other support. On the other hand, being back in the family of origin sometimes recreates old roles and resurrects value clashes. These reconstituted families become dysfunctional if the grandmother takes over as "parent" to the child *and* the mother, leaving the mother with little self-sufficiency and responsibility. If the grandmother and mother have inconsistent parenting styles, the child has trouble figuring out who's in charge.

  This same dynamic can exist when a single mom lives close to, but not with, her parents. Help from family is wonderful, but only if you are autonomous and clearly in charge of your life. Only you can judge whether moving home is appropriate in your case. Trust your intuition.

Find Less Expensive Child Care

Obviously, quality counts above all else in child care. I would never suggest moving young children to a less desirable or less convenient environment just to save money. At the same time, child care constitutes a major expense to single parents with small kids. If there's a way to reduce it without sacrifice, consider it.

Move to an Area with a Lower Cost of Living

My town never makes the list of the hundred best places to raise kids. I read newspaper articles comparing housing costs in other U.S. geographical areas, and my fantasies fly. For the price of my tiny home in the San Francisco Bay Area, I could occupy a comparative mansion in San Antonio, upstate New York, Alabama, or even California's nether regions. I could buy a house in the best school district, reduce my child-care expenses, and live more cheaply all around.

Why don't I? After twenty-five years, I'm just too firmly planted in the Bay Area. The combination of familiarity and variety comforts me. I know absolutely no one in any of those hundred best places. I could make a move, but I choose not to. I'd rather struggle with the cost of living here than pay the price of leaving my friends and support system.

You might differ. Maybe you'll move back to a place where you still have connections. Your college town. Your hometown. Even if you don't want to live *with* your parents, you might enjoy closer proximity. Or perhaps you're ready for an adventurous leap into the unknown. You'll have to follow your instincts on this one.

Paying for Your Child's College Education

Using formulas provided by a magazine and a mutual fund, I calculated that by the time five-year-old Christopher enters college, costs will total $87,500 for a state university, $196,000 for a private college, and $257,000 for an "elite" private college! My first thought after applying the smelling salts was, "Where do I get *that* kind of money?"

Average annual inflation is historically only 3–4 percent, but college costs increase at about 7 percent a year. Don't expect your home equity to pay the way. Most analysts expect housing prices to exceed inflation by only 1 percent or less over the next decade.

Yet I want my boy to attend college. Graduating from college nearly doubles the average monthly income of a high school grad. This adds up to a lifetime average of $600,000.

Ideally, your divorce settlement spells out who pays for the kids' education (see Chapter 1). Having an understanding from the beginning puts the obligation in the responsible party's mind and encourages him to start saving early. If your ex can't or won't fund higher education, however, you get the privilege by default. Naturally, you hope your brilliant child will win a full scholarship. If not, how will you save for both your retirement and his college?

A free Federal Student Aid Fact Sheet describes federal financial aid programs, and is updated annually, from Consumer Information Center, Pueblo, CO 81009.

Take Steps Now

- Send away for the free guides to investing for college published by some of the mutual fund families. These booklets help you estimate the total future costs and the monthly amount you need to save now in order to meet them. They also discuss the proper types of investment vehicles.
- Let grandparents and other potential gift-givers know that you have started a college fund. Suggest that contributions of any amount would be most welcome in lieu of new bedroom slippers or another sweater.
- Add as much as you can to that fund from your income. The longer you wait to start saving, the more you will have to set aside each month to meet your projected goal.
- Establish an automatic payroll deduction or savings plan.
- Consult your financial planner about whether to put the college account in your name or your child's. Depending on your situation, you may benefit tax-wise from having it in his name. You will set up a custodial account under the Uniform Gifts to Minors Act (UGMA) or Uniform Transfers to Minors Act (UTMA), naming yourself as custodian. This is as easy as can be—just check the right boxes when opening the account.

  Note two major disadvantages, however, to having the money in your kid's name: First, once deposited in his account, the money is *his.* No dipping into it for *your* needs or emergencies. If you might be tempted, do consider putting it into his name. Just remember, there is no taking it back if he goes to surfing school instead of college. You must give him full control at age eighteen or twenty-one, depending on your state. (Specify "custodian until age twenty-one" when you open the account, or he'll get the money at eighteen even if the state allows you to specify a later age.)

Second, under the federal student-loan guidelines, assets held in a child's name count against you more heavily in financial aid calculations. Your kid gets more aid if the money is in your name rather than your child's. Lenders expect children to contribute up to 35 percent of *their* money to college expenses, while parents need use only about 6 percent of theirs, depending on the current law.

- Look into prepaid tuition plans. Some colleges and states guarantee to cover future tuition, regardless of intervening hikes, if you contribute a lump sum now or a regular amount for a certain number of years. To make sure the plan makes sense, compare the rate of return you could make on investing the money to the rate of increase in college costs. Remember, also, that you may have a kid who decides to start up his own computer company or go off to make art in a warehouse without attending college. Or he might reject your choice of school. Most plans allow a refund of some sort in such cases, but read the fine print carefully before you sign on. For more details, call the College Savings Plans Network at 1-800-233-6734.
- Consider a "matching" program while your kid gets an allowance from you. For every sum he saves for college, you deposit a like amount, or even double.

Where to Invest College Money

Unless college is just a few years away, don't play it too safe with this money. Since college costs are rising faster than inflation, putting the money in CD's or other savings won't provide sufficient growth to cover expenses.

Consult your planner for advice, but most likely you will want to invest in a diversified portfolio of equity mutual funds, bonds, and cash. Proper allocation among the various types of investments accounts for over ninety percent of positive investment results!

When the Time Comes for College . . .

Even if you can't fully fund your kid's higher education, do what you can to help him through at least one year of college without working. Most dropouts occur during the first year, and keeping your child from having to work lets him adjust to college life, learn the ropes, and devote attention solely to school. After freshman year, he may have to do a work-study program or take a regular job.

> "Certainly there are lots of things in life that money won't buy,
> but it's very funny—
> Have you ever tried to buy them without money?"
>
> OGDEN NASH

- Apply for all applicable scholarships and grants, both governmental and private. Parents with more than one child in college qualify for more financial aid. This help may be based on financial need, scholastic achievement, religion, personal background, or particular qualifications relating to anything from parent's place of employment to intended major to quirky combinations—for example, Florida residents planning to major in swamp preservation whose parent works for the Scenic Everglades Tour Company. I made that up, but you get the idea. Books publish lists of these little-known scholarships. Money from these sources goes begging each year because no one with the requisite requirements applies.
- Start looking for scholarships *early,* during your kid's sophomore year in high school. Tracking down available financial aid takes a long time.
- Investigate all sources of loans. Apply for university loans as well as both state and federal government student loans, which we assume will survive political budget axes. At the moment, any family is eligible for government-backed student loans without regard to savings or income. If you show need, the government pays the interest while your child is enrolled. If not, you pay interest as you go. In either case, principal payment is deferred until the student leaves school.
- When you start applying for aid, make a chart of the many different deadlines and requirements. Don't disqualify by missing a date.
- Don't overlook relatives as potential sources of tuition loans.

- Home-equity loans, which charge lower interest rates than unsecured loans and may be tax-deductible, could be a good source of college funds.
- If you have whole life insurance, you may be able to borrow up to 95 percent of the cash value (but see Chapter 18).
- Note that you can borrow from your 401(k) retirement plan, but I would opt for the government loans instead. You have to repay (to yourself) whatever you borrow from the plan. While your children may be duty-bound to repay a government loan, the incentive to repay you rates lower. If they don't repay the plan, you'll have to. Imagine trying to repay it *and* make new contributions, which you'll have to do in order to have enough for retirement!
- Consider a local junior college for the first year or two. Tuition is lower, and your child can live at home. One single father enrolled his bright children in junior college courses while they were still in high school. Their credits transferred to a major university, and Dad had to pay for fewer terms at the higher tuition.
- Require a portion of your kid's summer earnings to go toward college.
- Encourage your child to think about career choices early and explore them through internships. This will ease his way into employment after graduation. Companies that hire student workers take about 17 percent of new hires from former interns, and that figure will probably increase.

You may have to make hard choices. Tia became a single mother by adopting an infant in her forties. As her son, Taylor, approaches college age, she grows ever closer to retirement. Her earning years will cease around the same time Taylor enters college. Citing the poor quality of urban public schools, Tia decided to send Taylor to private school for his elementary and secondary educations. The private school tuition will consume the money she otherwise would have saved for college. Nevertheless, that is the choice she made. She is gambling that a private-school education will improve Taylor's chances for scholarships and other financial aid. She believes private school will instill a love of learning that, aside from its intrinsic value, will motivate him to explore all alternatives for getting through college. Having worked her own way to advanced degrees, she believes Taylor could do the same.

Retirement

Preparing for your retirement proclaims that you count. Take advantage of all available retirement plans, where the money grows for years without interference from mean old Uncle Sam, the tax man.

- Retirement funds accumulate earnings *tax free* until you withdraw them when you retire and enter a lower tax bracket. This is a great advantage. Start *now* and contribute as much as possible, even if it's only a few dollars at first.
- Don't count on Social Security. Financial planners talk about the "three-legged stool" of retirement income: Social Security, employer-paid pensions, and earnings from savings and investments. However, many women rest on fewer than three of these legs. One in five relies solely on Social Security, which currently pays a monthly average of $561 to women and $735 to men.

A recent poll indicated that only 25% of Americans between eighteen and thirty-four believe Social Security will exist when they retire. In contrast, 46% believe in UFO's![15]

The Social Security Administration will calculate the benefits you can expect to earn at age sixty-five, based on your contributions to date. Ask for form SSA-7004, the Personal Earnings and Benefit Estimate Statement. To learn how much you are accruing in benefits each year, ask for Detailed Information Form SSA-7050; 800-772-1213.

- Various mutual funds sell low-cost (about $15) software for deciding how much to invest now for college or retirement.
- Vanguard Retirement Planner. 800-876-1840.
- T. Rowe Price Retirement Planning Kit (IBM format only). 800-541-6099.

National Center for Women and Retirement Research provides educational materials and a quarterly newsletter for $10 annually. 800-426-7386.

Today's working woman is unlikely to be better off than her mother and grandmother in old age.

Congress greatly underestimated retirees' life spans when initiating Social Security. Some experts project that today's baby boomers will net an effective 1 percent rate of return on all the money they pay into the system. Depending on the date of retirement, some will have a *negative* rate of return. This looks miserable compared to the average 10 percent return of the stock market.

Well-off single workers will fare the worst. An unmarried thirty-year-old today who pays the maximum tax and stays single will pay about $217,000 more into Social Security than he will receive in benefits!

- How much do you need to retire? The rule of thumb says that maintaining your current standard of living after retirement requires 75 percent of your pre-retirement income.

Like it or not, money plays a big role in your life. Either you don't have enough, you spend all your time making it, or you have to take care of it. It breaks up marriages, causes arguments, and destroys values. But you can't live without it.

You can take control of it, though, by educating yourself. Assess your weaknesses and get help—there's plenty of it out there. Budget, save, and invest for retirement—and for your children's future.

ORGANIZATIONS

The Institute of Certified Financial Planners: Makes referrals. 800-322-4237.

The International Association for Financial Planning: Provides the names of five planners within one hundred miles of your home. 800-945-4237.

Displaced Homemakers Network. 755 8th St., N.W., Washington, D. C. 20001; 202-347-0522.

Welfare Mothers Voice. Newspaper, $15 ($4 for mothers in poverty). 2711 W. Michigan St., Milwaukee, WI 53208; 414-342-6662.

BOOKS FOR PARENTS

Cohousing: A Contemporary Approach to Housing Ourselves, Kathryn McCamant, et al. (Berkeley, CA: Ten Speed Press, 1993).

Collaborative Communities: Cohousing, Central Living, and Other Forms of New Housing, Dorit Fromm (New York: Van Nostrand Reinhold, 1991).

Chapter 16

Teaching Your Kids about Money

Parents teach children about money in four ways: by modeling, by explicit instruction, by indirect instruction, and by practice with an allowance.

The Powerful Influence of Example

Not long ago, I ordered a salad at a friend's birthday lunch in an expensive restaurant, insisting I wasn't really hungry. In truth, I was famished. Before the waiter left, I changed my order and subsequently lingered happily over a delicious seafood risotto. Thinking about this later, I realized I had initially reverted to an old behavior. On the rare occasions my family ate out when I was young, we children somehow knew to order only from the cheapest menu items. Now, decades later, I fell back into that pattern, even denying my own celebratory feelings and inner sensations of hunger! The intermittent reemergence of my old money attitudes demonstrates the incredible power of my parents' influence, most of which they instilled by example, not instruction.

To my utter horror, at age four Christopher started prefacing requests with "Do we have enough money to . . ." While other kids screamed for favors, my child worried about their effect on the family finances! I've always been very open with him and given explanations for most of my actions. I realized I must have been telling him that we couldn't fly off for the weekend to visit our friends in Kuwait or have "a million" toy trains because "we don't have enough money." While true enough, other reasons also came into play. I always fulfilled his wishes in fantasy by adding that I wish we *could* just hop on a plane or order everything in the Lionel catalog. Still, my habitual first mention of money had invaded his small skull, and I felt terrible about passing along an attitude I've struggled to shed.

At least I became conscious of my statements and now think twice before offering lack of money as an immediate or primary reason for anything. As a result, Christopher no longer phrases requests in terms of affordability. In addition, I increased the number of small treats and "surprises" I bring him "just because." I want to teach him respect for money, but not deprivation. He also needs to see me spending money for the enhancement of our lives, and this requires me to stay mindful of my natural tendencies toward frugality.

On the other hand, over-spenders convey entirely different messages to their children, who sometimes act as though they're entitled to everything—*now.* Their kids don't stop to wonder whether money grows on trees or not—they *know* it comes from credit cards.

John, the custodial parent of his daughter Lynne, recounts story after story about her financial irresponsibility. In her early twenties, she inherited an unrestricted $75,000 and blew it in a year. Her closet boasted some wonderful designer clothes that season, and the sports car looked great zooming around town. Friends enjoyed her parties, too.

John, an attractive fiftyish man, seems too stable to have spawned such a spendthrift, and he despairs at her constant financial antics. Gainfully employed, he owns a home and seems the model of success. Or so I thought until I heard about his own relationship with money, which isn't much different from Lynne's. After his divorce and the sale of his business, he'd left California with a small fortune, which he then gambled away in Las Vegas. His home is mortgaged to the hilt, he participates in expensive sports, and he regularly patronizes fine restaurants. He clearly indulges himself, which is fine if he has the means, but I'll bet he doesn't indulge the retirement account. I'm quite certain Lynne learned her money habits through his example. Because he continually bailed her out of tight spots, she learned little about the consequences of irresponsibility. John's anger at his daughter's money madness probably masks feelings about his own similar behaviors.

With rare exceptions, based on well-reasoned and carefully explained grounds, you simply cannot behave one way and tell your children to act another. (See Chapters 7, 10, and 17.) Modeling is very powerful, which is why you need to get your own financial act together. Your kids see you deal with money practically every day. If you possess exemplary fiscal habits and attitudes, your children will absorb them. Of course, they're as likely to adopt bad habits as good ones. Make sure you set the best example you can, but don't expect perfection of yourself or your child. You both learn from your mistakes.

Teaching by Explicit Instruction

The little conscious instruction about money I received as a youngster focused on the value of saving. I had piggy banks and learned that I could turn certain combinations of change over to my dad and get a paper dollar. He warned me that if I spent my allowance on candy, I would "have nothing left for anything else." (No wonder I've found it difficult to treat myself!) At some point, my father took me to the bank to open a—what else?—savings account. A good saver, I basked in favorable comparison to others whose "money burned a hole in their pockets."

Most schools don't teach money management. Don't assume your child knows how checks or credit cards work or what a mortgage represents. The task of educating your kid about money falls squarely on you.

My parents failed to clue me in financially. Unsophisticated themselves, they were also secretive about money, as though even disclosing my father's salary would unleash an uncontrollable family desire to spend everything. In contrast, Tony grew up understanding basic investment principles. His dad reviewed family investments biannually with Tony at his side, explaining the why's and how's and openly sharing information about income and assets. By adulthood, Tony had observed risk pay off often enough to assume some of it willingly. Despite his episodes of manic spending and depressed recriminations later, Tony possessed a solid foundation in the workings of personal finance.

- Start talking to your kids about money as early as age three or four. If you've missed those early years, start now.
- Gear your explanation to your kid's ability to comprehend. Bring examples down to your child's level. Play at pretend grocery stores with a preschooler, for example. When he asks for an expensive new fire truck, tell him it costs as much as twenty cartons of his favorite ice cream, which would take until his next birthday to polish off. That will mean more to him initially than stating a dollar amount.

  Get help if you need to. Pay for an hour together with your financial planner, or suggest classroom instruction to your child's teacher. Don't structure this education too much. Just enjoy the process of casually teaching these valuable skills to your kid.
- Take everyday occurrences as triggers for education. Talk about money transactions as you and your child experience them. In response to one of my lack-of-money assertions, Christopher insisted, "Well, just go get some more at the grocery store!" He'd always seen me get cash back from the checker, not noticing that I first forked over a fat check. Likewise, ATM cards were the "open sesame" to a treasure trove of crisp twenties just waiting for the magic words. In very simple terms (and reluctantly because I thought his deductions so cute), I explained the sad truth to him—every penny from the grocery clerk comes straight out of my bank account. I'm sure only some of my explanation sank in, but that's fine—the subject will arise again.
- Explain comparison shopping, even if it's just between two brands of macaroni and cheese at the grocery store. Older kids can understand a more sophisticated calculation of per-ounce costs or price/value considerations.
- Let your child help you pay the bills. He'll be surprised to learn the number of money-eating gods you propitiate every month.
- When the restaurant check comes, demonstrate how it lists and totals the charges. Explain about tax and tipping and how to calculate them. Include useful shortcuts. For example, doubling the 8 percent tax where I live yields a normal tip amount.
- Teach an older child about saving and investments—certainly before a shower of credit cards floods his college mailbox. Help him open a savings account, and perhaps a checking account, and explain their workings. Give your child some money to invest in a mutual fund with a low initial minimum deposit or some shares in

a corporation whose name he recognizes. Or just track the stock in the business pages—the gain or loss may *really* be just on paper, but he'll get first-hand experience at investing.

- Incorporate financial information into family meetings (see Chapter 5). Let your child ask questions and have a say in how the family spends discretionary income. Discuss goals and major family purchases with him. Including him in this serious adult topic increases self-esteem and conveys your trust in him. It makes him feel loved and important.
- Inform him of how you plan to meet your financial goals. Show him the college account you have for him, for example. Perhaps it's even in his name in an UGMA or UTMA trust. (See Chapter 15). Although the account may seem pitifully small now, explain how it will grow through investment. Let him know that you'll make every effort to meet the goal, and discuss how he can help.
- Taking a cue from Tony's dad, I plan to open the family books to Christopher at an appropriate age, when it's meaningful and when he is mature enough to maintain confidentiality. I want him to feel like a trusted team member who understands our budget and goals and their impact on his life. Because the information is so relevant, teaching from real life hits harder and sinks deeper.
- If money is short, revealing that information, at least to an older child, should facilitate his understanding of why you can't buy him those $200 sneakers. It will take some pressure off you, too. No longer are you just the mean mommy or the stingy dad. Telling your child the true state of affairs opens the door to communication and negotiation. Maybe he can have those shoes if he gives up something else.

Teach about Money Indirectly

Become conscious of opportunities to instill good monetary values indirectly as well as by explicit instruction.

- Teaching your child to tolerate delayed gratification (see Chapter 9), for example, discourages over-spending and counters the need to "have" in order to "be." Television commercials bombard your kids not only to buy-buy-buy, but to do so *immediately* and before anyone else on the block.

When your child begs for something he just "has to have," telling him to put it on his birthday or Christmas list conveys the message that "wanting" doesn't necessarily mean immediate "having." Asking him to rearrange the wish list in order of preference teaches him to set priorities—an essential budgeting skill.

- Sometimes the points will be subtle. Christopher and I gave seven-year-old Steven a carefully chosen birthday present, which he eagerly ripped open. Without even looking at the contents, however, he demanded, "Is that all?" Sighing with embarrassment, Steven's mom, Edie, admitted that she gives him too much, too often, out of guilt because she often leaves him with sitters while working long hours. I imagine Steven in a few years as a compulsive shopper to whom "getting" equals love; when the sensation fades, he'll immediately look around for the next "hit." The irony is that Steven overlooked the genuine good wishes represented by our gift.

Allowances: Practicing with Real Money

Amazingly, only one-third to one-half of American children receive an allowance. The others miss a great opportunity to develop healthy money skills. Many parents cringe at the subject of allowances. They don't know:

- Whether to give an allowance
- Whether to tie it to chores, grades, or good behavior
- When to start
- Whether to restrict how it's spent
- How much to give
- How often to give it

Should You Give an Allowance?

Yes. Experience is a wonderful teacher, especially when mistakes won't cause a major crisis. You're not putting the kid in charge of Fort Knox, after all. His errors produce teeny little shock waves, and he learns from them.

Giving an allowance literally costs you nothing. Really! According to a 1995 survey, parents who don't give an allowance hand out the same amounts piecemeal as parents of children with regular allowances. The only difference is that kids without allowances don't learn how to manage money. They feel less confident about their abilities, and they express more dissatisfaction with the amount of their weekly receipts.

Allowances come with built-in "logical consequences" (see Chapter 5) that instill learning. If your kid spends it all, he can't buy anything else. Simple. You need do nothing further to get the lesson across except to communicate about what he's learned.

Should You Tie an Allowance to Chores, Grades, or Good Behavior?

Many child-development experts believe an allowance should not be contingent upon doing chores, achieving academically, or maintaining "good behavior" (whatever that means). An allowance represents an entitlement that your child gets in full, on time, no matter what. It's a money-management learning tool. Don't mistake it for a carrot or a stick. Don't require your kid to produce first, and don't dock him for screwing up. You give an allowance because you love him and he needs money to function in this world.

Grades and chores are matters of personal responsibility, but tying your kid's allowance to accomplishment conveys the opposite message—that he has to work only if paid. You can, however, pay your child *additional* money for extra work, such as baby-sitting or painting the house.

But what about "consequences" (see Chapter 5)? Can't loss of allowance be a consequence of, say, flunking geography? No. Geography bears no logical relation to receiving the money. This wouldn't be a consequence but a punishment. (Flunking geography carries its own consequences, by the way.)

Other experts believe that children can't learn the value of money unless they work for it. You'll have to follow your own instincts about which set of experts to believe.

When to Start an Allowance

No strict rules exist for when to begin giving an allowance. In general, begin when your child starts wanting things. Having his own money to spend reduces the amount of "have-to-have's" as he realizes buying all that bubble gum means he can't have the rubber snake. In a poll of *Money Magazine* readers, slightly over half of those responding thought allowances should start between ages five and seven.

Should You Limit How Your Child Spends the Allowance?

Some parents believe they have the right to forbid certain purchases. Other insist that the money belongs to the child and that he can spend it as he pleases, barring only illegal activities.

At first I agreed with the first alternative. After all, kids need limits, and I don't allow Christopher to eat ten pieces of candy at once when *I* pay for them. Why should he get to charge his sugar batteries just because *he* counts out the pennies? I'm still the mom. I soon came to believe, however, that I must give him a free hand if, as I had assured him, the money is truly his to spend as he wants. Besides, once that candy is gone, I don't have to listen to him beg for more. My candy-buying days ended when his began.

- Even if you don't control your child's spending, you can voice your opinions about his options. State expectations. Christopher knows I don't approve of the candy.
- Talk about how we have to budget and make choices. Teach your kid elementary budgeting by encouraging him to divide his money into short-term savings (which go toward specific goals such as a poster or tickets to a ball game), long-term savings (for big-ticket items like a trip or college), charitable contributions, and entertainment (activities, toys, and food treats). Consider offering to match any extra amount he saves for charity or long-term goals.

  Explain what the categories mean and why each is valuable. Do the math with him and set up separate piggy banks (and later, savings accounts) for savings and contributions. Dole out the allowance in appropriate change so he can feed the various piggies immediately. You'll help him establish life-long good habits.

How Much Allowance to Give, or Does Your Kid Have to Keep Up with the Junior Joneses?

The "right" amount for an allowance depends on your child's age, your financial condition, the local cost of living, what others give, and what you expect the money to cover. Most of these factors are self-explanatory.

- Contact other parents to determine local standards. You don't have to match the highest, but do give enough to enable your child to participate comfortably in the normal activities of his friends. He shouldn't have to save for weeks just to buy a few pogs. Conversely, wealthy parents should not necessarily give more than the norm, or they risk having their kids perceive money as a substitute for love and attention.

According to one survey, most kids with allowances receive extra cash during the week for special chores or for no particular reason. Some also held after-school jobs. I've seen various surveys listing suggested or actual median weekly allowance amounts for various ages. Some suggest a dollar for each grade of school. Putting them all together yields ranges like this:

AGES	WEEKLY AMOUNTS
3–6	$1
7–8	$2
9–10	$2–5
11–12	$5–9
13–15	$5–15
16–19	$30–100

- Some parents consider the allowance entirely available for "extras," while others expect it to defray certain living expenses too. Obviously, the choice influences the amount. A teen expected to budget for clothes and a private telephone line gets more money than one whose parent supplies them. When a kid must factor in such expenses, the budgeting becomes more complex, educational, and realistic. By the early teens, the allowance should cover most of the costs of entertainment, clothes, school supplies, and meals out. Giving your teen more power in these areas reduces struggles. It also forces you to relinquish some control, a good lesson to learn in the few years before he leaves the nest.

  One mother struck a bargain for school lunch money with her teenage daughter, whose allowance includes money for three hot lunches a week. The girl prepares a bag lunch from family food on the other two days. If she mismanages the funds, she has to make sandwiches every day. If she brown-bags it all week, the cash belongs to her.
- Your kid probably won't be satisfied with whatever amount he gets. Reevaluate and raise the allowance when you deem it appropriate. Or schedule raises at regular intervals, perhaps annually.
- When your child reaches age seven or so, give an increased allowance during the summer—money for the extra places kids go

during vacation. This keeps him from asking to go *everywhere* and forces him to budget. You would spend the money anyway, so you might as well let him practice financial management.

- If money generates anger between you and your child, think about what might underlie it. Perhaps he's frustrated that he can't compete with Junior Jones' BMW, for example. Maybe he doesn't "belong" because he didn't get the "real" sneakers. Explore the possibilities. Validate the concerns. Work with your kid to find ways to meet his goals. Stress the value of attributes other than ownership of material goods.

How Often Should You Give an Allowance?

Pay a young child weekly, a long time frame from his point of view. Get organized so you dole out the money on the same day every week. At age eleven or twelve, a kid becomes capable of budgeting for an entire month. Help him do it. Some parents move to yearly payments for older teens to prepare them for long-term budgeting in college or the work world. You'll know best when your child can handle larger but less frequent payments.

After-School Jobs

By working real-world jobs after school, teens expand their money savvy. Parents express different feelings about having their children work during the school year. Some approve the sense of responsibility it engenders, and some resent the pressure and loss of childhood. I suppose the final decision lies with the kids.

In any case, however, you should limit their work hours. A study found that a teen working twenty or more hours a week during the school year drops an average of half a letter-grade compared to one who works fewer than ten hours. Ironically, even if the money he earns goes straight into his higher education fund, that half a letter-grade could negatively affect acceptance at his college of choice.

After High School Graduation

With all this childhood financial training, your child should be ready for independent living.

- If he starts work immediately after high school, volunteer assistance with any money matters. Help with budgeting, for example, and encourage him to take immediate advantage of his retirement plan options. Suggest a savings and investment plan.
- For a college student, the outgo will far exceed the income. Help him budget to ensure his funding will stretch through the entire school year. Determine how you will transfer money to him, whether monthly, annually, or all at once. Discuss what, if any, further contributions you will make for special activities such as vacations, trips home, or money for holiday gifts. Make all contingencies and limitations clear. Reevaluate your decisions after a few months and make any appropriate adjustments.

  Your student will need a checking account, but experts disagree on whether a credit card is proper for college kids. Some argue that it only tempts them to over-spend, while others say it builds a credit history and protects the kids in emergencies. An equity credit card is a possibility since it fulfills the need without incurring the risk.

Boomerang Kids: They're B-A-A-A-C-K

If you've followed some of the suggestions in this chapter, your financially competent adult children normally shouldn't bounce back home looking for rent-free accommodations. Nevertheless, "stuff happens," and your son or daughter may need to move in with you to recover from divorce, illness, or loss of employment. During his absence, you've remodeled the house, adopted three of those long-haired cats that make him sneeze, and found a lover. Nonetheless, you take a deep breath and welcome him back.

- Do you charge him rent? If he could pay the going rate, he wouldn't be camping on your doorstep. Maybe you'd like him to make at least a small contribution as a reminder that you're no longer his sole source of support. In any event, he should contribute in other ways, through chores, cooking, errands, and special projects, and he should do so without reminders. Avoid returning to your former parent-child pattern. Communicate your requirements and expectations, and encourage him to do so as well. Don't forget that you count, too, however dire his needs.
- How long will he stay? While you willingly help, you don't want a permanent return. The goals of raising a child, after all, include

sending him on his independent way. Agree that you will discuss the situation at a certain future date, say in six months or a year. Even as young adults, kids may need a parent to set limits.

- Make intentions, obligations, and boundaries clear with a written understanding to refresh memories down the road.

The earlier you start teaching children about money, the sooner their skills develop, but it's never too late to start. The first step is getting your own finances in order so you'll model good money habits. Instruct your kids directly and indirectly, in age-appropriate ways. Finally, let them practice money management with an allowance. By the time they reach college or enter the work world, they should be highly functioning personal money managers.

BOOKS FOR PARENTS

Money Skills: 101 Activities to Teach Your Child about Money, Bonnie Drew (Franklin Lakes, NJ: Career Press, 1992).

BOOKS FOR KIDS

Kids & Money: A Learning Guide for Children. Free brochure from Fidelity Investments. 800-544-6666 (press #5).

The Kids' Money Book, Neale S. Godfrey (New York: Checkerboard Press, 1991) (grades 3 and up).

Kiplinger's Money Smart Kids: And Parents, Too!, Janet Bodnar (Wash., D.C.: Kiplinger Books) (to age 13).

Making Cents: Every Kid's Guide to Money, Elizabeth Wilkinson (New York: Little, Brown, 1989).

Money Matters for Young Adults and *Money Matters for College Students:* Free brochures from Citibank. 800-669-2635.

The National Center for Financial Education has a list of money books for kids and a free catalog; also sells the *Personal Money Book, Family Money Book,* and *Money Manager Book.* POB 34070, San Diego, CA 92163.

The Stock Market, Nancy Dunnan (Columbus, OH: Silver Press, 1990) (teens) (Dunnan has written other money books for teens).

The Stock Market Explained for Young Investors: The Perfect Stock Market Start-Up Kit for Any High School or College Student, Clayton P. Fisher (Milpitas, CA: Pacific Press, 1995) (grades 9 and up).

Young Investor Parents Guide: Free from Liberty Financial Co., 800-403-KIDS

Zillions: A kids magazine published by Consumers Union.

Part 4

Moving On

Chapter 17

Dating, Sex, and New Relationships for You

No "Right" Answers

How do you, as a single parent, find a new romantic relationship, and what do you do once you have it? This could be a very short chapter: Just do what feels right for you. Period.

That really *is* the ultimate conclusion. Everyone's values, morals, circumstances, and priorities differ. There are no "right answers," only complex questions that deserve more than spur-of-the-moment resolutions. Contemplate the issues ahead of time. Seek professional advice if you have trouble thinking them through. In the end, though, you will have to trust your instincts in:

- Dealing with your *ex's* new relationships
- Starting to date again
- Balancing your children with your dating, romance, and sex life
- Ending a relationship
- Remarriage and forming a blended family

Factors to Consider

How do you *know* what's right for you? Though no one can tell you how they add up for you, many factors enter into the equation:

- Your kids' ages. Younger children may not even understand the concept of your dating, but, depending on the circumstances, they may also jump to the conclusion that every new face is a replacement "parent." Older kids may be hostile, feeling threatened by your role as man or woman in addition to that of Dad or Mom. Overwhelmed by their own raging hormones, teens often feel threatened by anything that hints at a parent's sexuality, even his casual dating. On the other hand, some older children recognize loneliness in the parent and encourage him to seek a mate.

- Your kids' emotional states. They may still believe you will reunite with your ex. The death or divorce, especially a caustic, bitter one, may leave the kids so upset and confused that they simply oppose any more changes, period.
- Whether the kids are accustomed to social activity in your home. If so, they are more accepting of your social interactions.
- Who initiated the separation. If the kids think you blew the family apart, don't expect them to encourage you to build a substitute.
- The time since the separation or death. Obviously, the more recent your separation, the more likely your children will be hostile to your bonding with anyone else.
- Whether your ex has partial custody, providing you with free evenings away from the kids. If your children are with you all the time, it's harder to arrange a social life for yourself.
- The degree of civility between you and your ex. A supportive, or at least neutral, ex-spouse makes a new romance easier than an ex who resents your every conversation with the opposite sex, or god forbid, stalks or otherwise harasses you and your dates.
- The lay-out of your living quarters. Maybe that one-bedroom apartment with the kids on a sofa bed in the living room fits your budget and serves you well enough. It won't afford any privacy for a tête-à-tête, however, much less any physical intimacy.

Remain flexible and aware, as all these factors change over time.

Your Ex's New Relationship

Your child returns from her father's house with the news that, "Daddy has a new girlfriend." You express polite interest but, despite yourself, you're dying for details. Who is she? What does she look like? How did they meet? How old is she? Does she have any brains? You don't even know what answers you want. Your kid shrugs. "She seems okay."

- Strong feelings unexpectedly bubble to the surface, even though you detest your ex and never want to see him again. Or even though you're friendly and wish him the best. Even if it's been years since your divorce. Maybe you suddenly feel tingles of regret about your separation.

  Learning your ex-spouse has a new lover—or worse, a fiancé or new spouse—reignites old emotions, especially if *you* aren't dating. Rather than congratulatory, your thoughts may sound more like:
  –*Wait til she finds out what he's really like!*
  –*If he'd treated me that nicely, I'd have stayed with him.*
  –*He doesn't pay child support, but he can buy her a new car?*
  –*What does she have that I didn't?*
  –*He'll drop her when that body starts to sag.*
  –*She's just after his money.*
  –*Sure, they can travel; they've dumped the kids on me.*
  –*She'll get everything he promised me!*
  –*I'm going to lose my kid to a new mommy (daddy)!*

  And when your spouse expects a new baby with the new mate:
  –*Now he won't pay any attention to my child!*

You may fantasize about calling the new person to describe what your ex is *really* like. Or you may dream of reuniting with your former spouse. Whatever your immediate reaction, however, don't act on it.

Deal Appropriately with Your Initial Reactions

- Express all your negative feelings. Breathe. Scream alone in the car. Write in your journal. Refer to your ex by every name in the book. Be as catty and snide as you can. Vent strong emotions with a friend, a therapist, or a support group, *but not with your kid* (see Chapter 5). Keep in mind that disparaging a child's other parent amounts to disparaging *him* (see Chapter 1).
- Perhaps you can't identify what you're feeling. Maybe you're truly happy for your ex at some level. Still, strong emotions nag you. You can't get his new union out of your mind. Maybe you suddenly remember his virtues and forget his vices. You might even wish for another chance with him yourself, a common reaction even after lengthy separations.

  Whether angry or confused, spend some time simply breathing deeply and experiencing the emotions that arise. What can you learn about yourself from this experience? Get in touch with what the anger or confusion masks. Jealousy? Rejection? A sense of unfairness? Sadness? Fear that your kids will abandon you? Insecurity? These are all normal feelings.

Many of the emotions you experienced at the time of divorce recycle with this further step in establishing a separate life from your ex. Just sit with them. Don't act on them or repress them. If you need to, get help from a therapist. Remember why you're divorced. Accept that your ex has a new relationship. Be proactive. Get on with your own life.

- Remember, working through your own emotions allows you to detach and help your child handle his own reactions to the new person in your ex's—and your kid's—life. Let him know you can listen to how he feels about this without judgment and without obligating him to take sides. You can share some of your feelings if done appropriately. It's a gift to your child to know that the boundaries are intact, that he's free to form his own opinions.

Positive Aspects to an Ex-Spouse's Remarriage

In truth, having your former spouse remarry while you are single isn't the worst that can happen. Consider the positive aspects.

> One out of every six families getting together for winter holidays in 1992 was a blended family.[1]

- Living alone offers opportunities for personal growth that an ex-spouse who rushes into a second marriage doesn't have. You grow more independent and wiser about relationships. You learn about yourself and how you respond to adversity. You discover strengths and talents you didn't know you had. For some, just learning to live alone for the first time presents a major challenge. Personal growth can be hell, but in the long run, it's worth it. Self-knowledge will help you avoid repeating the same mistakes. Perhaps your hastily recoupled ex has *already* made them again!
- The situation can prove helpful to *you,* especially if your ex is uncommunicative or flaky around obligations to the kids. Though devastated at first, Caroline found her life infinitely easier when her ex-husband remarried. Suddenly there was someone on the other end who communicates! Who follows through on promises and commitments. Who plans ahead. The step-mom is flexible and

even volunteers actions for Caroline's convenience or her daughter's well-being. Take help where you can get it. In truth, stepparents can be very useful! They get so little credit—don't forget to show your appreciation.

- You are your child's only mom (or dad), the only one he will ever have. You have a special, unique bond with that kid. No matter how fun, exciting, or interesting, a stepparent can't duplicate it. No one can replace you. Think of a caring stepparent as one more teacher from whom your child can learn and benefit. Let go of any need to control your kid's experiences. You can't affect what happens at the other house anyway.

  Caution: It's another question, of course, if your child isn't safe at the other parent's home due to alcohol, drugs, or physical, verbal, or sexual abuse. If there is reason to worry about these factors, contact your lawyer or the proper authorities. (See Chapter 10.)
- Use your ex's pairing as a reminder of why you are no longer married to him. Congratulate yourself for all you've achieved since the divorce.
- You can't affect your ex's romances, and you'd be a masochist to try. Instead, concentrate on what you *can* influence. Maybe you'll be inspired to get a social life for yourself!

Starting to Date Again

Statistically, men remarry an average of one to two years after divorce. For women, the time is four to seven years. What accounts for this difference? My guess is that, despite trends toward joint custody, women often remain primarily responsible for the children. Or they feel more responsible. They may not have, or *take,* the opportunity to reenter the dating world as soon as their ex-mates. They turn to other women for post-divorce emotional support rather than seeking another male partner. At any rate, the possibility of dating and entering into new relationships eventually arises for most of us.

Getting Ready, Taking a Risk

For some people, reentering the world of dating comes naturally. They enjoy feeling footloose and free from an unhappy marriage. Others, traumatized by a death or the divorce process, isolate and bury themselves in work and child care. Some lose confidence in their looks or their dating skills after years of married life. Some lump all members of the opposite sex into one very tainted basket. Others feel guilty and undeserving because they broke up the original family. Still others doubt their own judgment to discern and act upon red flags that signal another potential marital mistake.

Many simply don't see how they'd find the time to look for a date. Even if they find one, the endless work of sole parenthood leaves them too exhausted for going out. Anyway, they've finally got life down to a routine that more or less works. Why add another factor that jolts everything back into chaos? Who has anything left over for the emotional drama that, for better or worse, always accompanies romance?

Very soon after Tony's death, my therapist surprised me by recommending that I start dating again. I had, he pointed out, separated from this unsuccessful relationship before the suicide, and I should not let the death keep me "in" it and cancel the growth I'd undergone. I needed to build on my independence and continue to focus on my strengths and myself. I half-heartedly agreed in principle but presented all the above arguments against dating. Moreover, the process was likely to fail. After all, I'd read that widows remain single an average of eleven years after the death of their spouses! My therapist issued a blithe denial that this statistic applied to me and pointed out that having a partner could *lessen* my burden. Novel idea!

Despite my protestations, I *did* long for someone with whom to share Christopher and myself. I wanted to stand arm-in-arm over my son's crib with someone who loved and appreciated him as I did. Someone who would thrill at his first sentence and exalt at his successful pee in the potty. How could Tony have chosen to miss this incredible unfolding of our new little being? How could anyone *else* want the experience if Christopher's own daddy had passed on it? Could someone who hadn't been involved from the beginning really care as I did? I wouldn't settle for less.

> Remarriage: "The triumph of hope over experience."
> SAMUEL JOHNSON (1709–1784)

I wasn't sure who I was anymore. I didn't know how to meet men, and I couldn't think of anything to talk about beyond suicide, legal woes, the wonder of my child, and the difficulties of being a single parent. Who would even want me? I doubted that men in my "older" age group would be willing to start over with a small child just as they were kicking their own grown birdies from the nest. I wouldn't mind being *in* a new relationship, I told my therapist, but the thought of *getting* into one was overwhelming. I wanted a perfect Mr. Right simply to drop through the ceiling and into my life.

Naturally, he didn't. I wasn't being proactive. Dating requires as much energy and commitment as anything else, and I wasn't ready to give them yet.

- First you must decide what you are ready for. Perhaps, like me, you need more time for solitary regrouping. Because kids are first priority, many single parents forego male-female relationships for lengthy periods. Forging successful, healthy, close bonds with the kids may be worth the sacrifice, at least for a time. It's your decision. You choose the priorities, and you can change them, too. If lack of time is your problem, consider where you can simplify, what other obligations you can eliminate.
- Staying home with the kids and the housekeeping feels safe after the trauma of divorce or spousal death, but you can't isolate yourself forever. Eventually you'll at least seek friendships with the opposite sex and have occasional casual dates. Humans are social creatures, and growth comes primarily from interaction with others. Take a risk and get back into the world a little.
- Don't expect a perfect experience. Ask yourself what is the worst that can happen if you "fail" in a given social situation. You suffer embarrassment or boredom, but you learn something from the encounter to use in the future. Detach psychologically and see yourself in this ridiculous new role of suitor or flirt—does it remind you of high school? See the humor. Laughing at yourself takes the pressure off.
- Remember, too, that taking care of yourself is taking care of your children. You need independent relationships to avoid relying on your kids for need fulfillment. Single parents often closely enmesh with their children, and as the adult, it's your responsibility to maintain the boundaries. Children should not feel responsible for their parent's well-being. They should not assume the role of partner in your life.
- You count, too. By allowing yourself some fun and romance, you bring new energy and vigor into family life. Your kids discover a new, more vibrant side of you. Model for your children how a happy adult exists in the social world.

- Act *entitled.* You are. The children will more easily accept your dating if you present it as a normal, necessary, healthy, grown-up activity, rather than as time you guiltily snatch away from them. Don't let guilt about the failure of your last marriage discourage you from having a social life. You can't change what happened. Forgive yourself and move on. Next time you'll do better.

Continue to Do Your Own Work

One key to having a successful relationship is working on your own emotional and psychological issues.

- You accept yourself as you are and don't buy into negative images and remarks. As a "whole" person, you bring more to a new relationship and can better resolve conflicts when they arise. Instead of seeking another to make you whole, first strive to find completeness in yourself, whether through therapy, spiritual growth, or other counseling. Just reducing stress and breathing help.
- As a healthy person, you don't depend on a partner to fill emotional gaps left over from childhood or prior romances. Emotional health means you don't act from guilt. You choose responses rather than reacting to others' behavior. You separate your issues from your partner's. You detach from the intense pull of emotions. You act in the present rather than reacting to past unresolved or even unconscious wounds. The healthier you are mentally, the better you see your past mistakes and avoid repeating them.
- Don't expect to "finish" this work before you begin dating. It's an ongoing process; enjoy it. There is always more to learn, another risk to take.

The thought of dating again overwhelmed me in part because in the past I'd expended time and energy fending off persistent men in whom I had no interest. How dense could they be, I wondered, not to leave me alone after I rejected them? I became angrier and more frustrated until I finally did something so mean they left. Meanwhile, my efforts exhausted me. Not until sharing this phenomenon with my therapist did I understand that I hadn't been sending "rejection" messages at all. For fear of hurting the man's feelings or incurring his wrath, I'd been oblique and indirect rather than forthright. This fear probably originated in childhood interactions with my father. Justified then, it no longer served as useful behavior. Other men aren't my father. Discovering this dynamic greatly reduced the time I spend with unsuitable men. It is still hard for me, but now I can say, "I enjoyed dinner, but I don't feel any chemistry between us, so I don't think we should go out again."

Most people appreciate such directness, which tells them unambiguously where they stand and avoids wasting *their* time. If they don't appreciate it, that's their problem, not yours. Another hard lesson to learn—you can only do your own work. You are not responsible for others' responses or psychology.

The Value of Transitional Relationships

> Marriage: "It's an experiment / Frequently tried."
> W. S. GILBERT (1836–1911)

Two years after her divorce, a man did drop into Megan's life, though not through the ceiling. She had slightly known Daniel before, and they renewed their acquaintance at a mutual friend's party. He was sensitive to her situation, and Megan enjoyed his company over the next few months. Though she didn't necessarily want to stop seeing him, she didn't share his vision of a future together, and when she made that clear, he said, "I guess I'm your transitional relationship."

- Transitional relationships serve the valuable function of getting you back into the world. This new person finds you attractive and interesting. His perspective is new, his sense of humor intact. He doesn't criticize or try to remake you. Your mannerisms intrigue rather than annoy him.

  In short, he undoes the negative images imposed by your ex. After years of hearing how "stupid" she was, Maria believed it. Her ex's negative label controlled and humiliated her. A different man, however, extolled her ingenuity and cleverness at establishing a small business. Of course, you don't depend on others' perceptions to make you accept yourself, but a compliment doesn't hurt! A new lover sees you in a different way and likes what he sees. That feels good.
- Transitional relationships also provide a chance to experiment with different types of potential mates this time around. Many single parents find that what attracted them before no longer looks inviting. People they would have rejected earlier now have qualities they seek in a partner for themselves and in a parent for their children. Flashy, exciting heartthrobs don't pass the first screening anymore.

- If you don't get what you want out of the new relationship, perhaps your goals are just incompatible. He wants a deep commitment, and you just want someone to take dancing. Or vice versa. Be open about your intentions. If this feels like a transitional relationship, say so. If you aren't explicit about your needs, you may end up blaming the other person or condemning yourself as a failure when the relationship dies a natural death.

  Of course, you may not *know* what you want right away. Fine. Communicate that, and then communicate again when you figure it out. Stay flexible. You may find a transitional relationship becoming more permanent.

Where Do You Meet New People to Date?

Every unmarried person I know agonizes over where to meet new people. The bar scene breeds discomfort. Fellow employees are married, or dating is prohibited within the company. Everyone rushes around. Dating services cost too much.

All of this may be true, but there are ways—if you look available and get yourself *out there.*

- Get organized, make a plan and follow through. Be open, creative, proactive, and flexible in your attitude. Take off rings to avoid ambiguity about your marital status. Get out of those sweats and into something more appealing when you run Saturday errands. Treat yourself to a cappuccino at midday and make eye contact with someone attractive. Attend an author's reading at a bookstore and start a conversation about the book. Keep your eyes open for other single parents when you take your kids to the zoo. Enroll in classes that seem likely to attract members of the opposite sex. Join an interest group. Some cater specifically to single parents.
- Some people seek romance among other single parents on the theory that they understand the pressures and complications and have a demonstrated interest in children. On the other hand, someone who likes kids but doesn't have any (or has already raised his) may be better able to give to yours. When Sarah mentioned to Andrew, a man she dated for a couple of months, that he hadn't taken an interest in her daughter, he said, "Well, I can't take that on. I invest all my emotions in my own kids." End of relationship.
- Look for singles-only events, such as bike rides, retreats, or theater nights. With a divorce rate exceeding fifty percent, more singles

emerge every day, and groups form to accommodate them. In my area, a church-sponsored, nonreligious singles program features an enormous Sunday-night mixer with free baby-sitting. The large gathering of several hundred people intimidates me, but smaller discussion and activity groups meet during the week in private homes or commercial locations. You enjoy an evening in someone's hot tub or share your interest in computer games. You make cookies or take your kids horseback riding. A small group goes dancing or discusses the politics of Angola. It feels risky to show up at one of these events, but most attendees experience the same awkwardness, even if they hide it well. And everyone is, by definition, available and looking to meet someone!

> The number of people who divorce and *remain* single has been rising. About 3% of the American household population was divorced in the 1960s. In the 1990s, that number has grown to about 10%.[2]

- In my locale, at least, the personals ads in weekly newspapers are fertile grounds for meeting other singles. Place an ad, which is free, rather than answering those of others on a 900-number. Experiment with different wording. The best ads tell about you instead of listing the qualities that your ideal mate must have or raving with dozens of others about "candlelit dinners and walks on the beach." Online computer services also offer personals connections.

  Of course, anyone responding to an ad is a stranger. Be cautious. Meet for a brief coffee-date at a neutral location before giving your full name or address.
- Ask for help in meeting people. Your friends and acquaintances are good sources, but you have to let them know you are ready. Ask for introductions to any singles they know. After Megan's "transitional relationship" with Daniel ended, he introduced her to Sam, graciously stating, "If I can't have you, I want you to be with someone special." Unfortunately, Sam didn't turn out to be that "special" from her point of view, but she appreciated Daniel's effort.

- Lower your expectation of finding the "perfect" mate. You may not even know what perfection means for you anymore. Keep yourself open to possibilities, and don't get desperate. Neediness drives people away. Stay positive. No one wants to date a demoralized grump!

How Do You Date?

After years in a marriage, you may doubt your knowledge of *how* to date. What do people do on dates these days? Who decides? *Who pays?*

- I found little agreement about that last question. The answer probably varies by age, culture, relative wealth, geography, and even politics. At a discussion group I attended, the men agreed that a woman's offer to contribute money is insulting. Testing that assumption, I let one of my dates pay when he invited me out, and eventually he mumbled that in this day and age, couples should split the cost of dating. (Never mind that I had reciprocated with home-cooked meals and a theater date on my season tickets. Oh, and the baby-sitting costs were my problem, too, if I couldn't engineer a trade or other free option.) Other men expected me to pay or to split the bill. Some offered to take care of the sitter in whole or in part!

  Faced with this jumble of views, I recommend a retreat to the tried-and-true tactic—communication. Having been out of the dating game for a time makes a request for clarification imminently reasonable: "Listen, it's been eleven years since I last dated. Who pays for what these days?" In my opinion, the cost of baby-sitting, which can add $20 to $30 to an evening out, enters into the equation, too. It's part of the cost of spending time together. Settling the money question up front seems difficult at first, but eliminating anxiety about it frees you to enjoy the date.
- The same goes for any other question of form or substance. Ask. Talk about it. Negotiate it.
- As for where to go, do whatever you both enjoy. Avoid the movies on a first date in favor of an activity that allows for getting acquainted through conversation. Anyway, sitting with a virtual stranger during a steamy love scene or a sentimental weeper can make you both squirm. You don't know this person well enough yet to share such "intimacy."

AIDS

Speaking of intimacy . . . If your last singles experiences date from Woodstock or another pre-AIDS era, you have much to learn. Both heterosexuals and homosexuals transmit the HIV virus that causes AIDS, and infected people usually look and feel healthy. Close to 1.5 million Americans carry the virus today. Don't add yourself to that statistic.

Don't be embarrassed to seek information from doctors, public health departments, the Red Cross, or other agencies. They're used to it. Here are the basics:

- Unprotected oral, vaginal, and anal sex transmit the disease. Kissing, touching, saliva, sharing food or eating utensils, coughing or sneezing, swimming pools, toilet seats, and bites from mosquitoes and other animals do not.
- Limit the number of your partners and always use a *latex* condom (others are not impervious to the HIV virus), but remember that even these are not foolproof if they break or slip off. Keep a supply on hand, even if it makes you seem calculating—you can't use them if you don't have them. Use each condom only once, and use it properly.
- Use only water-based lubricants, such as K-Y Jelly. Do not use Vaseline, vegetable oil, baby oil, cold cream, or mineral oil, as these cause condoms to break. Spermicides with nonoxynol-9 kill the HIV virus, so reduce the risk further by using them.
- Many singles insist that a partner produce written, negative HIV-antibody blood-test results before becoming sexual. While laws vary from state to state, public health agencies or AIDS service organizations usually provide the test anonymously, or at least confidentially, and at little or no cost. The human body may not produce HIV antibodies until six months or longer *after* transmission of the virus, however, so there's no guarantee your partner hasn't picked it up shortly before testing. A negative test result is just another layer of protection, not a substitute for safe sex.
- Find out all you can about your potential partner's drug use and sexual history. Does he practice celibacy between serious relationships, or does he heed the call of biology at every opportunity? Not that he can't lie, despite your feelings of trust. Face it, sex has always bred half-truths and untruths, especially in the heat of passion.

- Will your prospective lover commit to having sex only with you? If not, or if he resists using a condom, chances are good he has done the same with others.
- A partner who cares for you should willingly help you feel secure about health concerns. Be direct about safe sex. If *talking* seems awkward or embarrassing or too intimate, perhaps you should reconsider having sex with this person! Draw your lines—and stick to them. Watch out that alcohol or other drugs don't jeopardize your judgment and self-control.
- It's not just yourself who is at risk. Knowing the facts and observing precautions can save your life, the life of your child's parent! And you can give your kid accurate facts about the disease.

Your Ex's Reaction

When your social life picks up, you may find your ex suddenly angry and jealous. Or friendlier than he's been in years, bringing you flowers and gifts, accommodating your every wish, turning on the charm. You're flattered. You start to remember why you married him in the first place. He's changed, you think. Perhaps there's a chance you could make it again. People do marry the same person twice and live happily ever after.

Think very, very carefully about this one. It's a common phenomenon that has little to do with you and much to do with the other's psychology. The chase excites him. Or he wants to deprive you of enjoyment. Perhaps he subconsciously believes that convincing you to try again will negate his responsibility for the divorce.

People don't change overnight. Don't let fantasy blind you. For a taste of life after reconciliation, remember how it was just before your separation. Chances are *that* is what you would return to in short order. Unless you crave that, don't get involved. If you must explore possibilities with him, at least don't give up the rest of your social life.

Your ex may not explicitly state that he wants to reconcile, but if he suddenly showers you with gifts, recognize what's at work. Celia's former spouse suddenly developed a new attitude when she began dating. Every time he picked up the kids, he brought flowers and stayed for a chat. He expressed concern about her well-being, gave her extra money, remembered her birthday, and called sentimentally on their former anniversary. She felt she couldn't in good conscience accept his attentions and refused any further gifts, including the much-needed money.

Not everyone resists such temptations when an ex-spouse comes courting. Susan's short relationship with Rick faltered soon after he told his ex-wife he was dating seriously. Though they had separated two years before, Rick's ex suddenly had a strong urge to take a "family" vacation together. Rick agreed! That was it for Susan. I'm curious as to whether his ex's interest flagged once Susan was out of the picture.

Your Children and Your Romance

If you think finding a new relationship is complicated, just wait until you try integrating it into your "real" life with kids. You don't want the children thinking every date who walks through the door is a new daddy or mommy, but neither can you keep them completely in the dark until the wedding day.

Keeping your love life separate helps delay some problems, but it's not a permanent solution. For one thing, it tends to be exhausting, especially if you have full-time custody. For another, it deprives you of the chance to model healthy adult socializing for your children. Moreover, you and the kids are a package deal. You'll want to observe how the new person interacts with your children—and how he handles your diverting some attention from him to them.

When to Introduce the Kids

Frankly, I was surprised to learn that some experts recommend waiting three to six months, until you are certain the involvement is somewhat serious, before you introduce a date to the children. Rather than inviting him to your home or having him pick you up, they advise:

- Scheduling dates when the kids are with your ex or staying overnight with a friend
- Meeting at an agreed location
- Picking him up at home rather than vice versa
- Having him come by after the kids are asleep

> "More things belong to marriage than four bare legs in a bed."
> JOHN HEYWOOD (1497–1580)

Though I don't presently practice these arrangements, they make sense in many circumstances, and I may resort to them in the future. As always, be willing to adjust to changes in circumstance. If your separation is new, seeing you jump into an active social life may confuse and upset your child. If, by chance, an affair with your current lover broke up your marriage, expect antagonism.

I didn't have any of these complications. Christopher was under three when I started dating, and to him my dates were just more friends. We welcome a steady stream of acquaintances, both male and female, to our home. At five, my son easily accepts the appearance of a new "friend" to take me to dinner, especially when his sitter displays an interest in his toy trains.

When you start dating, don't talk about "finding a new daddy (mommy)." Avoid this language even when you're sure you've found Mr. or Ms. Right. If your ex is in your child's life, he's still the parent and can't be replaced. Your kid may wonder what's going to happen to his "old" mommy when a "new" one appears. Equally important, by raising expectations, you set your kid up for loss and disappointment if and when your new relationship ends.

So, throw all the factors into the hopper and decide what feels right for you. And don't be afraid to change your mind later.

Activities with the Children

To give a new relationship time and space to grow, you spend time together as a couple. Whenever it seems right, include the children in some activities. Do something they like, perhaps something active. Leave behind any expectations for instant bonding (or anything else).

Allow the kids and your new love to take one another's measure. Don't require them to "like" one another, although common courtesy must be observed on both sides. If you know of something certain to tick your kid off, forewarn your date. I tucked away for future reference one date's mention that his preteen twin boys hate people saying that they look nothing alike. As it happened, I didn't date this man long enough to use the information, but it could have obviated a disastrous first impression with his kids.

Feeling Pulled in Two Directions

You've explained to your child that all families are different and yours just happens to have no father, or a mother living apart. Your family is a complete unit, not a fractured whole. But introducing a love interest seems to belie that statement. Why do we need someone new, your kid may wonder, aren't I enough? (Never mind that *he* ignores *you* completely when *his* friends visit.)

- Bringing your child and your romance together makes you feel like a frayed rope in a tug-of-war. The kid inevitably tunes in to your attraction to the third person and demands more for himself verbally, through misbehavior, or by engaging the other's attention. He can be charmingly subtle or screamingly blatant. In either case, you constantly modulate your attention from one person to the other, never quite giving yourself to either. You get dizzy maintaining separate conversations and constantly worry you're slighting one of them. This stress takes its toll on you.

  The kid comes first. While even the most intense romances end, allegiance and commitment to your child are lifelong and primary. That doesn't mean he gets everything he wants or that you can't have a new partner. Nor does it entitle your kid to a vote on *your* romance. His negative behavior when you date can be conscious manipulation. Don't give into it out of guilt. You count. You deserve adult companionship.

  In some ways, young kids like Christopher are easier. They're cute and playful and accepting. Still, at times my son refused to go back to bed after I arrived home with a date. I tried going through the bedtime ritual while my date waited in another room, but Christopher later got up again for water and potty and another blanket and "just to say hi." If I placated him, I never got time alone with my date. If I didn't, the crying and screaming spoiled the ambiance of a glass of wine by the fire.

  Hostility toward the parent's dates can become brutal and direct with older kids: "I hate you," and, "Get out of here, *now*," and, "Leave my mom alone," and, "You're not my mommy," do not make for a warm welcome.
- Recognize the emotions that fuel the misbehavior or upset. Your kid's anger masks deep fears and insecurities. Adding another personality especially frightens an only-child used to having you all to himself. Your affection to anyone else threatens his very existence, especially if your ex isn't in the picture. If one parent disappeared, so can the other. Your child needs to feel secure in your love and certain he won't lose you to someone new. You are the only person in the world committed to his survival. He can't afford to have you lured away.

- What's the answer? On the practical level, you can keep your love life separate for a while. Date only during times that wouldn't otherwise belong to your child. Again, however, I don't regard this as a permanent solution.
- Communication is the best tool. Explain the rules of proper behavior that your kid must observe when your guest is present. How else will he know? Establish the consequences of breaking the rules. Encourage him to express his feelings verbally. Address his fears directly, even if he denies them. Frame the context for him: "If *my* dad started spending time with someone new, I'd be afraid he'd go off with her and leave me behind." Assure him these are normal fears and that he needn't worry. Regularly reassure him of your love and commitment, no matter what happens between you and that third person.

The Other Shoe

Don't forget, your lover may have kids of his own. That puts you on the receiving end of the issues we've been discussing. Respect his decisions about how and when you meet his children. To complicate this matrix even further, you decide together about introducing the two sets of kids. There are so many variables involved at this stage. Make the best choices you can and adjust as required.

> "Marriage is a thing you've got to give your whole mind to."
> HENRIK IBSEN (1828–1906)

Sex: Where and When?

Except for urging safe sex, I leave the *how* to you. (You do *remember* how, don't you? A small and completely unscientific inquiry leads me to believe that the frequency of sexual intercourse among single parents, both male and female, is amazingly low, often measured in months or *years.*)

Whether is also your choice. Because of AIDS or personal moral choices, some single parents opt for celibacy. If that's for you, mark a few complications off your list and skip right over this section.

If celibacy isn't an option, you face sticky dilemmas and contradictions: You want to be more open and honest with your kid about sex, but you're secretive about your own sexuality. You include your child in your new relationship but must exclude him from its most intimate aspects. Can you justify your sexual behavior with a temporary lover because Ms. Right hasn't appeared yet, when you counsel your adolescents to hold out for that special person?

- Your sex life is private. Obviously, whether you're single or married, don't directly expose kids to your sexual exploits. Accidentally observing or overhearing sex frightens and confuses small children and threatens older ones. Don't take chances. Only if your home's floor-plan assures privacy should you have sex when your kids are home or likely to wake up. If this means paying a sitter to stay at your house while you make love at his, then do it. Or farm the kids out for an overnight with a friend.
- What about indirect evidence of your sexual life? When your lover says good night and good morning without leaving the premises, teens draw the obvious conclusions, and even small children understand that this person is special in some way. One child-development professional told me that anyone appearing at breakfast appears to be "family." Presence at the morning table places the lover in too permanent a light and sets the children up for disappointment if the relationship ends. If you accept this theory, then you may have to boot your lover out of bed to drive home before dawn.

  On the other hand, if your relationship becomes serious, you may "go public" about it to your children. If so, be prepared to face the issues discussed previously about combining kids and relationships.

Ending a Relationship

Every time your child becomes invested in a relationship you develop with someone, he suffers a loss of his own when it ends. He also experiences loss on your behalf and tries to protect you.

Even a child who detests your lover will suffer. As egocentric beings, children often assume that whatever happens is their fault. When the fervently wished-for breakup occurs, the child internally takes the blame and feels responsible for hurting you. You can't stay in an unsuccessful relationship to spare your kid's feelings, but you can lessen the negative effect of a breakup.

- First and foremost, communicate. Whatever his relationship with your lover, assure your child that (like the divorce) the separation is not his fault and had nothing to do with him. Repeat this message often.

- Think of ways to influence the situation positively. If the breakup is friendly, for example, discuss the possibility of your departing lover maintaining some level of connection with your child. After Michael and Gaby stopped dating, he remembered her young son on birthdays and Christmas and even brought him back a toy from Mexico. During occasional social encounters, Michael still takes time to talk with the boy and admire his latest artistic projects.
- Most importantly, remember that your kids take cues from you about how to handle adversity and loss. Be a good model for them. Experience your feelings rather than hiding or stifling them (but don't let the kids see you out of control, as this frightens them). Admit your hurt, disappointment, and anger in appropriate ways. Recognize the other emotions hidden by your anger. Breathe and stay relatively calm.

  Discuss adult issues only with other adults, not with your children. Reassure your kids that you are still capable and loving despite the hurt. Assess what you've learned from this experience. And then move on with your life.

Making It (Forty Percent) Permanent: Blended Families

Remarriage is beyond the scope of this book, but that *is* where dating sometimes leads. Nearly seventy-five percent of divorced women eventually marry again. It takes much longer than you might think to meld a new "family" together—two to five years! You'll have to overcome the expectation of instant love. Forming a new family is a developmental process.

As the parent, you may get caught in the middle, blamed for everything by everybody, including yourself. If you're a long-time single parent used to dealing with everything on your own, fitting another independent person into the matrix causes conflict. Making room for him in the close ranks of the single-parent family takes awareness and communication.

Expect Emotional Repercussions

Moving two families in together changes existing dynamics, even if everyone has happily accepted one another up to that point. The adults have to rediscover confidence in their ability to sustain a lasting relationship and avoid the mistakes of the past. The children suddenly get a stepparent and, possibly, "siblings." Their birth order, often an important psychological factor, may change. Existing bonds have to loosen somewhat to allow others to form.

If possible, it's best for both new partners to move into a different house—neutral territory. When one moves into the established household of the other, the "old" children have to share existing space with the "new" kids. If one parent's kids live in the home full-time and the other's visit on a shared-custody schedule, must the latter get as much room as the former? No, but every kid *should* have his own private space, even if it's just a drawer or a corner. A box that locks can ensure privacy for "treasures." Treat the kids equally, given the circumstances. For example, display everyone's artwork on the walls.

Unless you reserve regular, special time alone with your own kids, they develop resentment at no longer having you all to themselves. Likewise, without consciously creating sufficient "couple time," one partner becomes jealous of the other's attention to the children. In addition, everyone has to get used to two "other" parents, your former spouses.

Don't be surprised if your remarriage is the occasion for grief about the first marriage, both for you and your children. Reunification fantasies can persist even after both parents have remarried. Sometimes the pain of the divorce doesn't surface with your child until later, when you break up from a subsequent relationship or marriage. Then the grieving is severe because it encompasses both breakups.

Parenting a Stepchild

The stepparent risks failure by asserting authority before building a relationship with the child, which can take a year or two. On the other hand, the kids must understand who is in charge. If the "real" parent constantly intercedes to avoid conflicts and acts as message-carrier, the stepparent and child never learn to negotiate their own needs.

- Again, communication is key. Family meetings are essential in blended families. Teach the children how to express negative feelings in a positive, respectful way. Show that any *feeling* about the new situation will be accepted, though not all actions will be.
- Sometimes one partner begins to scapegoat the other's child. He wants this second marriage to work and perceives all conflict with his new partner as a threat to the new union. The couple more easily tolerates open trouble between stepchild and stepparent than between themselves, so the kid becomes the problem instead.
- Holidays can be particularly stressful for blended families. Confused about where they fit in, kids may act out to get attention. Or they may become hostile to the "new" parent to prove loyalty to the "real" one living elsewhere.

    Negotiating details in advance helps mitigate holiday stress. Work out a solid plan among the adults for who will be where at what times. Agree on how to observe differing rituals. Be flexible and keep the kids' best interests uppermost. To give a feeling of security, explain the coming events to them in detail. State rules and expectations for behavior ahead of time, and maintain discipline. Relax. Exercise your sense of humor.

    In short, if you find yourself headed to the altar again, carry a good book on blended families down the aisle.

Next Time: Prenuptial Agreements

Do you ever wish you had your divorce settlement to do over again—with a clearer head and calmer emotions? Did you "just want to get it over with" and agree to less than you deserved? Did your ex hold your children "hostage" to get more than a rightful share of the assets? If you initiated the divorce, did you give up too much financially because you felt guilty?

In retrospect, I wish I hadn't accepted Tony's cavalier assertion that he "didn't believe in life insurance." In his opinion, the money "wasted" on premiums would benefit more through investment in the long run. Unfortunately, there wasn't a long run. Worse, whatever that "investment" earned was his separate property. Granted, my situation is not the dire hardship borne by many single parents. Still, if I'd had the foresight to insist on life insurance, or even to insure Tony's life myself, I could give my son so much more. (The suicide exclusions for life insurance usually expire after two years, in case you wondered.)

Well, I can't change any of this. No use fretting about it. I use my energy in more productive ways. If I ever marry again, though, I *can* influence what happens in case of death or divorce by entering into a prenuptial agreement.

Some people express outrage at a premarital contract about money "just in case" the marriage fails. It's so unromantic. It conveys distrust. If you love someone, you'll give him anything, right? Mine is yours and yours is mine. Until the divorce, of course. Then what's mine is mine and what's yours is mine.

- The divorce rate for second marriages is even higher than for first ones—sixty percent. The most common reasons for failures are conflicts over (1) money and (2) kids. Don't feel guilty about demanding a discussion or saying what you want.
- People are "funny" about discussing money, but fully exploring your attitudes and expectations about it *before* the wedding only solidifies your new union and produces a healthier relationship. Far from conveying any negatives, the ability to talk about this touchy subject exhibits trust and intimacy.

> "So they were married—to be the more together—
> And found they were never again so much together,
> Divided by the morning tea,
> By the evening paper,
> By children and tradesmen's bills."
>
> LOUIS MACNEICE (1907–1963)

- Whether your single-parenthood resulted from choice, death, or divorce, when your next marriage rolls around, you have children and, possibly, substantial assets from another life. So may your new partner. You may come together with greatly differing financial positions. In most cases, it's not as though you are both eighteen and starting together from scratch. You're older and more mature, and you have a history. If a second divorce eats up your assets, you have fewer earning years to re-accumulate them. You may wish to ensure that your kids get a fair share when you die, rather than enriching a new spouse who, statistically at least, might spend a relatively short time married to you. There are even ways to give your spouse the income during his lifetime with the principal going to other beneficiaries when he dies (see Chapter 18).

- Think carefully about what you want the prenuptial contract to say about your assets *and* your new spouse's. The agreement can be as broad or as narrow as you wish, specifying who pays what for raising the kids—his, hers, and theirs—for example.
- Normally you address what happens after death or divorce to assets each spouse *brings to* the marriage. How will you hold that property, jointly or separately? If you choose to maintain your property separately in a community property state, you retain the right to will the asset away, and it's protected from your spouse's debtors. If you do transfer existing assets to your new spouse, planners recommend doing so gradually over several years rather than in one lump sum.
- How will you hold property *acquired during* the new marriage? Will everything earned by each spouse after the marriage be separate or joint property? While most financial planners advise against transferring pre-existing separate property to joint ownership, some believe both partners *should* share the increase in its value. For example, the $100 a month your mutual fund earns becomes family income, but the principal investment itself remains solely yours.
- You can use either a do-it-yourself book or an attorney to draft the agreement. I highly recommend the latter for reasons discussed in Chapter 1. In either case, make sure the contract says what you want, that you understand every clause, and that all terms are completely acceptable. If not, don't sign it. Period. Especially if your intended partner sticks it under your nose for the first time after the wedding invitations have gone out or, worse, as you're dressing for that second walk down the aisle.
- Of course, you both have to agree, but if circumstances warrant, you can modify a prenuptial agreement later.
- If divorce comes, the costs and disputes diminish because you have a ready-made, "prenuptial divorce settlement."
- Later problems with a prenuptial agreement usually arise because you didn't take care of your own interests before signing.

Perhaps you thought this wonderful new partner would never really stick you with anything that inadequate. Or maybe you didn't realize the import of the agreement—"Courts never enforce these things, do they?" Indeed, they do. Perhaps pride raised its counterproductive head and insisted that you would do just fine on your own, thank you, if this marriage bottomed out. Maybe you have trouble asking for what you want and signed even though you felt dissatisfied. Avoid these mistakes. Take your time.

- Incidentally, couples entering marriage should also make new wills and consider whether to change beneficiaries on life insurance policies and retirement accounts.

Divorce the Second Time Around

Researchers estimate that fifteen percent of kids in divorced families will live through another divorce before age eighteen. Children experiencing more than one divorce suffer from higher levels of anxiety and depression, poorer academic achievement, and more troubled marriages of their own. The effect is cumulative: the more breakups, the worse the kids' disturbances.

A second divorce is highly disruptive, often requiring a change of schools, friends, homes, and "relatives" like stepsiblings and stepcousins. If bonds have formed with stepsiblings or a stepparent, those relationships usually disappear suddenly.

Factors that determine harm to the child in the second divorce are the same as in the first: the amount of conflict between the adults, how well the parent copes and can help the child through the process, and how much change occurs.

The bottom line about dating and new relationships? Think ahead. Consider all the issues raised here. Get help if you need it. Finally, realize that in navigating the opaque waters of dating as a single parent, you ultimately must rely on your own values and trust your own instincts.

ORGANIZATIONS

Stepfamily Association of America. 215 Centennial Mall South, Ste. 212, Lincoln, NE 68508; 402-477-7837 or 800-735-0329.

BOOKS FOR PARENTS

Making It as a Stepparent: New Roles—New Rules, Claire Berman (New York: HarperCollins, 1986).

BOOKS FOR KIDS

About Step Families (good answers to tough questions), Joy Berry (Danbury, CT: Children's Press, 1990).

Changing Families: A Guide for Kids and Grown-Ups, David Fassler, et al. (Burlington, VT: Waterfront Books, 1988) (workbook for ages 4 to 12).

My Mother's Getting Married, Joan Drescher (New York: Puffin Books, 1993) (ages 3 to 9).

My Real Family: A Child's Book about Living in a Stepfamily, Doris Sanford (Sisters, OR: Questar Publishers, 1993) (grades K–6).

"What Am I Doing in a Step-Family?" Claire Berman (New York: First Carol Publishing Group, 1992).

When a Parent Marries Again, Marge Heegaard (Minneapolis: MN, Woodland Press, 1993).

Chapter 18

Prepare for "Leaving the Picture"

Every single parent—especially those with sole responsibility for the children—should provide for his own incapacity or death.

Prepare for Your Possible Incapacity

Soon after Tony's death, I realized that if something happened to me, no one would be in charge. No father could step in. If I rode an ambulance from a crash site to the hospital, who would know to pick Christopher up at school? What would they tell him? Who would feed him if I spent a week unconscious in the ICU? Perhaps a public agency arranges these details, but I don't want my son spirited off to some foster home with people I've never met. I want him among friends who will love him, reassure him, and maintain his routine.

With their permission, I designated two well-organized and trustworthy friends as "point-persons" to take the lead in case of my incapacity. I thought it important that someone be in charge. I chose two in order to increase the odds that at least one can be reached immediately. She will take custody of Christopher, inform him what happened, and take him in for the night.

Then, using a list of people I provided, she will arrange his schedule until I recover. Friends and baby-sitters will care for him at their homes or mine. On the list I included everyone I could think of, and for each, I noted day- or nighttime availability, home and work phones, address, status (friends or paid baby-sitters), and any other information that would help. In most cases, I checked with the people in advance. When Christopher started school, I added a copy of the class roster, with parents' names, thinking that his friends' families might be able to accommodate him for a time. At the end were "last resort" possibilities—people who would probably respond if asked, though I hadn't sought a commitment. These included neighbors I knew slightly, friends who had faded from current relationships, teachers at his school, and so on.

Attached to my list is a "Christopher Care" memo containing all the relevant information about my son and how his life works. Fairly detailed, it lists safety measures, important numbers, schedules, habits, fears, rules, preferences, requirements for care, and so on. I revise this document from time to time as he grows. (I also give it to new baby-sitters. It saves explanation and provides a resource for unanswered questions.)

> About 1.8% of families lose at least one parent to death before the youngest child turns eighteen.[1]

I also included some executed medical consent forms in my emergency care packets so Christopher could get treatment if anything happened to *him.* Without signed, written permission, physicians and hospitals may not treat your child. I made up my own form, based on the one required at school.

I asked Christopher's school to notify my two designated friends if I unexpectedly fail to pick him up at the end of the day. In my wallet and car, I carry similar notices to contact these friends.

I update all these documents occasionally. With all this in place, I feel infinitely more at ease. My system won't prevent injury, of course, but it ensures that Christopher will have somewhere to go and someone to reassure him if I'm incapacitated.

Prepare for the Event of Your Death

If I don't pull through that car wreck, Christopher needs more than temporary care. No one likes to think about the possibility of his own demise, but every single parent must.

Your Will

Seventy percent of American adults have no will, and more than half die without one. Don't be like them. Having a will makes you proactive even in death—if you don't say who gets what, the state will decide for you. Though the state's decision could make you roll in your grave, it won't be enough to resurrect you—your would-be heirs will suffer the consequences of your intestate death. Express your preferences while you still can.

There is no good reason not to have a will. You can write your own simple one from a self-help book, but I recommend using a lawyer. Making a will is one time you get your money's worth from attorneys. They do them cheaply—a few hundred dollars at most—because they hope to probate the estate later on, and for that they'll earn a percentage of the assets. Your executor doesn't have to use that particular lawyer, but he often does.

- Make a will even if you think you have little to bequeath. You could own more than you imagine. For example, maybe you have equity in your house. Or a collection of vintage Barbie dolls you've never bothered to have appraised. Your estate may have a tort claim for major damages if someone else causes your death. Besides, unless your child's other parent is in the picture, you have to designate a guardian.
- If you had a will before becoming single again, your divorce affected it. In some states, a final divorce decree automatically revokes your existing will. In most states, however, divorce just revokes any provision that applies to your ex. Get a new will in any case. Update it with all changes in circumstance.
- A letter or other written document won't protect your final wishes unless it complies with formal and often very silly legal requirements left over from the middle ages. Let your lawyer earn his few bucks so you can count on the outcome, especially if you need a guardian for your children.
- Name an executor, someone you trust and wouldn't mind poking about in your personal stuff after you take the last exit from the freeway of life. Name an alternate, too. The complexity of the estate depends on what you leave behind. The executor will hire the lawyer, and they each take a percentage of the estate in payment. (When dividing your goodies, be sure to consider those deductions, as well as any gift and estate taxes and debts.)
- If you and your spouse have never "officially" divorced, see your estate lawyer for advice. You may need to follow through with the paper work. In most common-law states, a spouse automatically gets a portion of your estate, and you can't disinherit him without

his consent. In community-property states (Arizona, California, Idaho, Louisiana, Nevada, New Mexico, Texas, Washington, and Wisconsin), each spouse owns half of the community property acquired during the marriage—and you can leave your half (and all of your separate property) to anyone you please.

- To provide for a new spouse and still make sure your children inherit your nest-egg, you can set up a QTIP, or Qualified Terminable Interest Property trust. In essence, your spouse gets the income, but when he dies, the principal goes to your kids.
- Incidentally, if you want a significant other to inherit anything, you'll have to marry him or include him in the will. Otherwise, no matter how much you love each other or how long you've lived together, the law doesn't recognize his existence.

Guardians for Your Children

An ex-spouse with legal rights will take custody of your minor child if you die unless someone successfully contests his fitness. A judge will make the decision based on the best interests of the child. So, even if you detest your ex and designate another guardian in your will, your former mate will probably prevail. Likewise, if you and he should both die leaving wills that designate different guardians, the court will decide which, if either, represents the minor's best interest.

If, as in my case, no father exists, you *must* select a guardian for your minor children in the event of your death. The rights and procedure vary from state to state. Use an attorney to make certain you haven't overlooked a requirement.

- In California, parents actually designate two guardians, one "of the person" to raise the kids, and one "of the estate" to manage their money. Taking care of kids and taking care of money require different skills, and perhaps you won't find them both in the same person. Maybe your brother Joe would be a wonderful, loving parent, but he can't balance a checkbook. Or your finance whiz Barbara has no idea what to do with kids. Unless there's a good reason not to, however, most people choose one person for both functions.

  The money part is relatively easy. You can leave your vast fortune to a minor child in trust until he reaches a certain age (usually eighteen or twenty-one). The trustee or guardian simply opens accounts in his name "as custodian in trust for" your child under UTMA, the Uniform Transfers to Minors Act, or UGMA, the Uniform Gifts to

Minors Act, enacted in most states. He can open as many UTMA or UGMA accounts as he pleases, in banks, mutual funds, brokerages, and so on. The law prescribes how the trustee may spend the money and he has a fiduciary duty to your child, meaning he can't rip him off or waste the bucks on foolish furbelows.

- Choosing the guardian "of the person" presents a much harder task. You are, after all, naming a replacement for your wonderful self, parent to the one you love most. Starting with candidates somewhat like you makes sense.

  Consider the guardian's age. Grandparents may not be a good choice if they can't keep up with youngsters. Very young adults may not have the maturity you seek.

  A guardian with children of his own has parenting experience. Do you approve of his style and skills? How will your kid fit into his family? Conversely, can you satisfy yourself that a guardian without children can become a good parent for your child?

  > "When you die, you stay dead for the rest of your life."
  > MY SON CHRISTOPHER

  Does your child already have a relationship with the potential guardian? I read too many nineteenth-century novels to feel comfortable naming anyone Christopher doesn't know well. Those orphans always lived so miserably after being plunked down with a weird, distant, unknown third cousin after Ma and Pa perished in a buggy accident.

  Are the guardian's views on religion, discipline, education, and morals similar to yours? These areas mean quite a bit to you alive, and you should consider them for later, too.

  You may discuss your choice with an older child. Since the courts will give some consideration to his wishes, appoint someone he won't find objectionable.

  If you choose a *couple* to take over raising your child, name only one of them as the guardian to avoid disputes if *they* should ever divorce.

- Always ask potential guardians before naming them. The courts usually respect your choice, but that person doesn't have to serve. Surprise isn't the best strategy here. The person you designate must be willing to take on a traumatized, grief-stricken child at a moment's notice—and to stick with it until the kid is eighteen. Take time to discuss how you want your child raised and educated, and fill your designated guardian in on the finances.

Living Will

A living will authorizes someone you designate to pull the plug on life support and make other medical decisions if you can't. You may prefer to preserve your estate for your child instead of spending it on futile medical procedures. Executing a living will doesn't mean you have to make any particular set of choices, however. The form provides various alternatives and plenty of room to express your precise preferences. The living will also states whether you wish to donate organs. If you have feelings on these issues, make them known while you can.

Review any previous living will and replace your former spouse as designee.

Durable Power of Attorney

This document provides for a trustee to act for you in financial matters if you become physically or mentally incompetent. The trustee can (but needn't) be the same person as your executor. Don't worry, he doesn't get to declare your incompetence all by himself. The court oversees the process.

> "In this world nothing is certain but death and taxes."
> BENJAMIN FRANKLIN
> (1706–1790)

If you previously executed a durable power of attorney, replace your former spouse as trustee. Some states require periodic re-execution in any event.

Your Remains

If you want to be cremated and have your ashes dropped in paper airplanes over Mt. Kilimanjaro when the moon is in Capricorn, you'd better say so. Tell your executor where to find written instructions for the disposal of your body. Don't include them in the will, which may not be located or read until you're already in the cold, cold ground.

You may want to do some before-the-fact research on the legality of your final hurrah, especially if cremation is a part of it. Governments have some rather illogical (and often ignored) rules about what can be sprinkled where.

By the way, I found the Neptune Society to be caring, inexpensive, no-nonsense, and knowledgeable.

Where to Keep Your Will

Don't put it in a safe-deposit box, as that could be sealed at death. Your lawyer will keep the will if you wish (all the easier to get his hands on the probate assignment), or you can keep it in a file at home. Let your executor and others know where it is.

Life Insurance

The main reason to buy life insurance is to give your kids an income when you die. Keep it simple; don't let an enthusiastic salesperson talk you into anything fancy—that is, anything other than plain vanilla term insurance. Your well-being isn't necessarily his main motivation. His commission grows in proportion to the number of bells and whistles he sells you.

"Life insurance" encompasses different "products," as they say in the industry.

- One kind, "whole life" has a tax-deferred savings element as well as a payoff at death. You can borrow against the savings tax-free, though you pay interest for the privilege, and you never have to repay the loan. If you don't, however, the death benefit decreases by the outstanding loan amount. The premiums, while high, never increase. For retirement, you'll do better with a pension plan or IRA. As an investment, mutual funds will pay much more handsomely. For life insurance, you're better off with "term."
- "Term insurance" pays when you die, simple as that. If you cancel or let the policy expire before you do, all your premium payments belong to the insurer; you and your heirs get nothing. Term insurance starts out cheap and gets expensive later on as the statistical probability of your death increases. You need life insurance to replace your income as support for your children, or to ensure college funds if you die before saving enough. Because such an obligation ends at some point, you can buy the insurance for a "term," or a certain number of years, and drop it when the need decreases and the cost escalates.

  The variations and permutations of life insurance "products" will make you dizzy, and trying to compare them guarantees an ulcer. Unless the subject truly fascinates you, just buy renewable term insurance and spend your free time on something more exciting.

- How much should you buy? A rule of thumb says the death benefit should equal eight to ten times your annual gross salary, but if you expect your kids to attend college with the proceeds, you'll need more. For a more precise calculation, figure your current living expenses, taking into account your mortgage, if any, your job status, funeral expenses, estate taxes, and the number of children. Add in an amount that will grow to cover tuition costs (see Chapter 15). Then calculate your kids' income when you die, including pension and Social Security benefits, your savings, and any other sources of funds. The amount of life insurance you buy should close the gap between the projected income and needs.
- Whatever you decide, you'll designate one or more beneficiaries for the policy—your kids, most likely. If you already had insurance when married, confirm you still have it *and* that you removed your ex-spouse as a beneficiary.

> The odds of a family losing both parents to death before the youngest child turns eighteen are about 1 in 3,000.[2]

Pension Plan Benefits

Speaking of changing beneficiaries, remember to "X" your ex from all your retirement benefits, including pension plans and IRA accounts. If you don't live long enough to retire, the accumulated amounts go to the beneficiaries you designated when opening the accounts, which may have been long ago. Get your documents current with your present life.

This assumes, of course, that the divorce decree contains no restrictions against cutting your ex out, since pensions are assets subject to the divorce court's disposition.

Organize Your Important Records

Do your executor, if not yourself, a favor by organizing your financial records. Yes, this will take time, but it's a case of sharpening the shears before trimming the hedge. In case of death or crisis, having a central record of your finances ensures that nothing gets overlooked.

You or your executor can put your finger on information quickly when needed. Advisors—such as financial planners, CPAs, attorneys, or insurance agents—get a quicker, clearer picture of your situation and needs when you present everything together. In case of fire or other disaster, everything is in one place for evacuation. (I also keep a bare-bones summary in my disaster survival kits.)

A local financial planner suggests this method of record-keeping to all his clients:

Buy subject dividers and a large three-ring binder with a clear plastic cover. Label each divider with the tab number of the relevant sections listed below. Copy the table of contents from below for the cover. Insert relevant documents behind the appropriate tabs. If your information is bulky, use a summary page detailing important facts and indicating where to find the document itself. Tell your family, your executor, or a close friend of the existence and location of this binder.

Table of Contents

Tab 1. Key advisors. (This is a simple list that includes names, addresses, and phone numbers of your attorney, CPA, insurance agent, financial planner, doctors, therapist, parents, stock broker, clergy, employer.)

Tab 2. Instructions to physicians; durable powers of attorney and living will.

Tab 3. Instructions in case of death. (This tab includes an inventory of your possessions and the location of your safe-deposit box and key; copies of your will and the location of the original; instructions for the distribution of certain personal items; records of life and disability insurance policies and beneficiary designations; a list of important payments to keep current, with addresses, amounts, and relevant numbers (children's health insurance premiums, for example); the location of the deed to your cemetery site or any other arrangements and preferences for disposition of remains; and personal notes to survivors.)

Tab 4. Key information and a way to locate personal papers. Record Social Security numbers and birth dates for each family member here. Also include the locations of the following under this tab: birth, adoption, baptismal, and marriage certificates; divorce papers; military service records; naturalization papers and passport; employment records; educational records (transcripts, diplomas); medical and health records (medication, medical history, vaccinations); auto pink-slips and deeds (home, investment property); memberships (professional, religious, fraternal, union, other); and any other relevant personal papers.

Tab 5. Checking, savings account, and money-market fund statements. (You may want a separate "sub-tab" for each.)

Tab 6. Brokerage account statements and related documents; records of other securities.

Tab 7. Mutual fund statements. (You may want a separate "sub-tab" for each fund.)

Tab 8. Real estate records. (For your home and any investment property.)

Tab 9. Retirement account records. (IRA, SEP, Keogh, etc.; again, each may merit a separate sub-tab.)

Tab 10. Employer benefit plan records (Include statements for employee benefit plans, employee stock ownership plans, retirement plan statements, and so on; use sub-tabs if necessary.)

Tab 11. Tax records. (Current federal, state, estimated income tax and any gift tax returns go here; also, location of prior returns and backup documents.)

Tab 12. Current statement of assets and liabilities.

Tab 13. Statement of financial goals and action items for the current year.

You have to keep these documents somewhere. Why not neatly, all in one place?

Now that you're ready for the grim reaper, relax and have some fun in your life!

> "I shall have more to say when I am dead."
>
> EDWIN ARLINGTON ROBINSON
> (1869–1935)

Chapter 19

Where Do I Go from Here?

Single-parenting has no "conclusion," only more challenges—and rewards! It never gets easy, especially in a society that offers so little support. You're a pioneer, a member of the first generation to face this challenge and forge solutions. In earlier times, the stigma of divorce kept couples together, and widowed spouses remarried quickly instead of populating the ranks of single-parenthood. As a pioneer, you face your fears, question your abilities, and then take up the reins to move forward into the unknown.

Despite the difficulties, I'm happier now than ever before. Being a single mother brings me continual personal growth. I've broken through psychological roadblocks. My self-esteem skyrockets every time my parenting "works." I'm proud to be Christopher's helper as he unfolds. I set limits and provide information, and then back off to watch him experiment safely. My ability to self-nurture has strengthened. Balance between work and family life seems possible. Looking back over the few years since Tony's suicide, I give myself credit for how far I've come.

These idyllic words are true, but the day-to-day stuff can still be hell. Before taking Christopher to school today, I had to enforce logical consequences for the markers he scattered over my office floor, deal with tearful "hurt feelings" when I mentioned the ragged cuffs on the shirt he'd chosen, tear him away from a consuming art project, explain once again why we don't eat candy for breakfast, get him to open his mouth for tooth-brushing, face his assertion that every piece of fruit in the house is "too brown" for his lunch box, negotiate about him wearing a sock with a hole, and ponder the meaning of his insistence on that particular sock.

I reached for my Life Preservers, and we made it safely to shore. Neither of us remained hurt, upset, angry, or impatient, and we parted with a loving good-bye. My parenting wasn't perfect—it never is—but it was good enough. I constantly rely on skills and tips from Liz Hannigan, Cliff Crain, members of my single-parent support group, and other sources. This book has, I hope, given you some of those same resources.

Notice that throughout these pages, I avoided saying "try to" do this or that. Don't "try" . . . just *do* it. You can.

In a sense, becoming a single parent is a blessing. It contributes to your personal and spiritual development because the pain of getting there makes you decide who you are, what you can and want to do, and how you want to be. It forces you to ask not, "How did I end up here?" but "Where do I *go* from here?" However you became a single parent, the pain awakens you from a prior sleepwalking existence you didn't even know you were leading. It replaces one dream you thought would last forever with thousands more you never imagined possible.

Notes

Introduction

1. "Demographic, Social Pressures Are Changing Housing," *San Francisco Sunday Examiner and Chronicle,* 15 October 1995.
2. "One-Parent Families at Record High," *San Francisco Chroncle,* 1995.
3. "Single-Parent Families Keep Increasing," *San Francisco Chronicle,* 16 October 1995.
4. "Congress Pondering Rules on Collecting Child Support," *San Francisco Chronicle,* 1 May 1995.
5. "Single-Parent Families Keep Increasing," *San Francisco Chronicle,* 16 October 1995.

Chapter 1

1. "Families in Trouble All Over," *San Francisco Chronicle,* 31 May 1995.
2. "What's the Problem in Society? Dad's Missing," *San Francisco Sunday Examiner and Chronicle,* 30 April 1995.
3. "One-Parent Families at Record High," *San Francisco Chronicle,* 1995.

Chapter 3

1. "The Changing Profile of Unwed Mothers," *San Francisco Chronicle,* 7 June 1995.
2. "Families in Trouble All Over," *San Francisco Chronicle,* 31 May 1995.

Chapter 7

1. *San Francisco Chronicle,* 24 October 1995.
2. Ibid.

Chapter 8

1. "How Should We Teach Our Children about Sex?" *Time* magazine, May 24, 1993, vol. 141, no. 21.
2. From speech given by Jocelyn Elders, former U.S. Attorney General.
3. "How Should We Teach Our Children about Sex?" *Time* magazine, May 24, 1993, vol. 141, no. 21.
4. From speech given by Jocelyn Elders, former U.S. Attorney General.
5. Ibid.
6. Ibid.
7. Ibid.
8. Ibid.

9. Ibid.
10. Ibid.
11. "Yogurt Bacteria Help Women Fight HIV," *San Francisco Chronicle,* 14 February 1996.

Chapter 9

1. "Taming the Tube," *Sesame Street Parents' Guide*, April 1995.

Chapter 10

1. "Does Your Family Feel Safe?" *Sesame Street Parents' Guide,* July/August 1995.
2. Ibid.
3. *Health Magazine,* July/August 1995.
4. "Signs of a World Awakening," *Noetic Sciences Review,* Summer 1990.
5. Ibid.

Chapter 11

1. "Care around the Clock: Developing Child Care Resources Before 9 and After 5," U.S. Department of Labor, Women's Bureau study, April 1995.
2. "Careers Being Sacrificed to Preserve Family Life," *San Francisco Chronicle,* 29 October 1995.
3. "Emergency Child Care to the Rescue," *San Francisco Chronicle,* 24 October 1995.
4. "Flexing Your Work Schedule," *Sesame Street Parents' Guide,* October 1995.
5. "Care around the Clock: Developing Child Care Resources Before 9 and After 5," U.S. Department of Labor, Women's Bureau study, April 1995.
6. U.S. Department of Labor, Bureau of Statistics, *News,* 20 April 1993.
7. "Emergency Child Care to the Rescue," *San Francisco Chronicle,* 24 October 1995.
8. Ibid.
9. *Utne Reader,* May/June 1993.
10. *The Spirit of Community: Rights, Responsibilities, and the Communitarian Agenda,* (New York, NY: Crown Books, 1993).
11. "Pay Gap Narrowing—at a Penny a Year," *San Francisco Examiner,* 24 September 1989.
12. "Money Income of Households, Families, and Persons in the United States," U.S. Census Bureau, 1991.
13. *Valley Parent,* July 1995.
14. "Families in Trouble All Over," *San Francisco Chronicle,* 31 May 1995.

Chapter 12

1. Interview of Adam Robinson, *Bottom Line/Personal,* October 15, 1994.
2. Ibid.
3. Ibid.
4. "Schools Falling Short of Ambitious Goals," *San Francisco Chronicle,* 10 November 1995.
5. Interview of Adam Robinson, *Bottom Line/Personal,* October 15, 1994.

Chapter 15

1. "Few Parents Pay Support, U.S. Says," *San Francisco Chronicle,* 13 May 1995.
2. "Rich Americans Tend to Earn It, New Study Finds," *San Francisco Chronicle,* 25 July 1995.
3. "Few Parents Pay Support, U.S. Says," *San Francisco Chronicle,* 13 May 1995.
4. Ibid.
5. Ibid.
6. Ibid.
7. *Current Population Reports,* series P-60, no. 180.
8. *Statistical Abstracts of the U.S.,* 1992.
9. "Few Parents Pay Support, U.S. Says," *San Francisco Chronicle,* 13 May 1995.
10. Ibid.
11. "Congress Pondering Rules on Collecting Child Support," *San Francisco Chronicle,* 1 May 1995.
12. Center on Budget and Policy Priorities, 1993 report.
13. Ibid.
14. *Population Profile of the U.S.,* U.S. Census Bureau report, 1995.
15. *Columbia Investor,* July 1995, vol. 1, no. 2.

Chapter 17

1. "Avoiding Stepfamily Stress," *Sesame Street Parents' Guide,* December 1992.
2. "A House Divided," *San Francisco Examiner,* 30 April 1995.

Chapter 18

1. *Money* magazine, April 1993, p.147.
2. Ibid.

Index

A

C

E

N

O

P

S

U

V